Henry Stevens, East India Company

The Dawn of British Trade to the East Indies as Recorded in the Court Minutes of the East India Company

Henry Stevens, East India Company

The Dawn of British Trade to the East Indies as Recorded in the Court Minutes of the East India Company

ISBN/EAN: 9783744734332

Printed in Europe, USA, Canada, Australia, Japan

Cover: Foto ©ninafisch / pixelio.de

More available books at **www.hansebooks.com**

THE DAWN OF BRITISH TRADE
TO THE EAST INDIES
AS RECORDED IN THE
COURT MINUTES OF THE EAST INDIA COMPANY
1599-1603

Containing an account of the formation of the Company
The first Adventure and Waymouth's Voyage
in search of the North-West Passage

NOW FIRST PRINTED FROM THE ORIGINAL MANUSCRIPT

BY HENRY STEVENS OF VERMONT

WITH AN INTRODUCTION BY
SIR GEORGE BIRDWOOD K' CSI MD

LONDON
HENRY STEVENS & SON 115 ST. MARTIN'S LANE
Over against the Church of St Martin in the Fields
MDCCCLXXXVI

CHISWICK PRESS:—C. WHITTINGHAM AND CO., TOOKS COURT,
CHANCERY LANE.

PREFACE

HE original manuscript from which this volume is printed, is preserved in the India Office, London, where it is known as the first volume of the Court Minutes of the East India Company; and consists of 120 leaves foolscap folio, written in the old court hand of the Elizabethan period. Some few years ago it was sent, with other documents, to the Public Record Office to be calendared, and there fell under the notice of my late father, Mr. Henry Stevens of Vermont, who, ever watchful for new materials for history, especially American, immediately recognised its importance. Finding that only a very small portion had ever been quoted, he determined with the sanction of the Authorities of the India Office, to print it in full, and forthwith employed an expert to transcribe it exactly with all its peculiarities of spelling and contraction. This proved a work of time and of considerable difficulty, as the handwriting is extremely illegible in places, and in some cases several opinions were required to decipher certain passages.

The transcript, on completion, was handed to Messrs. Charles Whittingham and Co. of the Chiswick Press, with instructions to follow copy in the minutest particulars of spelling and contractions, a task which somewhat taxed their resources and ingenuity for peculiar types. The proofs, after careful correction with the transcript, were re-read with the original manuscript by an independent expert, and many and curious were the corrections which resulted.

Mr. Stevens's intention was to have written a lengthy essay by way of introduction, but he was unfortunately prevented by failing health and the pressure of other work. I may add, however, that from his memoranda it appears he was probably more interested in the volume from an American than from an Indian point of view. Perhaps this is pardonable when it is remembered how close were his sympathies and studies with the history and geography of the land of his birth; nevertheless, the importance of the British and Indian aspect of the volume must by no means be lost sight of. Finding that his memoranda were not sufficiently detailed to be capable of extension, Sir George Birdwood has kindly assented to my request to write an introduction.

Of the voyage for the discovery of the North-West Passage here recorded, very little has hitherto been known beyond the details given by Waymouth himself in his Journal, printed by Purchas, volume iii. pages 809-814. The present volume tends to contradict some of the statements there given, for in the opening paragraph of the Journal Waymouth says, his ships were "thoroughly victualled and abundantly furnished with all necessaries for a yeere and an halfe, by the right Worshipfull Merchants of the Moscouie and Turkie Companies," whereas we now learn that the expedition was undertaken at the sole instance of the East India Company, and certainly at first with some opposition from the Moscovie Company. George Waymouth was one of my father's most favourite subjects for study, and I have hopes that some interesting particulars respecting him may yet be gleaned from memoranda made for the introduction to an account of another of his Voyages which is also in the press.

Another point which greatly interested Mr. Stevens in this volume is the mention of the 'May flowre,' and I have heard him express a very decided opinion that the vessel here referred to was undoubtedly the veritable Pilgrim Ship. The mention of Hakluyt is also worthy of attention. On the 29th of January 1600 (see page 123) he is referred to as "Mr Hacklett the historiographer of the viages of the East Indies," and " was required to sett downe in wryting a note of the principall places in the East Indies wher Trade is to be had to thend the same may be vsed for the better instrucčon of o^r factors in the said voyage," and on the 16th of February (see page 143) we find that £10 was paid to him for his " advyses." The further payment of 30s. for three maps on the same date, raises the delightful query as to what maps they were, whether three different ones or three copies of Molyneux's " true hydrographical description of so much of the world as hath been hitherto discovered and is come to our knowledge," published just about this time and inserted by Hakluyt in some copies of his 'Principall Navigations,' but of which only some nine or ten specimens have come down to posterity. The last copy came to light in 1881, when it realised £131 at public auction. It would indeed be interesting if another copy should turn up amongst the East India Company's records.

The letters printed on pages 265 to 283, are probably draft letters of the " Company of Levant Merchants," and they commence at the opposite end of the manuscript volume to the minutes of the East India Company. From the first letter being dated March, 1599, while the first entry of the East India Company is September, 1599, it would appear that the book originally belonged to the Levant Company, but was afterwards used by both companies in common. This tends to show that the East India Company was partially an outgrowth of the

Levant Company, as several persons mentioned appear to have been prominent members of both Companies, notably Sir Thomas Smith, who held the office of Governor of each (see pages 62 and 281). Under these circumstances it was thought best to print these letters, although they do not pertain directly to the East India Company.

A word as to method of printing. The manuscript has been followed with the greatest possible care, though in one or two instances the greatest experts of the Record Office and others were at variance over a word or figure. The reader's indulgence is therefore requested should he discover an error. The words printed within brackets [ ] are struck through in the original as corrections, but have been printed here, as in many cases they tend to the better understanding of the sentence. The passages printed in italics are interlineated in the manuscript. The Index, which I undertook at my father's request, I have endeavoured to make as copious as possible.

HENRY N. STEVENS.

INTRODUCTION

"Qui mare teneat, eum necesse rerum potiri."—CICERO, *Ep. ad Att.*, x.

HE History of the East India Company is a work that has still to be written, although from its rise, at the close of the sixteenth century, to its disappearance thirty years ago, the Company was careful to provide all the necessary material for the task, and to place on formal record the simplest acts of its administration, and the reasons which prompted all its decisions. The value of these contemporary annals—for the Court Books, Factory Diaries, Consultations, and general correspondence, really constitute a continuous narrative—has been only impaired in a small degree by the ravages of time, and by the neglect of less careful custodians than the men who originally determined that their successors in office should gain by their example and experience, and that the Company itself should not suffer in the eyes of posterity from any ambiguity as to its proceedings. The present volume, printed as a labour

b

INTRODUCTION

of love under the direction and at the charge of the late Mr. Henry Stevens, is, so far as print can be made a facsimile of manuscript, identical with the first Court Book kept by the adventurers trading to the East Indies, who received from Queen Elizabeth in the last year of the sixteenth century a patent, or charter, recognizing them as the East India Company, with a monopoly of trade and specified privileges for a given term of years.

The first entry is of the names of those persons who subscribed on 22nd September, 1599, to "the pretended voiage to the Easte Indias, the whiche it maie please the Lorde to psper;" and the last is the report of a committee meeting on 28th June, 1603. Within those four years is contained the germ of every triumph subsequently achieved in the seas and lands of the East. The committees to which the adventurers entrusted the guidance of their affairs not merely laid down the countries with which it was desirable to trade, and the English commodities for which their markets might provide a vent, but they dwelt upon the inconveniences of the long sea route by the Cape of Good Hope to India, and listened with approval to any project, however visionary, for bringing London nearer to the wealthy kingdoms of Asia. As will be seen, their hopes centred in the North-West passage, which Robert Thorne had been the first to advocate in Henry VIII.'s reign as furnishing a road to Cathay and India, and which long continued to dangle before the eyes of the Company as a glorious possibility, never realizing its promise until in our time the discovery has been made, and the feat accomplished, not by naval skill and daring, but by the connexion of the two great oceans of the world by a line of railway. The early references to America contained in this volume will be of peculiar interest to the descendants of the Pilgrim Fathers of the *May Flower*,[1] who have so rapidly spread themselves over that mighty continent, and who have so brilliantly carried on the commercial traditions of the Mother Country of us all.

The present volume, the first Court Book, furnishes irrefragable evidence that the managers of the East India Company began their undertaking in a thoroughly practical and businesslike manner. They encountered a rebuff, however, on the very threshold of their enterprise, for after three meetings they were obliged to postpone their first voyage until the following year in consequence of the negotiations then in progress with Spain for the conclusion of a peace. The active life of the Company, therefore, did not commence until the meeting at Founders' Hall, on 23rd September, 1600, whereat it was announced that "it was her Ma^{es} pleasure that they shuld proceade in ther purpose." The first steps taken were the appointment of committees to select and purchase suitable vessels for the voyage, as well as the necessary stores and equipment. The *Susan*, or more

---

[1] The East India Company possessed in 1659 a ship called the *May Flower*, which I believe subsequently foundered in the Bay of Bengal. In my *Report on the Miscellaneous Old Records of the India Office* (H.M.'s Stationery Office, 1879), I ask whether it could have been the same ship as the *May Flower*, which landed the Dutch, Scotch, and English emigrants from Delft Haven, Southampton, and Plymouth, in New England, 25 Dec., 1620.

strictly the *Great Susan*, the *Hector*, and the *Assention*, were the first three vessels purchased, and then, after protracted bargaining with its owner, the Earl of Cumberland, the *Mare Scurge*, afterwards re-named the *Red Dragon*, was procured as the Admiral's ship. These four vessels constituted what is termed "the First Voyage," but a fifth, and much smaller vessel, named the *Guift*,[1] was added to them for the conveyance of some of the indispensable supplies of the squadron, and it was to be cast adrift at the discretion of the commander. The committees had to report to the Court every particular of their transactions with the owners of the ships, and these form the substance of the first half of the present volume. The inventories of the four ships named, given at pp. 15-20, pp. 22-4, pp. 42-4, are exceedingly curious, and mention everything on board from culverins and masts to " 1 pease pott & 2 gridirons." The *Mare Scurge*, of 600 tons burden, and twice the size of the next largest vessel of the fleet, the *Hector*, cost £3,700. The *Susan* was purchased for £1,600; but the prices given for the others are not stated. The *Guift* cost £300. These sums included everything on board, as well as the vessels themselves, and with regard to two of them it was stipulated that the seller should take back his ship at half price on its safe return.

The ships having been procured, the next thing was

---

[1] The received names of the ships here called *Mare Scurge*, and *Guift*, are *Malice Scourge* and *Guest*. The name of the *Assention* is usually spelled *Ascension*.

to make them ready for sea, and this was done with all dispatch—the workmen on the *Mare Scurge* being allowed a barrel of beer a day to prevent their running to the ale-house. They were then provided with their proper companies, the *Mare Scurge* having 200 men, the *Hector* 100 men, the *Susan* 80 men, and the *Assention* 80 men. The sailors received two months' wages in advance, and the officers were treated in an equally liberal manner. Great care was shown in the selection of the latter, and when the Lord Treasurer made a special appeal for Sir Edward Michelborne to be employed in the voyage the Court firmly refused " to imploy anie gent," and requested " leave to sort ther busines wth men of ther owne quality." Captain James Lancaster was appointed Captain of the *Mare Scurge*, and Admiral of the Squadron. Captain John Middleton commanded the *Hector*, with the succession to the chief command in the event of Lancaster's death. Both these officers were also appointed principal factors. The Master of the *Susan* was Samuel Spencer, and of the *Assention*, Roger Hankin.

The Company had difficulties of its own. Some of the adventurers were not prompt in paying up their instalments, and in April, 1601, the Company was £7,000 in default, and had to appeal to the Lords of the Privy Council for special powers to deal with those that " shewe themselves remisse & vnwillinge to furnyshe there promyssed contribucons," and this request was granted. The order is a characteristic one, and will be found at pp. 165-6. The Company issued warrants against the defaulters in accordance with this order, and we may assume that this summary mode of dealing was attended with satisfactory results as the subject gradually disappears from the Court Minutes.

On 1st May, 1601, the Court sanctioned the payment of "twentie merkes" to the King of Heralds for assigning Corporate Arms to the Company, but these were not the same Insignia[1] of Community, with the motto " Auspicio Regis et Senatus Angliæ," which, at a later date, became renowned throughout the East. Very stringent rules were also passed for the maintenance of order in the Court, and some of them would not be without their value in a more august assembly at the present day, as, for instance, the regulation providing that no brother of the Company should speak to any one matter " above three sundry tymes." The penalty of doing so was 3s. 4d., a considerable amount in those days. Penalties of different amounts were inflicted for uncivil or intemperate speeches and behaviour, for interruptions, such as private whisperings, &c., for breaking silence when enjoined by the Governor, for

[1] The earliest armorial bearings of the East India Company known to me are those stamped on the back of the bound volumes of the older —seventeenth century—records at the India Office. They are very beautiful, the shield being divided into three bands, the uppermost bearing conventional red and white Tudor roses on a gold ground ; the middle the conventional white lilies of France on a blue ground ; and the lowermost, three quaint heraldic ships sailing all in a line on an azure sea. The supporters are a blue sea lion on either side. The crest is a terrestrial globe, beflagged right and left ; and the motto " Deus indicat." And God did indeed fulfil the expectation of his trustful ones.

INTRODUCTION

leaving the Court without permission, and the refusal to pay these fines or penalties entailed a term of imprisonment. For further information on these points the reader must be referred to pp. 201-4.

It was in June, 1603, that news was received through a Frenchman that left the English fleet at sea of its safe return to European waters, but the first Court Book contains only special reference to the arrival of the *Assention*, from the officers of which vessel several letters were read in the General Court held on 6th June, 1603. Ten days later the reward of five pounds was assigned to Mr. Midleton of Plymouth "for his paines ryding hether wth the first report of the coming of the *Assention* out of the East Indies." Special orders were sent down to Plymouth that the ship was not to break bulk until anchored in the Thames. Warehouses suitable for the reception of its cargo were taken, tithes were paid to the Lord High Admiral for a prize captured at sea, and on the 16th June the entrance of the vessel into the river was publicly announced. Six pounds had then to be paid for pilotage and £917 for customs to the King (for James I. had succeeded "Good Queen Bess"), before the adventurers were in a position to know how their first journey had prospered. The Court Book says modestly that it afforded encouragement for a second venture, but for more exact and detailed information concerning the return of the East India Company's first squadron from Asia the reader will refer to the passages themselves.

Very soon after the sailing of the first fleet for India

by the Cape of Bona Speransa, the project of discovering a route to the East Indies by the North-West Passage was brought before the Court by " one George Waymoth [1] a navigator." The subject was considered in a dual form—first, whether the Company would take it up and be at the charge of fitting out two or three pinnaces, and secondly, if it would not accept this direct responsibility, would it leave the matter to private men, and reward their discovery by the surrender of the trade by this route for certain years? Whether from fear of losing any of the privileges and advantages of the monopoly of trade with China and the East Indies, or from pure public spirit, it was determined that " the finding out of the Northwest passage " shall be " consented unto for a voyage." The readiness of the Court to undertake this quest, and to seriously take up George Waymouth's idea can only be understood by realising the state of geographical knowledge at the time, and the hopes of the commercial classes of the discovery of new and short routes to the Indies as well as of new countries.

The discovery of the North-West Passage had been the first ambition of English navigators. Henry VIII.'s letters patent to John Cabot and his three sons in 1496 were for the discovery of this very route.[2] In the next reign Robert Thorne advocated the same project which Sebastian Cabot revived under Edward VI. and Mary, and the expedition of Sir Hugh Willoughby and Richard

---

[1] His name is afterwards spelt Waymouth and Waymouthe.
[2] See my *Report on the Miscellaneous Old Records of the India Office*, particularly p. 75 and pp. 91-92.

Chancellor to the White Sea, partly a failure and partly a success, was really another attempt to solve the same problem. The voyages of Martin Frobisher, in 1576-8, were the first to give any tangible ground of hope in the discovery of an inlet on the coast of Labrador running westward, and he was "highly commended of all men for the great hope he brought of a passage to Cathaia." These different attempts made in the course of a century, were so many endeavours to realise the predictions of Seneca and Pulci.[1] The latter clearly prophesied that across the Atlantic would be discovered not only a new world, but a new route to the East.

Political considerations confirmed the traditions kept alive by the bolder geographers and men of science of antiquity, and also of the renaissance. Da Gama's dis-

---

[1] Luigi Pulci, 1431-1487, "sire of the half-serious rhyme":—

"But see, the sun speeds in his western path
To glad the nations with unexpected light."

There was a general looking forward in the thirteenth, fourteenth, and fifteenth centuries, to the discovery of the American and the Australasian continents. The lines of Dante, 1265-1321, in the *Vision of Purgatory*, in which he alludes to the Southern Cross, are well known. I believe that the leading minds of ancient Rome had an equally clear, if not even a clearer conception of the as yet unrevealed lands lying indefinitely beyond the Atlantic and Indian Oceans. Pliny (Bk. II., Chap. 65) positively asserts the existence of the Antipodes: and records (Chap. 67) the tradition of "certain Indians, who sailing from India" for the purpose of commerce had been driven by tempests into Germany. If the story had any foundation in fact, these Indians could only have been North American Indians, such as the Esquimaux. Seneca's hackneyed line: "Nec sit terris ultima Thule" is not so vague a prophecy of the Americas as it appears separated from the context (*Medea*, Act II., lines 370-

covery of the Cape route to the Indies had been to the benefit of a Portuguese monopoly, not of the commercial interests of Europe at large. For a century the Portuguese enjoyed as undisturbed a supremacy east of the Cape as the Spaniards had for three-fourths that period on the Spanish Main. When the English navy was in its infancy that of Portugal had reached its prime,' and was, indeed, squandering the magnificent inheritance of Da Gama and Albuquerque. It seemed to English navigators and merchants that the only practical way of coping with the Portuguese in eastern seas was by the discovery of a new route thither of which. England might claim and possess the sole right of usage. In the sixteenth century English naval enterprise found its chief impulse in this consideration, and when the next century was marked by the beginning of an East India Company whose programme was to compete with the Portuguese and Dutch—for the latter had also, and

380): and he really seems to have anticipated the advice of the American humourist in not prophesying before he knew, when his poetical vision of the New World is compared with a prosaic passage, which I believe is now brought to light for the first time in this connexion, from his *Quæstionum Naturalium Libri Septem*. Herein he distinctly states that the distance from the west coast of Spain to "the Indies" was so short, that it could be sailed over, if the wind was favourable, in a few days. His actual words are : " Curiosus spectator contemnit domicilii angustias. Quantum enim est quod ab ultimis litoribus Hispaniæ usque ad Indos jacet? paucissimorum dierum spatium, si navem suam ventus implevit." It was always the quest and invention of the Indies that inspired Columbus and his English successors in the exploration of the New World; and they but picked up the Americas and the greater part of the Australasias as unconsidered trifles by the way.

before us, embarked on the same undertaking—in a trade by the Cape route, there were many who turned with unconcealed longing to the earlier scheme, as holding forth the promise of easier and more complete success. It was in this hankering feeling after a monopoly and a sway not to be disputed that men like George Waymouth and other advocates of the North-West Passage found their best opportunity and argument.

Such were the prevalent views when Captain Waymouth proposed a fresh search for the North-West Passage, and obtained the sanction of the Court to his design. Although a fleet had sailed only a few months before by the Cape route, then new to Englishmen, the generality of the Company showed every disposition to patronise another attempt to open a route peculiarly dear to the English, and identified with their name. Yet even in this matter, an unexpected obstacle presented itself in the alleged prior rights of the "Muskovia Companie," the parent of the Russia Company of our time. Delays and objections ensued as to the respective privileges of the two Companies, and the deliberations of chosen delegates did not greatly further any practical or definite conclusion. The discussion might have continued indefinitely had not the East India Company taken legal opinion as to their rights, and finding them ample for the purpose in hand sanctioned the scheme as their "Second Voyage" to the Indies. Finding them so firm, the Muskovia Company waived their loftier pretensions, and proceeded to associate themselves in the enterprise. For the purposes of this voyage, a special levy of one shilling for each pound deposited by the adventurers for the Cape experiment was ordered, and special terms, mainly dependent, however, on the result of his voyage, were made with Captain Waymouth. The objects of the journey itself are well expressed on pp. 198-9, whereat are recited some of the chief passages of Elizabeth's patent as well as the reasons which swayed the decision of the Court. The formal agreement between the Company and George Waymouth sets forth that the Governor and Company had deliberated on "the longe and tedious course wch hath benne hetherto houlden by all such as do trade or sayle from these parts of the world in to ye East Indies alonge the coast of Europe and Africa by ye Cape of Bona Esperansa and of the great adventures wch are borne in soe longe a viage by many kinds of daungers offered therin and beinge moved wth great hope that ther is a possibility of discovery of a neerer Passage into ye said East Indies by seas by ye way of the North-west yf the same were vndertaken by a man of knowledge in Navigačon, &c. &c," and had in consequence entrusted the task to Captain Waymouth. In a subsequent passage further details are supplied as to how it was thought this would be effected, and these constituted what would now be termed Captain Waymouth's sailing orders. He was to "sayle toward the coast of Groynland into that part of the open seas wch is described in sundry generall mapps by ye name of fretum Dauies and shall passe on forward in those seas by ye northwest or as he shall fynd the Passage best to lye towards the parts or kingedomes of Cataya or China, or y^e *backside of America*." Queen Elizabeth attached sufficient importance to the undertaking to write a special letter to the Emperor of China and "Kathia," the use of the double names for the one country implying rather the excess, or cautious completeness, of diplomatic courtesy than geographical ignorance.

Considering the great expense to which the Company went in the matter, the many hopes that were based on the enterprise, and the confidence of the commander himself, the speedy, not to say the ignominious return of the expedition, was extremely disheartening. The Court Book throws no further light on the causes of the failure of this well equipped expedition to achieve what was not then known to be impossible, than to attribute it to the intrigues of the minister or preacher, Mr. Cartwright. But Captain Waymouth endeavoured, and not unsuccessfully, to convince the Court to overlook his failure, and to take up new schemes for the discovery of another route, not by the North-west, but by the Southwest, or round Cape Horn. There is little doubt that he would have carried his purpose had he not allowed himself to be drawn into litigation with the Company about what he considered his just claims in the matter of the abortive voyage. These were firmly resisted, with the consequence that he failed not only to obtain his damages, but also to induce the Company to employ him on a fresh voyage, as had been intended.

The opposition of the Court to Captain Waymouth's demands and propositions was made the more inflexible by the safe return of the ships that had sailed by way of the Cape of Good Hope. The arrival of the *Assention* showed where the practically useful route to the Indies lay. It had its difficulties, delays, and dangers, but in comparison with a mythical North-West passage it acquired greater substantiality as one prosperous voyage regularly succeeded another. Hudson, Button, and Baffin followed at short intervals, and with more favourable results, in the footsteps of Waymouth; but even their successes went to demonstrate the impracticability of the main purpose of their voyages, the opening of a North-West Passage. The first Court Book, characteristic in every particular and important in most, is historically curious as officially marking the first indication of the waning hopes of the school of Cabot and Frobisher, and the rising expectations, soon to be confirmed by facts, of that of Lancaster and Middleton, of Saris and Marlowe. The North-West Passage was a great idea based on an error of fact. The long and tedious route by the Cape was a magnificent certainty which supplied English naval skill and daring with their most profitable and glorious field of enterprise. The pretensions of the Portuguese to a monopoly being steadfastly repelled, the opulent trade with the Indies became the prize in a fair and open competition of merit and energy. The present volume is evidence, not of the triumph of the English Company, but of the way in which they made up their minds to deserve and win it. The fruits of the victory they ultimately secured over all rivals, after a contest of two centuries, by the open ocean round the Cape of Good Hope, have been retained unimpaired now that the narrow seas from Gibraltar to Aden have become, since the piercing of the Suez Isthmus, the general thoroughfare to the Indies; and if the North-West Canadian Pacific Railway should realise the anticipations of its authors the practical solution of the old North-West Passage problem would leave the English-speaking races victors still in the secular and mortal struggle of the leading countries of the civilised world for commercial ascendancy, and political existence. The states which through degenerate weariness and faint-heartedness in well doing, fail in this implacable competition are foredoomed to forced decay.

Undying then should be our gratitude to the founders of the East India Company, for they were indeed the pioneers of the unparalleled colonial and mercantile supremacy of modern England: and we may be sure that wherever

"The strong hearts of her sons"

are not borne down, as they have been, for well nigh a whole generation among ourselves, by the miserable sense of constantly reiterated public shame, but are kept up by the high hopes on which they are perennially nourished in the invincible Republic of the West, and in the proud dominions of the British Crown in the great South Sea, there the names of these middle class Elizabethan merchant adventurers,—who so well understood, when occasion called, how by transgressing, most truly to keep the moral law,—will be for ever cherished and revered as of "brave men, and worthy patriots, dear to God, and famous to all ages."

Our own destruction, as a beneficent power among the nations, may be as inevitable, as our peril, arising mainly from the weakness of the historical instinct in the English democracy, at this moment seems imminent; but in the worst case we shall have bequeathed the secret of empire, in the New World and the Old, to more resolute inheritors of our common traditions and splendour.

GEORGE BIRDWOOD.

India Office, Westminster,
  "Queen Elizabeth's Day" [*17th November* [1]], 1886.

---

[1] The anniversary of the accession of "the Most Mightie and Magnificent Empresse Elizabeth" continued to be kept as a public holiday in England even within the last century, and it should still be so observed, at least in the India Office, and in British India, and the State of Virginia, in praise perennial of Her imperious Majesty's heroic memory.

"Cynthia prima fuit, Cynthia finis erit."

"Her deeds were like great glusters of ripe grapes
Which load the branches of the fruitfull vine,
Offring to fall into each mouth that gapes,
And fill the same with store of timely wine.

    *   *   *   *   *   *

Her thoughts are like the fume of Frankincence,
Which from a golden Censer forth doth rise,
And throwing forth sweet odours mounts fro thence
In rolling globes up to the vauted skies."

THE COURT RECORDS OF THE EAST INDIA COMPANY

The names of suche persoñes as haue writtin withe there owne 1599 handes, to venter in the pretended voiage to the Easte Indias (the whiche it maie please the Lorde to psper) and the Soñies that they will adventure the .xxij. Septembr̃. 1599. viz

1	Sr Stephin Soame, L° Mayor London	ł.	200	0	0
2	Sr John Harte and George Boales	ł.	1000	0	0
3	Sr John Spencer viij^c	ł.	800	0	0
4	Mr Nicholas Mosley alderman	ł.	300	0	0
5	Mr Paule Baynynge alderman	ł.	1000	0	0
6	Mr Leonarde Hallydaie alderman	ł.	1000	0	0
7	Mr Richard Goddard aldreman	ł.	200	0	0
8	Mr John Moore alderman	ł.	300	0	0
9	Sr Stephen Soame. Ric^{r}d Carter, &c°	ł.	400	0	0
10	Mr Edward Holmden alderman	ł.	500	0	0
11	Mr Robarte Hampson alderman	ł.	300	0	0
12	Mr Richard Staper	ł.	500	0	0
13	Mr Thomas Symonds	ł.	200	0	0
14	Mr John Eldred	ł.	400	0	0
15	Robarte Coxe grocer	ł.	250	0	0
16	Nicholas Leatt yremonger	ł.	200	0	0
17	Thomas Garwaye drap	ł.	200	0	0
18	George Holman grocer	ł.	150	0	0
19	Thomas Hiccocke	ł.	100	0	0
20	Robarte Sandye grocer	ł.	200	0	0
21	Nicholas Pearde cloatheworker	ł.	100	0	0

1599
22	Thomas Edwardes	t.	200	0	0
23	Nicholas Barnesley grocer	t.	150	0	0
24	William Dale	t.	100	0	0
25	Nicholas Linge	t.	100	0	0
26	Nicholas Style groc	t.	200	0	0
27	Lawrence Greene	t.	200	0	0
28	Edwarde Collins clotheworker	t.	200	0	0
29	ffraunces Cherie vintener	t.	200	0	0
30	Oliver Style grocer	t.	300	0	0
31	Richarde and James Wyche	t.	200	0	0
32	Thoms and Robte Midleton. Robt Bateman	t.	500	0	0
33	Nicholas ffarrer skynner	t.	200	0	0
34	ffraunces Terrell	t.	200	0	0
35	Thoms ffarrington vintener	t.	200	0	0
36	Richard Wragge	t.	200	0	0
37	Richarde Aldeworthe	t.	200	0	0
38	William and Ralfe ffreman	t.	300	0	0
39	William Romney	t.	200	0	0
40	Wittm Paule. George Cañynge	t.	300	0	0
41	John Newman. Reinold Greene	t.	200	0	0
42	John Woodwarde yremonger	t.	300	0	0
43	Baptiste Hick mercer	t.	400	0	0
44	Richarde Cockain and Comp	t.	3000	0	0
45	Clement Mosley. Jerome Suger	t.	250	0	0
46	Richarde Stephens	t.	200	0	0
47	Thoms Wheeler. Larance Wethrall	t.	200	0	0
48	William Chambre. Wittm Stoane	t.	500	0	0
49	Wittm Adderley and mr. thoms Henshawe	t.	300	0	0
50	Thoms Cambell. Miles Huberd	t.	200	0	0
51	Mr Wittm Garwaye drap	t.	500	0	0
52	Richard Cocke grocer	t.	200	0	0
53	Ralfe Hamor mchñttailor	t.	200	0	0
54	Walter ffletcher	t.	200	0	0
55	John Robinson senior mchñttailor	t.	200	0	0
56	Leonarde White	t.	200	0	0
57	Mr Thomas Cordell merc	t.	300	0	0
58	Mr Richarde Wiseman goldesmithe	l.	200	0	0

THE EAST INDIA COMPANY 3

59	Richarde Browne &c°	l.	500	0	0	1599
60	Roger Owfield	l.	300	0	0	
61	Wiłłm and Edward Turner	l.	200	0	0	
62	Thomas Cutteler grocer	l.	200	0	0	
63	Edwarde Jaymes	l.	200	0	0	
64	Robarte Bell John Potter	l.	200	0	0	
65	John Highlord and John Marris	l.	200	0	0	
66	Wiłłm Gore, and John Gore	l.	300	0	0	
67	Richarde Howse and Henrye Robinson	l.	200	0	0	
68	Thoms Bostocke. John Ramridge	l.	200	0	0	
69	Roger Howe	l.	200	0	0	
70	Wiłłm Harrison, and Wm Bonde m̃chn̄tay	l.	200	0	0	
71	Mr Robarte Lee alderman	l.	300	0	0	
72	John Buzbridge. James Turner	l.	200	0	0	
73	Vrye Babbington	l.	200	0	0	
74	Mr Thoms Smithe haḃrdasher	l.	200	0	0	
75	Nicholas Crispe and comp̃	l.	200	0	0	
76	Richarde Burrell groc̃ &c°	l.	200	0	0	
77	John Hewett	l.	333	6	8	
78	John Cornelis goldesmithe	l.	200	0	0	
79	Wiłłm Hallidaie merc̃. John Duckett	l.	200	0	0	
80	Humfrey Wymers. Richard Edmonds	l.	200	0	0	
81	Augustine skynner. Roḃte Brooke. tho. Westray	l.	300	0	0	
82	Thoms Haies. Roḃte Barley. Mathew Hamond	l.	300	0	0	
83	Rowland. Backhouse. barth and edw^{r}d Barnes	l.	400	0	0	
84	Sr Richard Saltonstall and his children	l.	200	0	0	
85	John Coghill Henrye Parkehurste	l.	200	0	0	
86	Thomas Juxon groc̃	l.	200	0	0	
87	Richard Barrett Wiłłm Allen merc̃	l.	200	0	0	
88	Barthilmew Barnes Edw. barnes. Row. backhous	l.	000	0	0	
88	Thoms Eaton Wiłłm Essington	l.	200	0	0	
89	John Cowp notarye	l.	200	0	0	
90	James Deane drap	l.	300	0	0	

1599
91 John Coombe t. 200 0 0
92 John Swynerton Junior t. 300 0 0
93 Giles Doncomb. Ricd Welbye t. 200 0 0
94 Edmond Nicholson groc̃ t. 200 0 0
95 Henrye Bridgeman letherseller t. 200 0 0
96 John Suzan Samewell Garrard t. 200 0 0
97 Wiłłm Barrell Walter Porter t. 400 0 0
98 Wiłłm Offeley the elder t. 200 0 0
99 John Harbie skynner l. 200 0 0
100 Ralfe Buzbie grocer t. 200 0 0
'101 Henrye Poalstedd george Whitmor t. 200 0 0

t. 30133 6 8

An assembly of the p̱sons heervnder named holden the xxiiijth of September 1599.

Sr John Hart knight	Nicħas Style
Mr Ald^n Moseley	Edward Collins
Mr Ald^n Bannyng	ffrauncis Cherie
Mr Ald^n Hollyday	Richard Wiche
Mr Ald^n Godderd	Roƀt Midleton
Richard Stap	Nicħas fferro^r
Thomas Middleton	Thomas ffarrington
Richard Wyseman	Thoñs Haiyes
John Highelord	Austin Skynner
Wm Rumney	Richard Aldworth
Thoñs Symondes	W^m ffreman
John Eldred	Raphe ffreeman
Roƀt Cockẽ	Reynold Greene
Nicħas Leet	Babtist Heckes
George Holman	Richard Cockein
Thomas Hickock	Wm Cockeyn
Roƀt Sandie	Clement Moseley
Nicħas Pierd	Richard Steephens
Thomas Edwardes	Thomas Wheeler
Nicħas Lynge	Wm Chambers

Thomas Henshawe
Thoṁs Cambell
Riċ Cockes
Walter ffletcher
Leonard White
Riċ Browne
Wm Turno^r
Roḃt Bell

Riċ Howse
Henr̃ Robinson
Thoṁs Bostock
Roger Howe
Joⁿ Busbridg̃
Vry Babington
Nich^o Cryse
Joⁿ Cornelis
Thoṁs Backhouse

1599
24 Sept.

HEREAS the severall psons abovenamed together wth divers others whose names ar Regestred in the begynnyng̃ of this booke, by the suffraunce of almightie god after Royall assent of o^r Soveraigne Lady the Queenes most excellent Ma^{ie} first therunto had and obteyned, do entend for the hono^r of our native Cuntrey and for thadvauncement of trade of merchaundize wthin this Realme of England vppon ther severall adventures accordinge to the severall proportions of the sommes of money by them severally sett downe and inregestred vnder ther owne handes, To set forthe a vyage this present yere to ye Est Indies and other the Ilandes and Cuntries therabout℈ and ther to make trade by the sale of suche commodities as vppon further delibation shalbe resolved to be provided for these part℈ or otherwyse by buying or barteringe of suche goodes wares jewelles or m̃chaundize as those Ilandes or Cuntries may yeld or afforthe. And for the better ordering and disposing̃ of the said viage intended and for thencoragem^t of all suche as have already determined to adventure in the same or shall before the viage set forthe determine to adventure therin, They have thought it meet to direct them selfes by certen Rules and orders to be holden and observed aswell in the preparing̃ of suche shipping̃ as shalbe thought fitt for this enterprice as of all other provision of wares merchandize bullion and suche other thinges as are to be provided and adventured in the same. And therfore at this assemblie it is agreed ordeyned and resolved as followeth.

1599
24 Sept.

First that noe ship shalbe receavid to be brought in by any adventuro^r in this viage to be imployed in the same as his stock or portion of adventure at any rate whatsoever.

Also that all shipping to be imploied in this viage shalbe bought and provided by suche as shalbe therto appointed for ready money onlie.

That noe commoditie shalbe accepted in the said viaĝ to be brought in as any mans portion of adventure but that all goodes wares and other thinges shalbe bought and prepared by suche as shalbe thervnto appointed as Comitties and directors of the said viage, for the buying and providing of shipping and merchaundize.

And this assemblie do electe nõiate and appoint theš fifteene persons heervnder named Comitties or directo^rs of this viage to manage order and direct the affaires belonginge to the same aswell concerning sewte to be made to her ma^ie for sole priviledĝ to be graunted to these adventuro^rs for soe manie yeres as can be obteyned and for such ỹmũyties and freedomes of Custome and other tollerations and favors as may be gotten as also for the providing for shippinge wares and merchaundize to be adventured in the said viage, Ratefying and allowing whatsoever the said Comitties or directors of the said viage or the greater nũber of them shall do or agree vppon in the premisses provided nevertheles that no factor or other officer to be imployid in the viage shalbe admitted or appointed therto but by a generall Assemblie of the adventuro^rs and ther elected by the consent of the greater nũber of them [elected] assembled.

Comitties or ye Directors of ye Viage.

Mr Ald^n Godderd
Mr Ald^n Moore
Mr Rich : Staper
Mr Tho Cordell
Mr Wm Garway
Mr Tho Midleton
Mr Tho Cambell
Mr Rich : Wiseman

Mr Tho Symondes
Mr Nich Style
Mr Nich Lyng
Mr Rich Wiche
Mr Roger Howe
Mr Wm Cockin
Mr Nich Leet

And the said Assemblie have chosen for ther Thre͞rs for the receaving̊ and paying̊ of the moneys imploied in the same Mr John Highlord and mr Wm Romney vnto whose handes the contributions of everie severall adventuror in the viage is to be brought in at two severall paymentç videlt the first payment by the   of November and the seconde paymt by the   of December.

1599
24 Septr
Treasurer

It is resolued at this assemblie that from henceforth no adventuror in this viage shalbe red to adventure in the same for a lesse some then 200li.

And it is generallie agreed that ther shalbe brought in to the handes of the Thre͞rs wthall expedition for the defraying̊ of some present pettie charges that shall be expended in the affaires of the said viage xijd vppon everie Cli sett downe and to be sett downe vppon every mans portion of adventure to be collected by him that warneth the adventurors to ther assemblies or otherwyse to be brought in by them selves to the Thre͞rs.

At an assemblie of the Comitties or ye directors of the viage the xxvth of Septembr 1599.

Mr Aldn Godderd	Mr Rich Wiche
Mr Aldn Moore	Mr Tho Cambell
Mr Rich : Staper	Mr Roger Howe
Mr Wm Garway	Mr Wm Cockin
Mr Nich Style	Mr Nich Lyng
Mr Tho Symondes	Mr Nich : Leet

1599
25 Sept.

HES Committies to whom the direction of the affaires of the viage is comitted beinge assembled together doe devide the present busines of the said viage to be followed and solicited by some of them at the Courte for the obteyning̊ of a priviledge and other liberties and freedomes therto belonging̊ and by some of them in surveying̊ and seeking̊ out of suche shipping̊ as is thought

1599
25 Sept.

meet for the viage to wch severall imploym^{ts} the said psons by mutuall assent *have agreed* to vse ther travell, viz.

to solicite ye ll. of ye Councell

Mr Aldⁿ Godderd
Mr Aldⁿ Moore
Mr Rich : Staper
Mr Tho Cordell
Mr Wm Garway
Mr Tho Cambell
Mr Tho Middleton
Mr Rich : Wiseman

to seek for shippes

Mr Nich : Style
Mr Tho Symondes
Mr Rich : Wiche
Mr Roger Howe
Mr Nich Lyng
Mr Nich : Leet
Mr Wm Cockin

And it is resolued that a petition shalbe exhibited to ye LL. of her ma^{es} most honorable privy Counsell in the name of the adventuro^r shewing ther honors that divers merchaunt℈ induced by the successe of the viage pformed by the Duche nation [who] and beinge informed that the duchemen prepare for a newe viage and to that ende have bought divers ships heere in England, were stirred vp wth noe lesse affection to advaunce the trade of ther native Cuntrey then the duche merchaunt℈ were to benefite ther Comon wealthe, and vppon that affection have resolved to make a viage to the est Indias yf her ma^{ie} wilbe pleased to add to ther entention the better to pforme the enterprise, these severall petitions or Request℈ following℈ viz.

To graunt to the adventures a priviledge in succession and to incorporate them in a Companie for that the trade of the Indias being so farre remote from hence cannot be traded but in a Joint and a vnyted stock.

That the shipping℈ of the adventuro^{rs} being℈ prepared for ther viages be not staied vppon anie pretence of [anie] service for y^t the stay of one moneth loseth the oportunetie of a whole yeres viage.

That it may be lawfull for the adventuro^{rs} anie Sta^t notwth-standing℈ to sende out forrein Coyne, and yf ther shalbe a want of forrein Coyne to furnishe this present viage that ther may be quyned in her ma^{es} mynt so muche forrein quyne as shall supply the want out of suche bullyon or plate as shalbe brought in by the adventuro^{rs} or by ther meanes.

That freedome of Custome be humblie requirid for all suche goodes as are carried out in 6 viages the rather for that many experiment^e are to be made before the Cuntrey shalbe fitted wth marchaundize vendible ther, and for that also the Duche m̃chaunt^e for ther better encoragem^t are freed for divers yeres bothe of Custome outward and inwarde

1599
25 Sept.

An assembly of Committies holden at m^r Ald^n Godderd the 4 of october 1599.

1599
4 Oct.

Mr Ald^n Godderd
Mr Ald^n Moore
Mr Rich: Staper
Mr Wm Garwey
Mr Thomas Cambell
Mr Tho Middleton

Mr Rich: Wiseman
Mr Tho Symondes
Mr Rich: Wiche
Mr Roger Howe
Mr Nich Lyng
Mr Nich: Leet

PETITION havinge bene deliuered to ye Ll of her Ma^{es} most honorable privie Counsaill accordinge to the agreement of the [said] Comitties in the last conference and the Ll. havinge re^d the same and favoringe thenterprise promysed ther furtheraunce to her Ma^{ie} for the obteyning^e of the thinges seet downe in articles mencōned [to] *in* the said Petition This assemblie doe resolve that a present course is to be taken to solicite ther honors againe for her Ma^{es} *answer* to the said Petition and articles and to that end the psons herevnder named are appointed to goe to ye L. Thr̃er and Mr Secretary yf they be in Towne and yf not to goe to the Co^{r}te to solicite ther honors and the residewe of Ll at the counsaill boarde.

Mr Rcih Staper
Mr Wm Garway
Mr Tho Cambell

Mr Tho Midleton
Mr Rich: Wiseman
M^r frauncis Chery

c

1599
16 Oct.

The 16 of october 1599 an assembly of ye Comitties.

<table>
<tr><td>Mr Aldⁿ Godderd</td><td>Mr Roger Howe</td></tr>
<tr><td>Mr Rich : Staper</td><td>Mr Rich : Wiche</td></tr>
<tr><td>Mr Wm Garway</td><td>Mr Wm Cockin</td></tr>
<tr><td>Mr Thomas Cambell</td><td>Mr Nich Leet</td></tr>
<tr><td>Mr Tho Symondes</td><td>M^r fra : Chery</td></tr>
</table>

Mr Hacklett

PPON the reporte of divers Comitties who have bene at ye Court of her Ma^{es} gratious acceptaunce of the viage and vppon like reporte that the Ll. do require that some of the Principall of the adventurors shuld resort to ye Court to morrowe to receave ther honors order for o^r further proceadinge It is ordered that the psons hereafter named shall repaire to the Court to attend ther honors direction at the Counsell boarde and as they shall finde fitt oportunetie to tender a Petition to ther honors conteyning̃ thes̃ severall request̃ following̃ viz.

That ther Ll. would by ther ho : order of ther assembly at the Counsell boarde geave the Companie a warraunt to proceade in the viage assuringe assuring them that they shall not be impeached in the same.

That they may have Warraunt to carry out in this first viage wthout charge v m^l weight of Bullion at the least.

That they may proceade wth the drawing̃ and preparing̃ in a redines of a graunt of priviledg̃ vppon suche point̃ as shalbe reasonable and fyt for suche a trade.

The Comitties above mencõned appointed to Solicite the Ll. for these favo^{rs} are

<table>
<tr><td>Mr Cordell</td><td>Mr Chery</td></tr>
<tr><td>Mr Stapers</td><td>Mr Symondes</td></tr>
<tr><td>Mr Midleton</td><td>Mr Wm Cockin</td></tr>
</table>

Mr Leet

M^d that by reason of a treatye of peace in hand betwene the Queenes Ma^{es} and the kinge of Spaine the Company soliciting̃ awarraunt from the ll. that they might p̃ceade in ther viage wthout anie impeachem^t; notwthstanding the said treaty and that by reason [of] thereof they shuld not be staied when ther shipping was p̄pared the ll. denied to geave them suche a warraunt as thincking it *more* beneficiall for the generall state of m̄chaundize to enterteyne a peace then that the same shuld be hindred by the standing wth the spanishe Comissioners [to breike the peace to holde the] for the mainteyning of this trade to forgoe the oportunety of the concluding of the peace. Whervppon the adventuro^{rs} fearing lest after they were driwen into a charge they shuld be required to desist ther viage did proceade noe further in the matter for this yere but did enter into the preparation of a viage the next yere following as hereafter may appeare.

1599
16 Oct.

At an assemblie in the ffounders hall the 23 of Septembe^r 1600.

1600
23 Sept.

HEREAS divers merchaunt₹ whose names are regestred in the begyning of this booke for the honor of ther natyve Cuntrey and for thadvauncem^t of the trade of merchaundize wthin this realme of England vppon ther severall adventures apportioned and sett downe of ther voluntarie assent have vndertaken to sett forthe a viage for the discoverye of the trade of the East Indias and to that ende have Solicited the Ll. of her ma^{es} most honorable privy Councell to move her most Excellent ma^{ie} for her gracious and royall assent to the said enterprise and for to further the same wth a graunt of [a] priviledge and other tollerations and favors [fytt] for the advauncem^t of the said trade. And whereas the said Ll. favoring so honorable an [enterprise] *attempte* have *accordinglie* moved her most excellent ma^{ie} for her gratious assent in this behaulf and having founde her ma^{ie} gratiously inclyned to [further the said viag] the furthering of the same viage and [to graunt] ready to graunt vnto the petition of the said adventuro^{rs} touching the pticler demaundes by them exhibited [in ther petition] did directe ther Lr̃es to the said

East India
[ship]
Viage

12   THE COURT RECORDS OF

1600
23 Sept.

Adventuro^{rs} [encoraging them to proceade in ther purpose] signefying therby that it was her ma^{es} pleasure that they shuld proceade in ther purpose assuring them that [noe occasion whatsoever shuld] they shuld not be staied or phibited therin [by any pretence of warres] wishing them to accepte of ther Certefycat of her ma^{es} pleasure as an ernest of a further warraunt wch afterwardes shuld be to them graunted by her ma^{ie}. Whervppon the said adventuro^{rs} in full and ample nūber assembled did geave ther generall Consent by erecting of handes (the [matter] *question* being putte to scruteny) that they would [proceade] *goe forward* in the [said voiage preparation of the] said viage, and to thende that they might the better dispose thereof and of *all* preparations necessarie for the same bothe for shipping merchaundize and money to be imployed therin they did [electe and chuse] *make choice of* the severall psons hereafter named to be Comitties and Directors, of all the [busines] preparations and busines concerning the said viage Reposing them selves wholy vppon ther fydelities [for the pre] and provident handling and ordering thereof wch Comittyes or the greatest number of them, from tyme to tyme assembled are [to] by the geñall Consent of the said adventuro^{rs} aucthorysid and warraunted according to ther discretions to *sett forthe and* mannage the whole viage vppon the proportion of stocke and adventure geñally Contributed and sett downe [by all the adventurors], and vppon any occasion [or necessarie service to b] for the furtheraunce of the said viage to vse the helpe of anie adventuro^r in any imploym^t requiring the same in tyme convenient.

Comitties
or directors
of the Viage

Mr Aldⁿ Bannyng   Mr Rich. Wyseman
Mr Aldⁿ Hollyday   M^r fra: Chery
Mr Aldⁿ Goddard   M^r   Allabaster
Mr Aldⁿ Smyth   Mr Roger Howe
Mr Rich. Staper   Mr Rich: Wyche
Mr Wm Garway   M^r Jo Eldred
Mr Tho Cordell   M^r Jo: Bate
M^r   Lancaster   Mr Wm Chamber
                M^r   Harryson

THE EAST INDIA COMPANY 13

The 25 of Septemb̃ 1600.

Mr Aldⁿ Bannyng
Mr Aldⁿ Hollyday
Mr Staper
Mr Wiseman
Capten Lancaster
Mr Howe

Mr Chambers
Mr Wiche
Mr Harryson
Mr Eldred
Mr Jo Bate
[M] Capteyn Davies

1600
25 Sept.

HE [parties] *Comitties* above named *or the most of them* havin̄g bene yesterday at Wolw^{ch} [debt] Deptford and Reddereth to viewe the severall shippes called the [Assention] Susan, the Globe the Paragon, the Phenix the Newcastleship the Liones the May flowre the Prousperous the Rowe Buck, and havinge pvsed them severally doe finde of the said shippes in respecte of ther burthens, that the Susan is the most [fittest] strongest and greatest burthen and so consequentlie most fittest for this viage and therfore in this assemblie [proceading̃] proceeded to bargaine wth m^r Aldⁿ Bannyng̃ for the same ship *wth her furniture expressed in the Inventory* exhibited and did agree wth him for the same at the rate of 1600^{li} vppon condition that he shall receave her againe vppon her retorne from the viage wth suche furniture as she shall brin̄g wth her at the rate of 800^{li} the wch he vndertaketh to geave for her againe.

The Susan bought

this condicion is discharged and a sale in writing sealed from mr Aldⁿ the 24 Januarie 1600

[And it is agreed that m^r Garway m^r Wyseman m^r Chery and m^r Howe shall goe downe this afternone to Deptforde *and* Reddereth to reviewe the Globe the Newcastle ship the may flowre and the prosperous and to make choice of suche of them as they shall thinke fittest for the said vyage and as neare as they can to drive a prise of suche *of them* as they finde to be most fittest for ther vse.]

The L. Admirall being̃ rode into Wilshire *and the messenger retornid from the court wthout delivering the l̃re directed to him* [and] m^r foulke Gryvell *Th̃rer of the Navye* being̃ moved by m^r Chery and Richard *Wright* for his furtheraunce in the L Admiralls absence for the vse of the Dockes of Wollw^{ch} and Deptford resorted hether to this assembly and promysed them

l̃res to my l. ō a messenger sent about ye vse of the dockes

1600
25 Sept.

to sende a messenger into wilshire w[th]all speede to my L. Admirall for his assent and that he in the meane tyme would take order the dockes shuld be prepared and made ready that the shippes may taken in at an instant after retorne of my L. aunswer.

Surveiors for the preparingof the shippes

It is ordered by the said Comitties that to everie ship that shalbe imployid in this viage ther shalbe 4 surveyors that shall take charge of the survey of eche ship in the sheething buildyng and all other provisions and to the shippes already bought [and apointed] these psons are severally appointed viz.

            Surveyors for the Hecto[r]
M[r] Wiseman   M[r] Leate
M[r] Burrell   M[r] [Pierde] Pierd
            Surveyo[rs] for the Assention
M[r] Garway   M[r] Hamersley
M[r] Bostock   M[r] [Lyng] Lynge
            Surveyors for y[e] Susan
M[r] Ald[n] Bannyng   Captein Middleton
M[r] Tho Richardson   M[r] [Lyng] Highlord

And it is ordered that the said [Comitties] *surveyor[s] being* apointed to the said shippes shall have aucthority [to] according to ther discretion wth thadvyse of the Carpenters to supply all defectes and [necessarie] repations *and all other necessarie provisions* of suche shipping as they are severally appointed vnto [and all other necessa]

The 26 of Septemb 1600.

1600
26 Sept.

M[r] Ald[n] Bannyng   M[r] W[m] Chambers
M[r] Ald[n] Hollyday   M[r] Rich : Wiche
[M[r]] Captein Lancaster   M[r]   Harryson
Capteyn Davies   M[r] Wysemen

FFER was made to thes Comitties by M[r] ferrers and m[r] Toppesfelde of a hulke called the Phenixe of the burthen of   Tuns at the prise of 1400[li] and to take her againe for 700[li] at her retorne orels at xijc[li]

ready w{th}out condition to take her againe wch offer is to be considered of and respited vntill another meeting.

1600 26 Sept.

Mr Alderman Bannynge is entreated by the resideu of the Cõmitties nowe assembled to deale wth m{r} Alderman Holmeden for the sale of the Cherubim and to make report at the next meeting howe he findeth him disposed for the sale of the same ship and what he demaundeth for her.

It is ordered by theŝ Comitties assembled that the officer apointed to Warne the adventuro{rs} of this viage shall Sommon them severallie to bring in their moneis viz the 3 part of ther adventure by the last of this moneth.

Mr Roger Howe is requested by this assemblie to travell in to the West Cuntrie to make provision for Dollers and victtelles for the shippes wherin he geveth no p̄nte assent but promiseth to advyse thereof and to geave his aunswere this daye.

An Inuentory of the Hector

Hector her inuentory

- A mayne maste a mayne tope maste and a tope gallante maste,
- A fore maste and a fore tope maste,
- A boate spreete and a spirrit saile tope mast &c.
- A missen mast and a mizen tope mast,
- A tope
- A mayne Course bonnet very good
- *A forecourse and bonnett*
- A mayne tope saile,
- A spirrite saile bonnet,
- A topp gallante sayle and a spirrit saile topp saile,
- 3[1] ankers and a kedger wherof one broake,
- 4 Cables good and bad,
- 10 wast clothes and a topp armor of bridgwaters
- 22 barrelles of powlder,
- 371 round shott,
- 400 base barr shott,
- 13 langerell shott,
- 13 lincke shott,
- 61 crosse barreshott,
- 18 musketę and 3 Callivers,
- 42 bandaleers musketę & callivers,
- 10 Swoards,
- A sturbowe and a bender,
- 44 musket arrowes,
- 20 casses barrshott,
- 2 steele targettę,
- Certen firewoorkę,
- 4 dozen of latten Cases,
- 10 longe pikes,
- 11 shorte pikes,

A smale barrell of smale shott
7 demy coulveringes ladles &
   6 sponges,
2 saker ladles and 2 sponges,
3 minion ladles and 2 sponges,
2 wadhook
3 saker 3 demycoulveringℰ and
   2 mynion formers &c.
Certen rowles of Match,
1 fier peeke,
A greate meltinge ladle and 1 small.
2 ancyentℰ and 28 pendauntℰ

and a smale [stage] *flag* for the boat spirrit
A boate skiffe wth 6 oars,
24 { 12 demicoulveringℰ / 10 sakers / 2 mynions
7 Crowes Iron,
All such rigginge as shee came from the sea wch besidℰ a newe maynetope mast shrowd a hawser cut out and made for mayne *shrowdes* and a smale rope.

The Inventory of the Asention

5 great ankers
2 Cables she rideth by,
2 Cables spiced together newe, one hath bene wett 6 tymes, the other never wett,
1 Cable never wett,
1 great warpinge hauser,
mastℰ and yeardℰ,

mayne Corse duble,
fowre Corse duble,
maine topsaile,
fore topsaile,
Sprit saile,
missonne
mayne bonnet,
fore bonnet,

2 top gallaunt sailes
All these are good sailes hauinge serued a strightℰ voiage,
1 duble foresaile,
1 maine topsaile,   } all newe
1 wayne bonnet duble at the Clivers,
30 Shiners of brasse,
All standinge rigginge and runninge ropes, as haue serued for a straightℰ voiage
9 demy Culueringes
13 Sackers   } wth their Carriages brechingℰ and tackels
2 fowlers
25 barrelles of powder,
shott rownd crosbar and langer sufficient for the powder,
10 Crowes of Iron,

40 musketƐ,
14 Calivers,
24 Pikes,
Spunges ⎫
Ladles ⎬ sufficient for such ordnaunce.
Ramers ⎭

The Inuentory of all such furniture and provision as belongeth to the good shipp called the great Susan.   Great Susan her inuentory

In primis 14 Demy CulueringƐ wth their carriages,
10 sakers wth their Carriages
1 hole newe shotte of cable never wett,
2 cables more she doth ryde by newe,
1 Cablett hawser,
3 warpes,
4 great ankers of 17^u 16^c & 14^c,
2 small ankers kedgers,
3 Catt blockes,
6 fidƐ and fid hamm^{rs},
1 newe mayne Course & bonnett,
1 newe mayne topsaile,
1 ould mayne topsaile,
1 newe fore course and bonnett,
1 other fore course bonnett and drabler,
1 fore topsaile,
1 sprit saile course and bonnett,
1 sprit saile topsaile,
1 mayne top gallaunt saile,
1 fore top gallaunt saile,
1 mizen course and bonnett,
  hir owningƐ fore and afte and hir mast clothes,
4 brasse shivers in her mayne knight,
4 brasse shivers in her mayne ramhed,
3 in her fore knight,
2 in her fore ram head,
2 in her cutt head,
2 in the knight of her mayne topsaile sheetƐ,

2 in her fore sheetℓ,
2 in hir boatℓ head and David,
2 in the fore shettℓ,
40 Coakes in blockes, wth all hir rigging well furnished wth mastℓ yeardℓ top mastℓ top gallaunte mastℓ and other hir appurtenaunces,
1 flag Antient, 7 pendauntℓ,
1 bell,
   the mayne shrowd,
   the mayne top mast shrowdℓ, the mayne top gallaunt mastℓ shrowdℓ the fore shrowdℓ fore top gallaunt mast rigginge, her sprit saile spritesaile top saile rigginge her mizen shrowdℓ and mizen topsaile shrowdℓ & rigging
8 barrellℓ of powder,
3 tanned hides and 2 peecℓ,
2 bondge barrells and som powder in one of them,
1 barrell of matche,
1 barrell wth pap Cartrages,
12 Dozen of Canvas Cartrages,
23 pottℓ wth powder,
24 [barrellℓ] *Ballℓ* wth fier woorke,
5 fier pikes wth stauves,
6 fier pikes wthout stauves,
2 trunkℓ wth fier woo^{r}ke,

18 swordℓ,
33 lattin cases,
1 latten budge,
1 close lanthorne,
30 musketℓ,
6 hargabush a Crocke,
12 mouldℓ for muskettℓ & hargabush a crocke,
2 meltinge ladles,
41 bandaliers,
4 dozen of tuchboxes,
6 steele targetℓ,
26 sponges for ordnaunce,

16 ladles for ordnaunce,
3 wadhookes,
4 furmers,
28 shorte pikes,
13 longe pikes,
12 billℓ,
9 boare speeres,
9 roddℓ for musketℓ,
1 leather for a budge barrell wth charges in 28 baggℓ for small shott,
1 sheepskin,
1 fawkenett ladle and sponge,

1 wadhooke,
320 demy culueringe round shott,
220 saker round shott,
47 Demy culveinge crosbar & saker crosse barr,
27 langrell and Chaine shott,
45 fawkenett shott,
24 breechinge for ordnaunce, part of a small coyle of rope
10 Lashers of ordnaunce,
46 takles of ordnaunce,
1 greate meltinge ladle, muskett shott in a box being full
24 leadℯ for peecℯ
11 crowes of Iron,
6 rope sponges,
1 great kettle of Copp to seeth vittles in for 80 men
1 pease pott. 1 skimer. 2 gridirons,
2 frieinge panns. 2 spittℯ. 1 trivitt,
1 paire of pott hookℯ,
1 mustard querne,
2 axes. 3 trayes. 1 fleshooke,
6 lanthornes, 1 tapborer, 5 gannchookℯ,
1 paire of bellowes,
1 great lanthorne for Admirall,
1 longe boat and a skiffe wth their oares belonginge to the boate,
1 standinge bed wth pillers vallens and curtaynes for the m̃chauntℯ,

7 Running glasses 7 Compasses,
18 newe top sailes sheett blockℯ for store
25 single blockℯ wooden pinnes.
25 duble blockℯ wooden pinnes,
26 Deadman eyes,
1 newe foretopsaile purrell,
1 newe top gallaunt purrell,
10 Iron esses for shrowdℯ,
10 Deadman eyes bound wth Iron hooke for hir Chamwellℯ,
2 pompes. 2. Iron brakes,
1 Iron hooke to hale vp boxes,
6 oares to the pinnesse wth mastℯ and saile
12 oares for the longe boate,
1 Winles ⎫ belonginge to the
1 David ⎬ boat wth a [rud]
1 Rudder ⎭ saile
lyne for Rutline,
3 boy ropes. 4 boyes. 2 haunsplugℯ,
2 dipsey leadℯ. 4 soundinge leades,
3 newe boate hookℯ, 4 luffe hookes,
Sennett and spun yarne and Canbins esteemed 1^c w^{tt},
1 dozen of platters 2 steepe tubbs,
6 burrecoes. 2 firkins wth tallowe,
1 great baskett for bread,
1 duble windinge blocke,
1 single windinge blocke,

1 snatche blocke,
4 brase shivers to the 3 blockes esteemed 1ᶜ wᵗᵗ
1 grinstone wᵗʰ his Irons and trough
1 windinge hawser newe,
1 table wᵗʰⁱⁿ the Cabbin, grateningℰ & nettingℰ fore

& afte,
16 newe chaynes and chayne bultℰ for the mayne shrowdℰ @ 3ᶜ 3�qʳ 9ˡ
12 newe platℰ of Iron for the mayne takles @ ᶜ wᵗᵗ,
1 settle bedd in the Cabbin,
6 small baskettℰ for bread,

The 27 Septemḃ 1600.

Mʳ Aldⁿ Bannyng	Mʳ Wᵐ Chambers
Mʳ Aldⁿ Hollyday	Mʳ Roger Howe
Mʳ Rich: Staper	Mʳ Rich Wiche
Mʳ Wᵐ Garway	Mʳ Harryson
Mʳ Rich. Wiseman	Mʳ Burrell

1000 Dollers of Mʳ highe-lorde

THIS assembly have contracted wᵗʰ mʳ Hilliard for 1000 Dollers at the rate of 4s. 6d. the doller to be taken [also] at that rate for his stocke of 200ˡⁱ, and the overplus beinge [repᵈ] 25ˡⁱ is to be pᵈ vnto him vppon the deliuery of his dollers, and yf the adventurors shall at thende of Two monethes mislyke to [take] hold them at the said valewe of 4s. 6d. then the said mʳ heliard is content and hath agreed to Receave the same againe at the same rate and to repay the xxvˡⁱ to him ḋd by the said adventuroʳˢ or ther Thr̃er.

The Mare scurge

Wher a motion hath bene made by mʳ Stap for the Buyinge of the Erle of Cumb̃landes ship called the Mare scurge the same ship being offered vnto them after they *have* furnished them selfes of the proportion of shipping agreed vppon by the gen̄alyty these Comitties cannot by any warraunt to them geaven proceade in the buying of the same ship her burthen being so great, wherby ther Tunage agreed vppon shalbe so greatly exceaded, but are of opinion that yf she were prepared and fyttid for service she would be a meet ship for the next [yeres ship] yeres viage but in any wyse not to doubt wthall for the present action in hand.

Mr Howe having bene moved at the Last meeting to take a iorney for the furthering of this viage into the West Cuntrey for the providing of Ryalls and to Joine wth Capten Davies for the provision biskett and syder, dothe very freindlie and kindly assent to take the same busines in hande and wilbe ready to ryde the next weeke, against wch tyme Remembraunces and instruccōns of the proportion of thinges to be provided are to be considered if, and howe the thinges provided shalbe p^d for together wth ther Charges to be defraied. *Mr Howe & captein Davies to go in to the west Cuntrey*

Mr Burrell is at this assemblie apointed and is contented to take the *generall* survey from tyme to tyme of all the shippes apointed for this viage, who may informe the Comitties of the wantes of the same shippes and what necessarie supplies belongeth vnto them. *Mr Burrell generall surveyo^r*

And it is ordered that Surveyors of the severall shippes wch are apointed to see the Supplies of the same [shalbe] shall before they proceade to enter into the said Supplies present vnto the Comitties in some of ther assemblies the pticlers of the wantes [and to be supp] and then to supply the same by order by the said cōmytties [to them to] be geaven to the said Surveyors. *Surueighers of ships*

[The] One of the owners of the Phenix being here before the Comitties who could of him self wthout his partno^r assent to ther offer of 1200^{li} for the same ship, tyme is taken vntill monday for the ferther agreem^t in the bargaine thereof, and wthall that in the said agreement be included certeñ furniture of the ship wch is not mencõed in the inventory exhibited, viz a Cable a cablet 13 coile of rope on coyle of white Ropes 8 barrelles of pitche 5 barr̃ tarre 18 boltes of Ipsw^{ch} Poldavies and x boltes of wormall Poldavies.

It is ordered that m^r Burrell shall provide timber for the wantes of the shipping and what money he shall disburce therin at reasonable rates shall be rep^d him by the Thr̃ers or one of them. *Provision of tymber by Mr Burrell*

22   THE COURT RECORDS OF

The 29 of September.

Mr Aldⁿ Bannyng   M^r fra^s Chery
Mr Aldⁿ Hollyday   Mr Wm Chamber
Mr Rich : Staper   M^r   Harryson
Captein Lancaster   Mr Allabaster
Mr Rich Wyseman   Captein Davies
[Captein Davies]   Mr Burrell

IT is resolved that Captein Davies shall drawe out a ꝓpor̃tion *of victualles* for 500 men for that is supposed that so great a nomber of men wilbe imploied in this viage.

It is alsoe agreed that Capten Lancaster Capten Davies Mr Chambers and Mr Harryson shall goe downe to morrowe morning to see what Pynnaces they can finde in the River fytt to be imploied in the viage and to morrowe in the after none to meet at Mr Aldⁿ Bannynges and ther to make report to ye residewe of the Comitties of ther opinions of suche Pynnaces as they have surveid.

An Inventory of such thinḡ as belonge to the Assention
28 September 1600.

<small>Assention her Inuentory</small>

A mayne mast fore mast and a mizen mast wth all their top mastẽ,
A mayne top, mizen top and sprit top saile,
Itm yeardes for all these mastẽ,
Itm a mayne course buble,
Itm a mayne bonnet double at the at the clewes,
Itm a newe mayne bonnet duble at the clewes,
Itm a mayne top saile,
Itm a newe mayne top saile,
Itm a mayne top gallaunt saile,
Itm a fore Course duble,
Itm a newe fore course duble,
Itm a fore bonnet and a drabler,
Itm a fore top saile,
Itm a fore top gallaunt saile,

Itm a sprit saile,
Itm a sprit saile bonnet,
Itm a sprit saile top saile,
Itm a mizen,
Itm a mizen bonnet,
Itm a flagge and an Antient,
Itm twelue ould pendauntℯ,
Itm scrowdes, stakles, pendentℯ, wth blockℯ &c belonginge to the mastℯ and sailes,
Itm thirty shivers of brasse,
Itm two Cables wch she rideth by,
Itm a shott of Cables,
Itm a newe Cable,
Itm a great hawser,
Itm a shete anker of eighteene hundreth,
Itm two other Ankers of 1500 p peece,
Itm an other Anker of 1300 p peece,
Itm an other Anker of 800,
Itm a boates Anker,
Itm a skiffes Anker,
Itm two pompes,
Itm two standardes of Iron,
Itm two pompbrakes of Iron,
Itm divers pompbockeses,
Itm two kittles for the fornases,
Itm an other kettle for victualles,
Itm a pitch kettle,
Itm nyne Demyculveringℯ,
Itm thirteene sakers wth their Carriages, Conies and bedes,
Itm two fowlers wth their fowre Chambers,
Itm a murtherer wth two chambers,
Itm takles and britchingℯ for the ornaunc,
Itm sponges and ladles for the ordnaunce,
Itm round shott crosse barr and langrell, and case shott indifferent store,
Itm 25 barrelles of powder,
Itm six brasse bales,

Itm Thirty cases for carriages,
Itm two tand hides,
Itm ten crowes of Iron,
Itm Thirty five muskettℓ,
Itm Thre hargabushes of croke,
Itm 16 Callivers,
Itm thirty bādalires,
Itm two lattin bugge barrelles,
Itm three Carriages of iron for shott,
Itm two dozen of pikes,
Itm five billes,
Itm muskett and caliver shott,
Itm a longe boate,
Itm a skiffe,
Itm ten oares,
Itm two paier of Canhookes,
Itm a bell,
Itm mast clothes of redd Cotten,
Itm a greate lanthorne for the poop wth six others.

The 30 September 1600.

Mr Ald^n Hollyday	Mr Rich. Wiche
Mr Rich : Staper	Captein Lancaster
Mr Wm Garway.	Mr Wm Chambers
Mr Rich Wiseman	Mr Harrison
M^r Jo : Eldred	Mr John Bate

Captein Davies

The thrers warraunt for ye payment of [moneys] moneys

IT is orderid that the Thrers of this felowship shall dysburce for the provision and furniture of the shippes and other necessarie occasions belonging to the viage suche somes of money as shalbe warraunted by order of [three] *fowre* of the Comitties at the least vnder ther handes and they shall not otherwyse wthout suche warraunt disburce vppon anie one occasion at anie tyme above the valewe of x^{li} vppon ther owne pill.

It is ordered that m̃ Allabaster shalbe entreated to take the Mr Allabaster
charge of keapinḡ of the Accomptes of this felowship yf his
leasure will pmitt him, and yf otherwyse then Julinus Beamishe
to be requirid to take the same charge.

At this assemblie m̃ Altham was present and did reade over The reading of the
and penne the booke of priviledges of this Soscietie havinḡ spent drawght of
all the forenone in the pvsinḡ thereof for the wch thes Comitties the pattent
appointed m^r Aldnⁿ Bannynḡ on of the Thr̃ers to [pay him]
geave him for his paines therein the somme of fowre poundes.

A warraunt signed to one of the thr̃ers to pay m̃ *Wyseman* Hecto^r 100^{ll}
[Staper] a hundred poundes for the provisyon of thingẽ necessarie
for the hecto^r.

A coppy of a l̃re written in the behalfe of Capten Davis to the
   right ho: the Erle of Essex.

Right honorable o^r dewties most humbly remembred vnto
yor good L: wheras wee and divers other m̃chauntẽ of London
were heertofore desirous to sett forth a viage to the East Indians in trade of m̃chaundize and for want of meanes to further
o^r intention haue bene hetherto staied, wee haue nowe at length
obteined not onely her ma^{ies} roiall assent to procead therin but
are promised such tollerations and favo^{rs} otherwise both for the
transportation of manyes the better to make o^r trade and other
ȳmüyties and priviledges to pas vnder the greate seale as that
wee are incorraged therby wth all expedition to enter into the
preparation of shippinge and furniture fitt for such an attempte
and beinge thus farre entred into o^r provision wee nowe rest
vppõ thassent of this bearo^r Capten Davies yor L: servant to be
imploied in the viage as a principall Director of the same whoe
havinge ben moved to that ende seemeth soe farr willinge to
·deale in the action as yor L. shall give likinge therto, whervppon
we humbly presuminge vppon yor L: redines to further anie enterprise wch may bringe hono^r to o^r country or benefit to the
com̃on wealth do herby humbly intreat yor L^s: favo^{rs} to be [to
be] added to this busines and to give your L: Consent for his im-
ployment in the same, in wch behalf wee shall accompte yor L:
an honorable patron therof and so humbly take o^r leave of yor
good L: London the last of Sept:

26   THE COURT RECORDS OF

1600.
The [2] *first* of october 1600.

Mr Aldⁿ Bannyng   Mr Rich : Wiseman
Mr Aldⁿ Hollyday   Mr John Eldred
Mr Aldⁿ Smithe   Mr Wm Chambers
Mr Rich. Staper   M^r   Harryson
Mr Wm Garway   Mr Rich Witche
Mr Captein Lancaster   Captein Davies
Mr Burrell

A propor-
tion of Vic-
tualles.

T this assemblie Captein Davies presented [a propor-
tion] in wryting a proportion of vittell both bread
meale beare [beavere] *ceyder* wyne Beefe Porke &c as
appereth by the pticlers thereof sett downe [after other thinges
in this meeting sett downe and agreed vppon] and redd at this
assemblie.

Proportion
of victualles
comitted to
Ald Ban-
nyng Cap
Lancaster
Cap davies
Mr Allabas-
ter

But the same *proportion* being pvsed and exaied in this assemblie it was thought fytt the same shuld be cōmitted over againe
to be further considered of by m̃ Aldⁿ Bannyng Captein Lan-
caster and Capteñ Davies together [at] wth m^r Allabaster at m^r
Allabasters house [shuld] *wher they may* meet to morrowe morn-
ing and ther [to] sett downe an exact proportion of the said vittell and other thing[[and] *in w^h conference* what soever proportion of vittell they shall agree vppon *this assemblie do agree* shall
stand for a Resolution of the whole provysion of vittell for the
viage.

Peas to be
prouided

Mr Garway acquainting this assemblie that he hath bene solicited for the accepting of a certeñ proportion of peas for the said
viag is requirid to talke wth the partie and to gett his lowest prise
for the same.

a proportion
of mer-
chaundize

It is alsoe orderid that the said m̃ Aldⁿ Bannyng Captein Lancaster m̃ Allabaster together wth m̃ Eldred and m^r ffitche shall
in ther meeting to morrowe morning at m̃ Allabasters house
conferre of the merchaundize fitt to be pvided for the viage and
to [make] sett downe ther opinions of the said marchaundize
that the same may be presentid to these Comitties at ther next
meeting to be further resolved vppon.

Mr Waldo resorted to this assemblie and solicited them for the imployment of one frauncis Wilson to be imployed in the viage as a Purser of one of the shippes, to whom this assemblie made aunswer that they would consider of his motion. frauncis Wilson his sute to be a Purser.

John Johnson dwellinge at lymehouse doeth offer him self to [them] this assemblie to be imploied as a m̃ in the viage.

The 3 of [Septemb] *October* 1600.

Mr Aldⁿ Bannyng	Mr Wm Garway
Mr Aldⁿ [Smythe] Hollyday	Mr Wm Chambers
Mr Aldⁿ Smyth	Mr Wm Harryson
Captein Lancaster	Mr Rich : Wiche
M^r Jo Eldred	Mr Allabaster
Mr Roger Howe	Capten Davies
Mr Burrell.	

THE adventure of the viage rysing͠ so farre above the proportion first expectid [Requiring] Requireth a larger proportion of shipping͠ then was formerlie agreed vppon and therfore this assemblie thinke it fytt the mare scurge wch is nowe taken in to the docke at wolw^{ch} shallbe surveyd and exaīed whether in state as she is she may be made fytt for this viag͠ in convenient tyme and yf she be founde in suche state as she may be made fytt then my L of Cumberland to be [further] delt wthall touching͠ the pryse of his ship wth suche as shalbe hereafter agreed vppon And for the Survey of the state of the said ship thes persons herevnder named are appointed [who hav] to go downe to morrowe and to serche into all her defectes and sett downe anote of the same in wrytinge wch done to present the same at the next meeting͠ of the Comitties. Mare scurge

Capteñ Lancaster	Mr Chambers
Mr Burrell	Capteñ Mydleton
Mr Wyseman	Mr Harryson

wth suche Carpenters as they thing meet to vse.

28   THE COURT RECORDS OF

<small>My l. thrers lre touching S Tho Michelborne knight</small>   A lre written from the L Thūrer to thes Comitties in the behaulf of Sr Edward Michelborne to be imployed in the viage as a principall Cōmaunder was reade wherin his L. vseth muche pswasion to the Companie to accept of his imployment yet soe as he is lothe to vrge them against ther likinĝ wch motion [because] this assemblie have [not] noe lykinĝ of for that they purpose not to imploy anie gent in any place of charĝ or cōmaundem^t in the said viage for that besides ther owne [conceipte] *mislike* of the imploym^t of suche they knowe the geñalyty will not indure to hear of such a motion [but] *and* yf they shuld be ernestlie prest therin they would wthdrawe ther adveutures, therfore this [Companie] *assembly* do intreat m^r Garway to [entreat] *move* his L : [not to expecte] to be pleased [that] noe further to vrge the imploym^t of this gent to the Companie, and to geave them leave to sort ther busines wth men of ther owne qualety and not to expecte that they shuld make any further motion of this matter to the geñalyty lest the suspition of the imploym^t of gents beinĝ taken hold vppon [will] do dryve a great nūber of the adventurers to wthdrawe ther Contributions.

[It is resolved at this assemblie that ther shalbe no pynnaces imployed in the viage but *onlie* suche *small* Lancher pynnaces as shalbe carried in the shippes to be putt out as occasion shall serve and to be taken in againe]

<small>A Comission for the provision of thinges in the West Cuntrey</small>   *Capteiñ Lancaster* m̃ Allabaster and m̃ howe are required to sytt together to morrowe morninĝ and to wryte a Comission to Captein Davies and suche other as shalbe imployed in the west Cuntrey for the provision of suche vittelles and other thinges as [that] those partes to yelde.

The iiijth of October, 1600.

<small>My Lorde of Comberland.</small>

M^r alderman Baynynge   Mr Willm Harrison
M^r alderman Hallidaie   M^r   Middleton
Mr Willm Garwaye   Mr Richard Wiseman
Mr John Eldred   Mr Richard Stap

Mr Willm Chamber Mr Roger Howe
Mr Richard Wyche Captein Lancaster
Mr Burrell

Y Lord of Combrland makinge an offer of his shippe called the Mall escourge, to the Companie to 3ve in this voiage to the Easte Indias, and the Comytties abouenamed havinge pvsed the Invetorye of the said said and made some estymate of her valewe, they did offer vnto his honor, ffor the said shippe and all her ordenance Sailes Cabls Anckers and all her fourniture as she is nowe, the sõme of three thowsand pound℗, the whiche *his* honor will not Accept, But did tell them yf they could thinke well of yt he would sell her vnto them for ffower thowsand pound℗ As she nowe is wth all her fforniture, affyrmynge that he would not take five hondreth pound℗ more, of enie other, and after muche dispute his honor and the Comitties abouenamed are agreed that fower Marchant℗ and [twooe] *fower* carpenters shall vewe and survey the said shippe, and vpon there Report℗ they will consider againe of the matter, and geue his honor a full answer. ^{Speche had wth ye Erle touchinge the Mall escourge}

These Comytties haue agreed that M^r alderman Baynynge shall deliR vnto M^r howe five hondreth pound℗, to be sent into the west contrey, there to be Imployed in suche busynes as apptayneth to the voiage, ffor whiche also divers of them haue subscribed a warraunte ffor his further discharge accordinge to the Comp order, and for the pvidinge of the said breade or enie other necessaries there is appointed to goe to Dartmowthe and Plymowthe, Thomas Baker and Robarte Pope to Joyne wth capteine John Davies ffor pvidinge all thing℗ there. ^{500^li to be deliuered Mr Howe to be sent to the West Cuntrey}

Mr Harrison is Requested to write to some of his ffrind℗ at Hull ffor the pvision of Peason, and that he will vndertake the fournishinge of them, and that they shall need one hondreth quarters of peason and fiftie quarters of Beanes, he saithe he will doe his beste therein but saithe it weare there best to send one downe expresse and so they should be assured to haue it well done, but he saithe he will write and geue order ffor it, and they haue agreed that *if* he will send downe *one* of purpose for pvision ^{Prouision of peas & Beanes}

THE COURT RECORDS OF

of the same pease and beanes he shalbe allowed ffor his paines and traveile.

Prouision for Caske

Capteine Lancaster, Capteine Middleton, M^r chambers, and M^r harrison are Requested to take care for p̃vidinge of all the caske that maie be needefull for the voiage wch is as follow^th.

The proportion of Caske.

caske ffor biere, 170 tõnes, to be of pipes bound wth ashen hoopes
The Wine to be in good caske, and to be Iron bound
30 Tonnes of caske ffor beeffe in newe hogeshed{s} Iron bound
40 Tonnes of hogeshed{s} ffor Porke
30 Tonne of drie caske ffor peason and beanes
12 Tonne of drie caske for Oatemeale
30 Tonne of caske for veniger, to Iron bound
3½ tonne of Iron bounde caske for aquavita
6 barrells ffor honie bound wth Iron
one Tonne of drie caske ffor mustard seed
one Tonne of drie caske ffor Rice
2½ Tonne in smale caske for Rape Oile Ironbound
Water Caske hooped wth Iron 150 Tonnes whereof 40 Tonnes of hogeshed{s}
8 Dozen of baricoes hooped wth Iron.

   in the Afternoone Did meete more

  Mr Staper   Mr Cordell
  Mr Wiseman   Mr Stephins
  Mr Burrell   Mr Burde
    nic° Symons

The said *Comitties* beinge desyered to talke and conferre aboute the price of the Mall escourge, had long conference aboute the same and in the end my lorde came againe him sellffe tellinge them he pceaved what paines they had taken about this busynes, but he said he would take no lesse then .iiij. m. ł whiche seeinge they would not geue, he would lose no tyme more aboute the same, but since they would not buye her he would ꝓceede about his owne busynes, and so prayed them to doe thers and so depted, but they offred him 3500^l—&c.

The 6 of october 1600.

Mr Aldⁿ Bannyng	Mr Roger Howe
Mr Aldⁿ Hollyday	Mr Wm Chamber
Mr Rich : Staper	Mr Rich. Wyche
Mr Lancaster	Mr John Bate
Mr Rich : Wiseman	Captein Dovies
Mr John Eldred	·Mr Burrell

MR Richard Stap and Mr John Eldred are required bothe by them selfes and by ther best meanes that they shall thinke meet [fitt] to vse, in the provision of all Clothes and kersies that shall be thought fitt to be sent in this viage. *Comitties for ye Prouision of clothe & Kersey*

Mr George Smythes and Mr Richard Yonson being admitted this day to adventure in the viage CC^{li} a peece they do promise to bring in ther said adventures in Spanishe money [at the rate] Ryalles of 8 at xviij^d the li proffite and yf the Companie do buy them at a lesse rate then they will accepte of lesse as other men do sell them. *Smythes & Yonson Gold-smithes to bring in 400^{li} in Royalles of 8.*

It is ordered that m^r wiche and Richard Wright shall compounde wth m^r Covell for the prouision of 60 or 70 quarters of peas white kylne dried, and to geave [som] him suche consideration for his travell therin as they can drawe him to accepte of *Prouision of Peas*

The 7 of october 1600.

Mr Aldⁿ Bannyng	Mr Allabaster
Mr Aldⁿ Hollyday	Mr Roger Howe .
Mr Rich : Staper	Mr John Eldred
Mr Wm Garway	Mr Wm Chambers
Captein Lancaster	Mr Rich : Wyche
Mr Rich : Wyseman	Captein Davies

THES Comitties entringe into Conference to drawe the [resolution] bargaine of the Malyce Scurge to a resolution [or ende] to the ende the preparation of the viage be not hindred by restinge in an vncertentie of o^r shipping they did in thende growe to this *TheMalyce Scurge bought for 3700^{li}*

32   THE COURT RECORDS OF

Conclusion that Mr Ald^n Bannynge and Mr Ald^n Holliday for the Companie, shuld Joine wth m^r Garway and m^r Allabaster who have Comission from my L of Cumberland to agree vppon the prise of the same ship, who departinge aside after some [offer] Loovinge and biddinge [thervppon] betwene them did agree vppon the price of three thousand seven hundred poundes to be p^d for the same ship wth all her ordnaunce Carriages tackle mastes sayles and all furniture whatsoever as well expressed in the inventorie as not therin mencōned wch anie way doeth belonge to the said ship, and the said parties havinge made this agreem^t amonge them selfes presented the same to the residewe of this Assemblie who did well allowe of ther said bargaine and accepted thereof accordinglie and afterwardes my L. of Cumberland him self cōmingȝ hether and beinge made acquainted what had past touchinge the bargaine of the said ship by the said Mr Garway and Mr Albaster did *for his part* assent to the said bargaine, and in like sort these Comitties for ther part. Soe as an absolute agreem^t was made by both parties to take the ship in the Companies charge wth all worke to her belongingȝ from this day.

Bargaines & sales of the 4 shippes to be made to feoffees in trust.

It was at this assemblie agreed that 4 severall bargaines and sales by writingȝ indented shuld be made betwene the severall owners of the 4 shippes and fowre of thes Comitties to take the bargaines and sales of the same shippes to ye vse of the generall adventuro^{rs} wherbie the propertie of the same shippes may be transferred out of the owners in dewe forme of Lawe and the parties to whom the *sale of the* said shippes shalbe conveied [vnto] are the persons heervnder named videlt

feoffees in trust for the shippes bought
}
Mr Roger Howe
Mr John Eldred
Mr Wm Chambers
Mr Rich: Wyche
Mr Governor

Thēs Comitties have also appointed for the surveyingȝ of the worke and prepation of the saide ship called the Malice Scurge,

THE EAST INDIA COMPANY 33

and for the providing of all thinges necessarie for the same ship the psons heervnder named viz.

Mr Thomas Cordall   Mr Robert Bell   Surveyors of
Mr Rich: [Wytche] Wyche   Mr Greenewell   ye Malice Scurge

Mr Aldⁿ Bannynge doeth geave his worde to this assemblie to be aunswerable for *Joseph Salamon* the Purser of the [susan] Susan, that he shall faithfully pforme anie trust that the Companie shall imploy him in the preparing of thingℓ necessarie for the same ship and in disposing of the same.   Josephe Salamon Purser of the Susan

M^r [Aldⁿ] Rich. Stap doeth in like manner geave his worde for the like fidelitie and trew service of George Parsons, the Purser of the Hector.   Georg Parsons Purser of the Hector

Mr Wm Garway doeth alsoe vndertake for the like fidelitie of the service of Wm Leake Purser of the Assention.   Wm Leake Purser of the Assention.

Wm Burrage Boatesoñ of the Malice Scurge to whose handes the Custodie of muche of the rigging of the same ship was cõmitted by my L. Cumberland came before thes Comitties [as] and was by them enterteyned to loke to the furniture [and] of the same ship and to the worke to be done vppon her in furnishing her for viage, the wch he is Content to do.   The Boateson of the Malice scurge

The viijth of October 1600.

Aldⁿ Bannyng   Mr Wm Chambers
Aldⁿ Hollyday   Mr Rich Wyche
Aldⁿ Smythe   Mr Harryson
Mr Staper   Capteñ Davies
Captein Lancaster   Capteñ Myddleton

T is agreed at this assemblie that ther shalbe p^d to Mr Wm Chambers the somme of one hundred poundes for the provision of Caske and yron hoopes, and a warraunt geaven to the Thr̃er vnder 4 of the Comitties handes for the paiment thereof.   100^{li} for provision of Cask

It is also ordered that m^r Richard Wiche and Richard Wright shall contract wth m^r Covell for the buying and provyding of xx^{tie} quarters of Beanes and 30 Bushelles of Musterd seed to   Beanes & Musterd seed

F

34 THE COURT RECORDS OF

be bought at the best rates he can [and] for the provision of the viage.

A Computation agreed vppon the 8 of octobo[r] 1600 for the victuallinḡ of the shippes followinḡ in a viage to ye Est Indies rated in Tonnage and men as hereafter followeth viz.

The Scourge allowed men	200	rated tuñz 600
The Hector allowed men	100	rated tuñs 300
Thassention allowed men	80	rated toñs 260
The Susan allowed men	80	rates toñz 240
The Pynnace allowed men	40	rated toñs 100
	Men 500	toñz 1500

Bread for 20 monethes this proportion altered 15 october by the Comit:yes then assembled.

Bread for 16 monethes of 30 daies p moneth
                       c   ℔   ℔   s   d
at 24[li] p man   1714 1 4   toñz 150   1028 08 0

Meale for 4 monethes at 30[li] p man p moneth
                                 li
                  535 2 24   toñs 30   267 17 4

Beare for 20 monethes Syder Wyne

Beare for 4 monethes at a pottle p man p day the hoggeshed accoumpted cleare of leakeage 80 gallons   gℓ 30000 toñs 170   510 00 00

Syder for 8 monethes at a quart p day at the former rate   gℓ 30000 toñs 170   680 00 00

Wine for 8 monethes at a pint p day at the former allowaunce   gℓ 15000 toñs 80   960 00 00

Beef for 4 monethes at [a] 1[li] p man p day
                   c   q   li
                538 2 14   toñz 30   428 10 00

Porke for 10 monethes at ¼[li] p man p day
Meate for 17 monethes
                 c
              669 2 16   toñz 40   669 12 6

Peace and beanes for porke adioyninḡ for 10 monethes at ½ pint for day p man is bushellℓ
1172   toñs 88   293 00 00

ffyshe for 3 whole monethes at a bacaliaw p man p day   45000 fishes toñs 25   225 00 00

THE EAST INDIA COMPANY 35

		li	s	d	
Otemeale for 3 monethes adioyning to fishe at ½ p day for a man makes bishelles 351 toñs 12		105	06	00	
Steele wheate extraordinarie and w^{th}out proportion for 3 monethes at ¼ pinte p man p day is bushell(351 toñs 9		87	00	00	No prouision for meate for 3 monethes in the Cuntrey wch the Cuntrey shall finde this prouision altered the 15 of october and reduced to 250 *bushells*
Cheese being olde holland cheese at discretion the whole fleet winds 20 toñs 2½		60	00	00	
Butter reparted vppon all the shippes firkins 80 toñs 2		72	00	00	
Oyle for 16 monethes at a quart p man p moneth gallons 2000 toñs 10		500	00	00	
Vineger for all the shipps to be repted 30 tons toñs 30		270	00	00	

Aquavite for all 14 hogsh^{de} viz

				li	s	d
The Scourge	6					
The Hector	3					
Thassention	2	hh(14	toñs 3½	175	00	00
The Susan	2					
The Pinnace	1					

		li	s	d
Honny for all the shippes together barr^{elle} 6 toñiz 1		56	00	0
Suger				
Spices sinamñ 30^{li} nutmegges 15^{li} Cloves 6^{li} suger 50^{li} pepper 12^{li}		16	05	00
Musterd seede for all the fleet bushell(32 tons 1		12	16	0
Rice for all the shippes 20 toñs 1		20	00	00
Rape oile for lampes for all the shippes hogshedd(10 10 toñs 2½		60	00	00
Candelles 250^{li} for 4 shippes couered in wax toñs [16] 2		16	13	4
Lampes for all the shippes 5 dossen 60 t		00	15	0
Candelles 100^{li} eche shipp ordinarie Candells toñs ½		8	6	8

Cookes prouision at discretion

A saine hookes fizgigƐ harping iron
Salt for all the whole 5 shippes 2 waigh toñs 2   7   00   00
Water Caske for all the fleete   toñs 150   150   00   00

                To all   toñs 1011   6600   4   10

     The merchaundiz to be sent in the said shippes viz.

                                       li   s   d
Yron   toñs 30 at   270   00   00
Tynn wrought   toñs 5   330   00   00
Tynn vnwrought iñ barres   toñs 5   420   00   00
Leade   toñs 100   1700   00   00

      Clothes 80 of thes sortes vizt
2 skarlettƐ   in 4 halfes
4 StammettƐ
8 blewes
8 Azures
8 PlunkettƐ
8 popingoies
4 grasse greenes
8 sadd greenes
8 venice greenes
4 olive Collers
8 Reading Clothes mingled 2 of eche colo^r
2 heare Collers
4 violettƐ
4 primerose Collers
—   li   s   d
80   at 16^{li} p cloth p esteme 1280   00   00
—
Deuonshire kersies of like Collers 80 peecƐ
               s
         at 50 p kƐ   200   00   00
hamshires of all collers   20 pecƐ at 3^{li} 10^s 65   00   00
Norw^{ch} stuffe 100 at discretion   250   00   00
     The present to be geaven to the kinge
A Belt or girdell
A Case of Pistolles   li
Some [Plumes] Plewmes   present 30

Looking glasses
Platters spones and toyes of glasse
Spectakelle̊ and Drinking̊ glasses of all sorte̊
An Ewer of plaine Silver   li   s   d

        To all   4545   00   00 $\frac{6600 \; 4 \; 10}{4545 \; 0 \; 0}$
                  11145 4 10

 Order is geaven [by] *in* this assemblie of the Comitties   Captein Davies his enterteynment.
before mencōned that Mr Ald^n Bannynge Mr Ald^n holliday
Mr Ald^n Smithe Mr Stap & Capteiñ Lancaster shall agree and
Compounde wth Captein Davies for his enterteynment in this
viage and to geave him therin all reasonable contentment and
having̊ compounded wth him to report what they have done
therin at the next assemblie of the Comitties.

   Mr Ald^n Bannyng   Mr Wm Chamber
   Mr Tho Cordell   Mr Rich Wiche
   Mr Wm Garway   Mr Wm Harryson
   Mr Roger Howe   M^r Jo Bate
   Mr John Eldred   Capteiñ Middleton

 At this assemblie the Comitties appointed to Compounde   The full agreement wth Captein Davies
wth Capteiñ Davies for his enterteynment in the viage have
deliuered in wrytinge ther said Composition wherto the said
Captein Davies hath Subscribed his name wch agreem^t is to
this effect, first they have agreed to geave him for his Charges
expended and to be expended in attending̊ the preparation of
the viage the somme of C^{li}, and to Lende him the somme of
CC^{li} to be rep^d againe to ye Companie vppon his retorne out
of suche allowaunce of proffit as is allowed him for his viage
W^{ch} they do agree to allowe him in this manner viz. That yf
the retorne of the viage do bringe forth and yeld for one, two,
then he to have of that profite five hundred poundes, and yf
the proffite of the viage doe bringe forth [out] Three for one
then he to have out of the said proffite one thousand poundes
And yf it bringe forth fowre for one then he to have out of
[that] *the said* proffite fifteene hundred poundes, and yf the
proffit of the viage to yeld for one five then he to have of
[that] *the* proffit the somē of two thowsand poundes for his full

recompence of the said viage. Wth wch enterteynment the said Captein Davies is verie well pleased and hath promised to p̱forme his indevo^r faithfullie in the said viage accordinge to his best knowledge and skill, and hath sett his hand to a note of this Composition wch remaineth in the Custodie of Richard Wright the Secretorie of the busines of this viage.

<small>The copie of a L̃re written by my L. Threr for credite of moneis to be dd in the West Cuntrey</small>

After my hartie com̃endacõns 1 am desired by divers of the merchaunt℞ of the East Indian trade that suche money as yo^u have in yor handes of he^r ma^{es} might be p^d unto them or suche as they shall depute in that behaulf for the receipte thereof They having great occasion to imploy the same money ther for the setting̱ forth of the same viage to the East Indies and they will pay here into her ma^{es} receipt presentlie so muche money againe as they shall receave of yo^u This offer of thers seemeth to me to be verie good for yo^u and as I make no doubte of ther sufficiency being̱ sundry aldermen and m̃chaunt℞ of great wealth that are to repay the same So nevertheles I do leave it to yor self to doe therin that wch yo^u shall thinke best for her Ma^{es} service and yor owne safetie and so I Commende yo^u to god this 8 of october 1600

Y^r verie Loving̱ frend

T: Buckhurst

To my verie Loving̱ frendes her Ma^{es} receivors of the Counties of Devon and Cornewell and to all the officers of the Portes wthin the same Counties.

<small>Syder</small>

Mr Chambers is intreated to deale wth one M^r fletcher for the p̱uision of suche sider as he can procure to be deliuered here in London at the best rate he can drawe him vnto.

<small>Captein Baker. A Comission for ye prouision in the West Cuntrey</small>

A Comission for Capteñ baker to goe downe in to the west Cuntrey for provision of victuall drawen by m̃ howe was read and he intreated to write it out againe that it may be signed by the Comitties.

<small>Peter frauncis a Portugall enterteyned.</small>

Mr Aldⁿ Bannyng̱ m^r Aldⁿ hollyday m^r Aldⁿ Smyth and m^r Richard Stap being̱ also aucthorised by the residewe of the Comitties to compounde and agree wth one Peter ffrauncis of Bridgewater in the Countie of Somersett a Portugall borne for his enterteynment in this viage in to the Est Indies Doe present vnto this assemble a Contract made wth the said Peter ffrauncis vnder his hand to this effect, That the said Peter is to have for his said viage x^li in hande to beare his charges vntill the shipps do enter into ye viage, and in the viage to have v^li p moneth to goe in the ship wher Captein Davies doeth goe, and to have 2 monethes wages p^d him before hande, and 4 monethes wages more to goe in stocke of proffite or losse of the viage and for this enterteyment he promiseth to pforme all his best endevo^r and skill for ye fortheringe the viage, And he is also enterteynid the meane tyme before the viage beginne, to loke to the workynge and repayringe of the shippinge and to be allowed vj^s viij^d p weeke for his diett.

The 10th of october 1600.

Mr Ald^u Bannyng
Mr Allabaster
Capteñ Lancaster
Mr Rich. Wyche
Mr Roger Howe
Mr Wm Chambers

Mr Wm Harryson
[Capteñ Middleton]
Mr Rich : Wyseman
M^r Jo Bate
Capteñ Midleton
Mr Burrell

AT this assemblie were directed hether severall tres of commendinge to the imployment of the Est Indie viage thes severall psons hereafter namid to be vsed as pursers videlt from Mr Thoms Midleton one—Robt Creswell from iñ Stap one—Richard Babington— and from Capteñ Midleton—[one] Henry Midleton his brother wch severall sewters beinge seene appeare psonall and fitt men for imploym^t Yet notw^thstandinge this assembly Consistinge but of a small nüber and for that the busines of the viage is not come so farre as to make election of men of Charge they thought it fytt to take a further tyme for thes matters.

Lres Commending of severall men to be imployed

Robt Creswell, Rich: Babington, Henry Middleton

ther is apointed by this assemblie to goe downe to see [the] howe the worke of the [shippinge] *Mallice scurge* goeth forward and to attend the same from day to day vntill the ships be ready thes persons followinge [viz] who shall lye at Wolw^ch all the

surveyo^r of the workes of the malyce scurge

weeke at the Companies Charge.　　Henr Mydleton
　　　　　　　　　　　　　　　　Edward Hylliard

The smith at Wolw^ch　　It is agreed that the Smythe wch dwelleth at Wolw^ch whose name is Justice mullett shalbe imployed in the yron worke ther soe as he vse Spanishe iron.

a warraunt to take vp shipwright　　Ther was dd at this assemblie to m̃ Burrell a Warraunt signed by my L. Thrẽr for the takinḡ vp of Carpenters and shipwrightℭ to be presentlie sett on worke in the shippes payinḡ them suche wages as they can be agreed wth all.

Beare allowed to the workemen in the Malice Scurge　　Order is geaven to the said henry Mydleton and Edward hylliard accordinḡ as they shall see cause for the better holdinḡ together of the workemen from runĩnḡ from ther worke to drinke, to allowe them of the Companies charge a barrell of beare everie day, and to have a speciall care they leave not ther worke to Runne to the Alehouse.

the boat belonging to the Malice Scurge　　It is ordered that a note be inserted in captein Bakers Comission who goeth into the west Cuntrey that he geave order to sende vp the shipe boate belonginḡ to the Malice scurge wch lieth at Plymouth or els wher in the west Cuntrey.

Robt Hughes Bolton Saylemakers　　It is agreed at the request of m̃ Burrell that one Robt hughes and 　　 Bolton shalbe vsed in the makinḡ of the sayles of the Mallyce scurge.

Comitties to ppare the genall busines.　　It is thought meet and a *meane of* speciall expedition and furtheraunce of the busines of this viage that some psons be selected out of the number of the Comitties who shall dailie meet together and conferre of pointes and Remembraunces meet to be propounded when the generall Comitties do assemble and in some sorte to prepare the businesses readie for the same Assemblie, to ye ende to avoide the Lonḡ dispute of [thing] questions wch we finde be experience doeth growe when matters are propounded to *the* whole [Companie] Comitties before they be in some sort prepared before hande.

　　　　Mr Ald^n Bannyng　　　　Mr Allabaster
　　　　Mr Staper Mr Cordell　　Mr Roger Howe
　　　　Capten Lancaster　　　　 Mr Wyche
　　　　　　to meet at m^r Ald^n Bannynges

Mr Allabaster being moved to take the Charge of the order- Mr Allabaster touching the Accoumptes
ing the Accoumptes of this viage, [doeth] ether by him self or
his servaunt doeth excuse him self by the multytude of his owne
busines to attende the same him self, but is contented that his
man shall attende the same busines and he will nowe and then
oversee what his man doeth wth wch this assemblie holde them
selfes satysfied, and in regard of this service wilbe thankfull to
m̃ Allabaster.

Order is geaven to m̃ Ald^n Bannyng Thr̃er to deliver to yron worke & caske 200^{li}
Capteiñ Lancaster and m^r Chambers 200^{li} to be imployed in yron
worke and Caske.

Lyke order is geaven to ye said m̃ Ald^n to deliver to Josephe 100^{li} for ye susan
Salamon Purser of the Susan to be imployed in the preparation
of thinges necessarie for the same ship the some of one hundred poundes.

Order is geaven to m̃ Allabaster to sende Comission to his ser- Moneis to be pvided at Callys
vaunt at Callis to take vp all the Royalles of plate he can at the
best rate he can gett although it come to [two or] three thowsand poundes and to sende the same over for England.

Prouision to be made by Comission in the west Cuntrey
geaven to Captein Baker.

Syder	100 ^{tons}
breade	1200 ^{kintalles}
Bockallrowe *fishe*	37500 great tale
wheate	351 bushelles Winchester
Meale	538^c

Sanies, *nettẽ*, hookes, fysgiggẽ and harpe Irons

A Commission drawen by m̃ howe for Capteiñ Baker and M^r A Comission in to the West Cuntrey
Pope being reade at this assembly was signed vnder the handes
and deliuered to m̃ howe for the dispatche of the said Capteiñ
Baker to goe away this after noone.

John Busbridge Lynnen Drap dwelling vppon London Bridge Prouision of iron
was [compounded wth] *compounded* [*moved*] wth by m̃ Ald^n Bannyng and m̃ Staper for 10 toñs of the best sort of English iron
ordinary barrs at xj^{li} p̃ toñ to be deliuered [bet] at Lo^n by the
first of December and for x toñ of small barres of like iron a-
bout C [or] barres or therabouts in a toñ [for w^{ch}] he asketh

xx m̃ke p̃ toñ but promiseth it shalbe better cheape yf can.

Malice Scurge

An Inuentorie of the thinges nowe remayninḡ wᵗʰ the Malice Scurge.

A fore course, bonnett and drabler little vsed
A maine cors̃e bonnett and drabler litle vsed
A maine Topsaile litle vsed
a missen and a missen bonnett litle vsed
a newe spritt saile little vsed
an olde maine corse bonnett and drabler
more another maine corse
more an olde forecorse
more a Top gallont saile
a spritt saile Topsaill
x Iron scantions
2 Iron Cheines   4 nettinges
3 Cables by wᶜʰ the shipp rides broken
2 ankers of 30ᶜ weight or therabouts̃ a peece
1 anker of 16 weight
1 anker of 12ᶜ weight
3 olde muckẽ
    a whole sute of rigginḡ as the ship cam̃ from Chatham savinḡ
    that the most part of the small rūninḡ ropes is spent and
    hath bene otherwise vsed
    A sewt of windinḡ tackle blockes wᵗʰ 4 shevers of brasse
    Brasse shevers more 50
x Iron pompe staves
3 Iron pompe brakes
3 Crowes of Iron
2 paire of Cañ hookes
1 paire of billowes
5 esses of maine cheines of iron
3 dead mens eies wᵗʰ cheines of iron
6 tackell hookes
5 port hinges
4 boat hookes
2 fidd hammers

2 fidd℮
4 capsquares for carriag℮
a Loose hooke
2 dipsy leades
1 harpinġ iron
1 fisgig
1 hawser of 7 inches
2 hawsers one of 7 inches ½ thother of 7 inches
40 guñers tackles
120 roles of matche decaied
4 dossen of plate Cartringes wch are in 2 chest℮
14 exceltries
17 plates of leade to lay over the peeces
5 great brasse bolles
3 old brasse ladles
36 sprigges and runners
4 ladles
2 wadhookes
300 weight of square shott
16 breechinges
1 table in the great Cabin wth 4 stooles and one chaire
2 earthen great pott℮ for water
1 pompehooke
  A Bell of brasse
  A Longe boate lying at Plimoth verie litle vsed
2 fornaces in the Cookerome wth iron worke to binde the Cookerome
  The top mastes and yerd serviceable
  Demi Cannott shott 49
  Culveringġ shott 162
  Demi Culveringġ Crosse barre 49
  Demi Culveringġ rounde 34
  Sacre Crosse barre 14
  Sacre round 12

	c	qr	℔		
1	60	0	0	} 6 toñs	Demy Cannons.
2	60	0	0		

44   THE COURT RECORDS OF

		c	q	lt		c	q	lt	
Culveringes 16	1	42	0	0	9	36	2	0	
	2	42	0	0	10	36	2	0	
	3	42	0	0	11	36	2	0	
	4	42	0	0	12	36	2	0	} 31 toñz 8ᶜ
	5	42	0	0	13	36	2	0	
	6	42	0	0	14	36	2	0	
	7	42	0	0	15	36	2	0	
	8	42	0	0	16	36	2	0	
		c	q	lt		c	q	lt	
Demy Culvering 12 pece	1	29	0	0	7	29	0	0	
	2	29	0	0	8	29	0	0	
	3	29	0	0	9	29	0	0	} 17 toñs 8ᶜ
	4	29	0	0	10	29	0	0	
	5	29	0	0	11	29	2	0	
	6	29	0	0	12	29	2	0	
		c	q	lt		c	q	lt	
Sacres 8	1	20	2	0	5	20	2	0	
	2	20	2	0	6	20	2	0	} 8 toñs 4ᶜ
	3	20	2	0	7	20	2	0	
	4	20	2	0	8	20	2	0	

Sm To^{all} of the toñz of ordnaunce, 62 toñz 27ᶜ

The 11th of october 1600.

Mr Aldⁿ Bannyng   John Eldred
Mr Rich: Staper   Rich: Wyseman
Mr Thomas Cordell   Erle of Cumbland
Capteñ Lancaster   Capteñ Middleton

Wm Broadebent

HES Comitties thinke that Wm Brodebent of Graveshend is a verie fitt man to take charge in this viage and to that ende resolve to sende for him and to see how he is affected to the said viage.

A Cheine pumpe for ye Scourge

The Erle of Cumberland adviseth that a Chaine Pumpe is verie necessarie to be vsed in the malice Scurge.

THE EAST INDIA COMPANY 45

Mr Wyche informeth this assemblie that Capteiñ baker told him that m̂ Sergeaunt heale would be content to deliuer vnto the Companie as ther assignes in the west Cuntrey to be p^d him here in London the somme of 400^{li} It is therfore thought good he be talkd wthall and to that ende m̂^{9} howe is intreatid to talke wth s^{r}geaunt heale. S^{r}geaunt heale to be talked wth for money

The Eare of Cumb^{9}land sealed a bargaine and sale of the malice scurge to m̂ howe m̂ Eldred m̂ wych and m̂ Chamb^9 and had 2 warraunt^p for 1700^{li} the one to m̂ Ald^n Bannyn^g for 1000^{li} the other to Ald^n Hollyday for 700^{li} to be p^d this day and his Lp hath putt downe him self an adventuro^r of 1500^{li}, [in the] and apointed m̂ Cordell an adventuro^r of 500^{li}, wch two somes of adventure together wth the 1700^{li} p^d him by the 2 Thiers make vp the whole somme of 3700^{li} being the price of the malice scurge bought of his Lp. Malice Scourge 1700^{li} p^d for the Scourge and the rest of the ships valewe sett downe by the Erle and by Mr Cordell.

A warraunt signed by 4 of the Comitties for the paiment of 600^{li} to m̂ fra: Elington for the provision of Cloth wch warraunt is directed to Ald^n Bannyn^g. 600^{li} for prouision of Clothe

Another Warraunt to Ald^n hollyday for the Purser of the Scurge for the paiment of 100^{li} 100^{li} to ye purser of the Scourge.

The 13 of october 1600.

Ald^n Bannyng   Mr Eldred
Mr Rich: Staper   Capteiñ Lancaster

T is thought meet by thes Comitties that ther shalbe noe adventuro^r refused that will adventure 200^{li} vntill the whole adventure do ryse above 55000^{li} for that it is supposed that somme [suche] wch have sett downe [that] ther contributions will drawe backe againe. howe farre aduentures shalbe re^d hereafter.

46   THE COURT RECORDS OF

The 15 of october 1600.

Aldⁿ Bannyng   Mr Roger Howe
Aldⁿ Hollyday   { Mr John Eldred
Mr Tho. Cordell   { Mr Wm Harryson
Mr Wm Garway   Mr Rich : Staper
Captein Lancaster   Mr Rich : Wyche
Mr Rich : Wyseman   { Capteiñ Davies
Mr Wm Chamber { Phiṗ Grove
                Mr Burrell

Proportion. THES[/] Committies [have] do resolve to alter the proportion of breade from the proportion sett downe in ther note of the generall provision, and do alter it from 16 monethes to xx^{tie} monethes provision so as by ther
Biskett present resolution ther is to be provided in byskett [2000^c   0^q 0^{ll} 280] 180^{mt}.
Meale And they do agree that ther shalbe provided in meale over and besides the provision in breade, 535 bushelles of Winchester measure being 8 gallons to the Bushell.
Wheate Wheate 250 Bushelles kill dried of like measure.
Syder 60 Toñs of Syder.
fishe 20 m^l newe [found] land fishe great tale.
Comission in to ye West Cuntrey to be altered Comission having bene geaven to Capteiñ Baker and m^r Pope for the provision of thes severall victualles above menc̃oed at the rates and proportions formerlie sett downe in the generall note of Proportion newe advyse is to be geaven them to make ther provision according to these rates above menc̃oned.
Mr Burrell Whereas Mr Atye semethe discontented and doeth not apply him self to furnishe suche provisions as belongeth to the preparing of the shippes [at *Wolwiche*] in suche sorte as the necessytie thereof requireth order is geaveñ to Mr Burrell to furnishe all suche provision of Tymber as the shippes stande neede of wthout depending vppon m^r Atye or enduring of any further delaies in this busines.
A newe boate for ye Malice Scurge Ordered that there shalbe made a [*newe*] longe boate Carvell fashion for the malice scourge to be sett uṗ in the Cuntry.

Order is geaven that ther shalbe p⁴ to Mʳ Burrell the somme of Cˡⁱ for provisions [and] of tymber to be used in the shippes by m͂ʳ Aldʳ Bannyng Thr͂er and a warraunt to that ende signed.

100ˡⁱ to be p⁴ to Mʳ Burrell.

The 16 of October 1600.

Ald Bannyng	Mʳ Wyseman͂
Ald Hollyday	Mʳ Howe
Mʳ Cordell	Capten Lancaster
Erle of Cumberland	

RDER is geaven by thes Comitties to Mʳ Aldʳ Bannyng to pay to Capten Davies to beare his charges in to the next Cuntrey the som͂e of 20ˡⁱ vppon an accompte of the pticlers of his charges in the said jorney.

20ˡⁱ to Captin Davies.

A Bill from Sergeaunt Hele to Warwicke Heale in the West Cuntrey wherby he is Required by the said sergeaunt to pay CCˡⁱ to Mʳ Roger Howe or his assigns at x daies sight is delivered to Capten͂ [to receive the leave wᶜʰ the said] [Davies to leave wᵗʰ] Mʳ Ellicott Baker or Pope to Receave the money accordinglie. Wᶜʰ bill doeth menc͂on that the money is already p⁴ to m͂ʳ Heale here in London althoughe he hath not yet reᵈ it. Wᶜʰ bill beareth date the 15 of October 1600.

Sergeaunt Heale

Composition͂ is made wᵗʰ Phillip Grove Pylote for to goe in this viage as he shalbe apointed. And he is contented to be imploied in the [same] viage according to the direction of the Comitties as Pilot to any ship apointed for the consideration of the somme of one hundred poundes to be pᵈ him to furnishe him self and to geave him the proffite of five hundred poundes as God shall blesse the viage. And vppon thes considerations he promyse to pforme all fidelytie and good service that Layeth in his power.

Phillip Grove Pylott.

Laus deo   London the 10ᵗʰ of October.

Lovinge frends etc As wee have Intreated you to take some

A Comission to Capten Baker and Mr Pope to goe in the West Cuntrey for Provisions &c.

paines for vs in the West Country Where now by Godſ grace you are to take yor Jornie for the procuringe and providinge of such victuallſ and other provision as wee in those partſ are to be furnished of for our pretended viage wch god prosper. The pticulers wherof herafter shalbe expressed soe wee hope that by your good and discreete meanes you will not onely take that good dilligent and provident Care in the providinge of that wch is very good well handled and in all respects soe orderly as the necessetie of so longe a viage importeth The first and most especiall thingſ that wee recomend vnto your care is for your bisket to see that the same be twice well dryed and that extraordinaryly for it is an extraordinary viage as you knowe and procure as neare as you may to have five Cakes to a pound and that they be whole and sound as neare as you may and for such Cakes as ffalle oute to be rather hollowe or broken that you appte them from the rest and keepe them be them selves that they may be first spent wee thinke it your best place to pvide the same in wilbe lañe Apsome Darmouth, Plimouth and the places to them adjoyninge for yor meale you may provide the same When you can gett the best driest and hardest corne and fittest for yor purpose and old corne is best yf you can gett it and being convrted into meale you are to take the branne out of it and soe packe it into good drie and sweet caske and to packe it verie hard and Closse and to see the same well hooped and packed cold. Nowe for the Syder you are to be carefull to provide that wch is good and beinge provided to wracke and for that it is newly made it wilbe good that that when you buy it to condicon wth them to recſ the same some 6 weekes after or sooner yf you please to your Choise the reason is for that in the meane tyme it may be settled and growe to be fine alsoe some it will excuse, it were not amisse you bringe yor owne Caske for yf you should remove it from hence it wilbe longe before it be fine againe. Alsoe you are to condicon wth them of whome you buy it that they at their charge deliver it at the water side I meane at the next convenient porte for ladinge of it Nowe the sider beinge bought doth accompte very much to have very good Caske and wel houped and three

Iron Hoopes vppon ech end of ech Cask for What prevaileth it to haue good suder and the cask be not good sweet and well hooped and this beinge effected to sent the same to Dartmouth wch must be the place of the assembly of all your prouisions the fittest place for the pvidinge of your suder is Colletton Seaton Axmouthe Newton Bushea and aboute Apsoñ and Dartmouth.

As for o^r Newland fishe if you are to pvide you are alsoe to be carefull to see yf the same not onely be good fish and well handled but also very Dry and that you take take not anie that ether head or tale be anie thinge moist as often tymes that fishe falleth out to be but yf you be forced to take anie in your ptide you may keepe them by them selues to be first spent And this beinge donne you are to lay the same in a good Close and dry Laughte and pvide good store of ffurre to lay vnder vppon and aboute the same to keepe the moist aire from yt and herafter you shall receaue further order from vs ether for the packinge of the same Cask or to bunndell it vpp 200 fishes in a bundell old corne wilbe best yf you can gett yt whether old or newe it must be keild dried and after packed in good cask℮ and as for saynes Hookes and Linnes you are to pvide them at the discretion of Capten Davis such and soe many as you shall thinke fitt and needefull further at your cominge into the Country you are presently to enquire and lerne what quantetie of wine and vinegre ther is tobe had and at what price and also the price of beanes and pease both white and gray also what store of Iron hoopes ther are to be had and at what price but not to buy anie untill you heare further from vs for that wee are ptly mynded to send you some from hence Likewise you are to write vs forthwth whether ther wilbe cask had ther sufficient and good to serue what you shall neade there or not for y^t yf you cannot fitt your selues thear wth such and as much there as you shall neede that then vppon notice therof from you wee may supply o^r want℮ from hence Alsoe you are to certefie vs of the state and price of all those pvisions that wee

you in charge to pvide and therwth all yor opiñions howe you shalbe able to effect and accomplish the same as neare as

H

you may wee are Informed as you knowe of a prize brought to
Plimouth wch some 40 tt₍° of Cassalla wines wch o^r desire is that
one of you wth as much speade convenient as you may for to
taste them and to knowe the lowest price of them and findinge
them good of that sorte of wines and such as will serue o^r tornes
to buy them yf you may haue them at a reasonable rate to say
not passing 10 or 11^{li} p tt₍° at the most but for lesse what you
may it is a kinde of wine not vendible here in o^r Country and
they haue benn sold here in London at 7^{li} p tt₍° very good wines
but yf you cannott gett them as aforēs^d then may you ꝑcure
the loest price of them and take the pties ꝑmise for some 12
daies respect in that tyme at your choise ether to take or leaue
them and so forthwth to certefie vs thereof yo^u may shew them
that yf yo^u buy them they shall have their present   for
them wch wilbe some cause to see them the better cheape and
yf at your cominge hether they be not landed out of the ship
wee would you could agree wth them to deliver them heere at
his charges and adventure though they cost vs the more as of
necessetie they will what further directions to give you presently wee knowe not for the ꝑvidinge of these thingꝭ and doe
referre vs to your good discretiõ and care for the managinge
and well orderinge of these businesses. By this you perceaue
what o^r desire is to haue donn wch yf you cannot accomplishe
as you would yet as well and as neare as you may.

Nowe resteth order and meanes to be taken for the furnishinge of you wth monies for the paiment of the ꝑvisions aforesaid

not exceed-
inge 1000^{li}
or two at
the most.

wch o^r desire ys that you take vpp in the country soe much
monie as you may and to give yor bills in Alde^r Banningꝭ Alde^r
Hollidaies for the repayment of it heer wth billꝭ wee will see
well p^d and for the better obteininge of monie ther wee haue
ꝑcured my Lo: Treasurers lr̃e to the receivers and customers
of Dovor and Cornewall to helpe you vnto such moneis as they

you are to
leaue this
lre wth M^r
Ellecot at
Exeto^r

haue in their custodie of her ma^{tes} as the said lr̃e doth import
wch wee delivered vnto yor   you may show as occasion
may serue to such as it is directed and what you doe receive of
them you may give them billꝭ in the Alderman aforesaid for
the repaym^t of yt heere wch shalbe well p^d and wth what by these

meanes you shall not be able to furnishe yor want{e} wee will vppon intellegence from you furnish you from hence from tyme to tyme in the best order wee may and for an earnest pennye wee will give order that you shall receive presently this next weeke in the country 5 o 600{li} but the more you cann pcure in the country the lesse charge and adventure wee shalbe at in sendinge downe of yt from hence ffurther for Royall{e} of plate wee pray you that you wilby all good meanes possible procure as many as yo{u} may of 8 &c 2 at the least Rate you may and for maym{t} of them ether to pay them ther yf you can get monies or else to give yor bill{e} as afores{d} or to take some short tyme yf wee may send the same downe yf they will not take their monies heer for such as you can gett to bagg them vp and seale the bagg{e} and make them and   them in some sure and trustye mennes hand{e} some in one mannes hand{e} and some viz in the hands of in another vntill o{r} further order also you are to pcure some Mr Ellicot out of Brittaine from Mort and St Mallowes both by your owne Mr Willīū Martin at meanes of yor frend{e} although you deliuer monies ther in their Excto{r} or Country to such mchaunt{e} as trade for them plac{e} before hand Mr Simes in Charde. beinge two sure men to some 200{li} and some 300{li} some more you must some lesse as you shall thinke the men to be of honesty and take bonds for such abilitie to performe such bargaine as they shall make wth you monies as wch must be for so much English monies as they binde them yo{u} geaue out to be selues to deliuer you so many Royalls of plate of 8.4. and 2. by repd by a such a tyme wch tyme must be at furthest the midle or end of day. novem{r} herof you are to certefye vs what you thinke you shalbe able to help vs vnto by that tyme and that as soone as you may for that wee cannot furnish o{r} selues ther wee may take some other order heere for o{r} bisket wee hold it very necessary that the bakers that bake it stand bund for the same shall continew good and sweet for 2 yeares at Plimouth ther is the malice skourges boate wch ship we have brought and therfore are to have the boate wch we pray you may be trimed and sent vp hether by the first convenient meanes you may and to se whether she may be worth triminge or no and to advise vs therof forthw{th} at Captin Davis his cominge downe wee will write you further whose opinion order and direction for the providinge and orderinge of o^r said victualls wee pray you to followe for that he is not onely well experienced herin but also is to spend and to take his pte herof in the viage.

The provisions as followeth

Bread 1200^c Syder 100 tt℔^o Meale 835^c Wheat 251 busshell℔ Newland ffishe 3785 Saynes Hookes Lynes &c. at Cap: Davies direction

Yo^r loving frend℔

Paull Bannyng	Ric Staper	Roger Howe	Jo Eate
Leonerd Hollyday	Ric Wyseman	Wm Harrysoñ	
James Lancaster	Wm Chamb^r	Ric Wyche	

Captein Davies Comission going into the West Cuntrey for provisions &c.

Lovinge freind Mr Davis since the makinge & geavinge of o^r former order & comission to Mr Backer and Mr Pope wth the wch you are acquainted notwthstandinge for yor better remembrannce herew^{ch} wee geve yo^u the Coppie wch is at lardge concerninge the providing of Victuals & Roials of plate in the West Cuntrie as to the said comission wee referre vs wee say since that tyme wee have had further conference & consideraĉon touchinge our said Commission for the proporĉon of suche victualls etc as wee gave order p̄ the same to provide & now havinge dulie considered there of wee have thought good to alter our former pretence & to lessen the proporĉon in some and encrease it in other some as hereafter shall appeare wth wch alteraĉon and now our determinĉon yo^u are at yor comige downe p^rsentlie to accquainte Mr Backer and Mr Pope ether by conference wth them or p yor l̃res and so to appointe a place of meetinge that yo^u may not onlie know what is done but also to take order for the accomplishinge of the rest and at yor meetinge wee hope you will so exactlie consider of all matters that you will lay your plate in that good order that our said Busines may be effected for our good & yor creditt℔ & espetiallie for you Mr Davies vppon whom wee do so muche rely & whom it doth so nere touche bothe in creditt and for your owne vse to see that wch is or shalbe provided to be good and well ordered eche proviĉon according to his qualetye As therof wee hold it needlesse to vse any further direcĉon for that wee know your experience & discreĉon to be suche that in these matters

you may rather directe vs but onlie hereafter to note somethinge
vnto you wch are as followethe.

First at yor cominge to the   wee pray you to conferr
wth Mr Thomas Syms and to know of him what Royalls of
plate he hath provided and what quantety he thincketh shalbe
able to provide and in what tyme and of him yo^u shall know
wher Mr Backe^r and Mr Pope are and at your cominge to
Exceter you are to make the like enquirie of Mr Ellecote and
Mr Martin concerninge Royalls of plate & to request them all
to procure vs as many as possible by any meanes they may and
for the payment of such as they shall provide to chardge us by
exchaunge accordinge to our former comission whose Bills
shalbe well paide   Also that Mr Ellecote & Mr Martin pcure
to take vpp as much moneys as they cann gett not passinge
and to charge us for paym^t thereof p their Billes as aforesaid
wch may serve for paym^t of our pvicon and Roials of plate as
occasion servethe and for such Roials as they provide of 8. 4.
& 2. that they make them vpp in canvas Bagge made of new
canvas   in eche Bagg & so seale them & lett them
remaine in yor custody untill o^r further order & for their paines
& labour in theise Busines they shalbe considered & for suche
Bondes or Billes as you shall have ther in the cuntrie made
vnto you ether for the accomplishinge of provicon or moneis
wee pray you that they may be all lefte wth the said Ellecote &
Martin takinge a note of their handes for all suche thinges as
yo^u shall leave in truste wth them and for such thinges I meane
Billes or Bondes that are for the pformaunce of matters ther
in the cuntrye you may leave the notes wth Mr Backer & M^r
Pope & for the rest you may bringe alonge wth you at yor Retourne wch wee would willinglie should be as soone as you may
for that wee shall have nede of you here for sundrie cawses
But duringe your beinge ther wee once againe pray you to
geve furtheraunce to all our Busines as well for provicon as
for Roialls of Plate as muche as possible you may.

If anie of yor freindes ther in the cuntrie are desirous to adventure in this our viadge you may accepte of them in such
order as wee here doe that noe one be les then 200^li and that

the moneis be provided in Roials of plate and paid to Mr Ellecote or Mr Martin p the fyne of November next at the furthest accomptinge their Roialls of plate at vj^d p pece and to make them suche further allowaunceſ as wee allowe vnto other men of whom wee ther buy them & for suche as do adventure lett them sett downe their names in a shete of pap vnder their owne handes as wee do here & so you may bringe the same alonge wth you that they may be admitted   But wee would not have you to take adventures not above 2 att most.

Wee vnderstand by one Mr Lecheland who dwelleth at Culleton that ther are some 100 Bushells of white pease to be had at some 2^s 8^d or 2^s 10^d wch yf you find them at that price wee pray you to buy them and althoughe you pay 3^s for them yf you like them & so thincke good   Wee understand that Porcke is also ther good cheape at your cominge downe lett not to write to vs presentlye how you find matters ther and what you thincke concerninge the effectinge of our Busynesses that accordinglie wee may go forward wth our Busines here   And thus wee leave you and all your endeavours to the direccon of Thalmightie.

O^r proporcon of Victuals is as followethe
200 Newland fishe great toele
60tſ sider & no more all to be sent to London in their caske
1800 of Biskett
535 Bushells of Meale Winchester measure of 8 gallens
250 : Bushells of Wheate of the same measure

Wee deliver yo^u herewth Mr Sergent Heale his Bill of exchaunge & a lre to Mr Warwicke for the receivinge of 200^{li}, at 10 daies sighte

Yo^r lovinge freindes
Pawl Baninge
Leonard Holliday
Richard Wiseman
Thomas Cordell
Roger Howe

A second comission to Captein Baker and   O^r Lovinge Freindes o^r former Comission directed to you bothe and delivered to Capten Baker wee have related to Captein Davies and to the end he may be accquainted wth all provisions touchinge the said viage wherin wee have appointed you to deale wee have geaven him a coppy of your said Commission But vppon further consideracon of our said provisions and the revewe of the ꝑticlers thereof wee are induced vppon good respectꝭ to alter the said proporcons enlarginge some of them and abridginge othersome of them accordinge to the rates herevnder ꝑticlerlie menc̃oed wch ꝑticlers wee do resolve shall stand for our provision wthout alteracon and therfore wee pray you to directe your proporcon of all the said victuall accordinge to these quanteties wch wee have delivered to Captein Davies Whervppon our desire is that you do all conferr together and dyspose of the provicon thereof as you may best sorte the same every one of you endeavoringe the good of the voyage as wee hope yo^u will wth good agreem^t and consent together.

^{Mr Pope altering the first proportion of victualles.}

The proportion of Victualles
20 thowsand newland ffishe great tale
60 Tons of Syder
180 thowsand Biskett
535 bushelles meale Winchester measure
250 bushelles Wheat of the same measure.

Yo^r lovinge frendes
Paull Bannyng
Leo Hollyday
Ric Wyseman
Thomas Cordell
Roge^r Howe.

21 October 1600.

WARRAUNT geven to Mr Ald^r Hollyday threī to pay to Mr Roger Howe to pay over to Sergeaunt Heele vppon a bill of exchaung to be p^d in Plymouth the sōme of 200^{li}.

^{200^{li} to S^{rg}eaunt Heele}

Warraunt geaven to Ald^r Bannyng threī to pay Mr Howe to pay over to Laurence Waldo for the like valewe vppon his bill of exchaung to be rep^d at Exceto^r the somme of 50^{li}

^{50^{li} to Laur Waldo.}

100ˡⁱ for Caske & iron hoopes. Warraunt for the paymᵗ of 100ˡⁱ to Mʳ Chambers to provide Caske and iroñ hoopes.

22 October 1600

Aldʳ Bannyng	Mʳ Wysemañ
Aldʳ Hollyday	Mʳ Harrysoñ
Mʳ Staper	Mʳ Wyche
Mʳ Cordall.	

30ˡⁱ Php Grove.   ARRAUNT geaveñ to Mʳ Aldʳ Hollyday to pay to Phiṗ. Grove vppon accompte of his wages the some of thirtie poundes.

100ˡⁱ Purser of the Scourge.   Warraunt is geaven to Aldʳ Bannyng to pay to Henr̃ Mydleton Purser of the Scourge for the defraying of charges aboute the same ship 100ˡⁱ.

the 23 octobʳ 1600.

Aldʳ Bayning	Mʳ How
Aldʳ Holliday	Mʳ Cordell
Mʳ Stapers	Mʳ Harrison
Mʳ Lancaster	Mʳ Chambres

1100ˡⁱ to Robert Steuens by letter off Mʳ Joh clacott.   ARRANT given to Mʳ Aldˀ Bayning to pay y 1100. to Robert Stephns; by vertew of a letter frõ Mʳ John Ellacott of Exceter of the 18 present, that hee hath in a more some made Imployment of In Ryalls of plate.

120ˡⁱ to ffr evington by bil of Robᵗ Pope.   Warrant given to Mʳ Aldˀ Holliday for payment of y 120. to ffʳ Evington; ffor a bill of exc̃ frõ Robᵗ Pope; that hee Rsᵈ towards pvyding of pvisions in the West countrey.

A leter to Joseph Sabbanck   Written a letter to Robᵗ Salbanck purser of the Susann to will him to suffer Mʳ Burrell to take such men as it shall please him out of his shipp towards the more speedy execution of the work of the malice scourge.

Thomas Wasse desyrous to bee Imployed,   By the motion of Mʳ Richard Candler it was ordred to sett down one Mʳ Thomas Wasse, who was desyrous to bee Imployed in this voyadg as a factor.

THE EAST INDIA COMPANY

Yt is at this Assembly accorded that Mʳ Sandy should contynew his wryting into the west countrey for pvyding of Ryalls of plate, warranting him that his bills should bee well payd.

prouyding of Ryals of plate in yᵉ west countrey.

The 25 october 1600.

Aldʳ Bannyng   Mʳ John Eldred
Mʳ Wᵐ Garway   Mʳ Roger Howe
      Mʳ Wᵐ Harrysoñ.

RDER is geaveñ by thes Comitties to Aldʳ Bannyng Threï for the paiment of the somme of 200ˡⁱ to Mʳ Coles for soe muche by him pᵈ to Roᵇᵗ Pope in the West Cuntrey.

200ˡⁱ to be pᵈ to Mʳ Coles by exchaung.

The like order is geaveñ for the paiment of one hundred markes to Mʳ Garwey for to be imploied in the necessarie repacõns of the Assension vppon accompte.

100 markes vppon repacons of the Assention.

Also order is geaveñ to the said Aldʳ Bannyng Threï to disburce vppon the necessarie repacõns of the Susañ vppon accompte the somme of fyfty poundes.

50ˡⁱ vppon repacons of the Susan.

The 27 Octobʳ 1600.

Aldʳ Bayning   Mʳ Lancaster
Aldʳ Holliday   Mʳ Harrison
Mʳ Garway   Mʳ Wyche
Mʳ Wyseman   Capt: Middleton
      Mʳ Cordell

T this Assembly it was ordred and determyned and a warrant given to Thomas Evesett to warne all the adventurers in this voyadg to bee at a court at ffounders hall on thursday the 30 of this moneth there to take notyce of hir Maᵗⁱᵉˢ pleasure signifyede by a letter frõ the lords of her maᵗⁱᵉˢ Counsayle.

Warraunt for a generall Court.

Yt is also appoynted that *Mʳ Aldʳ bayning Aldʳ Wattes* Mʳ Cordell, Mʳ Lancaster & Capteyne Middleton shall take

Chusing of Mʳˢ & mariners

58   THE COURT RECORDS OF

order in the choosing & appoynting of maysters ffor the shipps in this voyadg—

Captein Lancaster   Also that Mr Ald Bayning *Ald^r Hollyday, Ald^r Moore* Mr Cordell, Mr Garway & Thomas Alabaster *or any 4 of them* to deale wth capt. Lancaster ffor the taking of the government of this voyadg as the cheiff [generall] *commander* thereof.

Octob^r the 27th 1600.

50^{li} Nichas Holway   EVEN a warrant to [capt] M^r ald^r Holliday ffor payment of y 50li to Mr Nycholas Holway, by a bill of exĉ frõ Rob^rt Pope of the 19 hereof.

Comission for Royalles to Calleis & Roun.   Alsoe this day it is accorded that Mr Alabaster shall contynew his cõmission ffor Callais & Roane for the pvyding of Ryals of plate to the vallew of ffyve thousand pownds wth pmyse that his bills of exĉ shalbee payd & contented.

The 28 octob^r 1600.

Mr Ald^r Bayning   Mr Eldred
Mr Harrison   Mr Howe.

1000^{li} to Rob^{rt} Stephens by bil frõ Jno Ellacott   EVEN a warrant to Ald Holliday ffor paym^t of y 1000li to Mr Rob^{rt} Stephins in full of a bill of exĉ frõ Mr John Ellacott of Exceter ffor the vallew there Rsd to bee Imployed in Ryalls of plate.

44^{li} to peter sampson.   Geven a warrant to Mr Ald Holliday ffor paym^t of y 44li to peeter sampson by bill of exĉ frõ Mr John Sandy of Exceter; for the vallew there Rsd by him to the companyes vse.

A Gen^rall Courte.   The [last] 30 of Octob^r 1600 in the presence of the Comitties and Generalytie hereafter named viz:

Comitties.
{
Sr Johñ Hart knight   Mr Wm Garwey
Ald^r Bannyng   Mr Thomas Cordall
Ald^r Moore   Mr Richard Wysemañ
Ald^r Hollyday   Mr Wm Chamber
Ald^r Smyth   Mr Johñ Eldred
Mr Ric: Staper   Mr Roger Howe.
}

THE EAST INDIA COMPANY 59

Mr Johñ Eldred ⎫
Mr Wm Harrysoñ ⎭
  Gen^{r}alyty
James Deane
Edward Leanyng
Nicħas Leat
Nicħas Piece
Olyuer Style
Humfrey Smythe
Roƀ^t Sandy
Richard Pomtell
John Highelord
Humfrey Style
Nicħas Farrar
Thomas Farringtoñ
John Combe
Roƀt Offeley
James Turnor
Maurice Abbott
Leonard Whyte
Georg Chamƀleyn
John Cornelys
Raph Busby
Wm Jennyns
Roƀt Bell
Thomas Whyte
Nicħas Lyng
Wm Palmer
Nicħas Cryspe
Roƀ^t Cockes
Wm Wastall
Johñ Bate
Hugh Hamersley
Nathaniel Martiñ
Barthew Holland
[Richar Cockes]
Wm Stone

John Frier
Frauncis Dent
Richard Ball
Roger Hemmyng
Frauncis Evingtoñ
Thomas Westweawe
Daniel Marshe
John Midletoñ
Roƀt Gore
Raph Gore
Wm Cater
John Buzbridg
Thomas Horton
Wm Bond Mċhantailer
Augustin Skinner
Rich: Taileby
Robt Middletoñ
Roƀt Batemañ
Roƀt Waldo
Wm Dale
Lau: Waldo
Henry Bridgemañ
Samuel Armitage
Edward Harrysoñ
Edward Nicholsoñ
Clement Moseley
Humfrey Walcott
Reynold Greene
Roƀ^t Mildmay
Georg Chaundeler
Wm Burrell
Thomas Henshaw
Wm Ferries
Wm Hewett
Wm Fisher
Nicħas Salter
Wm Angell

Nicħas Barnesley	Henry Archer
Henry Polsted	John Casoñ
Andrew Bannyng	Richard Beale
Barthew Haggett	Richard Washer
Robt Buck	George Holmañ
Johñ Hodgesoñ	Frauncis Barker
Richard Piott	Richard Deane
Georg Coles	Richard Ironsyde
Raphe Hamor	James Dunkiñ.

HIS generall Assemblie being called together as well to acquaint them of the proceading̸ of the busines hetherto ҏformed in the preparatioñ of the voyage as to informe them of the slacknes of many of the Contributo^rs who had sett downe ther names and ther sommes pretended to be adventured and had hetherto brought in noe moneys to furnishe the provision, first the said Assemblie were putt in mynde of ther geñall Petition and projecte of the viage wch was offered in all ther names to the ll: of her Ma^es most honorable privy Counceℓℓ, wherby ther Lordships were humbly intreated by them to Solicite her ma^e in ther names, for her gratious Licence and assent that they might vndertake a voyage to the East Indies for the hon^r of o^r Cuntrey and for the advancem^t of the trade of merchaundize of this Realme conteyning in ther said Petition divers Clawses for the furtheraunce of the said viage. It was alsoe remembred vnto them that the Lordes having acquainted her ma^e wth ther said Petition did retorne them her ma^es gratious aunswer and free assent therunto geaving them incoragem^t to goe forward wth assuraunce that ther shuld noe staye be made of ther vyage wch was certyfyed vnder the handes of the Lord Threr̃ Lord Admirall L Chambleyn S^r [Robt] Wm Knowles Sr Robt Cycill and Secretery Herbert by a lr̃e bearing date the 16 day of Septc̃ber last. And they were further putt in mynde that vppon this Warraunt Certefyed by the lordes of her ma^es Assent and assuraunce to proceade the Companie had since

THE EAST INDIA COMPANY 61

mett together and at ther Gen^rall assemblie holden the 23. of Septemb̃ [last following] they, or the most of them having vnder ther owne handes sett downe ther adventures [had] did make choice of Seventeene of the said Contributors whom they appointed to be comitties to dispose and manage the whole busines and preparatiõn for the said viage. According to wch Coñiission geaven the said Cõmitties had hetherto proceaded and had defraied in the [said] preparation of the said viage and stoode ingaged to be aunswerd by exchaung and otherwyse for the soñie of xx m^l poundes at the least; The busines being thus farr proceaded in they were further geaveñ to vnderstand That many of the companie who had sett downe ther adventures begaune to wthdrawe ther purpose of pceading and wthheld ther paym^t of ther moneys vppon some Rumo^{rs} or doubtes geaveñ out that the viage was lyke to receave soñie stay for the removing and clearing of wch doubt that meanes had bene made by soñie of the Comitties to the lordes of the Councell for ther certifycat to the adventurers that they might wth full assuraunce proceade wthout any just cause of doubte, Who thervppon wrote ther lr̃es to Generalyty confirming ther former lr̃es of certificat that the said viage shuld receave noe stay or interruptioñ wch lr̃es being vnder the handes of the Lord keeper the L Thr̃er the L Admirall Sr Rob̃^t Cicell Sr John ffortescue, the L Chief Justice, and Mr Secretary Herbert were openlie read and beare date the 26 day of this instant october [and wthall it was delivered unto theñi]. In wch last recyted Lr̃es besides the warraunt of incoragem^t geaveñ to the Companie to proceade It was notid unto theiñ that the actioñ vndertakeñ by theñi was a publike action and not to be dallied wthall [and to that the] and therfore did require that the names of such as did ether wthdrawe them selfes or practise to wthdrawe others from proceading thein shuld be certefyed to ther Lorshipes that they might examine the reasoñ of ther discoragem^t. After the discourse of all wch severall matters and proceadinges all the said Assemblie by generall consent did agree to bring in ther moneys wch was by former [assent] order payable the most of theiñ being behinde but for the second paym^t wch was payable this present day and some of theiñ being behinde both for the first and seconde payment, [saving some] *amongest wch only* two or three of contributors, ther present denied to adventure at all viz Johñ Bate Robt Osseley *Nathaniell Martyn* and Hughe Hamersley the said Johñ Bate geaving his aunswer that he was disapointed by some that shuld have ioyned wth him in the adventure of CC^{li} and did fall from him, so that he could not adventure for his owne adventure above C^{li}, and the said Robt Osseley *Nathaniell Martyn* and Hughe Hamersley alledging that they held them selfes discharged by a clawse that was sett downe in the last geñ'all assemblie, wch was that he that brought not in his adventure by the last of September shuld not be pmitted to adventure at all.

The generalytie having thus agreed to bring in ther monies to further the expedition of the viage they required that order might be takeñ for all others wch wthheld ther contributioñs and came not at this assembly to geave ther assentes, that they might be called vppon to bring in ther money or to geave ther reason of wth holding it to thende, that according to the Councelles lres they might called before ther Ll: to aunswer the cause yf they did deny to adventure or would not bring ther moneys as by ther owne agreem^t they are to doe.

And forasmuch as the Pattent is already draweñ and in the handes of Mr Attorney ready to be pfytted by the course of wch Pattent the Companie is to consist of a governo^r 24 Comitties and the geñalyty this Court have by a most free Election, noiñted for ther governo^r Mr Thomas Smyth Ald^r whose name they do desire may be sett downe in the Pattent to be offred to her Ma^{ie}, and allowed for ther first Governo^r.

And whereas hetherto ther hath beene appointed by the geñ'alyty but 17 Comittyes to dispose and manage the affaires and busines of the trade, nowe forasmuch as by the Pattent ther is to be apointed 24 Comitties for that purpose Ther is choice made at this Assemblie of the full number of fowr and twenty whereof some part are of the former Comitties heretofore imployed in the said busines and the residewe are supplied

THE EAST INDIA COMPANY 63

out of the Geñalyty. Soe as the names of all the said Comitties as they are nowe agreed vppon be as hereafter followeth videlt:

Ald^r Bannyng
Ald^r Hollyday
Ald^r Moore
Ald^r Holmedeñ
Mr Rich: Staper
Mr Wm Garway
Mr Thomas Cordell
Capteñ Lancaster
Mr Rich: Wysemañ
Mr Fra: Chery
Mr Allabaster
Mr Roger Howe

Mr Richard Wyche
Mr John Eldred
Mr Wm Chamber
Mr Wm Harrysoñ
Mr Olyver Style
Mr Robt Sandy
Mr John Highelord
Mr Wm Rumney
Mr John Middletoñ
Mr Niclas Lynge
Mr Johñ Combe
Mr Robt Bell

This Co^{r}te havinge thus apointed ther Governo^r and Comitties they doe referre and Comitte to ther Governm^t *preparatioñ* and directioñ all matters whatsoever concerning the viage. Be it concerning shipping victualling merchaundizes moneys or appointing of officers to be imployed in the same. Allowing and holding for good all and whatsoever they or the most of theñ wth the Consent of the Governo^r shall direct or agree vppon.

The severall psons heervnder named do promyse to bring in ther adventures in this manner videlt:

Johñ Wastall will bring in his money in dollers at xviij^d the ^{ll}.

Daniell Marche offereth to bring in his money yf he may be imployed.

Augustine Skynner will bring in his money at xx^d the doller or els pay in Englishe money.

Wm Addersley his adventure shalbe brought in by Mr Henshawe

Niclas Salter will bring in his money
Thomas Ironsyde will bring in his money
Morice Abbott will bringe in his money the next weeke.

The 31 October 1600.

Ald^r Bannyng	M^r
Ald^r Hollyday	Mr Wm Chamber
Mr Olyver Style	Mr John Midleton
Mr Wm Garway	Mr Niclias Lynge
Capteñ Lancaster	Mr Robt Bell
Mr Rumney	Mr John Combe
Mr Roger Howe	Mr Rich Wyche
Mr John Highlord	Mr Wm Harryson
Mr Robt Sandy	Mr John Eldred

50^{li} to John Purnell

ORDER is geaveñ to Ald^r Bannyng Threr to pay to Johñ Purnell the somme of fyfty poundes for so much by him dd, in Spanishe Ryalles to Thomas Baker in Plymmothe.

24 to Wm Turnor

The lyke Warraunt is geaveñ to him to pay to Wⁿⁱ Turno^r the somme of twentie and four poundes for soe much dd by Richard Moone to Thomas Baker in Plymouth.

Robt Popes lres of advyse.

Lres from Robt Pope the one of 22 the other the 25 of this present froñ Plymouthe were reade wheriñ he geaveth the Companie divers advyses of his severall proceadinges in the Companies busines both for provysions and moneys. W^{ch} lres Mr Roger Howe is required to aunswer in the Companies name and having made aunswer thereof the same is to passe the handes of some of the Comitties to be sent him for his further Comissioñ.

Capten Baker's lres of advyse.

The lyke order is geaveñ to Mr Howe to aunswer another lre of advyse writteñ to the Companie by Captein Baker touching provision of money and other thingℓ menĉoned in his lre.

Mr Ellycot of Exeto^r

Lres of advyse froñ Mr Ellycot to Mr Sandy were read wherby it appeareth that he hath made provysion of Ryalles of plate for the Company but not in suche sort as the Companie entended for they Required his travell as an agent for them to ρvyde them moneys at the best rate he could and they would recompence his travell thankefully, but ment not that he shuld make a trade of theñ to buy theñ for his owne vse and to sell

THE EAST INDIA COMPANY

them to the Companie at the rates as the prise goeth in london as *it semeth by his lre* he p̃poseth to putt them̃ uppoñ the said Company Therefore it agreed that his lr̃es shalbe aunswered and a plaine course takeñ wth him ether to p̃vyde them̃ as other that are putt in trust in those partes do buy them̃ or els to desyst and provyde noe more.

Warraunt is geaveñ to Mr Ald^r Banyng to pay to the Purser of the Scourge to be imployed in the repayring of the same ship the som̃e of one thowsand poundes.   1000^{li} to the Purser of the Scourge.

Warraunt is geaveñ to the said Mr Ald^r Bañiig thei̇̃ to pay to Rob̃t Stevens by a bill of exchange from Mr Ellicott of Execeto^r the som̃e of one thowsand poundes.   1000^{li} by ex^e from Mr Ellycot.

Roger and Persevall Style are Sawtres to be imployed in this vioge.   Style.

[Warraunt is geaveñ to Ald^r Banyng threi̇̃ to pay to the Purser of the Scourge]

A Warraunt to Mr Ald^r Banyng to pay to Mr Richard Wysemañ to be imployed in reparat̃ons and provisions for the hecto^r the som̃me of one hundred pound₽.   100^{li} for ye Hecto^r.

Order is geaveñ and renewed to Richard Wyche and Ric Wright to deale wth Mr Covell in Tower Street for the provisioñ of the full of 70 quarters of peas and 30 quarters of beanes. according to former order.   provision of peas & beanes.

Order is geaveñ to Mr Ald^r Bannyng to pay to Wm Burrell Surveyo^r of the generall p̃vysioñ of shipping to be imployed in Timber the some of Two hundred poundes.   200^{li} to Mr Burrell.

Order is geaveñ to Ald^r Bannyng to pay to Joseph Salbancke Purser of the Susañ to be imployed in repat̃ons and other necessaries of the same ship the som̃e of 100 merkes.   100 merkes to the Susan

First Nouemb^r 1600.

Mr Ald^r Smyth go^r
Ald^r Bannyng
Ald^r Hollyday
Mr Olyuer Style
Mr Thomas Cordell

Mr Rich: Staper
[Mr Rob̃t Sandy]
[Mr Ald^r Smythe] Mr Ald^r Moore.
Mr John Combe

K

66   THE COURT RECORDS OF

  M^r Roḃt Bell.   Mr John Highelord
  Mr Wm Harrysoñ   M^r Roḃt Sandy
  Mr Thomas Allabaster [M^r Roḃt S———]
  Mr Wm Chambers   Mr Roger Howe.

200^{li} to Mr Speeke taken up by ex^e

ARRAUNT is geaveñ to Mr Ald^r Hollyday threr̃ to pay vnto Mr George Speake Esquier the soñe of two hundred poundes for soe muche takeñ vp in the West Cuntrey by Roḃt Pope.

lres unto the West Cuntrey per the Post.

L̃res *were* writteñ in to the West Cuntrey *severally* to Capteñ Davies Capteñ Baker and Roḃt Pope in aunswer of ther l̃res of advyse of ther proceading writteñ vp hether wch l̃res were signed by the Comitties being devysed by Mr Howe and were presentlie delivered to the Post of Exet^{or}.

lre to John Ellicot at Excetu^r.

Another l̃re was read writteñ by M^r Roḃt Sandy to Mr Ellycott of Exeto^r in aunswer of his l̃re whereiñ Mr Sandy writethe his myslyke of Ellicott(dryfte to be allowed xviij^d the ℔ for Ryalles seing the Company entended only to vse him for añ agent. to pvyde them̃ Spanishe money and not buy Ryalles of them̃.

A Warraunt from ye L. Threr. for the provysion & passing of pease & beanes.

It is agreed that a warraunt shall be made and offered to the L Threr̃ to obteyne his hande to ye same directed to the Justices of peace in Camb^rshire and Norff. for the Licencyng of Covell to provide and to bring out of those Counties wthout stay or impediment of 100 quarters of pease and 40 quarters of Beanes for the provysioñ of the voyage.

lres to Mr Sandy of Excetu^r

Another lr̃e read writteñ to Mr Sandy of Exceto^r and sent away by the Post in aunswere of a lr̃e by him directed to Ald^r Bannyng and Mr Stap touching the provysioñ of Royalles of plate wherin he is advysed not to exceade xij^d the ℔.

Captein Lancaster.

The Comitties formerly apointed to conferre wth Capteñ Lancaster touching his imploym^t in the voyage as the Chief Comaunder thereof are required to pceade therin as sone as they cañ, to thende his aunswer being hadd they may proceade to the electioñ of others. wch are to be imployed in speciall places in the viage ether as marchaunt(m^{rs} and other officers.

It is agreed by this Assemblie, in respecte of the great ex- Mʳ Aldʳ
perience of Mʳ Aldʳ Wattes in shipping and other directions in Wattes.
viages ther may be great vse of the opinoñ of the said Mʳ
Aldʳ Wattes in the further proceading of this viage That according to the warraunt giveñ by the geñalyty to the said
Comitties in that behaulf That the said Mʳ Aldʳ shalbe
warned to all meetinges and to be vsed as a Comitty in all
thingꝭ concerning the busines.

The 3 of Novemb̃ 1600.

Mʳ Aldʳ Bannyng	Mʳ Robt Sandy
Mʳ Aldʳ Hollyday	Mʳ Jo. Eldred
Mʳ Olyver Style	Mʳ John Middletoñ
Mʳ Rich: Staper	Mʳ Richard Wyche
Mʳ Rich. Wysemañ	Mʳ Robt Bell
Mʳ Thomas Cordell	Mʳ Wᵐ Chambers
Mʳ Roger Howe	Mʳ Wᵐ Harrysoñ

ROBT COBBE beinge one of them that is behinde Robt Cobbe
wᵗʰ his moneys was called hether. did for the securytie of his paymᵗ deliver vnto the handes of Mʳ
Aldʳ Bannyng bondes dated the 8 of the next
moneth wᶜʰ this company thought fyt to reteyne in ther handes
de bene esse not accepting theñ as his adventure.

Ordered that ther *be* provysioñ made of 130ᶜ byskett to Biskett.
carry the shippes into the West Cuntrey the care of wᶜʰ provysioñ is comitted to Mʳ Stap and Mʳ Cordell.

One thowsand of holland lynge to be provided for the vic- Holland
tualling of the shippes vntill they came downe into the West lyng
Cuntrey wᶜʰ provysioñ is comitted to Aldʳ Bannyng and Mʳ
Robt Bell.

Order is geaveñ for the provysioñ of 240 Tuns of beare of Beare.
severall brewingꝭ for the whole voiage to be apointed to be
brewed by the order of Mʳ Cordell and Mʳ Lancaster.

40 Tuñ of Syder is provided by Mʳ Chamber and Mʳ Harry- Syder.

soñ and bought of one Mr Fletcher and Company and 60 Tuns more is to be provided in the West Cuntrey by Capteñ Davies Capteñ Baker and Robt Pope.

<small>500^{li} to Mr Allabaster for provision of Royalles.</small>
Order is geaveñ to Mr Ald^r Hollyday Threr to pay to Mr Allabaster the somme of fyve hundred poundes to be exposed by him before hand to Calleis or other partes for the provysioñ of Ryalles for the voyage.

<small>400^{li} to Sr Hughe Portman p ex^{ee}.</small>
Lyke order is geaveñ to the said Mr Ald^r Hollyday to pay to Sr Hewghe Portmañ or to assignes the somme of fowre pounds for so muche by him dd in exchange to Robt Pope in the West Cuntrey Taking vp the Bill.

<small>Beef Porke.</small>
The provysioñ of beefe and *porke and* the Survey of the ordering thereof is comitted to Ald^r Bannyng and Mr Wysemañ who are content to vndertake the same.

The 5 of Novemb. 1600.

Mr Ald^r Smythe Go^r	Mr Olyver Style
Mr Ald^r Bannyng	Mr Wm Garway
Mr Ald^r Hollyday	M^r Jo: Highelord
Mr Ald^r Wattes	Mr Wm Rumney
Mr Ald^r Moore	Mr Wm Chambers
Mr Rich. Staper	Mr Robt Sandy
Mr Tho Cordell	Mr Nich Lyng
Mr Rich. Wysemañ	M^r Jo: Middletoñ
Mr Fra Chery	Mr Robt Bell.

Mr Wm Harrysoñ

<small>200^{li} to be p^d by Exchaung to Ellis Crysp for Tho: Jones.</small>
ORDER is geaveñ to Ald^r Hollyday Threr to pay vnto Ellys Cryspe for soe much re^d by Capteñ Baker of Thomas Jones of Plymouth by Exchaunge to be p^d in Londoñ, the someñ of two hundred poundes vppon paiment whereof he is to take vp the Bill.

<small>Wm Taverno^r mariner.</small>
Mr Staper maketh report to this Assemblie that he and Mr Wysemañ hath compounded wth Wm Taverno^r to be imployed

THE EAST INDIA COMPANY

in this viage by the Companie in what ship or place they wyll assigne him for the enterteynm^t of sixe pounde sterling p moneth geving him the somme of fourtie poundes before hand vppon his wages for wch enterteynm^t he promiseth his vttermost endeavo^r to be pformed wth all fidelyty.

Warraunt is geaveñ to Ald^r Bannyng Thre^r to pay vnto Rob̃t Stephens the somme of Nyne hundred pounds for soe muche re^d of him by Exchaung p^d to Mr John Ellicott at Exceto^r vppon Two severall Billes the one of fowre hundred poundes the other of five hundred poundes. vppon the payment whereof he is to take vp̃ the Two severall Billes *900^{li} to be p^d to Robt Stephens p exchaung.*

Mr Ald^r Wattes Capteñ Lancaster Mr Cherie and Mr Chamber *are required to make* [have made] Composition wth Roger Hankiñ marino^r to goe in this viage for a m^r in one of the shippes for this enterteynment [vĩz] in the best sort they can for the good of the Company and what Composition they shall make the Company will accept thereof. *Roger Hankyn marino^r.*

Warraunt is geaveñ to Ald^r Bannyng to pay to Mr Thomas Bowles of Tavestock the sõme of thirtie poundes sterling for so muche by him p^d to Capteñ Baker in the West Cuntrey by a bill of exchaung wch bill is to be takeñ vp vppon the paiment thereof. *30^{ll} to be p^d to Tho. Bowles by exchaunge.*

It is resolved that all the shippes shalbe Symented vppoñ ther sheething before they come out of the dockes and to that ende order is geaveñ to Mr Burrell to see the same prepared. *Symonding of the shippes.*

The 6. of Novemb̃ 1600.

Ald^r Smyth Go^r
Ald^r Bannyng
Ald^r Hollyday
Mr Staper
Mr Richard Wysemañ
Mr Wm Rumney
Mr Wm Chamber

Mr Rich : Wyche.
Ald^r Wattes
Mr Tho Cordell
Mr Wm Garway
Mr John Highelord
Mr Rob̃t Sandy
Mr Roger Howe.

The Erle of Cumbland

THE COURT RECORDS OF

<small>110ˡⁱ to John Stanfield for John Painter by exᶜᵉ.</small>

RDER is geaveñ to Aldʳ Bannyng Threʳ to pay vnto Johñ Stanfeld or his assignee the somme of one hundred and tenn poundes sterling for so muche takeñ vp̃ by Mʳ Sandy of Dertmouthe of Johñ Painter of the same Towne to be pᵈ by Bill of exchaung to the said Stanfeld vppoñ the payment whereof he is to take vp̃ the Bill of exᶜ.

<small>That the marinoʳˢ shall have 2 monethes pay & 2 monethes wages in adventure.</small>

It is ordered by the generall consent of this assemblie that for the commoñ and ordinarie mariners that are to be enterteyned for the voyage they shalbe severally allowed for the better provysioñ of every severall mariner to see he shall have Two monethes wages before hande. And for the better advauncemᵗ of his sallarie, that everie the said mariners shall have two monethes wages in adventure as his stocke provided that for his wages takeñ before hand every one geave such cawtioñ to the Threʳs of the viage or the Purser of the ship wherin they serve that the said Marinoʳ shall not depart from the voyage to the disapointing therof but be ready when the shippes shalbe sett forward.

<small>The proportion of victualles.</small>

It is ordered that Mʳ Aldʳ Wattes shalbe joined wᵗʰ the other Comitties apointed for the proportioñ of victualles and to exãe what provisioñ hath bene made according to the proportioñ sett downe, to thende that to see howe the preparation of the viage doeth presentlie stande.

<small>100ˡⁱ to the Purser of the Malice Scurg.</small>

Order is geaveñ to Mʳ Aldʳ Bannyng Threʳ to pay to the Purser of the Malice Scurge the sõme of one hundred poundes to be imployed in the building preparatioñ and provisioñ of the same ship.

<small>Roger Hankyn.</small>

Warraunt is geaveñ to Mʳ Aldʳ Wattes *Mʳ Chery & Mʳ Chambers or 2 of them* to proceade in the concluding [by agreemᵗ] wᵗʰ Roger Hankiñ for his imployment in this viage And yf they cañ not bringe him to *consent to be holden an* adventurer in the voyage for the sõme of one hundred poundes or vnder wᵗʰout wages theñ to agree wᵗʰ him for 50ˡⁱ to be geaveñ him freely and teñ poundes p̃ moneth for his wages. as was yesterday agreed vnto.

THE EAST INDIA COMPANY

It is ordered that Ald^r Bannyng Ald^r Hollyday [Mr Cordell] Ald^r Wattes, Ald^r More Mr Cordell Mr Gorwey Mr Allabaster or anie 3 of them̄ shall compound wth Capteñ Lancaster and to offer him the offer agreed vppoñ yesterday as the geñall offer of the Company wch will not be encreased and to take his aunswer directly *to* accept or refuse the same offer that the Compañie may resolve what course they may rest vppoñ.

Capten Lancaster. the offer is knowen but not sett downe.

It is ordered that Mr Wyseman̄ *and Mr Burrell* shall take and vse the mast that lyeth on the key at Savages wch was Ald^r Bannynges mast and the Compañ will save him harmeles therin and satisfie the proprietors thereof.

A mast for the Hector

It is ordered that ther shalbe p^d *by Mr Ald^r Hollyday* to Peter Grove according to the compositioñ made wth him the some of seventy poundes in full paym^t of the Agreem^t of the money to be dd̄ him.

70^{ll} to Peter Grove.

The 7. of Novem̄b 1600.

Mr Ald. Bannyng
Mr Ald^r Hollyday
Mr Ald^r Wattes
Mr Ald^r Moore
Capteñ Lancaster
Mr Rich : Staper
Mr Olyver Style
Mr Wm Rumney

Mr Tho. Cordell
Mr John Highelord
Mr John Eldred
Mr Rob̄t Sandy
M^r Jo. Combe
Mr Riche Wyche
Mr Wm Chambers
Mr John Middletoñ

T this Assemblie was signed a Bill of the Receipte of the severall peeces of Tymber herevnder men-cōed wch was borrowed of her Ma^e out of the Storehouse at Wolw^{ch} for the repairing of the Scourge

N^o.	Feet	N^o.	Feet
1	33	5	24
2	49	6	45
3	28	7	64
4	24	8	39

peeces of timber marked wth

```
 9 ——— 45        14 ——— 61
     ———         15 ——— 26
         350     16 ——— 60
10 ——— 46        17 ——— 33
11 ——— 61        18 ——— 32
12 ——— 15        19 ——— 60
13 ——— 44
                         440
```

of feet in all ——— 791

In tons of 40 ⎫ tons   feet.
foote p tuñ   ⎭ 19 — 31

At this Assemblie Consideration was had of the number of meñ that shuld be shipped in the severall shippes of the viage bothe of factors and mariners and have resolved that they shall be manned severally wth thes numbers following viz.

```
In the Scourge    ——— 180 ⎫
In the Hecto^r    ——— 100 ⎬ meñ.
In the Ascentioñ  ——— 080 ⎪
In the Susañ      ——— 080 ⎭
```

440

A reviewe of the proportion of victuall.

It is also agreed that Mr Ald^r Wattes and Capteñ Midletoñ shalbe ioyned wth Mr Ald^r Bannyng Capteñ Lancaster Capteñ Davies and Mr Allabaster who formerlie sett downe the proportioñ of victualles. and they altogether to enter into the reviewe of the same proportioñ; and to consider what is prepared thereof *and* what is further to be done in enlarging or abridging thereof and whatsoever they shall doe therein the Companie will allowe thereof.

Tho. Eldred of Ipesw^ch

Mr Johñ Eldred acquainteth this Assemblie that one Thomas Eldred of Ipesw^ch a mañ of good report who hath bene imployed wth Capteñ Candishe is willing to be imployed in the voyage and would go as Capteñ or M^r of one of the shippes, to whoñ aunswer is made that the Companie will enterteyñ none vntill they see him and speake wth him, and have willed that M^r

Eldred shall wryte vnto him that he thinketh yf he come vp̃ the Company are likelie to enterteyñ him.

Order is geaveñ to Ald' Hollyday Threr̃ to pay vnto M' W'ᵐ Harvy of Bridgewater the somme of fyfty poundes sterlinge for so muche re'ᵈ of him by Robt Pope to the use of the voyage by a bill of exchange vppoñ the payment whereof he is to take vp̃ the bill.   50ˡⁱ to W Harvy

The like order is geaveñ to the said Ald' Hollyday threr̃ to pay vnto James Prockter of Londoñ the somme of one hundred poundes sterling for so muche re'ᵈ by Robt Pope of Thoñis Trowbridge in the West Cuntrey to the vse of the voyage by a bill of exchaung vppoñ the paym't whereof the bill is to be takeñ vp.   100ˡⁱ to James Prockter

[M'] *Capteñ* Lancaster having bene alreadie talkd w'ᵗʰall by some of the Comitties w'ᶜʰ were yesterday apointed to that ende, and noe agreement fully made w'ᵗʰ him he beinge present at this Assemblie and the matter havinge bene something debated amongest theñ he yeldeth in the ende to comitt the absolute agreement of his enterteynment to the consideratioñ and finall ende of M' Ald Smythe Governo' Ald' Bannynge Ald' Wattes Ald' Hollyday Ald' Moore M' Cordell and M' Allabaster or any 6 of theñ. And this Assemblie in the behaulf of the Company do lykewyse referre theñ selfes to ther Censure, shewing ther assent by erecting of handes.   Capt'n Lancaster

The viij'ᵗʰ Novemb' 1600.

Ald' Bannyng   M' John Highelord
                    M' W'ᵐ Chambers
M' Garway   M' Roger Howe
Captein Lancaster   M' John Eldred
M' Rich: Wysemañ   M' W'ᵐ Harrysoñ
    M'. John Combe

THE COURT RECORDS OF

<small>lres out of the West Cuntrey.</small>

IVERS lres out of the West Countrey, brought by the Post of Exeto^r the one a generall lre from Capten Davies Capten̄ Baker Mr Pope, and Mr John Sandy were read mencōning ther severall proceading in the Busines wch lres are delivered over to Mr Howe to be noted and aunswered, and the aunsweres reterned by the Post.

<small>40^{li} to Wm Harvey p ex^c</small>

Warraunt is geaven̄ to Ald^r Bannyng Threr̄ to pay vnto Mr Wm Harvy of Bridgewater or his Assigne the somme of fowrtie poundes sterlinge for soe muche re^d of him by ꝓ exchaunge delivered to Rob̄t Pope, wch bill is to be taken̄ vp̄ vppon̄ the paiment made.

<small>100^{li} to Wm Lacy p ex^c</small>

The like Warraunt is geaven̄ to the said Threr̄ to pay vnto Wm Lacy of Hertrowe or his assignes the somme of one hundred and tenne poundes sterling for soe muche by him delivered ꝓ exchaung to Rob̄t Pope vppon̄ the paiment whereof the bill is to be taken̄ vp̄.

<small>100^{li} Malyce Scurg</small>

Warraunt is geaven̄ to Mr Ald^r Hollyday to pay to the handes of Edward Stephen̄s Carpenter the somme of one hundred poundes sterlinge vppon̄ accompt of Tymber for the Malice Scurge.

<small>80^{li} the Susan.</small>

Warraunt is geaven̄ to Ald^r Bannyng to pay to Joseph Sulman̄ Purser of the Susan̄ to be imployed in the p̄paration of the same ship vppon̄ an̄ accompt the somme of four score poundes.

<small>200^{li} to Mr Burrell.</small>

Warraunt is geaven to Ald^r Hollyday Ther̄ to pay to Mr Burrell Surveyo^r of the shipping to be imploied in preparing therof vppon̄ accompt the somme of Two hundred poundes.

November the 10th.

Mr Ald^r Halmden	Mr Harrison
Mr Style	Mr Sandy
Mr Lancaster	Mr Middleton
Mr Wych	Mr Combe
Mr Wyseman	Mr Howe

Mr Ald: Bayning:

THE EAST INDIA COMPANY 75

T this assembly it was ordred & appoynted ffor the provyding of all the pvisions to these men there seuerall pvisions aff° viz.

To M˙r How & M˙r Sandy M˙r *Combe* ffor these pvisions
    ffor 13 Hogesheads aquavitæ   Aquavitæ: 13 hh^ds
    ffor Spyces viz 112℔ sūgar   Spyces: 225^lb
               30℔ synamon
               15℔ nŭtmeggs
               6℔ clowes
               50℔ ginger
               12℔ pepper
    ffor Ryce 20c   ryce 20c
    ffor sault 16 tonns   sault 16 tonns
To M˙r Cordell and Stapers
    ffor 240c of bread at london   bread 240c
To M˙r Cordell and M˙r Wych ⎰ 75 tonns smale   beere 150 tonns
    ffor 150 tonns of beere— ⎱ 75 tonns of 50ˢˢ p̄ tonn
    To M˙r Harrisson, Combe & Sandy, & M˙r Howe & M˙r Bell & M˙ Lancast˙r
    ffor 66 tonns of wyne.   Wyne 66 tons

            November 1600 the 10th
To M˙r Ald bayning and M˙r Wyseman
    ffor C 707. —. 16 ,, beeff   Porck C883. 3.20.
    ffor C 883. 3. 20 ,, porcke   Beefe
To M˙r Wych and M˙r Wryte
    ffor pease & beanes 1031¼ bushells   Peas beanes
To M˙r Ald bayning:
    ffor 1000 : of ling great tale   lynge
To M˙r Ald Holliday
    ffor 10000 stock fish great tale   stock fishe
To M˙r Ald Bayning
    ffor 30 quarters oatmeale is 240 bushells   Otemeale
To M˙r Wych to speake to M˙r Covell
    ffor 70 bushells oatmeale   Otemeale
To M˙r Sandy, M˙r Harrisson & 2 pursers
    ffor 20 way of cheese   Cheese
    ffor 70 ffirkens butter   Butter

76   THE COURT RECORDS OF

	To Mr Ald bayning, Mr How, Mr Garway, & Mr Eldred
Sweete oyle	ffor 2000 gallons sweete oyle
	To Mr Combe, Mr Howe, & Mr Sandy
Vineger	ffor 24 tonns of vineger
	To Mr Sandy; Mr Howe & 2 pursers
Hony.	ffor 6 barrells of honey
	To Mr Wych
Musterd-seed	ffor 30 bushells musterd seed
	To Mr Wyseman, Mr Bell, Ald Holliday & Mr Chambres
Candells	ffor 1200 lb candles covered wth wax
	ffor 400 lb Ordynary candles
rape oyle	ffor 10 hh^{ds} rape oyle ffor lamps
	To Mr Chambres & Mr Harrisson
Caske	ffor 8 dozzen barrycods
	ffor 150 tonns water caske
	ffor 150 tonns ffor beere wth ash hoopes
	ffor 44 tonns ffor beeff
	50 tonns ffor porck
	150 tonns syder & strong beere
	24 tonns ffor vineger
	13 tonns ffor oyle & aquavitæ in barrells
	2 tonns ffor honey & Rape oyle
	6 tonns ffor tarr in yron hoopes
	10 tonns ffor oat meale
	2 tonns ffor musterd seed & ryce
	26 tonns ffor beanes & pease

Novemb^r 1600 the 11th.

Ald^r Smith governour	Mr Eldred
Mr Ald^r bayning	Mr Style
Mr Ald^r Holliday	Mr Chambres
Mr Wyseman	Mr Cordell
Mr Lancaster	Mr Sandy
Mr Wyche	Mr Chambres

Mʳ Harrison
Mʳ Combe
Mʳ Highlord
   Mʳ Alabaster

Mʳ Linge
Mʳ Middleton
Mʳ Rumney

THIS Assembly gave cōmissions to every of the cōmissioners ffor the pvyding of their severall coñissiers as are before written on the 10ᵗʰ hereof as appeareth. *Comissions for victuals:*

Mʳ Ald Bayning, Mʳ Ald Watts, Mʳ Alabaster, Mʳ Ald Holliday, Mʳ Ald More, Mʳ Cordell, Mʳ Style, Mʳ Combe Mʳ Rumney appoynted to agree wᵗʰ Capt Middleton about going on this voyadg *to agree wᵗʰ Capt : Middleton*

The names of such as are sett down & mencioned to goe factors on this voyadg. *factors nominated.*

Capteyn Jnº Middleton
John Haiward
ffrancis barnes
Robert Pope
William Brend
Elkana Cole
William Wilford
Thomas Dassell
Roger Style
William finchcomber
Edward lokar
Danyel Tucker
Thomas Salter
Richard Collimore
William russell
William Starkey
Robert Cressell

Henry Annis
Daniel Marsh
Robert Chamberlayne
Thomas Tudd
William Rutton
John Taylor. will vent 200ˡⁱ *Elkana Cole*
Tho: Morgan
Hollywell
Phillip Winchecombe
Robt Greene
Edm. Scott
Giles Georg
Tho Hickes
Hugh Wryte
Tho Hurlestoñ
Tho. Hickes
Henry Midletoñ
   John Wray

At this Assembley it was ordred that Mʳ Smith governour Mʳ Ald Holliday, Mʳ Ald Watts, Mʳ Ald More, Mʳ Cordell, Mʳ Garway and Stapers, should bee suyters to the lord treasurer *5000ˡⁱ to bee coyned*

78   THE COURT RECORDS OF

ffor a warrant ffor the ꝑvyding & coyning of y 5000ˡⁱ in the towar; & ffor ꝑvyding of bulleyne for the same & for the finishing the Pattent

A Warraunt for yᵉ transportation of Victualles from the Portes.
    The sayd cõmittyes appoynted to make suyte to the Lord treasurer for a lycence to transport ꝑvisions in the west countrey according to a letter of Mʳ Jnᵒ Sandy

November 1600 the 11th.

Mʳ Ałd bayning	Mʳ Chambres
Mʳ Ałd Holliday	Mʳ Lancaster
Mʳ Garway	Mʳ Alabaster
Mʳ Wyseman	Mʳ Middleton

Maisters & Officers
    AT this Assembly it was agreed and concluded that the committyes *and the maisters* ffor euery shipp shall take the charge of provyding [maisters &] other officers in the same shipps: wᵗʰ maryners, & what they shall doe herein shalbee well done.

The 12 Novemb 1600.

Aldʳ Bannyng	Mʳ Wᵐ Rumney
[*Aldʳ Holmedeñ*]	Mʳ Robt Sandy
Aldʳ Hollyday	Mʳ Johñ Combe
Aldʳ Wattes	Mʳ Rich Wyche
Mʳ Aldʳ Holmedeñ	Mʳ John Middletoñ
Mʳ Rich: Staper	Mʳ Robt Bell
Mʳ Wᵐ Garway	Mʳ Nich: Lynge

100ˡⁱ to yᵉ Purser of the Malice Scurdge
    ORDER is geaveñ to Aldʳ Bannyng to pay vnto Henr Mydletoñ Purser of the Scurge to imploy in the provysioñ and preparatioñ of the same ship vppoñ accoumpt the sõme of one hundred pound℔

40ˡⁱ per exᶜ to Joː Wyndeham
    Order is geaveñ to the said Aldʳ Bannyng to pay vnto Mʳ Johñ Wyndhañ. vppoñ a Bill of exchaung the somme of

fowrtie poundes for soe much paid by the said Bill to Robt Pope, in the West Cuntrey to the vse of the voyage.

It is agreed that a Warraunt for the transportation of all provysions made in the West Cuntrey for this voyage vnder the L Thre͠r hande to the officers of the Portes and other officers shalbe solicyted, and to be sent downe in to the West Cuntrey wth all convenient speede.

<small>Warraunt to be procured for the shipping of all pvision in the West Cuntrey.</small>

It is ordered that Mr Hilliard Mr Sandy Mr Chambers and Mr Grove, shall consyder of the small and extraordinary merchaundize of glasses knyves and Norrom boroughe ware fytt for the voyage and to bespeake suche things as are newlie to be made

<small>Glasses knyves Norrom borow ware &c.</small>

Mr Sandy Mr Bell are appointed for the provysion of Leade and Tynñ who together wth Mr Grove shall consider of the Quantety and of the kindes of the same comodyty.

<small>lead & tynn</small>

Novemb^r the 14th 1600

Mr Ald Bayning   Mr Roger Howe
Mr Ald Watts   Mr Olyver Style
Mr Ald Holmenden   Mr Linge
Mr Ric̄ Wyseman   Mr Robert bell

T this Assembly given severall warrants in Mr Ald Bayng for payment of these severall somes ffollowing to say.

Off y 50	to Nyc^o Symons for timb^r for ye Susann	£50: to Nyc^o Symonds.
y 66 ,, 13 ,, 4	to Joseph Salbanck for necessaryes & wages for the same shipp	£66.13.4 to Salbanck
y 39 ,, — ,, —	to Roger Gibbons by a bill of exc^r for Mr Robert pope.	£39: by bill for pope.
y 100 ,, — ,, —	to Mr Richard Wyseman for the hecto^r provision.	£100: to Mr Wyseman for the Hecto^r

THE COURT RECORDS OF

The 15 November 1600

Mr Ald^r Bayning	Mr Combe.
Mr Ald^r Watts	Mr Rumney
Mr Tho: Cordell	Mr Highlord
Mr Fra: Lancaster	Mr John Middleton
Mr John Eldred	Mr Nicholas Ling
Mr William Chambres	Mr Richard Stapers
Mr Wm Harrisson	Mr William Garway

g 30^{li} to Wm Kemp for Capt. baker

EVEN a warrant at this assembly ffor paym^t of y 30. to William Kempe by bill of exc^r for Thomas Bakar frõ Plymouth;

Order for carrying the shipps into dock for payment of the charg

Also it is agreed that Mr Wyseman shall see the bills of chargs ffor bringing in of the shipps into the docks dischardged & payd.

ffor provyding of 5000^{li} of bulleyne.

Also it is ordeyned that *Mr Ald Bayning* Mr Ald Holliday together wth Mr Wyseman shall take the charge for the p̄vyding of 5000^{li} of bulleyne ffor the coyning of the lyke vallew & also Mr Stapers to assist thereunto.

The 18. Novemb^r 1600.

Ald^r Smythe Go^r.	Mr Wm Chamber
Mr Ald Bannyng.	Mr Nich: Lyng
Mr Ald Hollyday.	Mr Wm Rumney
Mr Ald^r Wattes	M^r [Robt] *John* Comber
Mr Rich: Staper	M^r
Mr Wm Garway	Mr Rich: Wysemañ
Mr Robt Sandy	Mr Thomas Allabaster
Ald^r Holmeden	Mr Rich: Wyche
Mr Olyuer Style	Mr Robt Bell
Mr Wm Harrysoñ	

40^{li} to Thomas Northeover

RDER is geaveñ to Mr Ald^r Bannyng the^r to pay to Mr Thomas Northeove^r the somme of fowrtie poundes for so muche by him dd in exchange to

Robt Pope in the West Cuntrey vppoñ paiment whereof the bill is to be takeñ vp.

Lyke order is geaveñ to the said Threr to pay vnto Johñ Lant of Excetor the somme of one hundred and fyfty poundes sterling for so much by him dd in exchange to Robt Pope in the West Cuntrey vppoñ payment whereof the bill is to be taken vp. 150li to Jo: Lant of Excetor

This [Companie] *Assemblie* falling into Delibatioñ of some generall Course to be takeñ in the enterteymt of [the] *three* principall factors for three of the shippes and of the other sortes of factors vnder the principall in ther severall Degrees and places. They do resolve of ther severall rates of allowaunce and enterteynmentf following viz. that the 3 principall factors shall have every of theñ one hundred poundes geaveñ theñ to provide theiñ to sea and every of theñ the gaine of 200li adventure [as thowghe they had severally had putt in] and for the the 4. severall seconde sorte of factors they will allowe theñ severally fyfty poundes apeece to provide them to sea, and the [adventure] gaine of the adventure of one hundred pound a peece, and and for the 3 sorte of factors ther is allowed to theñ 30li a peece to be geaveñ theñ for ther provysion and the gaine of 50li adventure and for the fowrth and Last sorte of factors they will allowe theñ twenty poundes apeece and the gaine of *the adventure of* fowrtie poundes a peece. The enterteymnt of all thes factorⁿ

The allowaunce and enterteynmt of the said factors beinge resolved vppoñ the said Comittees proceaded to the Election of the 3 principall factors of the said voyag wherevppoñ electioñ being made by Scruteny vppoñ seaveñ of the Chieffest Sewtors to the Companie to be imployed as factors in the said viage. Choice was made of Capteñ Mydletoñ. Johñ Havard. and Frauncis Barme. for the said 3 principall factors [to be imployed in the said shippes] to be sorted and placed in the shippes as hereafter it shalbe considered by the said Comitties. Of wch severall factors only Johñ Havard beinge present was called in and acquainted wth the Electioñ and wth the enterteynmt is well contented therwth and doeth willingly accept thereof. The election of 3. principall factorⁿ
Capten Midleton
Jo: Havard
[Fra.Barme
Wm fisher

M

THE COURT RECORDS OF

The 19 Nouemb̃ 1600.

Mr Ald^r Smyth Go^r
Mr Ald^r Bannyng
Mr Ald^r Moore
Capteiñ Lancaster
Mr Wm Rumney
Mr Roger Howe.
Mr Richard Wyche
Mr Wm Harrysoñ
Mr Ald^r Wattc̃
Mr Rich: Wysemañ
Mr Olyuer Style

Mr Wm Chamber
Mr John Eldred
Mr Robert Bell
Mr John Combe
Mr Frauncis Chery
Ald^r Hollyday
Mr Nichãs Lynge
Mr Rich: Stapers
Mr Tho. Cordell
Mr Rob̃t Sandy
Mr Wm Garway

M^r Jo: Highelord.

40^{li} to M^r Joⁿ God per ex^{ce}

RDER is geaveñ to Mr Ald̃ Bannyng Threr̃ to pay vnto Mr Johñ God the somme of fowrtie poundes sterling for soe muche by him p^d and delivered in exchaunge to Robt Pope in the West Cuntrey vppoñ the payment whereof the bill is to be takeñ vp

100^{li} p^d to ffrauncis Covell for provision of peas and Beanes

Order is geaveñ to ye said Threr̃ to pay vnto ffrauncc̃ Covell towardes the providing of Peas and Beanes for the voyage the somme of one hundred poundes sterling vppoñ accompte of that provisioñ vppoñ payment whereof take his receipte.

The Election of the 4. second sort of factors. Robt Pope Wm Brand Tho. Saltern Wm Starky

The seconde sorte of factors being putt in Election at this assembly and eight sewtors for the fowre places being sorted out and putt to Scruteny the Comitties p̃ceded to the Electioñ of 4 of theiñ. In wch election ther was choseñ for the places of the seconde sort of factors thes psons following viz. Rob̃t: Pope Wm Brand Thom̃s Salterne and Wm Starky to be sorted and placed in the severall shippes according to the Discretioñ of the said Comitties.

500^{li} to Mr Allabaster for provision of Royalles.

Order is geaveñ to Mr Ald̃^r Bannyng Threr̃ to deliver vnto Mr Thom̃s. Allabaster the somm̃e of five hundred poundes sterling to be imployed by exchaung in provisioñ of Royalles of plate.

The said Assemblie proceading to the Election of the third sort of factors to be imployed in this voyage ther were propounded eight severall sewters for the said places vppoñ wch the Comitties proceaded to scruteny and did elect these severall psons following for the supplying of the places of the third *sort* of facto^rs videlt. Thomas Hickes Henr Mydleton Wm Wilford nathaniell [Gumbrell] Gamrym to be sorted and placed in the shippes by the discretion of the Comitties.

<small>The Election of the third sort of factors. Thomas Hickes Henry Midleton Wm Wilford Natha: Gamrym</small>

The Election of the fourth sort of facto^rs being pceaded in by the said Comitties ther were also propounded the names of Eight sewters. out of wch by scruteny were chosen. these severall psons whose names are subscribed to be sorted and placed in the shippes at the disposition of the said Comitties viz Percivall Stragling Thom^s Morgān Phillip Winchcomb and Thom^s Tudd.

<small>The 4 sort of factors. Percivall Stradling Tho Morgañ Phillip Wynchecomb. Thomas Tudd.</small>

The 21 November 1600

Mr Ald^r Smythe Go^r
Mr Ald^r Hollyday
Mr Ald^r Wattes
Mr Staper
Mr Olyuer Style
Mr Rich: Wysemañ
M^r Jo: Highelord
Capteñ Lancaster

Mr Wm Chambers
Mr Rob̃t Sandy
Mr Rich: Wyche
M^r Jo: Eldred
M^r Jo: Midletoñ
Mr Nic̃has Lyng
Mr Wm Harrysoñ
M^r Jo: Combe

Mr Rob̃t Bell.

ARRAUNT is geaveñ to Ald^r [Bannyng] *Hollyday* Thre͞r to pay vnto Richard Stratford by a Bill of exchaunge from Johñ Sandy for so muche by him takeñ and re^d of John Eydes *at Exceto^r* the somme of fyfty poundes.

<small>50^li per ex^e to Ric Stratford for Jo Eydes.</small>

Lyke warraunt is geaveñ to the said Thre͞r to pay to Mr Johñ Ellecott the somme of five hundred poundes sterling vppoñ his bill of exchaunge. to be rep^d at Exceto^r to the vse

<small>500^li to be p^d to Jo: Ellecott to be rep^d</small>

at exceto^r to ye vse of ye Company.	of the Companie vppoñ the paym^t whereof he is to receave his billes.
100^{li} p^d to Edw: High-lord purser of the Scourge.	Order is geaveñ to Mr Ald^r Hollyday Threr̃ to pay to ye Purser of the Scourge the somme of one hundred poundes vppoñ accoumpte to be imployed in the preparing of the same ship
40^{li} p^d to Rich: Wal-toñ p ex^c.	Order is geaveñ to the said Ald^r Hollyday Threr̃ to pay vnto Richard Waltoñ the somme of fowrtie poundes sterlinge for soe much by him p^d and delivered in ex^{ce} to Mr Johñ Sandy at Exceto^r vppoñ paiment whereof the bill is to be takeñ vp
Go to be p^d to Rich: Rudd by ex^c.	Lyke order is geaveñ to the said Ald^r Hollyday Threr̃ to pay vnto Richard Rudd the somme of sixtie poundes sterling for so muche re^d of the said Rudd at Exceto^r by Mr Johñ Sandy to the vse of the voyage vppoñ payment whereof the bill is to be takeñ vp
50^{li} to be p^d to Nicħas Rantoñ by ex^{ce}.	Lyke order is geaveñ to the said Ald^r Hollyday Threr̃ to pay vnto Nicħas Rantoñ the somme of fyftie poundes sterling for so muche re^d of him, by the handes of Johñ Sandy to the vse of the voyage vppoñ a bill of ex^{ce} vppoñ paiment whereof the bill is to be takeñ vp
Mr. Alla-baster.	Comissioñ is geaveñ to Mr Thomś Allabaster to take suche Course as he shall thinke meet for the conveyaunce of suche Bulleiñ or Royalles froñ Callyce as shall be sent froñ thence by exchaunge to the vse of the voyage.
300^{li} to Mr Sandy to be rep^d by him at Exceto^r.	Order is geaveñ to Mr Ald^r Bannyng Threr̃ to pay vnto Mr Robt Sandy the somme of three hundred poundes sterling to be rep^d by him at Exceto^r to the handes of Mr Johñ Sandy to the vse of the voyage.
40^{li} to be p^d to Rich: Gregory by ex^{ce}.	Order is geaveñ to Mr Ald^r Hollyday Threr̃ to pay vnto Richard Gregorie or his Assignes the somme of fowrtie poundes sterling for soe much re^d by Robt Pope at the handes of the said Gregorie in the West partes *by exchaunge* to the vse of the Companie. vppoñ paiment whereof the bill is to be takeñ vp.
Order for suche as re-fuse to	At this Assemblie order is [geaveñ] takeñ that the names of as many of these as have sett downe ther [names] handes and

sommes of adventure and have since denied to pforme the same, shalbe called vppoñ to geave ther resolutioñ what they will do, to thende some course may be takeñ wth them before the Pattent be putt to ingrossing. *bring in ther adventure.*

A lre from the L. Threr̃ in the behaulf of one Henry Aneys. to bee imployed in the said voyage was read vppoñ the reading whereof. aunswere was geaveñ to the bearer w[ch] was M[r] Suckley my L. secreterie, that the Companie were sorie that they had not notice of his L[ps] pleasure before the Election of ther factors [were] *was* past, yet notw[th]standing they will endevo[r] vppoñ anie occasioñ of the Refusall of anie of them that are choseñ. or vppoñ anie other occasioñ to [pleasure] imploy the said Anys yf they cañ finde fytt vse of his service *Henry Anys comeded by the l. Thrers lres.*

The 22 of the Novemb[r] 1600.

M[r] Ald[r] Smyth Go[r]   M[r] Wm Chamb.
Mr Ald[r] Hollyday   Mr Robt Sandy
Mr Ald[r] Wattes   Mr John Combe
M[r] Wm Garway   Mr Rich: Wyche
Mr Olyuer Style   M[r] Wm Harrysoñ
M[r] Jo: Highelord.   Mr Robt Bell.
                Mr Roger Howe

RDER is geaveñ to Ald[r] Hollyday Threr̃. to pay vnto W[m] Mallett gent or to his Assignes the some of threescore and tenñ poundes sterlinge for so muche by him paid by exchaunge to the handes of Robt Pope in the west Cuntrey vppoñ the paiment whereof the bill is to be takeñ vp. *70[li] to be p[d] to W[m] Mallett by exchaunge*

Order is geaveñ to the said Threr̃ to pay to the handes of M[r] W[m] Garwey the somme of two hundred poundes sterling vppoñ accoumpte to be imploied in the repairing and preparing of the Assentioñ. *200[li] to be dd M Garway for the Assention.*

The like order is geaveñ to the said Threr̃ to pay vnto W[m] Burrett Generall Surveyo[r] of the repairing and preparing of *100[li] to be p[d] to M[r] Burrell.*

86   THE COURT RECORDS OF

the shippes the somme of one hundred poundes sterlinge vppoñ accoumpte for the provisioñ of Timb^r and other necessaries for the shippes.

Poll Davies for bagges. It is ordered that Mr Roger Howe shall buy Poll Davies for the making of bagges and to putt them out to making that they may be sent into the west Cuntrey

All facto^{rs} to putt in sewrties. It is ordered by the generall Consent of this Assemblie that all factors. imployed in this voyage shall geave securytie to the lykinge of the Comitties before he be putt in to anie charge. that he shall pforme all faithefull service to the generalitie and shall abstaine from all private trade

Roger Style. Roger Style one that hath bene brought vp vnder Mr Olyver Style doeth make this humble sewte to the Companie that wher in the Electioñ of the 16 factors his name was putt in choyce and failed he is content to be imployed wthout Salary. so as he may be imployed as a facto^r yf anie of the rest shuld dye in the voyage, and is also content to be Left in the Cuntrey of the East Indies vntill the retorne of a seconde voyage in wch residence he is content to apply him self to lerne the language wch motioñ is well lyked of and shalbe further delt in hereafter

The 25 of Novemb 1600.

Mr Ald^r Hollyday   Mr Wyche
Mr Tho. Cordell   Mr Wm Harrysoñ
Mr Wm Garway   Mr John Combe.
Mr Wysemañ   Mr Roger Howe
M^r fra: Chery   Mr John Highelord
Capteñ Lancaster   Mr Robt Sandy
Capteñ Middletoñ   Mr Wm Chambers

Meale brought in the prize. WARRAUNT is geaveñ to Capteñ Mydletoñ and Mr Robt Bell to buy the Spanishe meale takeñ prize by the L. Willoughbies ship and to goe throughe wth the bargaine thereof as good cheape as they cañ leaving the sume to ther discretioñ.

50^{li} to Order is geaveñ to Mr Ald^r Holliday Threr to pay to Edward

Stephens principall [tymber] *Carpenter* in the Scourge the somme of fyftie poundes sterling to be imployed by him in the repayring of the same ship. And to geave an accoumpte thereof. for wch his receipte is to be taken — Edward Stephen for ye Scourge.

It is agreed that the enterteynment of a fourth M^r wch is not yet done shalbe referred to Mr Staper Mr Cordell Mr Garway and Capteiñ Lancaster. and that they also may proceade to Compound wth anie other officer of the shippes at the best rate they cañ — Order for the hyring of a M^r & other officers.

It is also ordered that Mr Garway Mr Cordell Mr Stap and Richard Wright shall attende and solicyte my L. Threr̃ for suche bullyoñ as *is* in the tower being about the valewe of 3000^li and to procure as much respite and Libertie of tyme as they can gett for the bringing in of the Like quantety of bulleiñ againe into the Tower — Bullyon to be had out of ye tower.

27 Novemb. 1600.

RDER is geaveñ to Ald^r Hollyday Threr̃ *by advyse from Rob̃t Pope* to pay vnto Johñ Portman Esquier or his Assignes the somme of two hundred poundes sterlinge for so muche to him delyvered by *the said Threr̃* in exchaunge to be p^d to the vse of the voyage. to the handes of Robert Pope in the West Cuntrey vppoñ payment whereof a Receipte is to be takeñ at the handes of Mr Portemañ or of him that receaveth the money as his Assignee: to make paym^t accordinglie — 200 dd p ex^ce to Mr John Portman

Order is geaveñ to Ald^r [Hollyday] *Bannyng* Threr̃ to pay vnto the handes of Edward Highlord Purser of the Scourge the somme of one hundred poundes sterling to be imployed in the repayringe of the shipp scourge vppoñ accoumpt vppoñ payment whereof yo^u are to take his receipte — 100^li to the Scourge.

The 28 Nouemb 1600.

The Erle of Cumbland   Mr Ald. Wattes
Mr Ald^r Smythe Go^r   Mr Ald Moore

88 THE COURT RECORDS OF

      Mr Olyver Style   Mr Wm Chambers
      Mr Robt Sandy   Mr Rich: Wyche
      Mr Tho. Allabaster   M^r fra: Chery
      Mr Johñ Highelord.   Mr Wm Harrysoñ
      Mr Ald^r Hollyday   Capteñ Lancaster
                    Capteñ Myddletoñ

y 112^{li}: to Wm Dale by exc frõ robt Pope

ARRANT is given to Ald Bayning ffor payment of y 112^{li} to Wm Dale by a bill of exc^e of the 15 hereof in tantonn frõ Robert Pope ffor the lyke vallew by him Receyved of Wm Macy

Pattent read.

At this Assemblie the Pattent of the previledges for the East Indie voyage was read and order geaveñ to the Secretorie to solicite the Queenes Attorney to make an end of the same.

100^{li} to ye Hecto^r.

Order is geaveñ to Mr Ald^r Hollyday threr̃. to delyver and pay vnto the Purser of the Hecto^r the somme of one hundred poundes sterling to be imployed in the repayring and preparing of the same ship vppoñ accoumpte.

             The 29 Nouemb 1600
      Mr Ald^r Hollyday   Mr John Highelord
      Mr Tho Cordell   Capteñ Midletoñ
      Capteñ Lancaster   Mr Wm Chambers
      Mr Olyuer Style   Mr John Combe
      Mr Rich: Wysemañ   Mr Niclas Lynge
      Mr Roger Howe   Mr Wm Garway

4^{li} p^d in recompence to a poore man for boulging his Crane wth the Scourges Anker. Advyse in to the West Cuntrey.

ORDER is geaveñ to Ald^r Hollyday Threr̃ to pay vnto a pore mañ in recompence of the boulging of his Crane by an Anker of the Scourge the somme of fowre poundes sterling.

Order is geaveñ to Mr Howe to write to Mr Pope, Mr Baker and Mr Sandye that they provide noe more biskett or meale for that vppoñ the viewe of the perticlers of provysion of breade and meale the full quantety is accomplyshed

100^{li} to M Cole dd in ex^{ce}.

Warraunt is geaveñ to Mr Ald^r Hollyday Threr̃ to pay to Mr Johñ Colles Esquier the somme of one hundred poundes

THE EAST INDIA COMPANY

sterlinge by exchaunge to be rep{{d}} againe by him or his Assignee in the West Cuntrey to the handes of Robt Pope to the vse of the voyage vppoñ the delivery of w{{ch}} money the bill of ex{{c}} is to be re{{d}}.

The like Warraunt is geaveñ to the said Ald{{r}} to pay to the handes of Capteñ Lancaster the somme of one hundred poundes sterlinge vppoñ the Reckoning of his enterteynment for the voyage.

100{{li}} to Capten Lancaster.

The p{{r}} December 1600.

M{{r}} Ald{{r}} Holliday
M{{r}} Ald{{r}} Wattℓ
M{{r}} Ald{{r}} More
M{{r}} Tho: Cordell
M{{r}} Rich: Stapers
M{{r}} Richard Wyseman
M{{r}} Capt. Lancaster
M{{r}} W{{m}} Chambers

M{{r}} Rich: Wych
M{{r}} W{{m}} Harrison
M{{r}} Rob: Sandy
M{{r}} Jn{{o}} Combe
M{{r}} Rob: bell
M{{r}} Jn{{o}} Meddleton
M{{r}} Hihlord
M{{r}} Style—

AT this assembly written a letter to m{{r}} Denman & m{{r}} Hale of the bridghouse to delyver to m{{r}} W{{m}} burrell 2 peecs of tymber, eyther taking his receipt w{{th}} promyse to redelyver the lyke, or to take money of him ffor the same.

M{{r}} Denman & M{{r}} Hale for 2 peces timber to be dd m{{r}} burrell.

Also it was at this tyme agreed & appoynted that the officers of the shipps [are to] *should* bee *hyred & placed* in the order ffollowing & their wages to bee agreed as also ffolloweth—

Carpenters	ffor the scourge	4	to bee hyred by m{{r}} Bŭrrell & their wages to bee allowed & agreed vpon, vpon his report of what he hath done at the table	Carpenters
	ffor the hecto{{r}}	3		
	ffor th'assension	2		
	ffor the susann	2		
Cawkers	ffor the scourg	4		Cawkers
	ffor the hecto{{r}}	3		
	ffor the assension	2		
	ffor the susann	2		

Gonners.	Gonners ffor the scourge 10;	the cõmittyes & m^r Lancaster to agree wth them
	ffor the hecto^r 6	the own^{rs} that were, to agree wth them
	ffor the sũsann 5	
	ffor th'assension 5	

Stewards — Stwewards ffor ech shipp himself and his mate
Cookes — Cookes ffor ech shipp one and his mate
Surgeons — Surgeons ffor ech shipp twoe & a barber

Generall, pilot major & m^r Bradbanck. — Also it was ordeyned that the generall the pilot major & m^r bradbanck maister shoũld goe in the Scourge.

To deale wth m^r Beare. — Also it was ordeyned that m^r ald Watts m^r Cordell & m^r Stapers should take in hand to deale & conferr wth m^r Beare to bee one of the 4 chief maisters.

The prim° December 1600.

£172.7.9 d vpo ald Holliday to pay to m^r ffor 95 quarters 6 bushels & 10^{lb} meale.

Geven a Warrant vppon ald Holliday to pay y 172^{li} . 7^s . 9^d to . . . . in ffull ffor 95 qwarters 6 bushells & 10^{lb} of meale bought by m^r Bell of one m^r gawldsmith being taken a pryze at xxxvj^s the qwarter amounting to the sayd some—.

The 4 of Decemb 1600.

Ald^r Moore :	Mr Olyuer Style
Capten Lancaster	Mr Rich. Wysemañ
Mr Rich : Staper	Mr Wm Chambers
Mr Wm Garway	Mr Wm Harrysoñ
Mr Tho Cordell.	Mr Johñ Midletoñ.

T is ordered by these Cõmitties that the psons heer vnder named shall conferre wth Capteñ mydletoñ touching his enterteynment in this voyage. and whatsoever they shall agree vppoñ to be geaveñ him shall be pformed by the generalyty and the said Capteñ mydletoñ for his part submytteth him self to ther agreem^t.

THE EAST INDIA COMPANY

The Erle of Cumbland
Mʳ Aldʳ Moore
Mʳ Tho Cordell   } or any 3. of them.
Mʳ Wᵐ Garway
Mʳ Rich Wyseman

It is also ordered that mʳ Stap Capten Lancaster mʳ Tho. Allabaster and Richard Wright shall conferre together touching *suche* lres as shalbe solicited from her maⁱᵉ to suche princes and Potentates as are in the places of the Este [whether] wher trade shalbe sought *(Touching lres to be writt from the Queene to the East Indies.)*

And it is ordered that Aldʳ Hollyday and Richard Wright shall sett downe the names of [such] all those that shalbe mencoñed in the Pattent and Carry them to Mʳ Attorney that the booke may be ingrossed.

And lastly it is ordered that vppoñ munday next a generall Coʳt shalbe called to enforme the generalyty of the proceadinges of the Comitties and how farre the busines is in a redines.

The 5 of Decembʳ 1600.

Aldʳ Bannyng   Capten Lancaster
Aldʳ Hollyday   Mʳ Wᵐ Chambers
Aldʳ Wattes   Mʳ Ry Wyseman
Mʳ Olyuer Style   Mʳ Wᵐ Harryson
        Mᵗ Nich. Lynge.

T this Assemblie it was resolved that mʳ Thomas Allabaster his Comission for prouision of Ryalles shalbe contynued the same to be provided from suche partes as formerlie it was ordeyned

Warrauntes were geaven to mʳ Aldʳ Hollyday for the paiment of these Sommes followinge viz.

five hundred poundes to *mʳ* Thomas Allabaster for provision 500ˡⁱ.0.0
of Ryalles
one hundred poundes to mʳ Wᵐ Garway for the provysion   100.0.0
of thassension.

100ˡⁱ.0.0   One hundred poundes to Mʳ Wᵐ Chambers for the provision of Caske.
120ˡⁱ.0.0   Warraunt is geaveñ to Aldʳ Bannyng to pay one hundred [poundes] and twentie poundes. to Josephe Salbanck

The 6 of December 1600.

Mʳ Aldʳ Smythe Goveʳ   Mʳ Jo : Highelord
Mʳ Aldʳ Hollyday   Mʳ John Eldred.
Mʳ Thomas Cordell.   Mʳ Wᵐ Chambers
Mʳ Olyuer Style.   Mʳ John Midletoñ
Capten Lancaster   Mʳ Nicħas. Lynge
      Mʳ Robt Bell.

80ˡⁱ to Mʳ Wᵐ Burrell

WARRAUNT is geaveñ to Aldʳ Hollyday to pay to mʳ Wᵐ Burrell for the provisioñ of Tymber and other necessaries for the shippes the soṁe of fowrscore poundes sterling to be dd him vppoñ accoumptes.

80. to Mʳ Nich: Symondson

The Like Warraunt is geaveñ to Aldʳ Bannyng to pay to nicħas. Symondsoñ for provisioñ of Tymber and paiment for ware the somme of fowrscore poundes sterling

50ˡⁱ to Wᵐ Angell, fishemongʳ

Another warraunt is geaveñ to *the said mʳ Aldʳ Bannyng to pay to* Wᵐ Angell fishemonger vppoñ accoumpt of fishe the soṁe of fyfty pounds sterling

Order is geaveñ for the warning of a generall Court vppoñ munday next to informe the geñ'alyty of the present state of the voyage for the better proceading wherein thes pticler [pointes are to] thinges [touching] are to be notyfyed vnto theṁ touching the handling of the busines hetherto. viz.

The Choice of factoʳˢ in ther severall places.
The Choice of the severall Mʳˢ
The redines of the shippes to come out of ther Dockes.
The present necessitie of the bringing in of money to pay wages because the officers and mariners are to [come] appointed to ther shippes.—&ℭ

THE EAST INDIA COMPANY

A Gen^rall Court the 8. Decemb̃ 1600
in the presence of

Mr Ald^r Smyth Go^r	Mr Roger Howe
Mr Ald^r Hollyday	Mr Rych : Wysemañ
Mr Ald^r Moore :	Mr Wm Chambers
Mr Tho. Cordell	M^r Jo : Combe
Mr Wm Garway	Mr Wm Harrysoñ
M^r olyuer Style.	Mr Nich : Lynge
M^r Jo Middletoñ :	Mr Rob̃t Bell.

And of a great nũber of the gen^ralyty whose names are forborne to be noted for the shortenes of the tyme.

T is agreed by the generall assemblie for the better advauncem^t of the voyage that whosoever is behinde wth his whole adventure by him sett downe and shall not wholie bring in the same by the 13 of this moneth beinge Satherday next that whatsoever damage shalbe susteyned by the deteyning of the shippes heare soe long wch are only deteyned by the not bringing in of the adventures shalbe laid vpponñ those that by the want of bringing in of ther moneis have bene the occasioñ of so great a damage. *for the bringing in of the adventures.*

The said Generalitie beinge made acquainted *by m^r governo^r* wth the redines of the preparatioñ of the shippes victualles and all other furniture belonging to the same and also wth the Choice of the principall facto^{rs} who are to be imployed in the said viage (the placing and sortinge of wch facto^{rs} being pticlerly noted and declared vnto theñ) the said generalyty were of opinioñ that in the disposing of some of the principall places and sorting of the facto^{rs} in the same, the said cõmitties had neade better to informe theñ selfes, theñ they have done for that in the seconde sort of factors ther is *placed* one Mr Brund a grave and discreet mñchaunt and one wch hath the arabyañ Spanishe and Portugall Languages wch may better deserve [a principall] *the* place of a principall facto^r then some of those wch are placed in the first place and therfore the generalyty do wyshe the Comitties in ther next assemblie to *The eleccon of one of the principall factors.*

advyse better of the same election and that they would consider thereof when they are mett in most ample number assuring them that m^r Brunde will not accept of a Second place especially the first being supplied by younger men and of *lesse* experience and desert then him self

The 10th of Decemb 1600

Mr Tho: Smythe Go^r	Mr Capten Lancaster
Mr Ald^r Hollyday	Mr John Eldred.
Mr Ald. Moore	Mr Robt Sandy
M^r olyuer Style	Mr Rich: Wyseman
Mr Tho Cordell	Mr Wm Chambers
M^r fra: Chery	M^r Jo: Middleton.
Mr John Highelord	Mr Niclias Lynge
Mr Wm Chambers	Mr Wm Harryson.
Mr Rich: Staper	Robt Bell.

Henry Napper.

T is ordered that Capten Lancaster and Capten Midleton shall conferre wth Henry Napper touching his imployment in the voyage to goe therin as they and he can agree the former Composition made wth him by Mr Staper notwthstanding. and as they proceade in the same conference. to acquainte the Comitties therwth at ther next meeting.

This assembly proceading to the reviewe and reexaiation of the former election of the .4. first principall factors places. according to the order of the last generall Court did in this meeting vppon good delibation enter into consideration of the matter and did wth a generall Consent by Scrouteny make choice of Mr Wm Brunde to be one of the fowre principall factors in this voyage *and* to be [sorted placed] sorted as heerafter followeth [viz] And it ys *also* agreed that the Generall and [principall] other the said principall factors shalbe sorted and placed as hereafter followeth viz

Capten Lancaster in the Scourge.
Capten Midleton in the Hecto^r.
Wm Brund in the Assention
John Havard in the Susan.

THE EAST INDIA COMPANY

Order is geaveñ to Ald^r Bannyng theī. to pay to henry mydletoñ purser of the scourge the some of 300^{li} vppoñ accoumpt for the provisioñ of the Scourge vppoñ paym^t whereof he is to take his receipte. _{300^{li} to ye Scourge.}

Lyke order is geaveñ to the said m^r Ald^r Bannyng to pay to Wm Walthall 224^{li} 2^s 0 for 29 fodder 4^C 1^q 16^{lb} of Peate Lead bought at vij^{li} xiij^s iiij^d the ffodder. _{224^{li} 2^s c^d for lead bought of Wm Walthall.}

Further order is geaveñ to the said Mr Ald^r Bannyng to pay vnto Edwyñ Babingtoñ the someˉ of 100^{li} sterlinge in part of payment for Canary Wynes provided for the voyage. _{100^{li} to Edwin Babington for wynes.}

Order is geaveñ to m^r [Thom$\tilde s$. Allabas] Ald^r. Hollyday to [pay] deliver to m^r Thom$\tilde s$ Allabaster vppoñ accoumpte the somme of five hundred poundes sterling to be imployed by him for thexchaunge of Royalles. for the vse of the voyage. _{500^{li} to Mr Allabaster for Royalles}

The like order is geaveñ to the said m^r Ald^r to pay vnto Edward Stepheñs Carpenter of the Scourge the somme of fyfty poundes sterling vppoñ accoumpte to be imploied in the Repairing and preparing of the same ship _{50^{li} to ye Carpenter of the Scourge.}

The 11th of Decemb^r 1600.

Mr Ald^r Hollyday	Capteñ Lancaster
Mr Wm Garway	Capteñ Middletoñ
Mr Rich: Wysemañ	M^r Jo: Combe
Mr Wm Chamber	Mr Robt Bell
Mr John Eldred.	Mr Rich: Wyche
M^r olyuer Style	Mr Nich: Lyng

Mr Wm Harrysoñ.

RDER is geaveñ to Ald^r Hollyday ther^r to pay vnto Raphe Salter Surgeoñ enterteyned for this voiage the somme of thertie and two poundes sterling being allowed vnto him by Compositioñ for the furnishing of his Chest wth all kinde of necessaries and remedies belonging to a Chirurgioñ to be vsed in this viage vppoñ paiment of wch money [you are] he is to take his acquittaunce. _{32^{li} to Raphe Salter Chirurgion.}

Ther is also order geaveñ to Ald^r Bannynge to pay vnto M^r _{100^{li} to}

THE COURT RECORDS OF

<small>frauncis Covell for peas & beanes.</small>
frauncis Covell the somme of one hundred poundes sterling vppoñ Accoumpte for the provysioñ of peas and beanes. vppoñ paiment whereof he is to take his receipte

<small>100ˡⁱ to the Hectoʳ</small>
The like order is geaveñ to the said Aldʳ. Bannynge to pay to mʳ Richard Wysemañ the somme of one hundred poundes sterlinge to be delivered to the Purser of the Hectoʳ for the Charges of provisioñ and p̃paratioñ of the same ship vppoñ accoumpte.

<small>The Scourge is hearafter to be called, by the name of the Red Dragoñ.</small>
It is ordered that the great ship called the Scourge wᶜʰ is to be lanched this after none. shall be called heerafter by the name of the Redd Dragoñ. and noe more to be knoweñ by the former name of the Scourge.

The 12ᵗʰ of Decemb̃. 1600.

Mʳ Tho. Cordell   Mʳ Rob̃t Sandy.
Mʳ Rich: Staper   Capteñ Lancaster
Mʳ olyuer Style.   Capteñ Middletoñ
Mʳ Rich: Wyseman   Mʳ Wᵐ Harryson
       Mʳ Nicħas. Lyng.

<small>71ˡⁱ. 13. 4ᵈ to Mʳ Attorney and his Clerkes.</small>
RDER is geaveñ to Mʳ Aldʳ Bannyng threr to pay vnto mʳ Rob̃t Sandy the somme of seventie *one* poundes *xiijᵗ iiij* sterling for somuche by him dysbursed for the Charges of oʳ Pattent and the Warraunt for coyning dewe to Mʳ Attorney and his Clerkes for the drawing and ingrossing of the same pattent and Warraunt. I say seventie one poundes thirteene shillingℓ and foure pence.

The 13 of Decemb̃ 1600.

Mʳ Aldʳ Wattes   Mʳ W: Rumney
Mʳ Aldʳ More   Mʳ Rob̃t Sandy.
Captein Lancaster   Mʳ Wᵐ Chamber
Mʳ Tho. Cordell.   Mʳ Nicħas Lyng
Mʳ olyuer Style   Mʳ

RDER is geaveñ to Ald^r [Hollyday th] Bannyng ther to pay vnto John Busbridge *lynnen*drap the somme of one hundred twentie and five poundes tenñ shilling₽ sterling for Lynneñ Clothe of him bought by Mr Stap and Mr Lyng for the vse of the voyage. whose pticlers appeare. and are to be ďď wth the warraunt for the paiment of the money. 125^{li} 10^s for lynneñ Clothe.

Order is geaveñ to Ald^r Hollyday ther to pay vnto Wm Cater. and George Cater. the somme of twentie eight poundes fourteene shilling₽ for 24 peeces of Roañ Cloth viz 475 elnes at xiiij^d oƀ p elne bought of them by m^r Nicħas Lyng. vppoñ payment whereof he is to take his receipt in fułł. 28^{li} 14 0 for Roañ Canves.

Order is geaveñ to m^r Ald^r Hollyday to pay vnto Mr Roger Hankin M^r of the Assentioñ the somme of thertie sixe poundes [three shillinges] and fowre pence for the fraight ballast and other Charges dewe thervppoñ of two hoyes. to goe to the severall shippes of this voyage vppoñ paiment whereof he is to take his receipte. 36^{li}. o. 4^d for ballast for the shippes and for the fraight of 2 hoyes to go to the shippes.

It is ordered that all the Pursers of the severall shippes shall be warned to appeare vppoñ twesday before the Comitties and to bringe in ther accoumptes of the disbursem^{tes} of moneys delivered theɱ to be imployed aboute the shippes and other occasions of the Companie. Pursers to bring in ther Accounptes.

Mr Wm Chambers made a motioñ to this Assemblie in the behaulf of one Walter Poyner to be imployed in the voyag: as a facto^r at large wthout salarie wth this hope that if anie facto^r faile, that he may supplie his place or the place of some other of the facto^{rs} that shalbe removed to the place of the decessed or to be left in the Indies as a resident facto^r whose motioñ is well lyked of and the matter to be further considered of at soɱe other meetinge when the Companie shall [consider] assemble them selfes to take a Survey of the facto^{rs}. Walter Poyner.

The like motioñ is made by m^r Sandie in the behaulf of m^r w^m martens sonne of Exceter for to be imployed in the voyage. for whose fidelyty his father wyll geave good security to the Companie. and is content to be imployed as the [said] Companie shalbe pleased or left in the Indies for a facto^r resident ther. Wm Martin

THE COURT RECORDS OF

The 15 Decemb' a°. 1600.

Mr Tho : Cordell
Mr Ryc^r Stapers
Mr Robte Saundye
Mr W^{ma} Chamb^{rs}
M^r Jn° Highlord.

m^r Alderman more
captaine lancaster
m^r ollyver style.
m^r wiche.
m^r fraunces Cherry

m^r Ryc: Wyseman.

26^{li}. 13^s. James Lovering [Daniel Lee] Chirirgeon of ye hecto^r.

ORDER is geven to m̃ Ald^rman Baninge to pay vnto [Daniel Lee] James Lovering surgeon of the hecto^r entertained for this viadge the some of twenty fyve pounds sterł beinge alowed him by Composicion for the furnisshinge of his chest wth all kinds of remedyes and necessaryes belonnginge to a chirurgeon to be vsed vpon this viadge. vponn paim^t of wch monney yo^u are to take his acquyttance.

20^{li}. to Xpofer newchurch surgeon of the Assencon

There is also order geven to m̃ Alderm̃ Banning to pay vnto chrystopher newchurche surgeon of the Assencon for twentye pounds stri Allowed him by Composicion for the furnishinge of his chest wth all kind of remedyes and necessaryes belonnginge to a chirurgeon to be vsed vpon this viadge. vpon paym^{tt} of his monney yo^u are to take his acquyttance.

20^{li}. to Jn°. gamond surgeon of the susann

There is also order geven to m̃ Aldermann baninge to pay vnto Jn° gamond twentye pound stri allowed him by composycon for the furnishinge of his chest wth all kind of remedyes and necessaryes belonnginge to a chirurgeon to be vsed vpon this viadge ; vpon paym^{tt} of this monney yo^u are to take his acquyttance.

The 16 of Decemb 1600.

Mr Staper
Mr Garway
Mr Cordell
Capten Lancaster
Mr Wysemañ
Mr Howe.

Capteñ Midletoñ
Mr Harrysoñ
Mr Eldred
Mr Chamber.
Mr Highelord.
Mr Sandy

Mr Chery

R Ald^r Wattes Mr Cordell Mr Wysemañ Mr Howe and Mr Harrysoñ or any. 3. of them are appointed Auditers to receve the Accoumptes of the Pursers and to examine the same and as they finde the said accoumptes to stande to Certefie ther opinions to the residewe of the Comitties to thende yf anie thinge fall out in the same accoumptes worthie the consideratioñ of the said Comitties [the] order may be takeñ therin by them. _{Auditors}

Order is geaveñ to m^r Ald^r Bannynge to pay vnto the Purser of the Hercules the somme of one hundred poundes sterlinge. vppon accoumpte to be imployed in the preparatioñ and repayring of the same ship _{100^{li} to the Hecto^r.}

The like order is geaveñ to m^r Ald^r Holliday to pay vnto ye Purser of the Assentioñ the somme of one hundred poundes sterling vppoñ accoumpte to be imployed in the preparatioñ and repairinge of the same ship _{100^{li} to ye Assentioñ.}

It is agreed that whereas the proportioñ for the provisioñ of iroñ was formerlie agreed to be but 30 tuñz it is nowe resolved that ther shalbe provided 20 tuñz more so that the whole quantetie of iroñ shalbe 50 tun^s. and that ther shalbe provided furthe some convenient quantety of faggot iroñ being in small barres fitt to be converted in to nayles. _{yron to be provided 50 tuñs in the whole.}

The same day in the after none.

Mr Ald^r Smyth Go^r	Capteñ Lancaster
Mr Ald^r Hollyday	Mr Highlord.
Mr Ald^r Wattes	Mr Chambers
Mr Ald^r Moore.	M^r Jo Combe.
Capteñ Lancaster	Mr Nich : Lyng
Mr Thomas Cordell.	Mr Rich : Wyche.
M^r olyuer Style.	Mr Wm Harrysoñ
Mr Rich : Wysemañ	Mr Robt Sandy
Mr Wm Rumney	Mr Wm Burrell

Mr Wm Garway.

HIS assemblie beinge [be] mett in conference for the placing and sorting of the Principall officers to be imployed in the voyage. they have agreed that they shalbe severallie sorted in the said shippes in manner and forme followinge viz

The sorting of the principall factors & other officers

In the red [Lyon] *Dragon*. Admirall.

Capteñ Lancaster generall.
Capten Davies   Pylott Maio^r of the fleet
Wm Broadbent   M^r of the same ship

In the Hector.   Vice Admirall.

Capteñ Midletoñ. principall facto^r in that ship
Henry Napper. M^r of the same ship.
Phillip Grove [Pylott] second Pilott of the fleet.

In the Assention.

William Brunde. principall factor in that ship.
Roger Hankin M^r of the same ship

In the Susan.

John Havard principall factor in that ship.
Samuel Spencer M^r of the same ship.

The 17th of Decemb 1600.

Mr Ald^r Smithe Go^r	Mr Wm Rumney.
Mr Ald^r Hollyday	Mr Rich. Wyche
Mr Ald^r Wattes	Mr Rob̃t Sandy
Mr Ald^r Moore	Mr Nich: Lynge
Mr Rich: Staper	Capteñ Middletoñ
Mr Thomas Cordell	Mr John Combe
Mr Rich: Wysemañ	Mr Fra: Chery
Capteñ Lancaster	Mr Wm Chambers
M^r olyuer Style	Mr John Highelord

Mr Roger Howe.

THE EAST INDIA COMPANY 101

HE choice of the factors formerlie made being interrupted by reason of the [refusall] *falling of* some of them ther was a newe proceeding in the election of [some] *divers* of the said factors wch geaveth occasion to make some alteration of the sorting and placing of the second, third and fourth sorte of *them*. [factors the the same factors] wheruppon at this Assemblie the said severall factors are sorted and disposed in manner and forme [following viz] menčõed on thother syde.

<small>A newe placing and disposing of the 2.3. and 4 sort of factors.</small>

Robert Pope who hath bene imployed in the West Cuntrey in the provysion of victualles moneys and other necessaries for the voyage. being come vp and present at this assemblie forasmuche as he hath taken paines in the said preparations and is one of the second sort of factors. appointed for the voyage: this assemblie have added to the ordinarye allowaunce geaven to the rest of the said seconde sort of factors to be [geaven] *paied*, to the said Rob̃t Pope the some of fyftie poundes sterling^e over and besides his Charges hetherto expended wch money shalbe p^d him before his going forthe.

<small>50^{li} to Robt Pope factor.</small>

The names of the seconde third and fowrth sort of factors. and ther places as they are appointed to be shipped

Robert Pope ———————— in the Red Dragon ⎫
Wm Starkey ———————— in the Hector   ⎬ 2 sort of factors
Tho Salterne ———————— in Assention
Henry Middleton ———————— in the Susan. ⎭

Nathaniel Gamram ———————— in the Dragon   ⎫
Thomas Dassell ———————— in the Hecto^r.   ⎬ 3. sort of factors
[Rich: Collymer] *Roger Style* —— in the Assention
Wm Wilford ———————— in the Susan.   ⎭

Xpofer Stradling ———————— in the Dragon.   ⎫
Tho. Tudd ———————— in the Hecto^r.   ⎬ 4. sort of factors
Phillip Winchecomb ———————— in the Assention
Tho Morgan ———————— in the Susan   ⎭

The names of suche facto^{rs} as are admitted to goe wthout Salarie to [be] take place

102   THE COURT RECORDS OF

yf anie of the former enterteyned factors do dye. or to be left in the Cuntrey as residentȝ ther to lerne the Language. and to looke in to yᵉ trade of those Cuntreis at the discretioñ of the Generall and other principall factoʳˢ

D.	John Smythe.	
H	Walter Poyner.	
S.	[Roger Style] George Allyñ.	to be placed in the shippes at the dispositioñ of the Chief Generall and principall factors.
A	Roger Martiñ.	
A	Thomas Warde.	
D.	Thomas Webbe.	
H.	Hughe Hule.	

The 19 December 1600.

Mʳ Aldʳ Holliday   Capt. Lancaster
Aldʳ Watts   Mʳ Wyseman
Aldʳ Moore   Mʳ Style
Thomas Cordell   Mʳ Chambers
Wᵐ Garway   Mʳ Howe
John Eldred   Mʳ Sandy.

y 800. vppõ ald bayning to robt stevens

EVEN a warrant vppõ aldʳ Bayning ffor paymᵗ of y 800. to Robᵗ Stevens in full of a bill of y 1400. frõ mʳ John ellacott of exceter.

y 600. vppõ ald: holliday to Robt stevens.

Geven a warrant vppõ ald Holliday ffor paymᵗ of y 600. to Robt Stevens & Roger Howe in full of a bill of y 1400. frõ mʳ John ellacott of exceter

y 241. vppõ ald. holliday

Geven a warrant vppõ ald holliday ffor paymᵗ of y 241. to mʳ ffrancis west by a bill of excȇ frõ John Sandy frõ exceter

y 105. 12. 4 vppõ ald holliday to walter clarck. mʳ alabaster not to proceed in ryalls.

Geven a warrant vppõ ald [holliday] Bayning for paymᵗ of y 105. 12:4ᵈ to walter clarck ffor lyke vallew Receyved in exceter by John sandy in Ryall of plate as ꝑ the bill.

Yt was at this assembly ordeyned that mʳ thomas Alabaster should not proceed any ffarther in provision of Ryalls frõ callais.

THE EAST INDIA COMPANY 103

Order is given to m͏ͬ Roger How to take the charge in answering of certayne letters Rhd̄ frō the factors in the west countrey & to give a Remembrance to m͏ͬ Roḃᵗ pope bound thither ffor the manadging of the busynesse there concerning [all] as well Ryalls of plate as all other provisions their made & to take an accōpt of euery of the rest of the factoʳˢ there wᵗʰ such other directions as hee shal thinck meete for these busynesses.

Given a warrant vppō ald̄ Bayning for paymᵗ of y 30. to   30ˡⁱ to wᵐ
Wᵐ Wilford for his salary in this voyadg   wilford one
                                                        of the factors·

The 20 december 1600.

M͏ͬ Goüernoür	M͏ͬ richard stapers
M͏ͬ Aldʳ Moore	M͏ͬ Harrison
M͏ͬ Richard Wyseman	M͏ͬ Chambres
M͏ͬ olyver Style	M͏ͬ Combe

M͏ͬ Lancaster.

EVEN a Warrant vppō ald̄ Bayning ffor payment of   231ˡⁱ.10ˢ.—ᵈ
y 231 . 10 . — . to george hangar ffor 22 pypes of   to m͏ͬ
canaria wyne at 10£ . 10ˢ — ᵈ p pype.   hangar.

The 20 december 1600.

Geven a warrant vppō ald̄ Bayning ffor paymᵗ of y 378. to   378 ˡⁱ to m͏ͬ
m͏ͬ wᵐ harrisson ffor 36 pypes of canarya wyne at y 10 . 10 . harrisson
— p pype.

Geven a warrant vppō ald̄ Bayning ffor paymᵗ of y 160. to   160ˡⁱ to m͏ͬ
m͏ͬ Edwin babington in full for 26 pypes of canary wynes at y Babington
10 p pype.

The 22 december 1600.

M͏ͬ Gouernour	M͏ͬ
M͏ͬ Cordell	M͏ͬ Eldred
M͏ͬ Wyseman	M͏ͬ Lancaster
M͏ͬ Style.	M͏ͬ Middleton
M͏ͬ Rumney	M͏ͬ Stapers

M͏ͬ highlord

EVEN warrants vppõ ald^r Bayning ffor paym^t of these soñies ffollowing to say—

    100^{li} to Lewes Tate smith ffor smithery by him delyvered

    100^{li} to henry middleton purser of the Redd dragoñ.

    50. to Roger hanckey m^r of the assension vppõ accõpt of his wages.

    100^{li} to william Burrell ffor pvision for the shipps

    40^{li} to John coles by exc^e for Lewes pope in absence of Robert pope to the hands of gyles Barrey.

    200^{li} to m^r wyseman to pay ffor wax candles & provision for the hecto^r.

Geven a warrant vppon ald^r Holliday ffor paym^t of y 100. to Richard Hart smith ffor smithery ffor the assension.

    The 24 Decemb^r: 1600.

Mr Ald^r Watts	Mr Sandy
Mr Cordell	Mr Harrison
Mr Cherrey	Mr Howe:
Mr Style	Mr Lancaster
Mr Wyche.	Mr Ald^r Hollyday
Mr Wyseman	Mr Middleton
Mr Eldred	Mr Highlord.

EVEN at this assembly warrants vppõ ald^r Bayning ffor these soñies ffollowing viz

    y 30: to thomas dassell ffor his wages in this voyadg

    y 100: to william Bradbanck maister of the dragon vppõ accõpt

    y 150: to John Būzbridg vppõ accõpt of yron by order of mr. sandy

    y 100: to Rob̃t warner vppõ accõpt of 35 tonns of yron

    y 210: to m^r Robt savadg ffor 20 [tuns] pypes of canaria wyne

    y 100: to m^r william Chambres towards provision of caske &c:

THE EAST INDIA COMPANY   105

The 24 December 1600.   1600
Geven warrants vppõ aldⁿ Bayning ffor payment of these   24 Dec.
somes ffollowinge—
l 10. 5. 8, to henry lambard ffor 89 black iacks
l 50.—.—, to xpofer [Smith] thomson smith vppõ accõpt of yron wark for the hecto^r
l 17. 4. 11, to ffrancis covell in ffull of provisions made by him as by accõpt
l 50.—.—, to william Dixson purser of the Redd dragon for the vse of that shipp
Geven warrants vppõ aldⁿ Holliday ffor payment of these somes ffollowing viz
l 100. to m^r w^m Garway for the assention
l 150. to w^m Candish vppõ accõpt of lead by order of m^r Sandy.
At this assembly it was determyned that Roger Style should   RogerStyle.
take the place of Richard Collymore ffor one of the third sort of ffacto^{rs} & to have the same allowance & salary as the other of that sort are allowed, and vppõ this agreem^t m^r olyver style hath in his behalf ,pmysed to adventure l 200.—.—
Also it was ordered that every sort of ffacto^{rs} before elected to   Bondes of
take chardge in this voyadg [vnder] *in* the number of the sixteene   the factors.
should give in bonds ffor their truth & good behavio^r as followeth—
The ffirst ffower to give bonds of l 500.—.—
The second fower to give bonds of 500 marcks
The third sort to give bonds of 200^{li} p peece
The fforth sort to give bonds of 100^{li}

The 27 of Decemb^r 1600.   1600
                                                                  27 Dec.
ARRAUNT is geaven to Aldⁿ Bannyng *thēr* to pay   500^{li} to M^r
vnto Rob̃t Stephens for the vse of John Ellicott the   Ellicott for
some of [one h] five hundred poundes sterling in   royalles.
part of paiment of seven hundred poundes. taken vp by him in Ryalles of plate.

P

106 THE COURT RECORDS OF

1600
27 Dec.

25ˡⁱ pᵈ to John Sheir for money by exchaunge.

The like warraunt is geaven *to Aldⁿ Hollyday* thër to pay vnto Laurence Waldo the somme of Twentie and five poundes sterling̊ and is for somuch taken vp by exchaunge of John Sheer of Exeter and pᵈ to the handes of John Sandy to the vse of the Company.

200ˡⁱ to y Purser of the Scourge

Another Warraunt is geaven to the said Aldⁿ Bannyng̊ to pay to Edward highlord Purser of the Read Dragon vppon accoumpte for provision and preparatioñ of the same ship the somme of Two hundred poundes sterling̊.

50ˡⁱ for timber for the read Dragon

There is also another Warraunt made to the said Aldⁿ Bannyng̊ to pay the somē of fyfty poundes to Edward Stephens vppon the accoumpt of Tymber for the red dragon

1600
29 Dec.

The 29 December 1600.

Mʳ Tho Smythe Goʳ   Mʳ John Highelord
Mʳ Aldⁿ [Wattes] Hollyday   Mʳ John Eldred.
Mʳ Aldⁿ Wattes   Mʳ Roḃt Sandy
Mʳ Wᵐ Garway   Mʳ Wᵐ Chamber.
Mʳ Rich: Staper   Mʳ Wᵐ Harryson.
Mʳ Tho Cordell.   Capteñ Lancaster
Mʳ Rich: Wyseman   Capteñ Midleton.

700ˡⁱ to Mʳ Allabaster for royalles.

ARRAUNT is geaven to Aldⁿ Bannyng̊ to pay vnto Mʳ Thomŝ Allabaster towardes the payment of certen billes of exchaunge. the somē of seven hundred poundes sterling̊ in part of payment of the said billes wᶜʰ do come to 880ˡⁱ being for the provision of royalles.

50ˡⁱ to Wᵐ Starky.

Another warraunt is geaven to Aldⁿ Hollyday to pay vnto Wᵐ Starky one of the factors the somme of fyftie poundes sterling̊ for so muche allowed him [vppon] *for* his enterteynment for his preparation [of] *in* the voyage.

100ˡⁱ in gold to be geaven in gratuity.

It is ordered that ther shalbe geaven according̊ to this conference the somme of [one h] Two hundred angelles in gratuyty from the Companie to suche psons as mʳ Garwey and Richard Wright by this assembly are directed to attende for that purpose. And it is ordered that

THE EAST INDIA COMPANY

It is alsoe ordered and Warraunt is geaven to m^r Ald^r hollyday to pay to the handes of Richard Wright for the provideing of the said 100^{li} in gold and for 50^{li} more in silver to pay other Charges for the passinge of the Pattent and the Warraunt for Coyning the Signet the privy seale and great seale.

1600
29 Dec.
50^{li} for the charges of the bookes.

The 31 December 1600

Mr Ald^n Smithe Go^r	Mr Wm Chambers
Capten Lancaster	Capten Midleton
Mr Tho. Cordell.	Mr Nich : Lynge.
M^r olyuer Style	*Mr Staper.*
Mr Robt Sandy	Mr Wm Garway
M^r Jo : Combe.	Mr Robt Bell.

1600
31 Dec.

WARRAUNT is geaven to m^r Ald^n Bannyng to pay vnto to pay vnto John Gover. for viij hh. of Aquavite cn^{tg} 482 gallons. [of Aquavitæ] the somme of nynty six poundes viij^s at iiij^s the gallon / in full payment.

96^{li}. 8^s. for aquavite

It is ordered that the Thre͞rs accoumptes shalbe pvsed wth all expedition and to see what moneis hath bene p^d in by the adventuro^{rs} and what remaineth in ther handes . to thend that yf ther appeare a want of money wch cannot be otherwyse supplied then by the encrease of the gen͞all adventure, that then the gen͞ality may be called together and ther is apointed for Auditors. Mr Cordell m^r Style. Mr Wyseman. Mr Harrison.

Auditors for the Thre͞rs accomptes.

It is agreed that the goodes shipped by the Companie and the Caske shalbe m͞ked wth this gen͞all marke in the mergent and that an Iron be prepared wch shall make the said marke

Order is geaven to Mr Sandy to provide CCCC ½ of Castle Soape.

The 2 of January 1600.

Mr Ald^n Smithe Go^r	Mr Ald^n Hollyday
Mr Ald^n Bannyng	Capten Lancaster

1600
2 Jan.

1600
2 Jan.

Mr Tho Cordell.
Mr Garway
M^r oliuer Style
Mr Rich: Wyche.
Mr John Combe.
Mr John Eldred

Capten Middleton
Mr Niclas Lyng
Mr Robt Bell
Mr Wm Harryson
Mr Rich: Staper
Mr Robt Sandy.

100^{li} to ye Purser of the Read Dragon.

ORDER is geaven to m^r Aldⁿ holliday thrēr to pay vnto Wm Dyckes Purser of the Read Dragon the somme of one hundred poundes sterling to be imployed vppon necessary provision of the same ship vppon Accoumpte.

250^{li} to the Purser of the Susan.

Order is geaven to Mr Aldⁿ Bannyng thrēr to pay vnto Joseph Salbanck Purser of the Susan. to be imploied in the necessarie provision of the same ship the some of Two hundred *and fyftie* poundes sterling vppon accoumpte.

100^{li} to Robt Stephens by bill of exchaunge from Jo: Ellicott

The lyke order is geaven to m^r Aldⁿ holliday thrēr to pay vnto Robt Stephens the some of one hundred poundes sterling by a bill of exchaung of John Ellicott directed to Robt Sandie written in the West Cuntrey vppon paiment whereof [yo^u are] *he is* to take his acquittaunce together wth the Bill.

Streamers Flaggs & Auncients.

It is ordered that ther shalbe provided for eche of the shippes 12 Streemers. 2 fflagges and one Auncient wth all convenient speede, and that the same shalbe provided by the severall Comitties formerlie appointed to the said severall shippes for the provision of thinges necessarie for the same.

30^{li} to Roger Style factor

Ther is order geaven to Ald^r [Hollyday] *Bannynge* to pay to Roger Style one of the third sort of factors. the somme of thirtie poundes sterlinge. being the allowaunce graunted by the Companie for his provision.

1600
8 Jan.

Edm: Scott admitted to go in the voyage.

The 8 of Januarie 1600

EDMUND SCOTT is admitted to goe in the voyage putting in Two hundred poundes venture: whereof C^{li} is to be p^d in hand and the other C^{li} at 14 daies next following . and where he was willinge rather then not

THE EAST INDIA COMPANY   109

to be imploied in the voyage to have geaven X^li to the Com- 1600
pany for his diett aboard they are content to remitt the said   8 Jan.
X^li in hope of his good service in the choice of Drugẽ and
spices wherin he pretendeth to have knowledge.

A generall Court holdeñ the 9 of Januarie 1600. in   1600
                the presence of   9 Jan.

Mr Ald Smithe go^r   Mr Robt Sandy
Sr John Spencer   Mr John Eldred.
Mr Ald^n Bannyng   Mr Johñ Middleton
Mr Hollyday   M^r fra Chery
Mr Ald^n Wattes   Mr Roger Howe
Mr Tho Cordell.   Mr Rich: Wyche
M^r olyver Style   M^r Jo: highelord
Captein Lancaster   M^r Jo: Rumney :
Mr Rich: Wyseman.   And the greater part of
                              the geñalyty.

ARRAUNT is geaven to Ald^n holliday *thrẽr*   100^li per
to pay vnto Robert Stephens the somme of one   ex^e from
hundred poundes sterlingẽ vppon a bill of Ex-   Jo: Ellacot.
chaunge from Johñ Ellicott out of the west
Cuntrey Directed to Mr Robt Sandie vppon the
East Indie accoumpte.

At this Courte the Pattent [it is ordered th] vnder the great   Admitting
seale was read [and] to the generalitie wherby it appeareth that ther   of freemen.
is power geaven to the generalyty to admitt in to the priviledges.
of the Company suche as [shal] they shall thinke good from tyme
to tyme according to wch power forasmuche as divers have of
late contributed to the voyage 200^li a peece whose names are
not conteyned in the said Pattent therfore accordingẽ to the
warraunt geaven the Companie by the said Lrẽs Pattentẽ this
Court have ordered that the same Contributors shalbe holden
to all ententẽ and purposes as free as [all] anie other [the]
whose names are expresselie mencõned in the said graunt—the
names of wch Contributors [are heervnder written viz] are

1600
9 Jan.

The want of the necessarie supplie of the adventure howe it is to be raised.

hereafter to be presented [at the next geñall Court and] then to be confirmed as free brothers of this felowship.

This Court was informed that the comon adventure sett downe for the voyage falleth out too short by the some of fowre or five thousand poundes. of that wch shall be necessarie to be sett forth considering the great preparation of the Ductche wch are ready to goe to the same places of the East Indies to wch o^{r} voyage is directed, and that also some of the adventure^{rs} wch have sett downe ther contributions have brought in noe part thereof and other some *do* defaulte of that wch they sett downe alledging that will not adventure so muche as they sett downe *at the first.* by wch meanes the adventure will fall short of that wch is necessarie *to be* [still further] *adventured to make a good voyage* by the some of eight or nyne thowsand poundes in the whole vppoñ wch information this Court falling into the delibation howe in best sort they may supply this present want. It was agreed [that] therfore by this geñall Court for the advancem^{t} of this voyage and for the avoyding of the preiudice that may happen by the want of a convenient proportion of adventure [for this present voyag̃ enterprise], *and that* by the generall assent of this assemblie and establyshed as a Lawe Warraunted by the said lres Pattentes that for the present dispatche away of the shippes and the full augmentation of the Stocke and adventure to be sett forthe ther shalbe enlarged by every contributo^{r} according to the proportion of his adventure ij^{s} vppon the pounde wth this Cawtion notwthstanding that yf the full adventure can be otherwyse supplied by any voluntary [supply] *enlargement* of mens voluntary encrease of ther adventures and by the vrging of those that are behinde wth all or part of the adventures to bring them in according to that wch they have sett downe that then all the overplus wch shalbe brought in by the enlargem^{t} of ij^{s} the pound. shalbe proportionally restored backe againe to the Contributors and be vsed the meane tyme as money lent. And it is also ordered that a present information and Complaint *shalbe* made to the Ll of the Councell of suche as have disapointed the preparation of the voyag̃ [shalbe] *that they may be* called before ther Lord-shippes to receave suche order as to ther honors shalbe thought meet. And to thende that this order and decree agreed vppon may be executed wth all spede the said rate of ij^s the li shalbe brought in by everie adventuro^r according to his proportion by the. 15. of this moneth vppon payne of forfeyture of Double the valewe to be Levied vppon them according to the aucthoritie of the [said] graunt of priviledges. before mencōned provided all waies and it is agreed that yf any man shalbe willing voluntaryly to encrease his adventure already sett downe above the rate of ij^s the li that then he shall not be w^thin the Compas of this acte of enlargem^t of ij^s the li by way of Lone.

<small>1600 9 Jan.</small>

At this Court according to the warraunt geaven to the Companie for the election of the . deputie to the Governo^r of the same. they have proceaded to the election of the said deputie and by geñ'all consent have nōiated and chosen m^r [John] *William* Rumney to execute the same office.

And for the better expedition of the setting forthe of the shippes on ther voyage. and for the redresse of the wronge wch suche as have not brought in ther moneis *have offered to the voyage* order is geaven that m^r governo^r and Comitties shall apoint suche as they thinke meete to goe to the Co^rt to [offer] *exhibite* ther information and Complaint to the Lordes.

   10 &. 12. 13. January severall Warraunt^(entred Mr Allabaster's booke viz.

300^li to John Busbridge for yron.
100^li to Wm Dixon purser of ye dragon.
60^li to xpofer Thompson Smythe for the Hector
100^li to Mr Wyseman for the Hector
20^li to Nich : Lynge for charges.
213^li 6. 8. to Andrew Bannyng for oyle
100^li   to Wm Dixon for the hecto^r.

  A Geñ'all Court holden the 14 January 1600.
      Present
Mr Ald^n Go^r   Sr John Hart

<small>16co 14 Jan.</small>

1600
14 Jan.

Mr Aldⁿ Hollyday
Mr Jo : Wattes
Mr Cordell
Mr Wyseman
Mr fra Chery
Mr Jo: Highelord

Mr Wm Chambers
Mr Robt Sandy
Mr Rich: Wyche
Mr Nich: Lynge
Mr Wm Chambers
Mr Olyuer Style.

And the geñalyty or the greatest part

HIS Court was called vppon occasion of the [vrgent] order takeñ by the Lordes of the Councell touching those that have sett downe ther Contributions. and have not brought in the same. ether in part or all and the assemblie being gathered together *the said* order taken by ther Lordships was published and read to the geñalyty wch order being vnder the hande of [the] one of the Clerkes of the councell and enregestred in the Councell booke doeth followe in thes wordes. viz.

1600
11 Jan.

At the Whytehall the xjth of January 1600.
Present.

L. Keaper
L. Threasurer
Mr Comptroller

Mr Secretory Cycill
Sr Jo : Fortescue
L. Chief Justice

Mr Secretory Herbert

Vppon complaint made to ther Ll̃p by the newe aucthorised Companie of merchaunt℘ preparing to trade to the East Indies that certen persons wch had heertofore promised and assured by ther subscriptions when the said voyage was first proiected to advaunce certen sommes of money for the proceading in the same vppon confidence [had] and Assurance Whereof the preparation for the said voyage hath bene vndertaken and advaunced to a full redines and yet nevertheles that the said psons would since vppon some vndue pretences retract ther former promyses in that behauIf whereof would ensue that by the want of ther promised contributions the voyage must breake Ther Ll̃p vppon due consideration howe greatlie it doeth import the hono^r of the Realme and the state of the present affaires thereof that the said voyage shuld not be hindred or overthrowne by any

THE EAST INDIA COMPANY

such default [or accident] and indirect meanes and consideringe also howe weake allegations of excuse have bene made by the persons refusers It hath bene therfore this day ordered by ther LLp̄ that notw^{th}standinge the pretences of the foresaid psons they shall w^{th}out further delay and namelie by satherday next furnishe ther promysed contributions or otherwyse that order shalbe taken by the LLp̄ wth suche as shall refuse the same to Comitt them to prison vntill they Conforme them selfes and make satisfaction accordinge to their subscriptions

   This is a true copie of ther LLp̄ order wch by ther LLp̄ cōmaundem^t is entred into the Regester of the Councell.
           Thomas Edmondes.

1600
14 Jan.

Vppon the hearing of wch order it was conceaved by divers of the generalytie that yf the moneis dewe by the said refusers were brought in accordinge to the said order that then ther shuld be no neade of the supplyinge of ij^s in the ħ vppon everie adventuro^r as was intended by the last geñall Court but when it was related vnto them that notw^{th}standinge all the contribution wch was sett downe would fall too short to supplie [the] a convenient adventure by 4 or 5 thousand poundes . and that of [necessitie we] necessitie the ij^s in the ħ was to be brought in the geñalytie did wth one assent confirme ther former order and were content to bringe in the said supplie accordinglie.

It was also ordered that a Common seale shuld be made for the vse of the Companie and the rather that the same beinge made everie contributo^r might have a bill of adventure of his Contribution vnder the Comōn seale of the Companie.

A comon seale.

      the 15 January 1600.
Ald^n Bayning :   William Harrison
Tho : Cordell.   Robert Sandy
Rich : Wyseman.   Rich : Wyche
Olyver : Style :   Jeames Lancaster
John Eldred   William Chambers.

1600
15 Jan.

1600 15 Jan.	
l 100 : to John Ady.	
l 80: to W^m ffisher.	
l 194 : 5 : 6 to W^m garway.	
l 150: to Wm Garway for the assention.	
l 70 : to Wm Harrisson ffor 7 tonns vineger :	
120 oxen for victualling the shippes.	
150^li to Wm Dixsy for the redd dragon.	
20^li to bee coyned.	
l 200 : to Thomas Barbar.	
1600 17 Jan.	

EVEN a warrant to Ald^n : Bayning : for paym^t of l 100 : to John Ady carpenter vppō accōpt of Timber hee delyvered to the vse of the hecto^r & Assention.

Geven a warrant to Ald^n Bayninge : ffor paym^t of l 80 : to W ffisher ffor 24 barrells of candy oyle at 3^li . 6^s . 8^d p barrell

Geven a warrant to Ald^n Halleday : ffor paym^t of l 194 . 5 . 6 // to w^m garway ; ffor 58 barrells 4 gallons 3¼ tt at l 3 . 6 . 8 p barrell.

The 15 January 1600.

Geven a Warrant to Ald^n Halleday ffor paym^t of l 150. to w^m garway ffor the vse of the Assention towards repayracion of hir.

Geven a warrant to Ald^n Bayning ffor paym^t of l 70: to william [garway] Harrisson in ffull ffor 7 tonns vineger at l 10. p tonn.

It is ordered that m^r Ald^n Bannyng and m^r Wyseman shall provide 120 oxen. for the provision of the voyage for that vppon Computacōn made of the beef Cutt out and salted for the victuallinḡ of the shippes ther appeareth a want of so muche as the said number of oxen doeth come vnto.

Geven a warrant to ald^n halleday ffor paym^t of l 150. to w^m Dixsy purser of the Redd dragon ffor the repayration & vse of that shipp.

At this assembly it was ordeyned & determyned that there should bee coyned in the towar over & above the l 6000. already appoynted the vallew of twenty pownds st^rling money to bee delyvered vnto m^r wryte to bee distributed vnto the lords & other as vnto him shall seeme good.

Geven a warrant to ald^n Bayng ffor paym^t of l 200. to thomas Babar ffor & on accōpt of canvas ffor the shipps.

The 17 January 1600.

M^r deputy rumney :	Mr Eldred :
Mr Stapers :	Mr Lancaster :
Mr Garway :	Mr Harrison

THE EAST INDIA COMPANY

Mr Highlord Mr Style   1600
Mr Sandy   Aldⁿ Halliday   17 Jan.
Mr Combe   Aldⁿ Watts
            Aldⁿ Moore

EVEN a warrant vppõ aldⁿ [Halleday] bayning ffor paym^t of [ł] 133^{li} 6^s 8^d in ffull of his ⅙ pte of the assension I say to Robert Rickman pte owner of the sayd shipp. ┆ 133. 6. 8. to Robt Rickman.

Geven a warrant vppõ aldⁿ Bayning ffor payment ł 128 . 1 . 8 to m^r robert sandy in ffull ffor sondrey disburcements made by him as p the warrant pticularly appeareth. ┆ 128. 1. 8. to Robert Sandy.

Geven a warrant vppõ aldⁿ Bayng ffor paym^t of ł 200. to Robert stevens ł 100. by a bill of exc̄ & ł 100 by order of the sayd ellacott ffor the vallew, in himself. ┆ 200 : to Robt Stevens.

Geven a warrant vppõ aldⁿ Bayng ffor paym^t of ł 500. to S^r hugh portman by a bill of exc̄ for Robt Pope of the 2 January

Geven a warrant vppõ aldⁿ Halleday ffor paym^t of ł 500 to S^r hugh portman by a bill of exc̄ for Robert Pope of the 10 January

┆ 1000 : to Sr Hugh Portman.

It is ordered that Mr Aldⁿ watts m^r Aldⁿ Moore m^r *Wyseman* m^r Chery and Richard Wright Secretorie shall goe to the Court to morrowe morning and ther to exhibite the names to the LL℘ of suche that have not brought in the^r moneis according to ther LL℘ order and to aunswer the peticōns of suche as detract ther paiment℘ by some colorable pretences.

Order is geaven to Aldⁿ Hollyday Thr̄er to pay to ye handes of m^r Wm Burrell the somme of one hundred poundes sterling vppon accoumpte to be imployed in the provision of boat℘ and other necessaries. 100^{li} to Mr Burrell.

Warraunt is geaven to aldⁿ Hollyday to pay vnto Anthony moseley the somme of 25^{li} 10^s 0 for 4 tuñs and 1 hogg^{hd} of vineger bought by Mr Combe and m^r Howe. 25^{li} 10. 0 to Anth: Moseley for vineger.

The Like warraunt is geaven to the said thr̄er to pay to Humfrey Phipps [for] the somme of 20^{li} sterling for tuñs of wyne vineger bought by him of m^r Combe and m^r Sandy. 20^{li} to Humfrey Phips fo wine vineger.

116   THE COURT RECORDS OF

1600
17 Jan.
14ˡⁱ 12ˢ : to
Mʳ Combe
for wine
vinegar.

The like warraunt is geaven vnto the same thēr to pay vnto mʳ John Combe the somme of xiiijˡⁱ xijˢ for so muche pᵈ by him to a mariner for 2. Tuñs of wyne vineger at 7 6 p tuñ.

69ˡⁱ 8. 2 to
Mʳ Wasse.

Another Warraunt is made to the said Thēr to pay vnto Mʳ Cristopher Wasse by order of mʳ Cherie for a silver fountaine and a *Case* [silver Bowle or basen] the somme of [fourscore] 69ˡⁱ poundes eight shillinges and 2ᵈ sterlingẽ in full paiment.

Looking glasses.

It is ordered that 2 faire *Costlie* Looking glasses shalbe prouided to be geaven a way as presentẽ yf cause do require.

Pursers wages.

It is agreed that the Generall Wages of all Pursers imploied in the voyage. shalbe xlˢ the monethe to be accoumpted from the tyme of the settingẽ sayle to the shippes and for ther imploymᵗ in harborowe. they are to be allowed xxˢ the moneth besides ther borde wages wᶜʰ is already allowed. And it is ordered that the Scourge shall have 2 Pursers.

26. 13. 4 to
a Preacher.

Warraunt is geaven to Aldⁿ Hollyday to pay to Thomas Pulleyñ preacher apointed to goe in the voyage the somme twentie six poundes 13ˢ 4ᵈ for his provision to Sea.

1600
19 Jan.

The 19ᵗʰ January 1600.

Thomas Cordell   Jnᵒ Combes
Wᵐ garroway   Robte Sandy
Ryc̄ Staper   Ryc̄ Wytche

30ˡⁱ to Mʳ
Spencer mʳ
of the
Susann

RDER is geven to Aldermann banninge to pay to samuell spencer mʳ of Susann the some of thirtie pounds sterlinge and is for his advauncemᵗ aforehaund accordinge to agremᵗ

1600
21 Jan.

The 21 January 1600.

Mʳ deputy rumney   Mʳ Style :
Mʳ Stapers :   Mʳ Sandy :

Mʳ Harrison   Mʳ Middleton   1600
Mʳ Lancaster   Mʳ Combe   21 Jan.
                  Mʳ Bell.

AT this assembly it was appoynted and concluded that
peeter ffrancis a portugall who goeth on this voyadg   peter francis
should goe in the susann wᵗʰ mʳ John havard and   a portugall.
ffor his wages to have ffyve pounds p month so long as hee
serveth in that voyadg

Given a warrant vppō aldⁿ Bayning ffor payment of ł 333.   333ˡⁱ 6ˢ 8ᵈ
6. 8 // stʳling money on the last of ffebruary next to wᵐ skid-   to wᵐ skidmore
more in ffull of his ¹ pt of the assention.   ffor ⅓ of th' assention.

Order is given at this assembly ffor the provyding of a
bason and an ewer of playne whyte silver poiz 100 ounces by
mʳ wyseman & mʳ style   3 peecs of

Also order is given to the sayd mʳ wyseman & mʳ style   plate.
ffor the provyding of 2 standing cupps & 2 other peecs of
other whyte plate that should way about 30 ounces p peece.

Order is given to these ffollowing committyes ffor to take
the care of provyding of necessaryes ffor the shipps ffor the
Gunners stewards cookes and boatswaynes *and Carpenters* stores
viz   necessaryes
    To capteyn middleton ffor the hectoʳ   ffor the
    To mʳ Jnᵒ Havard; ffor the Susann   ships.
    To mʳ Ric Wych; ffor the Dragon
    To mʳ William Harrisson ffor the Assention.

Geven a warrant vppō aldⁿ Bayning ffor payment of ł 200.   1 200: to
stʳling money to Joseph salbanck purser of the Susann ffor the   Joseph salbanck
provision of that shipp to bee Imployed vppō hir

Geven warrants vppō aldⁿ Halleday ffor payment of these
somes ffollowing—

ł 250 : to wᵐ Dixson purser of the Redd dragon.
ł   6. 13. 4 // to thomas Symonds.
ł 250.—.— to Ric wyseman ffor the purser of the
            hectoʳ.
ł 150.—.— to [wᵐ garway ffor] wᵐ *leake* the purser of th'
            assention *for men's wagꝭ*.

118   THE COURT RECORDS OF

1600
21 Jan.

† 250.—.— to Jnᵒ havard ffor the Susann ffor mens wages.

† 19. 6. 3 to george Davyes ffor chests ffor cloth

le 21 January 1600.

Order is taken that mʳ [Aldⁿ] Richard stapers & mʳ sandy should enter all the goods and pay the custom of them and to make a cargazon ffor the whole.

Also order is given to mʳ Sandy ffor provyding ffor ech shipp these pcells ffollowing vīz :

    1 hhd of prunes
    1 barrell of currents
    1 barrell of Reysons solis

1600
22 Jan.

The 22 of Januarie 1600

Mʳ Wᵐ Rumney deputie Mʳ Nich : Lynge
Mʳ Aldⁿ Moore   Mʳ Wᵐ Harryson
Mʳ Rich : Staper   Mʳ Wᵐ Garway
Mʳ [Rich] Tho Cordell Mʳ Roger Howe
Mʳ olyuer Style   Mʳ Robᵗ Bell
Mʳ Robᵗ Sandy   Capte Lancaster
    Capte Middleton.

Plate for presents

T is agreed that ther shalbe prepared for presentes or otherwyse disposed 4 standing Cuppes of bigger and lesser sizes to be carried in the voyage the same to be chased white vnguilt. the 2 greatest at 30 oz̃. the 2 lesser at 15 oz̃. the wᶜʰ are agreed for at 5ˢ. 6ᵈ the oz̃.

Mariners shares of reprisalles

Wheras this assemblie were acquainted that ther hath bene some question made by some of the mariners [for] what allowaunce they should have vppon suche reprisalles as may happen in the voyage. It is vppon that question aunswered that ther is noe intention to [enterteyn anie] make anie attempte for reprisalles but onlie *to* pursue the voyag̃ [wᵗʰ] in a m̃chauntlike course. Yet notwᵗʰˡⁱstanding yf anie oportunety be offered wᵗʰout preiudice or hassard of the said voyag̃ [the] Captein Lancaster is to take

suche co{r}se therin as he shall thinke meet and thervppon to [so] make suche agrement wth the mariners for shares as he thinketh good. vppon suche oportunety yf anie suche happen.

1600 22 Jan.

Vppon advyse required out of the West Cuntrey for the conveyinge of suche Spanishe moneis as is in the West Cuntrey to be brought on ship boarde order is geaven to m{r} Sandy to write to m{r} Ellicott and m{r} Robt Pope to conferre together and to take the best co{r}se therin that they can proceading therin according to ther discretion at the Companyes adventures.

Shipping of o{r} moneys in the West Cuntrey

Warraunt is geaven to [the Widowe Bennett] Ald{n} Hollyday th{er} to pay vnto Widowe Bennett vppon accoumpte for iron for the shippes and the voyage the some of one hundred poundes sterling.

100{li} to Widowe Bennett for iron.

The Like warraunt is geaven to the said Th{er} to pay to Percevall Stradling one of the fourth sort of factors the some of xx{li} agreed to be geaven him for his enterteynm{t} to provide him self before his going forth

Percivall Stradling 20{li}.

A warrante ys granted to Alder{n} Holledaye to paye vnto S{r}geant helle, the some of fyve hundred pound{es} for so moche he cawsed to be payd at Exeter to m{r} John Ellecote, for the vse of the Companye the 23. Jañ 1600.

500{li} to sargeant Hale.

A warn{t} vpon m{r} Alldermañ bannyng to pay to Henry plvmpton threeskor & *seven* [nyne] pounds nyne shillyng{es} & was ffo{r} 7 peec{es} of Rape oyle bought of him by w{m} Chamber ffo{r} the vse of the Company this 23th January 1600.

67 . 9 . 0 to Henry Plvmpton fo{r} Rape Oyle.

The 24 of January 1600.

Mr Ald{n} Smythe Go{r}
Mr Ald{n} Bannyng
Mr Ald{n} Halmeden
Mr Rich : Staper
Mr Lancaster
Mr olyuer Style
Mr Ald{n} Hollyday

Mr frauncis Chery
Mr John Eldred
Mr Robt Sandy
Mr Rich : Wyche
Mr Wm Chambers
Mr Wm Harryson
Mr Robt Sandy.

1600 24 Jan.

1600
24 Jan.

T is resolued that ther shalbe sent from hence in to the West Cuntrey Two of the Comitties to see the shipping of o^r moneys and victualles when the shippes shall come thether to thende [they] vppon ther returne the Companie may be satysfied howe [ther] ther busines is [disch] dispatched and cleared vppon the departing of the said shippes from the coast. And it is thought [meet] that m^r howe and m^r Sandy in respecte that they have had the dealing and directing of the West Cuntrey busines, that they are the meetest men to be imployed in the said busines.

It is resolved that especiall care be taken and m^r Aldⁿ Hollyday conferred wthall that the full valewe of vj mł łi. in money be coyned in the Tower. rather wth [an] *a large* overplus then *ther shuld appeare* any want of the said somme . to thende all quarrelles or questions of breache of Coveñnte may be avoyded. that might geave impediment or damage to the voyage.

50^{li} to Tho. Salterne one of the 2 sort of factors.

Warraunt is geaven to Aldⁿ Hollyday to pay to Thom̅s Salterne the somme of fyftie poundes sterling for his enterteynm^t to be p^d him in money by agrem^t made wth him as one of the Second sort of facto^{rs}.

30^{li} to Roger Style oñ of the 4 sort of factors.

Warraunt is also geaven to m^r Aldⁿ Bannynge Thrēr to pay vnto Roger Style one of the 3 [4] sort of factors imployed in this voyage the somme of thirtie pounds sterlinge for so muche agreed wth him *for his* enterteynm^t in the voyage.

250^{li} to Jo: Dixon Purser of the Dragon.

Order is geaven to m^r Aldⁿ [Holliday] Bannyng to pay vnto [the] Wm Dixon Purser of the Read dragon the somme of twoo hundred and fyftie poundes sterling vppon accoumpte for the provision [of the] and preparation of the same ship.

The sale of the Susan sealed.

Whereas the 26. of September Last m^r Ald Bannyng solde to the Comitties the ship called the Susan at the rate of 1600^{li} vppon condition to take her againe at her Retorne wth her furnyture and to geave for her 800^{li}. It is nowe agreed that the bargaine and sale of the said ship shalbe absolute . and the condition discharged, and thervpp̃. an absolute sale in wryting was sealed this day to m^r howe to m^r Eldred m^r Chambers and m^r Wyche by m^r Aldⁿ Bannyng.

THE EAST INDIA COMPANY

Warraunt is geaven to m{r} Ald{n} holliday thēr to pay vnto phillip winchecombe one of the fowrth sort of factors the somme of Twentie poundes sterling for so muche allowed him for his provision and preparation to sea according to [his] agreament.

1600 24 Jan. 20 to phillipp wynchecombe one of the 4 sort of factors.

Order is geaven to m{r} Ald{n} Bannyng to pay vnto one Bradley for Ballast. the some of Twentie Nobles. in full demaunde . who by vertue of a pattent claymed the ballasting of all the 4 shippes or to be p{d} therfore whether he found ballast or not.

6 13 4 to one Bradley for Ballast.

The 26 of Januarie. 1600.

Mr Wm Rumey deputy
Mr Ald{n} Bannyng
Capten Lancaster
Mr Wm Garway
Mr Midleton

Mr John Eldred
Mr [Jo] Robt Sandy
Mr Rich. Wyche
Mr Wm Chambers
Mr Wm Harryson.

1600 26 Jan.

IT is ordered that the provision of suche cordage pitche tarre and other thinges of that kinde that the Company shall have occasion to vse shalbe re{d} and ·provided wth one Browne and Companie yf they shalbe well vsed ther yf otherwyse to take it wher they may have it at the best hand.

provision of cordage pitche tarre &c :

Warraunt is geaven to m{r} Ald{n} hollyday to pay to George Persons Purser of the Hecto{r} the somme of one hundred poundes. for provisions by the motion of Capten Lancaster.

100{li} to the purser of the Hecto{r}.

The like warraunt is geaven to the the said Ald{n} to pay to Patrick Johnson for 12 way of Salt the somme of xxxviij{li}.

38{li} for 12 way of salte

Complaint beinge made to this Assemblie that some abuse hath bene offered to the Companie in provysion of thinges for the voyage by requiring and putting to accoumpte more then is paid for thinges provided and the matter being exāīed It was confessed by Peter fenton that the Carpenter of the Susan had re{d} of the Company 3{li} 6{s} for a mast more then he p{d} for the same. and for another smale mast that cost but 20{s} he re{d} of the Company 25{s}.

Deceipt vsed by the Carpenter of the Susan

R

THE COURT RECORDS OF

1600
27 Jan.

The 27 of Januarie 1600.

Mr Ald Smyth Go^r   Mr Aldⁿ Bannyng
Mr Wm Rumney deputy   Capteñ Midleton
Mr Tho Cordell   Mr Roger Howe.
Capten Lancaster   Mr Nich: Lynge.
M^r Jo : Eldred.   Mr John Combe
Mr Wm Chambers   Mr Wm Harryson
Mr Rich: Wyche.   Aldⁿ Wattes.

326. 134 to Simon furner for powder.

ARRAUNT is geaven to m^r Aldⁿ hollyday to pay vnto m^r Symon furner the 10th of marche next the somme of three hundred twenty six poundes 13^s 4 for 98 ba^{les} of ordinarie powder cñ^{tg} [100^{li}] five score^{li} neat in eche barrell at viij^d p li

20^{li} to Tho: Tudd on of the 4 sort of facto^{rs}.

Warraunt is geaven vnto Ald^r holliday Thrēr to pay vnto Thomas Tudd on of the fowrth sort of facto^{rs} enterteyned for the voyage the somme of twentie pound℄ sterling for soe muche agreed to be geaven him for his enterteynm^t and to make his provision.

Moneis reported to be shipped in the shippes.

Ald^r Hollyday pro*p*oundeth to this assembly a forme of repτition of the moneis in his Custody provided to be shipped for the voyage wch being considered of at this assembly is well lyked and allowed of and is as followeth

Newe moneys.

In the read Dragon 3 chests cñ^{tg} 8 bagges a pece cñ^{tg} ech bag 500 pec℄ of 4^{ss} steř wth the proffit amounteth to aboute   2600 . ^s . ^d

In the Hecto^r 2 chest℄ cñ^{tg} ech chest 8 bagg℄ and 500 pec℄ of 4^{ss} in ech bag and amounteth wth the proffit   1733 . 6 . 8

In the assention 1 chest cñ^{tg} 8 bagges of 500 pec℄ of 4 p bagg amounteth   866 . 13 . 4

In the Susan—1 chest cñ^{tg} 8 bagg℄ of 500 pec℄ of 4^{ss} p bag amounteth   866 . 13 . 4

Spanishe money.

In the read Dragon 2 chest℄ cñ^{tg} 8 bagg℄ p chest and in ech bag 500 peic℄ of 8 Riolles amounteth   1733 . 6 . 8

THE EAST INDIA COMPANY

In the Hector—2 chestes cñ{ts} 8 bagg{e} p
chest and in ech bag 500 peec{e} of 8 Royalles
amounteth   1733 . 6 . 8
In the Assension 1 chest cñ{ts} 8 bagg{e} and
500 p{e}c{e} of 8 Ryalles in the bag   866 . 13 . 4
In the Susañ 1 chest cñ{ts} 8 bagg{e} and 500
pec{e} of 8 Ryalles in ech bag   866 . 13 . 4

    Whereas ther are shipped in the shippes severally certeñ peec{e} of vnwatered Chamlett{e} cñ{ts} 60 peec{e} in alle. wch are shipped w{th}out any geñ{er}all order of the Comitties it is ordered that the same Chamlett{e} shalbe taken vp againe [and] by him that entred and shipped them vppon payne of suche forfeiture as shalbe assessed vppon him for an offence of privat trade being m{er}chaundize not allowed to be shipped by the Company.

    It is ordered that ther shalbe allowed and deliuered to Samuell Spencer m{r} of the Susan a barrell of oyle for his provision to sea for that he eateth in ordinarie salte victualles that is provided for the Companie.

    Order is geaven to Ald{r} hollyday to pay vnto John Havard one of the 4 principall factors the somme of one hundred poundes sterling{e} for soe much allowed for his enterteynm{t} to be imployed in the voyage

Margin notes: 1600 27 Jan. · Chamlettes shipped w{th}out warraunt. · Samuel Spencer. · 100{li} to Jo: Havard one of the 4 principall factors.

    The 29 of Januarie 1600.   1600 29 Jan.

Mr Wm Rumey deputy	Mr Robt Sandy
Mr Ald{n} Bannyng	Mr Robt Bell
Mr Ald{n} Moore	Mr Wm Harryson
Mr Rich : Staper	Mr Rich: Wyche.
Mr Jo. Highelord	Capteñ Lancaster
Mr Rich : Wyseman	M{t} Jo : Midleton.

RDER is geven to Ald{r} Bannynge ther to pay vnto m{r} [Ald{r}] Wattes in full paiment [of] for 22 shirtes of mayle the somme of 36 . 10 . 10. to be p{d} the 28 of Marche next.

    Mr Hacklett the historiographer of the viages of the East

Margin notes: 36 . 10 . 10 to Mr. Wattes for shirtes of Maile. · Mr Hacklett.

1600 29 Jan.	Indies, beinge here before the Comitties and having read vnto them out of his notes and bookes divers instrucc̃ons for provisions of Jewelles . was required to sett downe in wryting a note of the principall places in the East Indies wher Trade [was] is to be had to thend the same may be vsed for the better instrucc̃on of o^r factors in the said voyage.
prises of tymber.	It is ordered that Mr Wyseman m^r harryson and M^r wyche shall agree wth the Carpenters for the prises of Tymber dd for the shippes whervppoñ some difference resteth for the said prises.

1600 31 Jan.	The 31 Januarie 1600.

<table>
<tr><td>Mr Ald^n Smithe Go^r</td><td>Mr Ald^n Hollyday</td></tr>
<tr><td>Mr Wm Rumey deputy</td><td>Mr Ald^n Wattes.</td></tr>
<tr><td>Mr Rich : Stapers</td><td>Mr Wm Chamber.</td></tr>
<tr><td>Mr Rich : Wyseman</td><td>Mr Nich : Lynge</td></tr>
<tr><td>Mr Roger Howe</td><td>M^r Jo Combes.</td></tr>
<tr><td>Mr John Eldred</td><td>Mr Rich : Wyche</td></tr>
<tr><td>Mr Rob̃t Sandy</td><td>Mr Wm Harryson.</td></tr>
</table>

Augustine Skinner.	T is ordered that m^r Augustine Skinner his adventure of 200^{li} shalbe re^{cd} in the West Cuntrey in Ryalles according̃ to his lr̃es directed to Mr Ellecot dated the 30 p̃nte. wch lr̃e is [directed] delivered to Mr Sandy. to be sent to Mr Ellecott.
Private trade.	It is ordered that the p̃sons herevnder named together wth the Secretorie shall devyse and sett downe certen ordenaunces for the avoiding̃ of private and p̃ticler trade in this voyage. And the same ordenaunces to be Considered of by the Comitties and afterwardes p̃sented to the generalitie to be Confirmed as Lawes to be holden and observed for the Common good of the voyage.

Comitties for to devise orders against private trade.
{ M^r olyuer style
  Mr Thomas Cordell
  Mr Tho : Allabaster
  Mr Rich : Wyche
  Rich : Wrighte.

60. Tho : Shere.	Warraunt is geaven to Ald^n holliday thrẽr to pay vnto

THE EAST INDIA COMPANY 125

Thomas Shere of Exceto^r threescore poundes sterling for so muche re^d of him by M^r Jo : Sandy to be imploied in Ryalles in the West Cuntrey.
_{1600
31 Jan.}

Warraunt was geaven to Aldⁿ Bannynge to pay vnto Thomas Parkins for 32 Jarres of honny. twentie poundes one shilling sterling.
_{20^{li} 1^s for honny to Tho Parkins.}

It is ordered that Aldⁿ Wattes shall conferre wth of Colchester touchinge the dammage required for the [amo^t of] hurt done to his ship by the Anco^r of the Scourge.
_{Damage for the hurt done by the Anco^r of the Scourge.}

It is ordered that Mr Governo^r shall gratifie [m̃] one Wm Walter who dedicated to the Companie the book of the flemynge voyage. wth the some of xx^s and to be rep^d the same by one of the thẽrs.
_{xx^{li} to Wm Walter.}

It is apointed that the Comitties apointed for the shippes wth suche as Were owners of the same before they were bought shall go to the severall shippes and take an Inuentorie of all the furniture as well formerlie sold wth the shippes as bought since for the said shippes for the preparation of the voyage.
_{Comitties for the shippes.}

Warraunt is geaven to Aldⁿ Bannyng thẽr to pay vnto Leonard Shawe thirtie seven poundes [sterling] xv^s vj^d sterling for Chese bought by m^r Sandy and 14^{li} v^s fo^r butter being in the whole 52^{li}.
_{52^{li} to Mr Shawe for butter and chese.}

The 3. of february 1600.
_{1600
3 Feb.}

Mr Wm Rumey deputy   Mr Wm Harryson.
Mr Rich : Wyseman   Mr Ald. Bannyng
Mr John Eldred.   Mr Rich : Staper
Mr Wm Chambers   Mr Robt Bell.

ORDER is geaven to Ald^r Holliday thẽr to pay vnto Mr Wm Brunde oñ of the Principall factors of the shippes the somme of one hundred poundes sterling for somuch [by] to him allowed for his enterteynm^t to be p^d him for his provisioñ to sea :
_{100^{li} to Mr Brund one of the principall factors.}

Whereas Thomas Johnson servaunt to the Earle of Oxford is secretlie departed from his [said] service being imployed in office of trust wthout geving vp anie accompt intending to goe
_{The erle of Oxfordes man Run away.}

1600 3 Feb.	to sea. Therfore it is ordered that inquisition shalbe made in the severall shippes for the said John and suche order taken that he shall not be pmitted to go in anie of the shippes.
The Comitties of the shipps to call the officers of the shippes to accoumpt.	It is ordered that the Comitties of the severall shippes shall have aucthoritie to call before them all officers of the said shippes and to take an accompte of them. what provisions of anie of the said shippes hathe bene re^d or brought into anie of the said shippes by them or anie of them and wher the same hath bene had and *at* what prises.
20^{li} to Thomas Morgan.	Order is geaven to Mr Aldⁿ Bannyng ther to pay vnto Thomas Morgan on of the fowrth sorte of the facto^{rs} of this pnte voyag^e: the somme of twentie pound€ sterling for so muche agreed to be p^d him for his enterteynm^t to provide him to sea.
180^{li} to M^r Jo: Lacy by assignm^t of the Moskovia Company.	Order is geaven to m^r Aldⁿ *Bannyng* [holliday thrēr] to pay vnto m^r John lacy by the Assignm^t of [m^r] the Company of the Moscovia the somme of one hundred fowrscore and eight poundes sterlinge vppon accoumpte of cordag€ wch hath bene had of the said Companie for the provision of cordage for the [sai] voyage: [vppon] the money to be p^d the Last of Marche next.
100 to the Purser of the Assention.	Order is geaven to m^r Aldⁿ Holliday to pay vnto *Mr Garway or* the Purser of the Assention the somme of one hundred poundes sterling vppon accoumpt for the provision of thing€ necessarie for the same ship.
	It is ordered that m^r Andrewe Bannyng shalbe required to pay the 200^{li} sett downe for Jeffrey kirby for that the 200^{li} sett downe for Barthew Haggett thes comitties are content to forbeare and to suspend his admission for a further tyme vntill they shall be aunswered ether that he will bring in money or els to exclude him from the pviledges.
90^{li}, 10^s. to Mr Robt Bell for Paper.	Warraunt is geaven to Mr Aldⁿ Holliday to pay vnto m^r Rob̃t Bell the somme of fourscore and tenn poundes [sterling] and tenn shilling€ sterling for paper bought of him for the vse of voyage.

Mr Gouernour	Mr Stapers
Mr Deputy	Mr Wyseman

Mʳ Aldⁿ Holleday   Mʳ Highlord   1600
Mʳ Sandy   Mʳ Bell   3 Feb.
                Mʳ Linge.

Order is appoynted that mʳ lancaster & mʳ middleton should end and agree wᵗʰ him ffor his charges & enterteynmᵗ in this voyadg.

Geven a warrant vppõ aldⁿ Bayning ffor paymᵗ of ł 300 : to Mʳ John davyes pylott maior ffor his salary to goe this voyadg.

Geven a warrant vppõ aldⁿ halleday ffor paymᵗ of 188 . 16 . 3. to mʳ george smithyes ffor plate bought of him.

                The 5. February 1600.   1600
Mʳ Rumney deputy   Mʳ Lynge   5 Feb.
Mʳ Tho : Cordell   Mʳ Roger Howe
Mʳ Ric Stapers   Mʳ Ricᵈ: Wych
Mʳ Ric : Wyseman   Mʳ Highlord
Mʳ John Eldred   Mʳ Sandy
                Mʳ Bell.

T is ordred that mʳ chambres & mʳ harrisson shall agree wᵗʰ mʳ ffletcher & his company to reckon wᵗʰ them and so make an end and cleere accõpt wᵗʰ them. — Cleering of accõpts wᵗʰ mʳ fletcher.

Also that mʳ Richard wyseman should cleere accõpt wᵗʰ mʳ william Burrell. — wᵐ burrell

Also that mʳ aldⁿ Halleday should cleere accõpt wᵗʰ william Angell. — wᵐ Angell

Also mʳ Sandy to cleere accompt with mʳ peard. — mʳ peard

Also to cleere accõpt wᵗʰ Mʳ Howe. — mʳ Howe

To make maurice Abbott creddito' by Mʳ Rickman ffor 100ˡⁱ.

Also mʳ aldⁿ halleday to cleere accõpt wᵗʰ Mʳ Gosson.

Order is geaven to mʳ Aldʳ Bannyng to pay vnto Wᵐ Dixon Purser of the [hector] redd Dragon the some of two hundred poundes sterling vppon accompt for the provision of the same ship. — 200 to the dragon.

It is ordered that the psons heervnder named shalbe conferred wᵗʰall for the going in to West Cuntrey to see the — West Cuntrey.

1600 5 Feb.	discharge of the shippes there to thende that two of them at the least may appointed to that imployment.

        Mr Rob̃t Sandy   M^r Jo: Combe
        Mr Roger Howe   Mr Nich: lyng
        Mr Wm Chamber

Damage required for hurt done by the Anker of the read dragon.	It is ordered that m^r Cordell and m^r highlord shall attend my l. of Cumberland concerning the demaunde [of] made by the shippes for the damaǧ susteyned by the Anker of the read dragon and to pray his lordship to take some co^{r}se wth the Judge of the Admiralty therin signifying vnto him that it seemeth that one of the officers of the Court followeth the cause as a solicito^r being interested by [Comission] Composition for that wch may be recovered therein.

~~~

1600 7 Feb.	The [6] 7. of February 1600.

        Mr Wm Rumney deputy   Mr Ald^n Hollyday.
        Mr Ald^n Bannyng   Mr Rich: Wyche.
        Mr Ald^n Wattes   Mr Nichãs Lyng
        Mr Tho: Cordell   Mr Wm Chamber
        Mr Rob̃t Sandy   Mr Wm Harryson
        M^r Jo Combe   M^r frauncis Chery.

Wm Brodebent M^r of the Dragon 100^{li} lent vppon Land morgaged	UPPON the ernest request of [the Co] Wm Brodebent to deliver him of a preiudize wch he is like to vndergoe vppon the morgage of certen landes in the handes of m^r Hughe Beeston [ther is] it is agreed that ther shall be lent vnto him the sõme of one hundred poundes vppon the like assuraunce made of the same land to m^r Cordell and m^r wyche to the vse of the Company for the repayment of the money at 6 monethes and to that ende warraunt is geauen to Ald^n Hollyday thẽr to pay the same money to the said m^r Brodebent.
M^r flemyng	It is ordered that ther shalbe stay made of [an iron] a Smithes Bill of wares made for the voyage who hath re^d his iron of m^r fflemynǧ and paieth him not for it And the Smyth is content that m^r fflemynges money shalbe p^d viz the 17. of feb: 1600 he agreed therto.

THE EAST INDIA COMPANY

Order is geaven to Ald^u Bannyng͠ th͡er to pay vnto Josephe Salbanck Purser of the Susañ the some of one hundred poundes sterling͠ vppon accoumpte of the Charges imployed for the provision of the voiage.   *1600 7 Feb. 100^{li} to the purser of the Susan.*

Order is geaven to Aldⁿ Holliday to pay vnto the Assignee of Thom̃s Billett Costemer of Poole the som̃e of two hundred poundes sterling͠ for soe much taken vp by ex^{ce} in the West Cuntrey by Rob̃t Pope for the vse of the voyage.   *200. to Tho: Billett by exⁿ.*

Lyke order is geaven to the said th͡er to pay vnto Thomas Lieth Pewtero^r the som̃e of sixtie eight poundes xviij^s vppon a bill of p̃celles of Pewter bought of him by m̃ Sandy and m̃ Bell.   *68 18 for pewter.*

Another warraunt is geaven [to the] to Aldⁿ Bannyng th͡er to pay vnto m^r Ald^r Wattes the som̃e of thirtie and six poundes sterling for iron hoopes bought of him for the vse of the Companie.   *36^{li} to Ald Wattes for iron hoopes.*

Warraunt is also geaven to m^r Aldⁿ Holliday th͡er to pay vnto Rob̃t Warner the some of ffowrtie three poundes 16 . 6 sterling͠ vppon a bill of p̃celles of glasses re^d to the vse of the Companie amounting to 143 16 6 whereof 100^{li} is already p^d.   *43 . 16 . 6 for Glasses.*

A Gen^rall Court the xth of february 1600.   *1600 10 Feb.*
Present.

Mr Thomas Smythe, Aldⁿ Go^r   Mr Rich : Staper
Mr Wm Rum̃ey
Mr Rich : Wyche   & a verie great nūber of
Mr Nich : Lynge   the geñalyty.

T this Co^rt the companie accordinge to ther priviledg͠ p̃ceading͠ to establish and enacte certen Decrees and lawes fitt for the present occasion. and to be vsed as directions. for the guiding͠ of the trade and traffique belonging͠ to ye present voyage. nowe to be sett forth Do at this assemblie ordeine and Decree thes severall ordinaunces to be holden and kept as standing ordinaunces [for] to be vsed in [ther] the

s

THE COURT RECORDS OF

1600
10 Feb.

That all thinges be mannaged as a iointe stocke, & noe priuate Trade to be vsed.

voyages wthout alteration or chaunging the teno^r whereof hereafter ensue videlt.

It is ordayened and decred that all the preparation of moneis merchandizes and other provision for [the saide] *this present* voiadge and all Comoditýes moneis Jewells and other merchandize retourned in the saide voiadge shalbe holden reputed and accompted and be carried mannaged ordered and handled as one entyre Joynte and Comon Stocke of adventure wherein no private traffique barter exchaunge or merchaundizinge shalbe vsed practized or admytted by any pticuler Governo^r Capten merchaunte Agent facto^r m^r marriner officer or other pson whatsoever imployed in the saide voiadge or permitted to goe in the same vppon payne of the losse & forfeiture to thuse of the Generall Companie and Adventures in this voiadge of all somes of money Jewells warres goodes or mchandizes wch shalbe founde in the saide shippes or els where, carried forthe or retourned home by any private or pticuler man and not contayned and brought in to genall and comon accompte & ioynte adventure of the saide voiadge And to thend this prejudice of private traffique may the better be avoyded It is alsoe ordeyned & appointed y^t due inquisicon be made in all and euerie the seuall shipps of the saide voiadge and els where by serche of all such Chestes boxes Packes Packetts bookes wrytings and other meanes whereby discoverie may be made of the breache of this present ordinaunce.

The prevencon of priuate traffique

Againste fraude in the genall venture & the penaletie.

And yt is in like manner ordayned and decred for the avoidinge of all vnfaithfullnes and deceipte to be vsed in the saide voiadge in the defraudinge of the genall adventure wch is prepared and sett forth that the greate Costs and Chardgs of such as repose there trust and confidence in the officers and mynisters imployed in the saide voiadge that what pson soever shalbe found vnfaithfull or vniust in the saide voiadge by ymbesselinge or wthdrawinge of any the goodes wares merchaundizes Jewells or other comodityes Whatsoever ether belonging to the adventure sent out or beinge pcell of the retourne of the same wch was is or shalbe ether prepared bought or belonginge to the comon or generall Stocke or adventure that such p̄son shalbe barred and concluded to demaunde of the Governo^r & Companie of the saide merchaunt℈ of London tradinge into the Eaſt Indies any accompte rekoninge or paym^t of any wages salary contract or entertainm^t for his imployment in this voiadge wherevnto he was or otherwise might have binne interessed yf such offence had not binne comytted And further *that* everie such p̄son soe offendinge shalbe [p̄sented] *prosecuted* by the saide Governor & Companie of the saide m̃chaunt℈ of london tradinge into the East Indies accordinge to the qualetie of his offence in that behalfe by the lawes and Statut℈ of this Realme.

1600
10 Feb.

And further more yt is ordeyned that yf vppon the deliũie of her Matie lr̃es to the prinnces of those places where our shipps shall arrive [yõ] *the generall and* [*merchaunt℈*] *factors* shalbe peaceablie received & entertayned as m̃chaunt℈ to commerce and traffique wth the people of those Cuntries or places and be secured & warranted hereafter to frequente and visite those p̄tes Then yt is ordayned and agreed that *ther* shalbe selected out of the yongest sorte of *the* facto^{rs} *or others* entertayned or voluntarily suffred to goe in the voiadge such and soe manye of the aptest and towardest of them as [yõ] *o^r principall merchaunt* shall thincke meete and *w^{ch}* shall have best approved them selfes fitt for [such our] *the* imploym^t *of the Companie* to resyde & abide in the saide places where [yõ] *they* shalbe soe peaceablie received yf [yõ] *they* may be p̄mitted therevnto takinge sufficient and carefull order for the [dischardginge] *defrayinge.* and supplyinge of there Chardge vntyll those places shalbe hereafter visited by another fleete sent frõ hence And leavinge wth them such advyse and direction for ther better informaçõn howe to carrie them selves in those places as by *the* [yor] good direction *of o^r principall merchaunt* wth thadvyse of suche as [yõ] *he* shall consulte wth*all* thereof shalbe thought meete and as tyme and experience of those places shall directe [you] them whilest the shippes Do lye in thes partes.

Leavinge of factors in the East Indies.

At this court was read a Cõmission conceaved by the Comitties to be Delivered vnto the generall *or principal merchaunt℈ & others in succession* vnder the Cõmon seale of

A Comissyon for the Gen^rall & in succes-

THE COURT RECORDS OF

1600
10 Feb.

sion vnder the Comon Seale.

the Companie concerning the managing of the trade by avoyding of private traffique & vnfaithfull Dealing and *to geave order for the* Leaving of fitt factors to reside in the East Indies vntil the retorne of [the next] *a seconde* fleet *thether* wch Comission was well lykd of and agreed to be written in fowre severall ptes and vnto everie part the Comon seale of the Companie to be [annexed] added to thende that *in* everie ship one of the said Comissions may be kepte in the handes of the principall mchaunt$\tilde{e}$ of [the] everie ship wch Comission doeth followe in thes wordes. viz :—

The Commission to the Generall or principall marchant.

Whereas wee the governo^r and Companie of the mchaunts of London . trading into the East Indies have chosen yõ Mr James Lancaster for the chief governo^r or geñall to governe or Rule all suche merchaunt$\tilde{e}$ marrine^{rs} office^{rs} and other her Ma^{ies} Subiet$\tilde{e}$ wch are ymployed by vs or are or shalbe shipped in anie of the fowre shippes by vs prepared and sett forthe for this p̃nte intended voiage towardes the East Indies   And whereas the Queens most excelent Ma^{ie} approvinge and allowinge of our Choice of yo^u to the said government and favouringe the said enterprise hath by her gratious Lres pattent$\tilde{e}$ vnder the great Seale of England the better to enable you to keepe yor whole Companie in good agreement one towardes another and in obedience and dew respect towardes you geaven you aucthoritie to chastice and correct such offences as shall arrise in the said voyadge accordinge as in the said Lres Pattent$\tilde{e}$ at large appearethe wch L̃res Pattent$\tilde{e}$ extendinge onlye to the generall governm^t of yor whole Companie shipped in the said shippes for their Croill behaviour whilest they are abroad in the said viage and not vnto the mannaginge and orderinge of the trade of merchaundize for wch the said voyadge is principallie appointed and sett forthe wee therfore by these our pnte Lres [Pattent$\tilde{e}$] or Comission vnder our Common Seale for the orderinge and disposinge of all such merchaundize gold pearle Jewells and other Commodities wch are to be bought bartered procured, exchaunged or otherwyse obteyned in this pnte voyage do for yor remembraunce and direcc̃on in that behaulfe sett downe theise Clawses ordeñnc℥ and decrees hereafter followinge declaringe hereby our purpose and entenc̃on how wee appointe and ordeyne that the traffique of this p̃nte voyadge shalbe ordered and carryed wch ordeñnces and decrees wee will and require you to observe and keape and do geave you power and aucthoritie to see the same executed and putt in vse accordingly videlt wee do ordeyne and decree that all the preparac̃ons of moneis m̃chaundizes and other provision for the said voyàge and all Commodities moneis Jewells and other merchaundize retourned in the said viage shalbe holden reputed & accompted and be carred mannaged ordered and handeled *as* one entire Joint and Common Stocke of adventure wherein no private traffique barter exchaunge or merchaundizinge shalbe vsed practized or admitted by any pticler Governo^r Captein m̃chaunt Agent facto^r Mr Marrine^r officer or other pson whatsoever imploied in the said viage or pmitted to go in the same vppon paine of the losse and forfeiture to thuse of the generall companie and adventurers in this viage of all som̃es of moneis Jewells wares goodes or merchaundizes wch shalbe found in the said shippes or els were carried forthe or retourned home by any private or pticler man and not Conteyned and brought into the generall and common accompte and ioynte adventure of the said viage And to thend this preiudice of private traffique may the better be avoyded wee do ordeyne and appoint that due inquisic̃on be made in all and everye the severall shippes of the said viage and els refer by searche of all such chest℥ boxes pack℥ packett℥ book℥ writing℥ and other meanes whereby discovery may be made of the breache of this present ordeñnce And wee do in like manner ordeyne and decree for the avoydinge of all vnfaythfullnes and deceite to be vsed in the said voyage in the defraudinge of the generall adventure wch is prepared and sett forthe att the great cost℥ and charges of such as repose their trust and confidence in the office^{rs} and mynisters imployed in the said viage that what pson soever shalbe found vnfaithfull or vniust in the said voyadge by embesselinge or w^{th}drawinge of anie the good℥ wares merchaundizes Jewells or other commdoties whatsoever other belonginge to the adventure sente

1600
10 Feb.

1600
10 Feb.

out or beinge pcell of the retourne of the same wch was is or shalbe ether prepared bought or belonginge to the common or generall stocke or adventure that such pson shalbe barred and concluded to demaund of the Governo^r and Companie of the said merchaunt℈ of London tradinge into the Est Indies any accompt reckonige or payment of anie wages salary contract or entertaynm^t for his imployment in this viage wherevnto he was or otherwyse might have bene enteressed yf such offence had bene comitted. And ffurther that every such pson so offendinge shalbe prosecuted by the said Governor and Companie of merchaunt℈ of London tradinge into the East Indies accordinge to the qualety of his offence in that behaulfe by the lawes and Statut℈ of this Realme.

And furthermore wee do ordeyne that yf vppon the delivery of of her Ma^{ies} Lr̃es to the prinnces of those places wher our shippes shall arrive yet shalbe peacably received and entertayned as merchaunt℈ to Commerce and traffique wth the people of those Cuntries or plac℈ and be secured and warraunted hereafter to frequent and visitt those ptes then wee do ordeyne and agree that you shall select out of the yongest sort of our facto^{rs} *and others* entertayned by vs or voluntarily suffered to go in the voyage such and so many of the most aptest and towardest of them as you shall thincke meet and as shall have have best approved them selves fitt for such our employment to reside and abide in the said places wher yo^u shalbe so peaceably received yf you may be pmitted therevnto takinge sufficient [order] and Carefull order for the defrayinge and suppliinge of their charges vntill those places shalbe hereafter visited by another fleet sent from hence and Leavinge wth them such advise and direc̃õn for their better enformac̃õn how to carry them selves in those plac℈ as by y^r good discrec̃õn wth thadvise of such as you you shall conferre thereof shalbe thought meet and as tyme and experience of those places shall direct you.

And forasmuche as the daies of manns liefe are lym̃ited and the certeintie thereof for their continuance and end onlie knowen vnto God Wee the said Governour and Companie of merchaunt℮ of London tradinge into the East Indies do hereby ordeine and provide that yf it shall happen you the said James Lancaster to depte this mortall liefe before the retourne of the said shippes then from and after the decease of yo^u the said James Lancaster wee do by this o^r p̄nte Comission vnder our Com̄on Seale constitute and appointe yo^u Mr John Middleton to be the cheife Governo^r or generall of the said merchaunt℮ marrine^{rs} officers [and other officers] and other her Ma^{ius} subject℮ by vs ymployed or otherwise shipped in the said viage willinge and requiringe you and gevinge you like power and aucthoritie to putt in execuc̄on the said ordennc℮ and decrees concerninge the orderinge and disposinge of the traffique and merchaundizinge of the said viage as wee have done to the said James Lancaster and yf it shall happen by god℮ appointment that both you the said James Lancaster and John Middleton shall decease in the said viage then wee ordeyne and appointe the principall and generall government of the whole Companie therein imploied or shipped in this p̄nte viage vnto you Mr William Brund beinge also one of o^r fowre principall merchaunt℮ whom we have chosen and entertayned for the orderinge and disposinge of the merchaundizes and traffique of the said viage Requiringe you yf you shall fortune to survive the said James Lancaster and John Middleton to observe and keape the same o^r ordeñnc℮ and decrees before menc̄oed ordeyned and appointed by vs for the traffique and merchaundizinge of the said voyadge geavinge you the like aucthoritie to execute the same as is formerlie herein geaven to the said James Lancaster and John Middleton or ether of them and yf you the said William Brund shall fortune to decease in the said viage then wee do appointe the ymediate succession and execuc̄on of the said charge and governm^t aforesaid vnto you Mr John Havard one other of our said principall merchaunt℮ requiringe you to see our said ordeñnc℮ and decrees to be kept and pformed geavinge vnto you the same power and aucthoritie as wee have hereby geven to the said James Lancaster Jo: Middleton and William Brund *or any of them* And yf it should fortune that all the said severall psons imploied by vs as our principall merchaunt℮

1600
10 Feb.

1600
10 Feb.

in this p̃nte viage to decease then wee ordeyne and appointe the whole governm^t and Charge before menc̃oed to be vndertaken by one of you fowre wch are of the second sort of merchaunt℘ or facto^{rs} by vs imployed in the said viage the same to be taken and executed successively [by] one after another as anie of you shall happen to decease after the said Charge by the trew meannge hereof shalbe cast vppon you wch Charge wee do ordeyne shall succeade in this manner videlt *first* to our second merchaunt shipped in the Redd dragon next to our second merchaunt or facto^r shipped in the Hecto^r thirdly to our second merchaunt or facto^r shipped in the assention and lastlie to our second merchaunt or factor shipped in the Suzan [Reposinge in you our severall m̃chaunt℘ and all you our severall officers appointed and entertayned in this viage espetiall hope trust and confidence that you will accorde and agree together and ioyne in freind shipp and amyty to do and execute yor vttermost endeavo^{rs} for the benefitt of the voyadge wthout contenc̃on discord or emulac̃on to be vsed amongst you guidinge yor selves therein by that generall Reigment and Sea government wch our Englishe fleet℘ do vse when they sorte themselves togeather And so wee commend you and yor travilles to god & providence who guide you wth his feare and defend yo^u from all daungers.]

And wee do further Ordeine that as wee have appointed a Succession of o^r Principall merchaunt and governor of the Whole Companie imploied or shipped in this viage so wee do order and decree that vppon soever the said governm^t in succession shall fall by the decease of anie the psons before named that he shall or may shipp or imbarke him selfe in the Admirall of o^r fleete and enioye and receive such place Cabbin easement and commandm^t therein as o^r said generall and principall governo^r formerlie did.

And Lastlie whereas her Ma^{ie} by her Commission vnder the great Seale haith onlie appointed the generall governm^t of all her Subiect℘ imploied in the said viage vnto the said James Lancaster wthout anie appointinge of Succession by like Warraunt to any that is imploied in the said viage and that it lieth

THE EAST INDIA COMPANY

not in vs to geave anie warraunt for the Correcc̃on of offencẽ by pennall lawes to be executed vppon the bodies of anie her Ma^{ies} Subiectẽ wee do in that behaulfe as to menn havinge reason and discrec̃on and to men that feare god offer vnto you^r good Considerac̃ons the benefitt of order and peaceable agreement in matters and enterprises vndertaken for a Common good Reposing̃ in yo^u o^r seũall m̃chauntẽ and all yõ o^r seũall officers appointed and entertayned in this voiadge a specyall hope trust and confidence y^t yõ will accorde and agree together and Joyne in freindshipp and amytie To doe and execute yor vnttermost endeavo^{rs} for the benefitt of the voiadge w^{th}out Contenc̃on discorde or emulac̃on to be vsed amongest yõ guidinge yo^rselves there in by that gen^rall Reigem^t and Sea govermet wch o^r Englishe fleetẽ doe vse when they sorte themselves haveinge a specyall and due respect to him that is yor princypall or cape merchant And soe we comende yo^u and yor travailes to gods providence who guide yõ wth his feare and defende yõ frõ all Daungers.

1600
10 Feb.

Whereas by an order of Court of the 9 of Januarie last It was agreed that he *that* [shall] did not bring in by the way of supply *to be added* to his adventure formerlie sett downe ij^s vppon everie pound [of his adventure by him so sett downe] *of his stock or contribution* by the 15. of the same moneth should forfeit x^{li} vppon *everie* the Cth *of the said adventure* notw^{th}standing w^{ch} [lawe] order ther are divers that have not brought in ther said supplies by wch meanes ther resteth forfeited out of ther said stockes the said ij^s in the pound wch cometh to [xx^{li}] x^{li} vppon everie c^{li} [sett downe *and whereas* notw^{th}standing wch penaltie divers of the Companie were still behinde and have not yet brought in ther said Supplie by meanes Whereof] the voyage is *still* [for no] in a great afterdeale and want of moneis to supplie present and necessarie paimtẽ [by the want whereof] *by meanes whereof* the shippes are deteyned here *at the companies great charge*. It is therfore ordered for the avoyding̃ of the daunger [that] wch thes delaies of bringing̃ in of moneys may bread [that] and for the encoragem^t of suche as wilbe forward to supply the wantẽ thereof that [whosoever] *as many* of the Com-

An act touching the bringing in of the supplie of 2^s in the li.

T

1600
10 Feb.

pany *as* will bring in to the handes of the Thrēr the some of xx^{li} to be added to his *or ther* owne adventure formerly sett downe having brought in his full principall and his supply *of ij^s the li* by the said recited act agreed vppon, shall for the said xx^{li} by him or *them* voluntaryly brought in have not only the benyfyte of the gaine thereof but the [benefytt or] *principall and* gaine of the some of xx^{li} by the said act forfyted by some one that hath not brought in his supply of ij^s the li. And to that ende thursday next is geaven to all those wch are behind wth ther said supplies ether to bring them in or els to lose xx^{li} [vppon or] out of [ther] every cc^{li} of ther stocke to be added to the stockes of them wch will supply it for them [&] in ther default, the same to be sett over at the next genall Courte wch is intended to be on fryday next [And is]

1600
11 Feb.

The xjth of february 1600.

Mr Ald. Wattes   M^r Jo: Highelord
Mr Rich: Staper   Mr Robt Sandy
Mr Rich: Wyseman   Mr Wm Chambers
Mr Wm Garway   Mr Wm Harryson.

207 to fraunces Parrott for Norromborghe ware.

ORDER is geaven to m^r Ald^n Bannyng to pay vnto fraunc€ Parrett for Norromborowgh ware bought of him the somme of Two hundred and seven poundes sterling pcell of 407^{li} arysing to that some by the pcelles delivered to the handes of m^r Allabaster wherof the said 207^{li} is presentlie to be p^d and the resideue the last of Aprill.

Order is geaven to Ald^n Bannyng to pay vnto George Davyes for chest€ filled wth showes shirtes Cassock€ and breeches the some of Eleven poundes [sterling] one shilling sterling.

Order is geaven to Ald^n Holliday to pay vnto m^r Derick Lypson for steele bought [by] *of* him by m^r Wm Garway the somme of fowrtie fowre poundes sterling as apereth by a bill of pticlers of the same.

Order is geaven to the said Mr Ald^n Hollyday to pay vnto Phillip Grove the somme of Eleven poundes sterling for his Charges of diet and boat hire expended in the travelling of the Companies busines.

The xijth : of Febr : 1600.

		1600 12 Feb.
M^r W^m Ruṁey deputy	Mr Rich : Wyche	
Mr Rich : Stapers	Mr Wm Chambers	
Mr Wm Garway	Mr Wm Harryson	
Mr Rich : Staper	M^r Roƀt Bell	
M^r Jo : Eldred	M^r Jo : Midleton	
M^r Roƀt Sandy	Mr Tho : Cordell.	

[Motion is made]

IT is ordered that Phillip Grove shall have a bill of adventure for the Composition wch is made wth him for his enterteynm^t in the voyage. — *Phillip Grove.*

Warraunt is geaven to m^r Ald^r Holliday to pay to Nathaniell Jamryn one of the 3 sort of factors appointed for the voyage according to the agreem^t made wth him for his enterteynm^t the soṁe of xxx^{li} sterling. — *Nath: Jamryn 30^{li}.*

Warraunt is geaven to Ald^r Hollyday thẽr to pay to Mr Wyseman to be đđ over to the Purser of the [hercules] Hecto^r the somme of one hundred poundes sterling for the paym^t of mens wages in that ship. — *100^{li} to the Purser of the Hecto^r.*

Warraunt is geaven to Ald^r Holliday thẽr to pay to Wm Done Cowper for worke done for the voyag vppon the rest of a geñall Reckoning of 53^{li}. 7^s. 7^d in full paym^t the soṁe of xxxviij^{li} vij^s vij^d. — *38^l. 7^s. 7^d to Wm Done Cowper.*

Warraunt is geaven to Ald^r Hollyday thr̃er to pay vnto Mr Wm Segar one of the herrault$?$ for the wryting of her ma^{rs} Lr̃es. to the kinges of the East Indies the soṁe of xiij^{li} vj^s viij^d and xij^d for a boxe bought by him to putt in the same lr̃es. — *13^{li}. 7^s. 8^d to Wm Segar for the Q^{es} lres.*

Warraunt is geaven to Ald^r Bannyng thẽr to pay vnto Capten Lancaster vppon the Companies Agreem^t w^h him vppon his enterteynm^t the somme of two hundred poundes. — *200^{li} to CaptenLancaster.*

The like warraunt is geaven to the said thrẽr to pay to the said Capten Lancaster. for soe much by him [deliuered] laied out vppon the Companies occasions the somme of Eleven poundes vij^s viij^d. — *11^{li}. 7^s. 8^d to Capten Lancaster.*

Another Warraunt is geaven to the said thrẽr to pay to the [Purser] Wm Dickson Purser of the Read Dragon for the — *200^{li} to the Purser of the Dragon.*

140   THE COURT RECORDS OF

1600
12 Feb.
provysion of the said ship vppon accoumpte the somme of two hundred poundes.

[Order is geaven to Ald^r Hollyday thēr of the to pay vnto m^r Richard Wyseman.]

100^{li} to Capten Midleton.
Order is geaven to Ald^r Holliday *thēr* to pay vnto Mr John Mydleton for his enterteynm^t in the voyage the somē of one hundred poundes sterlinge for soe much allowed him by Composition.

100^{li} to ye Assention.
Order is geaven to Ald^r Hollyday thrēr to pay vnto Mr Wm Garway vppon accoumpte for the provisyon of the Assention, the somme of one hundred poundℓ.

8^{li}. 3^s. 7^d
Order is geaven to Ald^r Hollyday thrēr to pay vnto Capten Mydleton vppon a Bill of pticlers of charges by him disbursed in the Companies occasions the somme of viij^{li}. iij^s. vij^d.

1600
13 Feb.
The 13th of february 1600.

Mr Wm Rumney deputy   Mr Wm Chamber
Mr Aldⁿ Wattes   M^r Jo Combe
Mr Wm Garway   Mr Rich Wyche
Mr Tho Cordell   Mr Wm Harryson
Mr Rich : Wyseman   Mr John Middleton
Mr Roger Howe   *Mr Aldⁿ Moore*
Mr Aldⁿ Hollyday   Mr Nich. lynge
M^r Jo : Highelord

Mr Roger Howe M^r Jo Combe xx^{li} a peece.

R. Roger Howe and Mr John Combe having bene delt wth all to travell into ye west Cuntrey [for] to see the discharge of the shippes having otherwyse as they constantly affirme ernest busines of ther owne doe notwthstanding assent to be imployed to doe anie good office for the voyage [and] vppon whose assent it is resolved by this assemblie to gratyfye them wth the consideration and gratification of xx^{li}. a pece to bestowe vppon them in plate or otherwyse at ther pleasure and to beare all ther Charges for them and ther servauntℓ.

400^{li} to M^r
Order is geaven to m^r Aldⁿ Hollyday thrēr to pay vnto one

Mr William Harvy or his Assignes the somē of fowre hundred poundes sterling for soe muche re^d of him in the West Cuntrey by the handes of Rob̃t Pope by bill of exchaungẽ dated the 18 of Januarie.

<small>1600
13 Feb.
W Harvy
per ex^n.</small>

It is informed this Assemblie that o^r shippes are too deeply Laden and therfore moved that some smale ship shalbe hired to stowe the spending victualles and to followe the shippes some part of the voyage and to retorne againe, but it is resolved that the shippes shall all fall downe to Gravesend and then they shalbe surveyed what necessitie ther wilbe of the provision of suche a smale ship and then accordinglie order to be taken.

<small>a small ship for the spendinge victualles.</small>

Order is geaven to Ald^r Hollyday to pay vnto m^r Pope sergeaunt of th'admiraltie vppon a bill of charges for the buriall of those wch were slaine in the Hecto^r the somē of Liij^s.

<small>2^li. 13^s. o^d to Mr Pope sgeaunt of the Admiralty.</small>

Warraunt is geaven to Ald^r Holliday to pay vnto Henry Mydleton one of the seconde sort of factors vppon the Composition made wth him for his enterteynment in the voyage the somme of fyftie poundes sterlingẽ.

<small>50^li to Henry Midleton, vpon his enterteynm^t.</small>

It is ordered that Mr Garroeway and Richard Wright shall resorte to the l. thrër and m^r Secretorie and to entreat ther honors warraunt to deliver out of m^r Governo^rs howse the plate and other presentes wch are prepared for the voyage. Whose pticlers hereafter followe viz.

A founteyne wth a bassen white of 205 oz̃.

A standing Cup wth a Cover	63 oz̃.
2 standing Cuppes wth Covers	64 oz̃.
2 standing Cuppes wth Covers	32 oz̃.
A Bason & ewer.	102 oz̃.
A ship basen & ewre.	30 oz̃.

2 fans of fethers.
2 plumes of fethers.
3 Looking glasses
A Target and headpece belonging to ye Muskovia company
A Comõn Seale of the Companyes.—
Order is geaven to Ald^n [Bannyng] Hollyday and Mr Eldred to

142   THE COURT RECORDS OF

1600
13 Feb.

see the moneis provided to be shipped out of the Port of London and reported by a repertition made at an assemblie of the Comitties the 27. of Januarie last and the same [being entred] *to enter* in the Custome howse *and to see it* to be waterborne and carried downe to the shippes at Gravesend and ther to be delivered a board eche ship that the same may be safely shipped and stowed accordinglie.

1600
14 Feb.

The 14. of february 1600.

Mr Wm Rumey deputy	Capten Middleton.
Mr Rich : Staper	Mr Roger Howe
Mr. Thomas Cordell	Mr. John Combe
Mr Wm Garway	Mr Rob̃t Sandy
Mr Rich. Wyseman	Mr Nich : Lynge
Capten Lancaster	Mr Wm Chamber.

361^{li}.15^s.0^d
to Mr Simon
furno^r for
powder.

ORDER is geaven to Mr Ald^n Hollyday to pay vnto Mr Simon furno^r 371^{li} . 15^s . 0^d rest of of 698 . 8 . 4. dewe to him for powder Brimston and Saltepeter delivered for the shippes whereof *for* 326^{li} . 13 . 4 Warraunt is formerlie geaven and the said 371^{li} . 15^s . 0^d is to be p^d at three monethes after the date hereof.

61^{li} . 5^s . 9^d
to Simon
Yomans for
butter &
cheese

Lyke warraunt is geaven to the said Thrẽr to pay vnto Simon Yomans Chaundeler for 52 fk̃e of butter at 19^s the ff and for x^c q̃ xij^{li} of chese at xxiij^s the Cth ; the somme of sixtie and [two] *one* poundes [nyne] *fyve* shillinges [three] *ix* pence.

86 . 0 . 0
to W^m
Vffington
for wax
candelles.

Lyke warraunt is geaven to the said Thrẽr to pay vnto Wm Vffington waxe Chaundeler for 1310^{li} of wax Candells *at* xv^d ob̃ the ti and for viij Chestẽ and 4 boxes. the somme of fowrscore and six poundes sterling̃.

34^s . 3^d.

Geven by warraunt vpon [Ald^n Hallydaye] *Mr Chambers* to pay vnto Capten Mydleton . as by a bill of pticulers.

100^l to m^r
Wisman for
the Purser
of ye Hector

A warrant geven vpon Ald^n Hallyday to paye to m^r Wiseman [for] to be geven to the purser of the hector. for defrayeinge of charges the some of one hundrethe poundẽ by direction of Capten Mydleton.

THE EAST INDIA COMPANY. 143

Munday 16. february 1600.

Wm Romenij Depute
Mr Ald^n Watt(.
Mr Cordell
Mr Style
Capt. Lanckester

Capt mydleton
M^r wiche.
Capt. Davis.
Mr Linge
Mr Combes.

1600
16 Feb.

OMPLAYNT beinge made of the overchargenge and pesteringe bothe of the Susan and the rest of the Shippes. but espetially of the Susan. it was ordered that that a hoygh or some other ship of one hundred Tuns or more should be bought to goe a longe wth the shippes as farre they shuld it fytt and then to take suche co^rse wth the ship so bought as they shuld thinke meet; and Mr Cordell and   were intreated to seeke out for suche a ship.

Order is geaven to Mr Ald^n Bannyng to pay vnto Thoms Parkins Cowper in full paym^t of Caske as by his accoumpte audited by Mr Chambers and m^r Harryson appeareth the somme of threescore and eighteene poundes sixtene shillinges and fowre pence sterling.

78.16.4
to Tho:
Perkins for
Caske.

Order is geaven to Ald^r Holliday to pay vnto m^r Wm Candyshe in full paym^t and Clearing of his accompt for leade the some of fowrtie and Nyne poundes sterling.

49^li to W^m
Candishe

Order is geaven to Ald^r Holliday to pay vnto James Emerson *for the just and* in full paym^t of Fyve hogg^hds of aquavitæ the somme of [three] thirtie poundes sterling for wch ther hath bene p^d him already the somme of xxx^li:

30^li to James
Emerson for
Aquavitæ.

Ther is geaven to M^r [Ald^r] Hackett by thassent of this assemblie for his travelles taken in instrucc̃ons and advyses touching the preparing of the voyage and for his former advyses in setting the voyage in hand the Last yere the somme of tenn poundes and xxx^s for 3 mappes by him provided and dd to the Companie the same money to be p^d him by Mr Ald. Hollyday.

11^li. 10^s. to
be geaven to
Mr Hack-
lett.

Ther is geaven to Mr Henrie Napper m^r of the Hecto^r in consideration of his extraordinarie travell and paines taken in the preparation of the shippes and for his expences [taken]

20^li to
Henry Nap-
per for his
paines &
expences

1600
16 Feb.

expended in attending the same the somme of Twentie poundes to be p^d him by m^r Ald^n Bannyng.

1600
17 Feb.

The 17th of febr 1600.

Mr Wm Rumney deputy   Capten Midleton
Capten Lancaster   Mr Robt Sandy
Mr. John Combe.

100^li to the Purser of the dragon

RDER is geaven vnto Mr Ald. Holliday to pay vnto Wm Dixon Purser of the Read Dragon vppon accoumpte the one hundred poundes sterling to be imploied in the pparation and clearing away of the same ship.

50^li to the purser of the Hector.

The like warraunt is geaven to the said Three to pay vnto Mr Wm Garway or to the Purser of the Assention vppon accoumpte the somme of fyftie poundes sterling to be imploied in the preparation and clearing away of the same ship.

The 17th of feb 1600.

Mr Wm Rumney deputy   Capten Middleton
Mr Ald^n Hollyday   Mr Rich: Wyche
Mr Tho Cordell   Mr John Combe
Mr Rich: Wyseman   Mr Rich: Staper
Mr John Eldred   Mr Wm Harryson
Mr Wm Garway   Mr Robt Sandy
M^r olyuer Style   Mr Ald^n Wattes
Mr John Highelord   Mr Ald^n Moore
M^r frauncis Chery   Mr Robt Bell.

T this Courte was reade two severall formes of Billes of adventure to be geaven to every adventuro^r in the voyage and to everie facto^r enterteyned in the same to be passed vnder the Comon seale of the Company. for the better satisfaction both of the adventuro^rs and of the said factors and to geave testimony of ther moneys brought in [and] *by the adventures* and of the Contractes made wth the said factors. the teno^r of wch billes do followe in thes wordes viz:

THE EAST INDIA COMPANY

Whereas A. B.   is entertayned by vs the Govenor 1600
and Companie of merchaunt^s of London tradinge into the East 17 Feb.
Indies to go as one of our   facto^{rs} in this p̃nte voiage The forme
nowe by vs prepared towardes the said Indies and is allowed of the Bills
                                                             to be giuen
for his imployment in the said viage the somme of   to euy ad-
           for his preparacon to Sea the wch he hath received before venturer.
his goinge forthe Nowe know yee that wee the said Governor
and Companie for the further allowaunce wch the said A. B. And to euy
                                                                  ffacto^r in
is to have and receive accordinge to o^r agreement wth him do the voiadge
acknowledge and testifie and do promise and agree by these p̃nt^s
that the said A. B.   shall have and enioy for his further
allowaunce and entertaynment in the said Voiage vppon the
gaine and proffitt wch god shall send by the retourne of the
same voiage (the principall adventure thereof and all Charges
of the voiage . first deducted suche rate and proporc̃on of proffitt as [if] he had bene an adventurer of the somme of
          and as yf he had putt in so muche readie money in
stocke in the said voiage the said rate and proporc̃on of proffitt
to be paied vnto him after his retourne into England in suche
manner and forme as the gaine and proffitt of the said viage is
paied to other the Adventur^{rs} generallie vppon the Somme of
          by them adventured So as he procead
in the said viage and do not retourne before the viage be ended.
And yf he happen to dye before the retourne of the said shippes
from the said East Indies havinge lived and Contynued in the
said voiage vntill the shippes shalbe laden or vntill he *or* [and]
other facto^{rs} shall have Contracted and made provision for their
Ladinge. then the said gaine proportioned the said rate of
          adventure to be paid to his Executo^{rs} adminis-
trato^{rs} or Assignes as it should have bene paied to him yf he had
retourned wth the shippes Provided alwaies that yf he decease
before the shippes shall arrive in the east Indies that then the
money imprested and delivered him before his goinge to Sea
shalbe vnto him a full recompence of his entertaynment agreed
vppon for the voiage And vppon theise condic̃ons and proviso
before menc̃oed Wee the Governo^r and Companie under o^r
Common Seale have geaven vnto the said A. B.   this
u

THE COURT RECORDS OF

1600
17 Feb.

p̄nte bill of Contract and adventure dated the   day
of february Anno regni R⁽ᵃᵒ⁾ Eliz. xliij^{cio}.

Whereas A. B.   one of the adventurers and one of
the Brethren of the Governo^r and Companie of Merchaunt€ of
London tradinge into the East Indies havinge sett downe for
his adventure wth the said Companie for their first voyage into
the east Indies the Somme of   sterlinge
hathe not onlye paied the said somme of   to
          Thrēr of the said Companie but haithe
supplied accordinge to the ordeīnce of the said Companie The
Somme of   sterlinge more wch is after the rate
of ij^s the pound of his said adventure Wee therefore the said
Governor and Companie do by this our p̄nte Bill of Adventure
promise and agree to and wth the said   That
wee the said Governo^r and Companie and our Successo^{rs} shall
and will vppon the retourne of the shippes or anie of them sett-
out by vs in this p̄nte voiage or w^{th}in Convenient tyme after
their said retourne in the same deliver vnto the said
          his Executo^{rs} and administrat^{rs} a[nd] trew and iust
accompte and payment of suche Stocke benefitt and proffitt of
Stocke as god shall send vppon the said voiage accordinge to
the generall distribuc̄on proporc̄on and alotment wch shalbe
alotted disposed and geaven to all and everye the severall adventurers in the said voiage proportionall to their severall adventurs
In Wittnes whereof the said Governo^r and Companie have heervnto annexed ther Common Seale the   day of Febr. 1600.

It is ordered that m^r Ald^n Hollyday shall carry downe to
Gravesend some convenient somē of money to the valewe of
4. or 5 *or 6* hundred poundes for the payment of Harboroughe
wages and other Reckoning€ for the clearing€ of the shippes.

1500^{li} to be taken at interest by the Thrers.

It is ordered that Mr Ald [hollyd] Bannyng and Mr Ald^r Holliday shalbe entreated to geave ther Credites for the Companies
vse forthe taking vp of fyfteene hundred poundes sterling for
three monethes and the Companie shall save them harmeles.

61^{li} for Caske.

Order is geaven to Ald^n Hollyday to pay vnto Henry Ryvell€
Coop for Caske in full paym^t of his accoumpte audited by m^r

Chambers and Mr Harryson the some of threescore and one poundes. 1600 17 Feb.

The lyke order is geaven him to pay vnto John Hardway Coop for Caske in full payment of his accoumpte audited and allowed by Mr Wm Chambers and Mr Wm Harryson the some of ffyftie and seven poundes fyfteene shillingℓ. 57{ll}. 15{s}. o{d} for Caske.

At this Court Richard Hart a Smythe to whom the Company are to pay money for yron worke is content that the rest of money dew to him vppon his reckoning shalbe staied in the thrērs handes and p{d} to m{r} Flemyng in part of payment of the said Hartes debt dewe to him for yron. Hartes debt for yron to be p{d} to Mr flemyng.

Order is geaven to Ald{n} hollyday to pay

It is agreed that m{r} Cordell m{r} Wyche and m{r} Bell shall proceade in the auditing of the Pursers accompte and all other accoumptes appteyning to the read dragon. The accompte of the read dragon to be audited

At this Co{r}t is read the Copie of a Comission geaven to m{r} Howe and m{r} Combe and allowed and liked of and they required that it might be written over againe wth some of the pointes altered according as Direction was geaven them and the Comitties at ther next meeting will signe it. A Comission to Mr Howe & Mr Jo. Combe to go in to the West Cuntrey.

It is ordered that the psons heervnder named shall goe downe to Gravesend to see the discharge of the shippes and to take order in suche thinges as shalbe necessarie to be dispatched ther and order is geaven them to dispose of all accedentℓ and occasions that shall be fytt to be determined ther according to ther discretions and whatsoever they shall doe therin the Companie will ratefie and allowe thereof Comitties apointed to go to Graueshend

 Mr Wm Rumney deputy Mr Wm Garway
 Mr Ald{n} Hollyday   Mr Rich : Wyche
 Mr Ald{n} Wattes   Mr Wm Harryson
 Mr Ald{n} Moore.   Mr Robt Sandy.
 Mr Tho Cordell   Mr olyuer style.

At this Co{r}te m{r} Cordell maketh report that he Captein Lancaster and others have bought of Mr fraunce Chery and of Ratclyff a ship called the guift of the burthen of 6 score tun for the somme of three hundred pounds sterlinge to be p{d} one hundred poundes the Last of this moneth The guyft bought for 300{li}:

1600 17 Feb.	another Cth ti. the last of m̃che and the third Cth ti. the last of May following wch bargaine the Companie do well allowe of, and do imploy the said ship in following of the fleete wth victualles.

The xviijth of february 1600.

1600
18 Feb.

    Mr Wm Rumney deputy   Mr Aldⁿ Moore
    Mr Aldⁿ [Moore] Wattes   Mr Rich : Wyche.
          Mr Aldⁿ Hollyday.

Phillip Grove.

BILL of adventure sealed vnder the Common Seale to Phillip Grove Pylott for [*the gaine of*] five hundred poundes adventure vppon the gaine of the voyage allowed him.

100^{li} to ye Purser of ye Susan.

Warraunt is geaven to Ald^r Bannyng *ther* to pay to [the] Joseph Salbanck Purser of the Susañ vppon accoumpte for the provision of the ship and the Clearing of her away the somme of one hundred poundes sterling.

40^{li}. 12^s to leonard Onnyslowe Coop.

Warraunt is geaven to Ald^r Hollyday thēr to pay vnto Leonard Onnyslowe Coop for Caske the some of fowrtie poundes twelve shillinges sterling in full paym^t his accoumpt being audited and allowed by m^r Wm Harryson.

19. 16. 0 to John Spencer Cooper.

Warraunt is geaven to Ald^r Bannyng to pay to John Spencer Coop for worke done in Caske wrought for the Companie as apereth by his Accoumpt allowed by the said Ald^r the somme of xix^{li} xvj^s iiij^d.

36^{li}. 19. 0 to Georg Chapman Cowper.

Lyke warraunt is geaven to [the said] Ald^r Hollyday thēr [the some] to pay vnto George Chapman Cowper the some of thirtie sixe poundes xix^s sterling for Caske wrought for the Company being rest of a former accoumpt [allowed] audited by m^r Harrison.

The 20th february 1600.

1600
20 Feb.

    Mr Wm Rumey deputy   Mr Wm Garway.
    Mr Aldⁿ Hollyday   Mr Robt Sandy
    Mr Tho. Cordell   Mr Rich. Wyche
    Mr Rich : Staper   M^r Jo : Combes.

BILL of adventure sealed vnder the Common seale to Mr John Ellecott for 220^{li} adventure put in stocke.

1600 20 Feb. John Ellecot his bill of aduenture of 220^{li}.

Geven a warrant vppõ Ald^r Holleday ffor paym^t of ł 29. to Thomas Duck ffor anchients & streamers to the dragon as p bill.

The 20th February 1600.

 BILL of adventure sealed vnder the Comon Seale vnto Wm Allen of London Esquier for 200^{li} adventure putt in stock.

Wm Allen esqr.

A Bill of Adventure sealed vnder the Comon seale vnto [Wm Starky and] Raphe Allen ñcer and Wm Starky Skynner for 400^{li} of adventure put in stock.

Raphe [Starkey] Allen W^m [Allen]Starky

Geiven a warraunt vppon Alderman Hollidaye for paym^t of fower score pound℔ to Josephe Page Baker for an accompte of breade.

Joseph Page Baker 80^{li}

A bill of adventure sealed vnder o^r Comõn Seale to Wm Starkie one of o^r seconde sorte of facto^{rs} of a 100^{li} [venture] adventure vppon the gaine of the voyage.

Wm Starkie

Geiven a Warrante vppon Alderman Bannynge for paym^t of 27^{li}. 6^s. 6^d to Robte Myddleton in full for sugar delified to the Shippes.

Robte Middleton 27^{li}. 6^s. 6^d

Geiven a warrante vppon Alderman [Bannynge] Hollidaye for payment of 7^{li} 10^s to John Pywell for head peces and morrens.

7^{li}. 10^s to John Pywell.

A Bill of adventure sealed vnder o^r comon Seale to Roger Style grocer one of o^r Third sorte of factors of fiftie poundes adventure vppon the gaine of the voyage.

Roger Style

A Bill of adventure sealed vnder o^r Comõn Seale to Phillipe Wynchcombe one of o^r fourth sorte of facto^{rs} of ffowrtie pound℔ adventure vppon the gaine of the voyage.

Phillipe Wynchcombe.

A Bill of adventure sealed vnder o^r Comon Seale to Thoms Salterne of the Cytie of Bristowe one of o^r seconde sorte of facto^{rs} for a hundred pound℔ adventure vppon the gaine of the voyage.

Thomas Salterne.

Geiven a warrant vppon Alderman Hollidaye for payment of a hundred pound℔ to Christopher Thomson Smithe vppon an accompte of yron.

Christopher Thomson Smithe 100^{li}.

THE COURT RECORDS OF

1600
20 Feb.
Wm Brunde.
A Bill of adventure sealed vnder o^r Comon Seale to William Brunde of London one of o^r princypall factors for two hundred pound℮ adventure vppon ye gaine of ye voyage.

John Hauarde
A Bill of Adventure sealed vnder o^r Comon seale to John Havard Grocer one of o^r princypall [merchant℮] facto^{rs} for two hundred poundes adventure vppon the gaine of ye voyage.

Captaine Lancaster.
A Bill of Adventure sealed vnder o^r Common seale to Captaine Lancaster The Geñ'all of o^r ffleete for fiftene Hundred poundes adventure or three hundred poundes sterling accordinge to the condition of the said Bill. vppon the gaine of the voyage.

The xxjth of february 1600.

1600
21 Feb.

Mr Wm Rumney deputy   Mr Robt Sandy
Mr Aldⁿ Moore   Mr Rych : Wyche
Mr Thomas Cordell   Mr Wm Harryson
Mr Rich: Staper   Mr Aldⁿ Hollyday.

Wm Wilforde
A BILL of adventure vnder the Common seale was sealed to Wm Wilforde one of the 3. sorte of facto^{rs} for 50^{li} adventure vppon the gaine of the voyage.

Nathaniel Jamryn.
A Bill of adventure vnder the comon seale was sealed to Nathanyell Jamryn one of the 3. sorte of facto^{rs} for 50^{li} adventure vppon the gaine of the voiadge.

John Myddleton a princypall factor.
A Bill of adventure vnder o^r comon Seale was sealed to John Myddleton gent one of the princypall sortes of facto^{rs} for ffowre hundred pound℮ of adventure vppon the gaine of the viage.

John Myddleton an adventurer
A Bill of adventure under o^r comon Seale was sealed to John Myddleton Gent for 220^{li} adventure put in Stocke.

Thomas Pulleyñ. Precher.
A Bill of adventure vnder o^r comon Seale was sealed to Thomas Pulleyñ preacher for the some of 50^{li} adventure vppon the gaine of the viage.

30^{li}, 10^s. to
A warrante is Geiven to Alderman Hollidaye for the pay-

ment of thirtie poundes tenn shillingẹ to Richarde Hall Smithe for two Ankers for the Hector his Bill beinge allowed by Mʳ Wiseman.

1600
21 Feb.
Richarde
Hall
Smithe.

At Graueshende. the xxiiijth;
[A distribution of the presentẹ· by the Comitties.]

1600
24 Feb.

Mʳ Wᵐ Rumey Deputy   Mʳ Wᵐ Garway
Mʳ Aldⁿ Hollyday   Mʳ Olyuer Style
Mʳ Aldⁿ Wattes   Mʳ Robt Sandy.
Mʳ Aldⁿ Moore   Mʳ Rich: Wyche
Mr. Tho Cordell   Mʳ Wᵐ Harryson.

DISTRIBUTION of the presentes prepared for [the] to be presented to yᵉ Princes of the East Indies wher trade is to be sought devided in *to* the severall shippes by the order of the Comitties above named as followeth viz in

The read dragon.
- A siluer fountaine & basen of 205 oż.
- 1 standing Cup wᵗʰ a Cover 63 oż.
- 2 looking glasses of the greatest.
- 2 Helmeetẹ
- 2 Plumes of fethers
- 2 lr̃es.

Hectoʳ
- A basen & ewre of   102 oż.
- 1 standing Cup of   32 oż.
- 1 lesser Cup of   16 oż.
- [1 Plume of fethers]
- 1 looking glasse smalest
- 2 lr̃es.

Assention
- 1 standing Cup of   32 oż.
- 1 lesser Cup of   16 oż.
- 1 fann of fethers
- 1 smale looking glasse.
- 1 Case of dagges.
- 1 lr̃e.

THE COURT RECORDS OF

1600
24 Feb.

Susan
{
1 ship basen & ewre of   50 oz.
1 fanne fethers
2 beltes imbrothered
[2 helmeets]
1 looking glasse.
1 lrc̃.
1 head pece & targett of the Moskovy Company.
}

1600
25 Feb.

The xxv[th] of februarie 1600.

M[r] Cordell   M[r] Wyche
M[r] Garway   Ry Wright } left at Graveshend

John Dauyes his bill of aduenture as Pylott maior.

Bill of adventure was sealed vnder o[r] Comon seale to John Davyes gent. Pylott maior of this viage for his [One hundred poundes] adventure vppon the gaine of the viage as yet shall arryse viz yf the viage yeeld two for one then he to have out of the clere pfitt all chardges deducted 500[li] yf three for one 1000[li] yf fowre for one 1500[li] yf five for one 2000[li] out of w[ch] paym[t] w[ch]soever shall fall *due* to him by the value of the retourne of the saide viage there is to be deducted 200[li] lent vnto him by the Companie before his goeing forth over and above 100[li] geiven him for his pvision.

John Dauyes his bill of adventure for a 100[li] put in Stocke.

A Bill of adventure vnder o[r] comon Seale to John Davyes gent Pylott maior of this viage 100[li] adventure put in Stocke.

Thomas Morgann.

A Bill of adventure vnder o[r] common Seale to Thomas Margann one of o[r] fourth sorte of factors for fortie poundes adventure vppon the gaine of the viage.

Henrie Myddleton.

A Bill of adventure vnder our Com̃on seale to Henrie Myddleton gent one of our seconde sorte of factors for 100[li] adventure vppon the gaine of the viage.

Robte Pope.

A Bill of adventure vnder o[r] Com̃on seale to Robte Pope one of o[r] seconde sorte of factors for 100[li] adventure vppon the gaine of the viage.

Christopher Stradlinge.

A Bill of adventure for Christopher Stradlinge sealed vnder o[r] Comon Seale and one of o[r] fourth sorte of factors for fortie poundes adventure vppon the gaine of the viage.

Thomas Dassell.

A Bill of adventure vnder o[r] comon seale to Thomas Dassell one of o^r Third sorte of factors for fyftie poundes adventure vppon the gaine of the viage.

1600
25 Feb.

The xxvjth of februarie 1600/

1600
26 Feb.

FOWRE seuerall comissiones to the generallie and other the factors in succession beinge all of one tenor was sealed vnder the comon seale of the Companie and seſtallie deliſied to the princypall factor of everie shippe.

Comissions sealed vnder ye Comon seale.

A Bill of adventure sealed vnder o^r comon seale to Wm Brodebent M^r of the Reade Dragon for One hundred pound€ adventur vppon the gaine of the viage and for twentie marke a monethe for his wag€ contracted wth him And whereas there was geiven him by the Companie One hundred pound€ sterling for his provision to Sea And the warraunte geiven to ye Thŕer for the payment thereof made menc͠on that [same] the saide hundred poundes was a paymente vppon his wag€ be it remembred that the saide warrant was mys taken and should have binne a warraunt of a One hundred pound€ ymprested & absolutlie geiven him for his provision to Sea and not in pte of paym^t of any his wages.

Wm Brodebentes byll of aduenture

A Bill of adventure *sealed* vnder o^r comon Seale to Thomas Tudd one of o^r fourth sorte of factors for fourtie poundes adventure vppon the gaine of the viage.

Tho: Tudd his bill of aduenture.

A Bill of adventure was sealed vnder o^r comon Seale to Roger Style on of o^r thirde sorte of factors for fourtie poundes adventure put in Stocke.

Roger Style his byll of aduenture.

Whereas the Companie did lende m^r William Brodebent the some of One hundred poundes for sixe monethes for w^{ch}[yt] was entended y^t certen howses should be morgaged for the companies securitie the saide william Brodebent before his depture from Graveshende beinge vppon an accompte to have received as dewe to him from the Companie the some of xxviij^{li} (as by the accompte of william dixon purser of the Reade Dragon appeareth) he the said Wm Brodebente hath lefte in the handes

Wm Brodebent.

1600
26 Feb.

of the saide Dixon to thuse of *the* Companie the saide xxviij^{li} in pte of paym^t of the saide 100^{li} And hath assigned m^r Thomas Cordell and m^r William Garwaye to paie to the Companie seventie & two poundes residue of the saide 100^{li} vppon the xxvjth of August next by wch payment and assignaçõn satisfacçõn is made to the saide Companie of the saide 100^{li} by them lent and the saide Mr Brodebent dischardged thereof.

100^{li} to the Purser of the Assention.

Order is geaven to Mr Ald^n Hollyday to pay vnto [m^r] Wm Leake Purser of the Assention for the paiment of half wages to mariners and for the clearinḡ of the ship from hence the somme of one hundred poundes sterling whereof he is to geave an accoumpte.

100^{li} to ye Purser of the Hector

The lyke order is geaven to the said Thrẽr to pay to *Georg psons* the Purser of the Hecto^r the lyke somẽ of one hundred poundes to the lyke vse.

100^{li} to the Purser of the Susana.

A nother warraunt is geaven him to pay *to Josephe Salbanck* the Purser of the Susan the lyke some of one hundred poundes to the like vse.

180^{li} to the Purser of the read dragon.

A warraunt is also geaven to Mr Ald^n Bannynḡ to pay vnto *Wm Dixson or Edward Highlord* the Purser of the Read Dragon the somẽ of one hundred and fowrscore poundes to the like vse.

1600
28 Feb.

The xxviijth of februarie 1600.

Mr Wm Rumney Depu: M^r Roḃte Sandye
Mr Thomas Cordell   Mr John Hyghlorde.
Mr Oliuer Style.   Mr Richarde wiche.

15. 7. 0 to Mt Duffield Bruer.

ORDER is geaven to Ald^r Hollydaye Thrẽr to paie to Mr Anthonie Duffeilde Berebreuer for. 59. barrells of bere deliṽed to the Scourge when she laye in docke whereof tenn barrells at iiij^s and the residue at v^s the barrell somẽ xv^{li} vij^s sterlinge.

300^{li} to Mr Chery & Mr Golding for the guift.

Order is geaven to the said Thrẽr to pay to Roḃt Golding of Radcliff mariner for the ship called the guifte bought of him and M^r frauncẽ Chery the somẽ of three hundred poundes sterlinge whereof by Agrcem^t one hundred poundes is deue this

THE EAST INDIA COMPANY 155

pñte day and another hundred poundes the Last of marche 1600
and the other hundred poundes the Last of aprill. 28 Feb.

Lyke warraunt is geaven to the said Thrēr to pay vnto 24ˡⁱ 19 0
James Bover and Richard Vale for spectacles and Boxes for to James
spectacles wᵗʰ ther cases the somme of xxiiijˡⁱ xixˢ. Bover for spectacles.

The seconde of Marche 1600. 1600
 2 Mar.

Mʳ Wᵐ Rumey deputy Mʳ Jo: Eldred.
Mʳ Aldⁿ Wattes Mʳ Robt Sandy
Mʳ Rich: Staper Mʳ Ry: Wyche
Mʳ Rich: Wyseman Mʳ Wᵐ Harryson
Mʳ Jo: Highelord Mʳ Nich: Lynge.

T is agreed that the persons heervnder named shall Mr Ady
viewe & determyne the reckoninḡ betwene Mʳ Ady forTymber.
and the Company for tymber deliuered for the
building and the repayringḡ of the shippes and to agree vppon
an indifferent rate of the pticler prices. Whervppon ther is
some variaunce. dependinḡ betweene the Companie and him.

To morrowe in the after-
none at Mʳ Aldⁿ Wattes
hys house.
⎰ Mʳ Aldⁿ Wattes
⎸ Mʳ Staper
⎸ Mʳ Cordell
⎨ Mʳ Burrell
⎸ Mʳ Garway
⎸ Mʳ Wyseman
⎸ Mʳ Jo: Eldred.
⎱ or any 4. of them.

And the same psons are required on the behaulf of the Ship
Companie [shall] to viewe and determyne the Reckoninḡ of wrightes
the other shippewrightt̄ for other tymbers dd to the vse of reckonin-
the Companie. ges.

[Warraunt is geaven to mʳ Aldⁿ Hollyday to pay vnto mʳ [200ˡⁱ to
Abraham Campion vppon accoumpte of 646. 15. [4] 2. dewe to Mr Campion for
him for beare deliuered to the shippes the some of two hundred beare.]
poundes sterlinge.]

156   THE COURT RECORDS OF

1600
2 Mar.
2ˡⁱ to the searcher.

It is ordered that ther shalbe geaven by way of gratifycation to Mʳ Worsenham the Searcher for the clearing of the shippes the some of xlˢ.

Thaccoumpte of the state of the Aduenture bothe for ther debt & Credyte.

It is ordered that mʳ Aldⁿ [Hollyday shalbe intreated to] Bannyng and mʳ Aldⁿ Hollyday shalbe sent vnto to geave order that to morrowe morning ther bookes of Accoumptes may be brought hether and Mʳ Allabasters man be warned hether to meete together to arme an accoumpte of the state of the busines and that the same accoumpte may be pvsed and audited by the psons heervnder named to thende some present order may be taken for the clearing of the Companies debtes. by calling in suche moneys as are vnpᵈ or some other course taken to avoyde the clamoʳ of suche as are vnpaid the billes and Reckoninge dew to them by the Company.

    Mʳ Staper   Mʳ Harryson
    Mʳ Wyseman   Mʳ Lynge.
    Mʳ Wyche   or any three of them.

1600
6 Mar.

The 6ᵗʰ of Marche. 1600.

    Mʳ Wᵐ Rumney deputy   Mʳ Wᵐ Harryson
    Mʳ Rich: Wiseman   Mʳ John Eldred
    Mʳ Oliuer Style   Mʳ Wᵐ Burrell
    Mʳ John Highlorde   Mʳ Thomas Cordell.

The state of the aduenture in debt and Credyte.

PPON conference had wᵗʰ the Thrers and an estimate made of the moneys in ther handes. and of the debte owing by the Company and of suche moneys as is dewe to the adventure not yet brought in to the Thrers handes.

9000ˡⁱ owing at this day.

It appereth by the said estimat as the state of the Adventure as it standeth at this day that ther is owing by the Company aboute the somme of ix m̄ˡⁱ, towardes the paiment Wherof ther resteth onlie in ready money in the handes of mʳ Aldⁿ Hollyday Threr. 814ˡⁱ or therabouts, that ther is owing by divers wᶜʰ have sett downe ther adventures, and have brought in no part thereof about 5000ˡⁱ that ther is also owing by such

as have brought in part of ther adventures and not the whole 1600
and for the Supplies of ij^s the li. aboute 2000^{li}. So as the state 6 Mar.
of the Busines standing in this case appeareth.

    Order is geaven to Ald^r Hollyday thr͠er to pay to [Josephe] 100^{li} to Lewys Tyght Blacksmythe vppon Accoumpte of yron worke   wys Tyght, smythe for
wrought to the Read dragon the somme of   yron worke to the Read
    The like warraunt is geaven to the said Thr͠er to pay to dragon.
Joseph Page Baker vppon Accoumpte of Biskett the somme 50^{li} to Joseph
of fyfty poundes sterling. Page Baker

    Another Warraunt is geaven to the said Thr͠er to pay 30^{li} to
frauncis Candell Painter vppon accoumpte for the paintinge of frauncis Candell
the read Dragon. the somme of thirtie poundes sterlinge. Painter of the Read Dragon.

    Another Warraunt is geaven to the said Thr͠er to pay vnto 161^{li} 13^s 1^d
Richard Hart Smythe for Nayles and iron worke deliuered to to Rych:
the Assention the somme of one hundred sixtie one poundes Harte
thirtene shillings and a pennye in full paym^t of all yron Worke Smythe.
by him d̄d̄ to the Company.

    Another Warraunt is geaven to the said Thr͠er to pay vnto 18^{li} to
Edmond Saunderson Turno^r for Launterns Platters and other Edm: Saunderson
Turno^{rs} ware d̄d̄ to the Reade Dragon. for Turnors worke to y^e

    Another Warraunt is geaven to the said Mr Ald^n Hollyday Read dragon
to pay to Mr Wm Burrell vppon accoumpt for paym^t of moneys 100^{li} to M^r
owing to divers men the somme of one hundred poundes Wm Burrell
sterling. vppon Accompt.

    Another Warraunt is geaven vppon the said Thr͠er to pay 16^{li} o 10^d
vnto Wm Bacon for smale mastes and other store for the to Wm Bacon for
shippes the somme of sixten poundes tenn pence in full paym^t Mastes.
of a bill of pcelles of xix^{li} vj^s x^d whereof iij^{li} vj^s is bated as soe 30. 12. 4^d
muche wherin the Company were deceaved by the Carpenter of to James Waters for
the Susan. gonners

    Another Warraunt is geaven vppon the said thr͠er to pay vnto pvision for y^e
James Waters Iremonger vppon a bill of pcells for the gonners Susan.
provision *for the Susan* the some of xxx^{li} xij^s iiij^d in full paym^t. 100^{li} to Nichas

    Another Warrante is geiven vppon Ald^n Bannynge Th͠rer [Harrison]
to pay to Nic͠has Symondson the som͠e of One hundred poundes Symondson for tymber
sterlinge in pte of paym^t of tymber and Planke and othe nec- &Plank for y^e
cessaries for ye Susann. Susan.

158   THE COURT RECORDS OF

1600
13 Mar.

The xiijth of Marche 1600.

M^r W^m : Rumney Deputie   Mr Rob̃t Sandy
Mr Rich: Staper   Mr Wm Chambers
Mr Wm Garway   Mr Wm Harryson.

34. 16. 8
for lighter-
age & port-
age to W^m
Kimber at
Gully key.

RDER is geaven to Ald^r Hollyday Thēr to pay m^r
Wm Kymber Wharfeinger of Gully Key for Lighterage and portage of goodes to the shippes from the
same kay the somme of xxxiiij^{li} xvj^s viij^d [as] being dewe to
him vppon his bill of p̃celles. audited and allowed by Mr Highlord m^r Harryson and Mr Lynge.

34. 13. 8
for portage

The lyke order is geaven to the said Thrēr to pay to the
Porters of the Grocers haberdashers Salters and Skynners for
Portage and Lading of the fowre severall shippes thes severall
sommes following amounting in all to the somme of [xiij] xxxiiij^{li}
xiij^s viij^d sterling. as appereth by ther severall billes audited and
allowed by the Comitties of the shippes videlt for the read
dragon xiij^{li} ij^s xj^d for the hecto^r viij^{li} iiij^s for the Assention
six poundes tenn shillingℓ j^d and for the Susan vj^{li} xvj^s viij^d.

11^{li} 6. 8
for wharf-
age to Robt
wood at
wooll key.

Another warraunt is geaven to the said Thrēr to pay to
Rob̃t Wood Wharfeinger of wooll key the somme of xj^{li} vj^s
viij^d for wharfage and lighteringe of goodes shipped from the
same kay.

42^{li} 8^s 11^d
to M^r
Rumney
for money
disbursed.

Another warraunt is geaven vppon the said Thrēr to pay
to m^r Wm Rumney deputy [for] the somme of fowrtie and two
poundes viij^s xj^d whereof [40] 38^{li} 10^s 3 was by him p^d and deliuered at his going downe to graveshend to Capten Mydleton
for payment of mariners and the rest being ij^{li} xij^s was
disbursed in Charges by him and M^r wyche wth ther servaunt.

1600
21 Mar.

The 21 Marche 1600.

Mr Wm Rum̃ey deputy   Mr John Highelord
Mr Aldⁿ Hollyday   Mr Wm Harryson
Mr Rich : Staper   Mr Nicl̃as Lynge
Mr Wm Garway   Mr Wm Burrell
Mr John Eldred   Mr Thomas Cordell
            Mr Rich : Wyseman.

THE EAST INDIA COMPANY

RDER is geaven to Mr Wm Burrell to take vp the boate of thassention that lyeth at Blackwall and to make sale of the sale of the same for the most that can be gotten who hath vndertaken *to* do his best therin.

1600 21 Mar, The Assention's longe boate.

Order is geaven to Mr Harryson and Mr Burrell to gather together all suche provysions and thinges belonging to the shippes that are left behinde as 2 demi Cannons iron stanchions Anker caske and other thinges and putt them in some storehouse to be provided for that purpose to thende they may be solde for the most that can be made thereof.

A storehouse to be provided for the gatheringe together of thinges left behinde.

A Bill of Adventure sealed vnder the comon seale to Stephen Hodgeson for his adventure and supply of 220^{li}.

Stephen Hodgeson the bill

Order is geaven that all suche as depend in accoumpte wth the Company shalbe called vppon to bring in ther billes that ther accoumptes may be made vp and brought in to a certen state. of wch accoumptaunt^e thes persons following are to be called vppon—viz:

stayed.

Mr Pomtell & Rewler &c. [Jo: More] Nichas Pierd
[M^r fletcher] Ald^r Bannyng Mr Roger Howe
W^m [Rutter] Burrell. Rich: Gossen
Wm Angell Mr Staper.

Order is geaven to m^r Ald^n Hollyday thre͠r to pay vnto Thomas Hewys Clothworker for worke done to the Companie 12^{li}. 8. 6 in full for his said worke.

12^{li}. 8. 6 to Tho. Hewys Clothworker

2^s p lb further supply vppon the like pound in the former act.

xv^l at interest to be p^d Mr. Beareblock.

A Gen^{r}all Court holden the first of Aprill 1601.
Present of the Comitties

Mr Wm Rumey deputy Mr Ald^n More
Sr John Harte Mr Rich : Staper
Mr Ald^n Wattes M^r olyuer Style

1601 1 Apr.

160   THE COURT RECORDS OF

1601   Mr Rich. Wyseman   Mr Wm Harryson
1 Apr. Mr Robt Sandy   Mr Aldn Hollyday.
        Mr John Eldred
        Mi John Highelord   wth the greatest part of the
        Mr Rich: Wyche   Generality.

A newe supply of ijs the lb to pay Companies debtes.

THIS Cort being called vppon occation of the great debt and afterdett that hangeth vppon the voyage by reason of the severall sommes sett downe by [divers of] the adventurors and not brought in ether in the whole or in part and by divers other somes behinde by some of them as pte of ther adventures *sett downe and not brought in wholy* and also by other sommes behinde for the supplies *over and above the sommes sett downe and brought in* All wch do amounte [very neare] to the some of Nyne thowsand poundes and above the wch must of necessitie be pd the same being dewe to a nuber of poore men who importune the Comitties every day for payment vppon consideration of wch great arrerages and surplusage of provysion and charge that lieth vppon the voyage this Court resolving that every adventuror [was] is for his rate and proportion of his adventure a debtor for and towardes the whole Credite geaven to the voyage, Did therefore order and decree that a further supply of ijs the tt vppon every mans adventure shalbe brought in to the Thrers of this fellowship towardes the satysfaction of this debt depending vppon them [betwene] by the xth of this moneth And to thend the paymt thereof may be the better pformed It is agreed that as many of the brethren of this Company as shall faile in the bringinge in of ther moneis *at that day* [contrary this acte]. ether vppon the former supply of ijs the tt. wch by order of this Company was apointed and ordred to be brought in by a decree of a general Cort holden the 9. of Januarye *Last* or contrary to this present act for the further supplie of ijs the tt. more now presentlie decreed to be brought in shall forfeite *to the vse of the comon stocke* to be defalked out of his *privat* stocke bothe by the one decree and the other [in] wherein he shall [*be found to*] faile to make payment the severall somes of ijs vppon every tt of his adventure and it is alsoe ordered for the making good of this penaltie to the vse of the [Comon]

Gen^ralyty and the comon adventure that the Bookeap shall vppon the severall accoumptes of every adventuro^r that shall faile in the bringing in of ether of thes supplyes contrary to the trew meaning of both this and the former acte or ether of them defalte from the private stocke of every *suche* contributo^r the said penaltie of ij^s the ℔. soe forfeyted and make his stocke [credito^r] *lesse* by so muche as the said penaltie soe forfeited cometh vnto thend. that the same forfeitures [beinge] may be putt to the comon accoumpte of profit and losse [may goe to the advauncem^t of ther stockes wch have [brou] or shall [supply] bringe in ther supplyes. And it is also ordered that in the Billes of adventure that shalbe geaven out to every of them wch do not bring in their said supplies the valewe thereof shalbe defalked out of his said bill of adventure [and he holden credito^r for soe muche lesse as the penatie].

1601
1 Apr.

It is alsoe ordered that wher for the supply of necessarie paiment^s and provisions of the voyage before the going of the shippes out of the River Mr Aldⁿ Bannyng and m^r Aldⁿ Hollyday the thre^rs of this felowship did take vp at interest the somme of xv^{Cli} that the genalyty shall and will save the said thre^rs harmeles and stande chargeable for ther indempnitie both of the principall and the interest of the said somme of xv^{Cli}.

xv^c li. at interest by the Thers taken up to be discharged by the Company.

At this Co^rte the right honorable the Erle of Cumbland wrote his letter to the generalitie entreating them that he might assigne out of his stocke of adventure of xv^{Cli} the somme of 200^{li} to m^r Wm Beerblock goldsmithe and therwth that the Companie would admitt the said Mr Beerblocke not onlie an adventuro^r of so muche but to accepte *and admitt* him as a free brother of this Companie wch motion albeit both in the example [or] *and* president [it seemeth] and alsoe in the [admittaunce of 2 psons] admittaunce in to the freedome of the Companie of 2 psons vnder one adventure once entirely sett downe it may seeme *to be* and is prejudiciall *to order* yet at the request of so honorable a pson [they] *this Court* could not denye to yeld to the said motion and did agree both to the assignation of 200^{li} adventure to be sett over vnto him and to

Wm Beerblock admitted an adventuro^r of 200^{li} of the erle of Cumbland his stock of xv^c by way of assignation & also made free.

162   THE COURT RECORDS OF

<small>1601
1 Apr.</small>

admitt him also in to the previledges of the said Companie and he the said Mr Beareblocke did agree [to add] by way of increase of the said adventure of 200^{li} and for the supplies thereof according to the ordinaunces of this felowship to add therunto the somme of 50^{li} more and soe to stand an adventuro^r in principall and supplies of the some of 250^{li} wch is by the booke keap to be sett vppon the said m^r Beerblock and therwth 200^{li} to be taken from the Erle of Cumberland his adventure.

<small>1601
3 Apr.</small>

The 3. of Aprill 1601.

Mr Wm Rumey deputy   Mr John Highelord
Mr Rich: Wyseman   Mr Wm Harryson
Mr John Eldred   Mr Thomas Cordell
         Mr Rob̄t Sandy.

<small>M^r W^r
Megges
140^{li} for
rest of stock
& supplies.</small>

R Megges being warned before the Comitties for the bringing in of the rest of his adventure of 200^{li} and his severall supplies *havinge brought in* 100^{li} did insist a while vppon a discharg promised him by the bringing in of one Mr Clenche to sett down CC^{li} was not wthstanding overruled and in thend brought to assent to pay [in his CC^{li}] C^{li} for the rest of his adventure and to pay his supplies when others had p^d thers: or els he would procure a discharge to the Company for the valewe of C^{li} wch they are to pay to the Muskovia Company for cordage.

<small>1601
7 Apr.</small>

The 7. of Aprill 1601.

Mr Wm Rumey deputy   Mr Rob̄t Sandy
Mr Thomas Cordell   M^r Jo: Highlord
Mr Rich: Staper   Mr Niclas lyng
Mr John Eldred   Mr Wm Harryson.

<small>li s d
14. 7. 2
to Mr John
Highlord.</small>

RDER is geaven to Aldⁿ Bannyng to pay to Mr Highlord vppon a Bill of pcelles of moneis by him Laid out for the Companies vse the somme of xiiij^{li}. vij^s. iiij^d. [vppon present vse].

THE EAST INDIA COMPANY 163

The 9. of Aprill 1601.   1601
                                9 Apr.

Mr Wm Rumcy   Mr Rich : Wyseman
Mr Thomas Cordell   Mr Wm Harryson

RDER is geaven to m^r Ald^n Hollyday thrēr that   30^li Arnold
whereas he hath p^d to Arnold Mabanck Pullymaker   Mabanck
                                                   Pullymaker
for worke done to the shipps the somme of 30^li
w^thout Warraunt that he shall pay vnto him in full payment
of his whole whole worke done the somme of 24^li. 7^s. 9^d more
and take his acquittaunce for the whole 56. 7. 9.

The Like order is geaven to the said Thrēr to pay vnto   34^li 4^s 2^d
Xpofer Thomson *Smyth* the somme of 34^li. 4. 2 being rest of   Xpofer
                                                                Thompson
pcelles [of] amounting to 274. 4. 2. Whereof all the residue is   Smythe.
already *paid* as by a note of the accoumpte from the bookeap
appeareth So that this 34 4 2^li is in full paym^t.

Warraunt is geaven to Ald^n *Holliday* [Bannynge] thrēr to pay   16. 1. 8. Jo:
vnto M^r [Robt.] *Mr* [Thomas] John Hedland the somme of   Hedland for
                                                           Carriages.
sixten poundes one shillinges viij^d for making of cariages for y^e
shippes as appeareth by his bill of pticlers therof for wch he is
to take his acquittaunce in full paym^t, or to abate soe much
to Mr Thomas Symondc vppon his second supply because he
hath p^d the same 16. 1. 8. to ye said Jo : Hedland.

Warraunt is geaven to Ald^n Bannyng Thēr to pay vnto   12^li to Tho:
Thomas Duck for streamers by him served to the shippes in   Duck for
                                                            streamers.
full paiment thereof the somme of Twelve poundes.

Warraunt is geaven to Ald^n Holliday Thēr to pay vnto   100^li. 0. 0.
Lewys Tayte Smythe in part of paym^t of iron worke done for   to Lewis
                                                              Tayte
the shippes the somme of one hundred poundes.   Smythe.

Warraunt is geaven to m^r Ald^n Bannyng thēr to pay to   50^li to Edw:
Edward Stephens Shipwright for worke by him done vppon   Stephens
                                                         Shipwright.
the read Dragon the somme of fyftie poundes in part of
paiment.

Warraunt is geaven to Ald^n Holliday thēr to pay vnto M^r   100^li to
Thomas Barbor for Canvas for sailes the somme of one hun-   Tho: Barbor
                                                            for Canves.
dred poundes sterling in part of paiment of a mere somme.

Warraunt is geaven to Ald^n Bannyng thēr to pay vnto Adam   50^li to

1601
9 Apr.
Adam Wood
for deales &
mastes &c.
11ˡⁱ. o. o.
to Jo: Maxfield Brasier

Wood in part of paiment of deales mastes and timber served to the shippes the some of fyfty poundes sterlinǧ.

Warraunt is geaven to Aldⁿ Holliday thēr to pay vnto John Maxfield Brasyer for Copp vessellꝭ by him served to the shippes in full payment thereof the some of Eleven poundes sterling.

42. 15. 0
to Robt
Highoo for
Canves.

Warraunt is geaven to Aldⁿ Holliday thēr to pay vnto Robert Heighoo for 30 peecꝭ of Ipswᶜʰ Canves at 28ˢ. 6ᵈ the peece the somme of fowrtie two [pence] poundes xvˢ in full payment of the said Canves.

22ˡⁱ. 4ˢ. 0ᵈ
to fra:
Covell
Chaundeler.

Warraunt is geaven to Mʳ Aldⁿ Holliday to pay vnto fraunc꜡ Covell Chaundeleʳ for provision by him served to the shippes the somme of Twentie two poundꝭ fowre shillingꝭ in full paiment of the same provision.

1601
11 Apr.

A Genʳall Court holden the 11ᵗʰ of Aprill 1601.
Present

Mʳ Wᵐ Rumey deputy
Sʳ John Hart. knight
Mʳ Aldⁿ Wattes
Mʳ Rich : Staper
Mʳ Robt Sandy

Mʳ Nich : Lynge.
Mʳ Rich : Wyseman
Mʳ Wᵐ Harryson
Mʳ Wᵐ Garwey
Mʳ Jo : Eldred

Mʳ Jo : Highelord.
wᵗʰ the greatest pt of the genſalyty.

AT this Court was read an order from the LL of her Maᵉˢ most honorable privie Councell taking knowledge of the remissnes of the Companie in payinǧ ther debtes dewe by the voyage wᶜʰ importeth the honoʳ of the state being a publique action the tenoʳ of wᶜʰ acte doeth followe in thes Wordes.

At the Courte at Whitehall the xᵗʰ of Aprill 1601.
Present.

L : Archb : of Cant :
L : Keeper.
L : Treasurer.
L : Admirall.

Mʳ Comptroller
Mʳ Secr : Cecyll.
Sʳ John Fortescue
Mʳ Secr : Herberte

PON complaynte made this daye to their ll̃p̃ : by the Comyttyes of the Easte India Companie, that yᵉ debt℮ of the p̃ñte viage now by them sett forthe amountinge to Seaven Thowsande poundes above the contribuc̃ons sett downe by the adventureʳˢ are not paide, the same growinge by reason of the backewardenes and frowarde dispoṡic̃ons of dïṽse p̃sons that shewe themselves remisse and vnwillinge to furnyshe there promyssed contribuc̃ons and alsoe their porc̃ons of the supplyes wᶜʰ since at there generall meeting℮ at severall tymes have been agreed on to yeelde above there adventures a rate of fowre Shilling℮ in the pounde for the cleeringe of the saide debte, Their ll̃p̃: vppon due consideratĩon how muche yt ymporteth the honnor of the state, that so publique an acc̃on should not receive scandall or shamefull imputac̃on Have this daye ordered that forasmuche as the saide debt in all or in p̃te is proporc̃onablye due to be satysfied by everie contributoʳ of the viage That therefore the saide Companie and everie adventurer thereof shall wᵗʰout further delaye not only p̃forme and satysfie there full contribuc̃ons agreed vppon, promysed and sett downe vnder there handes, But alsoe there proporc̃onable supplyes accordinge to there agreemᵗˢ at there geñ'all Court℮, Or otherwyse yf any p̃son or p̃sons shall refuse to conforme themselves therevnto ; that then the Governoʳ deputye and comyttyes of the saide companye or any fower of them shall by vertue of this there ll̃p̃: order straightlye Injoyne and comande the saide p̃sons to make there ymediate appearance before their ll̃p̃: to the end there ll̃p̃: may proceed to yᵉ punyshinge of there contempte, by refusinge to accomplishe there one agreemᵗ and promyse, so muche importinge the publique, as their obstinacye and p̃versenes shall deserve, And to that end direction is geiven to a Messenger of her Maᵗⁱᵉˢ Chamber to attend the saide Governoʳ and Companie to bringe the saide p̃tye℮ before there ll̃p̃:

1601
11 Apr.
The long order for betterpaymt of the Companies debts dew by the voiadge. By bringing in Adventures and supplies.

     Concordat cum Registro.
       Tho : Edmondes.
Vppon the readinḡ of wᶜʰ act it was resolved that especiall

1601
11 Apr.

care and travell shuld be taken by the whole Company to free the viage from all imputation and discredit and y[t] the same might the better be effected forasmuche as M[r] Rumney the deputie of the Governo[r] to the Company is necessarielie for his health shortlie to take his iorney *to the Bathes* in whose absence the teno[r] of ther Lordships order cannot be executed vnlesse the present governo[r] of the Company were discharged of his imprisonm[t] and at Libertie to travell in the Companies occasions. Therfore for the better ordering of the affaires of this felowship and the gathering in of Contributions and supplies wherby ther debtes may be presentlie discharged w[ch] cannot endure the delay and expectation of M[r] Thoms Smythe the Late and present governo[r] his enlargem[t] This Assemblie did proceade to the Election of a nother Governo[r] to stande for the government of thaffaires of this felowship vntill the next day of election apointed by o[r] priviledges and divers being put in election for the supplying of the same place the said Election by Scruteny is fallen vppon M[r] Ald[n] Wattes who beinge present was placed in the office accordinglie.

At this Courte the generalytie did Noiate and chuse the psons heervnder named to be generall auditors of the Threīs Accoumptes and of all other the charges of the voyage to ioine wth the former Auditors apointed by the Comitties and vsed by them in the auditing of the said Threīs accoumptes and other the expences and disbursem[tes] of the voyage all W[ch] ioining together or anie six of them may audite the accoumptes of the state of the voyage and report the same to the generalyty when all the said accoumptes are disgested and agreed vppon.

Auditors

Auditors form[rly] apointed by y[e] Comitties.	Auditors apointed by the Gen[r]alyty.	
M[r] Thomas Cordell.	M[r] Rich: Bowdeler	
M[r] olyver Style	M[r] Jo: Harvy	
M[r] Rich: Wyseman	M[r] Greenewell.	Auditors.
M[r] W[m] Harryson	M[r] Tho Symondes	
	M[r] John fletcher	
	M[r] Nich: Leat	

After the rysinge of the generall Co͡rte warraunt was geaven by the Comitties to m͡r Ald͡n Holliday th͠er to pay vnto Joseph Page Baker for Biskett made and deliuered [by] to the shippes the somme of fourtie five poundꝯ [sterling͡] tenn shillinge xj͡d sterling in full paym͡t.

1601
11;Apr.
45^li.10.11^d
to Joseph
Page bak͡er

Lyke warraunt was geaven to Ald͡n Bannyng th͠er to pay vnto George Barbo͡r the somme of twentie seven poundes five shillingꝯ sterlinge [in full] for rest and in full paym͡t for [Pulleis] Sailes to the Susan having p͡d him xx^li before w^thout warraunt in part.

27. 5. 0
to Georg
Barbo for
sayles.

Another Warraunt to the said Ald͡n Bannyng th͠er to pay John Crane fower poundes Nyne shillingꝯ viij͡d. for rest and in full paym͡t for Pullies having p͡d him xvij^li before w^thout warraunt in part.

4. 9. 8. to
Jo: Crane
for Pullies.

The xx^th of Aprill 1601.

1601
20 Apr.

M͡r Ald͡n Wattꝯ Gouer :
M͡r Ald͡n Banninge ⎫
M͡rAld͡n Hollydaye ⎭ Th͠ers
M͡r Rich : Stapers.
M͡r w^m Garwaye.
      M͡r w^m Burrell.

M͡r Rich : wyseman.
M͡r John Hyghlorde.
M͡r Ro͠bte Sandye.
M͡r w^m Harryso͠n.
M͡r Nic͠lius Lynge

PON conference had wth the Th͠res there desire was to see the Accomptꝯ and an estemate to be made of the moneys in there hands to paye suche debtꝯ as farre as there moneys will extende.

Order was geiven to Ald͡n Hollydaye for payment of 200^li to Thomas Barber vppon an accompte of canvas dellivered to the shipps.

200^li to
Thomas
Barber for
Canvas.

The like order is geiven to the same Ald͡n to paye to William Hedger in full for buildinge of a pinnace for the Hecto͡r and di͠use other thingꝯ belongein to the rest of the shipps the some of sixe poundes.

6^li to
William
Hedger.

Order is geiven to *Ald͡n Hollidaye to paye to* Ro͠bte Huse saylemaker in full paym͡t of his Bill for makinge of sayles the some of fortye nyne poundes.

49^li to
Ro͠bteHuse
for sayles.

168   THE COURT RECORDS OF

1601
20 Apr.

49ˡⁱ to John Bowden for sayles.

42ˡⁱ. 5ˢ. 4ᵈ to Adam Wood Carpenter.

The like order is geiven to the same Aldⁿ to paye to John Bowden sayle maker the some of fortye poundes in full for sayles for the shipps.

Order is geiven to Aldⁿ Hollydaye to paye to Adam Wood Carpenter in full paymᵗ of his accompte the some of Fowrty & two poundℓ five shillingℓ fowre pence.

1601
22 Apr.

The 22ᵗʰ of Aprill 1601.

Mʳ Aldⁿ Wattes Goʳ   Mʳ John Highelord
Mʳ Aldⁿ Bannyng   Mʳ Nich: Lynge.
Mʳ Rich: Wyseman   Mʳ Rich: Wyche
Mʳ Roƀt Sandy.   Mʳ frauncys Chery
           Mʳ Roƀt Bell.

86. 15. 4 to Robt Bradbery Saylemaker

WARRAUNT is geaven to Aldⁿ Hollyday Thrĕr to pay vnto Roƀt Bradbury Sailemaker in full paiment of his billes for making of sailes for the dragon and the hectoʳ the somme of fowrscore and six poundℓ fyfteene shillingℓ and fowre pence.

42. 15. 0 to Robt Highhoe for Canuas.

Order is also geaven to Mʳ Aldⁿ Hollyday thrĕr to pay vnto Roƀt Highoe in full for Canvas he dd to the vse of the Assention as p bill the somme of fowrtie and two poundℓ fyfteene shillinges sterling [the same being paid]

46. 17. 0. to Mʳ George Bowles for Curraunce.

The like order is geaven to [the] Mʳ Aldⁿ Bannyng thĕr to pay vnto Mʳ George Bowles grocer in full payment for curraunce bought of him by Mʳ Roƀt Sandy for the vse of the shippes the somme of fowrtie and six poundes seventeene shillinges sterlingℓ.

27ˡⁱ — — to James Waters for iron.

The Like order is geaven to Mʳ Aldⁿ Hollyday thrĕr to pay vnto James Waters Iremonger in full paiment of his bill for iron Worke, deliuered to the vse of the shippes the somme of twentie and seven poundes   shillingℓ sterlingℓ.

13 0 0 to Hildebrand Sprusen saylemaker.

The like order is geaven to Mʳ Aldⁿ Hollyday thrĕr to pay vnto Mʳ Hildebrand Sprusen Sailemaker in full of his bill the somme of thirteene poundes sterlingℓ money.

The like order is given to Mʳ. Aldⁿ hollyday thr̃er to pay vnto Mʳ Peter Pett shipwright in full payment of his bill for worke and charges the somme of seventeene poundes [twelve shillingꝭ and six pence] sterlinꝫ money.

<small>1601 22 April. 17.[12.6] to Peter Pett shipwright.</small>

The like order is geaven to Mʳ Aldⁿ Bannynge thr̃er to pay vnto Wᵐ Denham shipwright in full payment of his bill the some of six poundes sterlinꝫ.

<small>6—0—0 to Wᵐ Denham shipwright</small>

The like order is geaven to Mʳ Aldⁿ Bannynꝫ thẽr to pay vnto James Marshe in full payment of his bill the somme of nyne poundes fyfteene shillinges sterlinge. for deales and planckes.

<small>9—15—0 to James Marshe for deales & plankes.</small>

The like order is geaven to Mʳ Aldⁿ Bannynge thr̃er to pay vnto Ffrauncis Covell in full paiment of his bill for provisions dd to yᵉ assention. the somme of twentie and two poundꝭ fowre shillingꝭ sterlinge.

<small>22—4—0 to francis Cobell Chaundeler for provysion.</small>

Warraunt is geaven to Mʳ Aldⁿ hollyday to pay vnto Mʳ Crosse vintenoʳ the somme of [x] fourteene poundes tenn shillingꝭ for a [Butt] Pyke of malliga Wyne geven to the L. Admirall in leiw of the deodand claimed for the hectoʳ.

<small>14—0—0 to Mʳ Crosse for sack geaven to yᵉ lː admirall.</small>

The Like warraunt is geaven to [yᵉ said] *Mʳ Aldⁿ Bannynge* to pay vnto ffrauncis Tailoʳ [Vintenoʳ] *Girdeler* for a Tun of Clarett wyne the somme of Eighteene poundes wᶜʰ wyne was geaven to the L. Admirall in Lieu of the deodand claimed for the hectoʳ.

<small>18—0—0 to</small>

It is ordered at this Assemblie that a Warraunt shalbe sent to the persons heervnder named that have hetherto denyed to bringe in ther Contributions, *subscribed* vnder the hand of the Governoʳ and 4. of the Comitties wᶜʰ warraunt shalbe shewed vnto them by a Pursevant to thend that vppon ther refusall to pay they may be carried before the LL: or els vppon ther assent to pay they may be appointed to come to Mʳ Governoʳ to geave ther Wordes to pay the same to the Thre̾r the tenoʳ of wᶜʰ warraunt doeth followe in these words videlt:

<small>A warraunt for the sõmoning of the Contributors denying to bring in ther Payments.</small>

Whereas yoᵘ the sefſall psons hervnder named have binne diuerse tymes required to bringe in yoʳ promysed Contribuc̃on towardes the settinge forthe of the Easte Indie viage and have not [done] yet done the same Wee doe eftesones require yõ to geive yoʳ

1601
22 April.

directe answer whether yō will bringe in to one of the Thřers of the Companie yor said contribuc̃ons or not (yf not) then accordinge to yor warrante of the LL. of her Maties privie counsell to vs in that behaulfe geiven Wee require yo^u to repaire to the Courte & yeald to there lordshipps a reason of yor refusall & yf yo^u will assent to paye yor contribuc̃ons then to repaire to me the Governo^r of the Companie & to geive yor word for the present paym^t of the same dated the 22th of Aprill 1601.

Richard Champion	Rob̃t Pennyton
Hughe Hamersley.	Ric Hearne
Wm Kellett	Wm Palme^r
Wm Barrett	Rob̃t Myldmay.
Bartl̃ew Haggett.	John Bates
Peter Helinge	Rob̃t Bowyer.

1601
27 April.

The 27. of Aprill 1601.

Mr Aldⁿ Wattes Go^r	Mr Wm Harryson
Mr. Alldⁿ Bannyng	Mr Rob̃t Bell
Mr Rich : Wyseman	Mr Nich: lynge
M^r Jo: Highelord	Mr Rob̃t Sandy
Mr Roger Howe	Mr Rich. Wyche
Mr Wm Chambers	M^r Jo: Combe.

Hughe
Hamsley

UGHE Hamersley being on of the persons that was convented before the LL : and by their honors comitted [vnto the chain] vntill he had geaven satisfaction to the Company to charg his Contribution sett downe. Did at this assembly appeare and praied the favo^r of the Company towardes him in respecte [whereof in thende] of wch submission and ptly vppon his owne offer to take vppon *him* to satysfie and discharge the Companie of the valewe of 240^{li} to any [the] to whom the Company were indebted This assembly did agree that yf he brought a discharge wthin thes 3 daies from the Agent of the Muskovia Company of the payment of 240^{li} wherby this Company may be discharged of so much for cordage owing them then he the said hughe hamersley shuld be admitted

THE EAST INDIA COMPANY 171

into the priviledge of this felowship and be discharged of his Cõmittement.   1601
27 April.

John Bate and Robert Bowyer [being] ther names having bene presented to the LL : as those that deny to bring in ther Contributions and supplies and ther LL : having geaven a warraunt for the Comitting of them yf they bringe not in the money before thursday next. Are required to geave ther aunsweres whether they will bringe in ther money accordingly or not who have severally taken tyme betwene this and thursday to advyse of that matter and to geave ther aunswer what they will doe.

The first of Maye 1601.   1601
1 May.
Mr Ald^n Wattes Go: Mr Eldred
Mr Rumney Depu :   Mr Sandy
Mr Stapers   Mr Highlorde.

 WARRAUNT is geiven to Ald^n Hollyday Thr̃er to paye to the kynge of Heraldes the some of Twentie merkes for assigninge a Armes to the Companie by the vertue of his office.   Twentye mkes to the kinge of Heraldes for assigning the companyes Armes.

The 8th of May 1601.   1601
8 May.
Mr Ald^n Wattes Go: Mr Ald^n Bannynge.
Mr Richard Wyseman   Mr John Highlorde
Mr John Eldred.   Mr Wm Harryson
           Mr Niclias Lynge.

RDER is geiven to Ald^n Bannynge to paye to Jeames Skelton in full for Tallowe deliûed to the vse of the shippes the some of nyne poundes Sterlinge.   9^{li} to James Skelton in full for Tallowe.

The like order is geiven to the same Ald^n to paye to Abraham Campion berebrewar the some of five hundred poundes vppon an accompte of bere deliûed to the shippes.   500^{li} to Abraham Campion Brewar.

The like order is geiven to Ald^n Hollydaye to paye to Roberte Savadge in full for wastẽ & deales One hundred & Two poundes sterlinge.   102^{li} to Roberte Sauadge for wastes & sayles.

172   THE COURT RECORDS OF

1601
8 May.
29ˡⁱ 1ˢ 4ᵈ
to Justice
Mallett
Smythe for
yron
worcke.
300ˡⁱ to
Thomas
Barbar
for canvas.
90ˡⁱ to
Elizabeth
Bennett in
full for
Nayles.
71ˡⁱ 15ˢ
to Nicholas
Symonson
carpenter
in full for
tymber.

The like order is geiven to the same Aldⁿ to *paie* Justice Mallett Smythe p the handℓ of Gyles ffleminge in full for yron worcke to the Dragon twentye nine poundℓ one shillinge fowre pence.

The like order is geiven to the same Aldeⁿ to paye to Thomas Barbar the some of Three hundred poundes stʳlinge vppon an accompte of canvas delivered to the Shippes.

The like order is geiven to the same Aldeⁿ to paie to Elizabeth Bennett in full for nayles &c deliũed to the Shipps as by her billes appeareth the some of ffowrscore & Tenn poundes stʳlinge.

The like order is geiven to Aldⁿ Bannynge to paye to Nicholas Symonson carpenter in full for tymber delivered to the Susann threescore & eleven poundes ffyfteene shillinges.

1601
15 May.

The 15 of May 1601.

Mʳ Aldⁿ Wattes Goʳ   Mʳ Wᵐ Harryson
Mʳ *Wᵐ Rumey Deputy*   Mʳ *Aldⁿ Bannyng*
Mʳ Rich: Wyseman   Mʳ Thomas Cordell
Mʳ Wᵐ Chambers   Mʳ John Highelord
Mʳ John Combe   Mʳ Roger Howe.

Accomptes
in the west
Cuntrey.

IT is ordered that mʳ howe and mʳ Combe shalbe warned to bring in ther accoumptes of the Reckoningℓ and disbursemtℓ of the west Cuntry to be audited at the next meeting of the Comitties to thende that those accoumptes being audited the Companie may proceade to the auditing and pfecting of the geñ'all Accoumptes.

3ˡⁱ 15 0
to Peter
Hilles
for Caske.

Order is geiven to Aldʳ Hollidaye to paie to Peter Hilles the some of three poundes fiftene shillinges in full for Caske deliũed to the Hector.

48ˡⁱ to
fraunces
Caudell
Painter

Order is geiven to the said Alderman holliday thrēr to pay vnto ffrancis Caudell Painter [for] in full of paintinge worke done by him vppon the Redd dragon the somme of fowrtie eight poundes sterling. vppon paiment Whereof his acquittaunce is to be taken in full paiment.

It is ordered by agreem{t} betwene thes Comitties and m{r} John Adye for a reckoning of tymber betwene the Companie and him that m{r} Wm Burrell for the Companie and James Marshe for him shall have the pvsing of the said accoumpte and loke what shalbe found to be dewe to him shalbe p{d} him by warraunt to be geaven to one of the threi̇́s.

1601 15 May. John Adye for Tymber.

Order is geaven to ye said m{r} Ald{r} hollyday thrĕr to pay vnto Wm Allom Lighterman for lighteradg of goodes sent *to* the shippes in full paym{t} the somme of tenn pound℈ sterlinge.

10{li} to Wm Allom for lightteradge.

The 22th of May 1601.

Mr Ald{n} Wattes Go{r}
Mr Ald{n} Hollyday
Mr Rich : Staper
Mr Olyuer Style

Mr John Highelord
M
Mr Roger Howe
Mr Jo Combe.

1601 22 May.

AT this meeting℈ m{r} Rogér howe and Mr Combe did exhibite to the Comitties present divers accoumptes and papers concerninge ther busines in the West Cuntrey w{ch} [the] are conteyned in 48 severall pticler Writinges [made] by way of Inventory noted vnder the handes of the said Comitties All wch writinges are deliuered over to the bookekeap to drawe in to ferme of accoumpte armed.

Mr Roger Howe. Mr Jo: Combe.

Geven a warrant vppon ald{r}man Bayning ffor paym{t} of ł 39. 16. 6 to Mr Richard wryte in ffull payment of his accŏpt ofcharge disburced ffor the vse of this voyadg as p the pticulers therein.

ł39. 16. 6{d}. to Mr Richard Wryte.

Two severall Warraunt℈ directed to the Pursevant that attendeth vppon the Companie for the warning of divers of the adventuro{rs} wch are behinde wth ther supplies to appeare before the LL : to aunswere ther Contempte.

Warrauntes for the Comitting of suche as deny ther suplies.

A warraunt geven vppon Ald{n} hollyday to pay to lewis Tate Black Smithe in full paiment of iron worke for the red dragon and Susan the soḿe of two [three] hundred [and] twentie and seven poundes sterling℈.

227{li} to Lewis Tate Blacke smithe.

Order is geaven to Ald{n} holliday to pay vnto Agnes Haselton to relieve her husband Richard haselton hurt in

xl{s} to Rich: Haselfoote.

1601
22 May.

the hecto^r in the Companies service the some of fowrtie shillinges.

29 10 0
to Charles
Anthony
for geaving
of stampes.

Order is geaven to Ald^r holliday thr̃ur to pay vnto Charles Anthonie her Ma^{es} Geaver for stampes made for the East Indie moneis the some of twentie nyne poundes x^s sterling.

1601
29 May.

A Gen^ral Court holden the 29th of May 1601.
Mr Aldⁿ Wattes gou^r   Mr Wm Chambers.
Mr Rich. Wyseman.   Mr Wm Harryson
         Mr Rich: Staper.

John Bate disfraunchesied.

WHEREAS ther hath bene some question betwene the Company and m^r John Bate touching the bringing in his contribution of 200^{li} by him sett downe wherin he hath wthstoode the Company for some dislyke he hath conceyved of the voyage and hath resolved not to be of the Company.

John Jackson made free.

And whereas m^r John Jackson clotheworker is content to supply all suche payment℈ as m^r Jo Bate shuld pay for his Contribution and supplies and to take the [place and] freedome of this felowship in the place of the said m^r Bate. Therfore this Court have agreed that the said m^r Bate shalbe disfraunchesied and from henceforth be holden an adventuro^r or brother of this Company and that m^r John Jackson shalbe admitted to the freedome of this felowship. whervppon the matter being put to question by erection of handes, the said Mr Bate is disfraunchesied and the said [John] m^r John Jackson admitted a free man to enioy all benyfites of freedome incident to this felowship as freely as yf he had bene nõiated in the Pattent.

W^m. Smythe

Whereas ther hath bene some question betwene the Comitties and m^r Wm Smyth touching his adventure by him sett downe wherin he pretendeth an agreem^t made wth him that for the paym^t of Cv^{li} [to be made to] *he shuld* stand an adventuro^r of C^{li} [he shuld] *and* be made free. wch agreem^t being denyed by the Comitties and the matter being referred by both ther Consent℈ to the generalyty at a general Court to be descyded   This Court being acquainted wth the question did fall into the delibation

THE EAST INDIA COMPANY

of the matter and in thende did resolve that they could not w^{th}out [any] *a geñall preiudice* to the Company by suche an example yeld to the desire of the said Smythe and therfore did resolve that the said m^r Smythe shuld be required to bring in the rest of his adventure and supplyes. 1601
29 May.

At this Court m^r hughe hamersley haberdasher is admytted into the freedome and Liberties of this felowship and hath satysfied 200^{li} for his adventure and xl^{li} for his Supplies according to former orders. Hugh Ham^rsleys admission

At this Court humfrey Milward haberśher who hath formerly denied to bring in his supplies doeth at this Court assent to bring in the same by the last of Julie next. humfrey Milward.

The 10th of June 1601. 1601 10 June.

Mr Ald^n Wattes. Go^r   Mr Rich : Wyche
Mr Ald^n Bannyng   Mr Nichãs lynge.
M^r staper   Mr Wm Harryson
M^r olyuer style   Mr Roger Howe.
Mr Rich : Wyseman   Mr John Highelord
M^r Jo : F.ldred   M^r [John] Robt Bell.
         Mr Robt Sandy.

AT this Court m^r frauncis Dent being desirous to set over his adventure and freedome vnto one George Bennet Salter doeth move the assent of the Comitties heervnto. But forasmuche as the name of M^r frauncis Dent is pticlerly expressed in the pattent thes Comitties cannot w^{th}out the consent of the geñ'alie disfraunchies the one and admitt the other in his place. therfore the said Comitties have referred both the said pties to the next generall Courte. fra: Dent Geo: Bennett.

It is ordered that the Secretorie shall make out Billes of adventure and supplies to everie adventuro^r and that the same be Delivered over to the two theïrs to deliver to the parties that haue Cleared ther adventures and supplies wth the said theïrs : and the threï shall receave for the vse of the Secretorie for everie bill of adventure [the] vj^d. Billes of Adventure.

176 THE COURT RECORDS OF

1601
23 June.

The 23 of June 1601.

Mr Ald^n Wattes gou^r M^r olyuer style.
Mr Wm Rumney deputy   Mr Rich: Wyseman
Mr Thomas Cordell   Mr John Highelord
              Mr Rich: staper.

Richard Taylby 73^{li}. 6, 8 assigned over to Mr Aty. 100^{li} assigned to the Moskvy Company of Rich: Taylbyes adventure. m^d that this bonde is the 21 Julie 1601. dd to Mr Stap to deliv over to the said agent.

RICHARD Tailby one of the adventuro^{rs} hathe promysed to pay vnto m^r Atye vppon Satherday next the somme of 73^{li}. 6. 8. for part of his adventure and supply by him vnp^d the wch some is assigned over to the said m^r Atye for money owing him by the Company.
  The said Richard Tailby is assigned over for C^{li} more of his adventure behinde to the Moskova Company to be p^d at micħas next by a bonde made to the Agent in the penaltie of CC^{ii}.

1601
4 July.

The 4th of July 1601.

Mr Gouernor   Mr Chambers   Mr Combe
Mr Deputye   Mr Highlorde   Mr Howe
Mr Ald^n Moore Mr Sandy   Mr Lynge.
M^r wiseman   Mr Harrisson

v^{li} to M^r ffletcher.

AT this Courte there was allowed to m^r ffecther v^{li} in consideraĉon of Rackinge of syder.
  Alsoe the rest of accompt of m^r Howe & m^r Combe beinge eyghtene poundes seven shillingẽ two pence is allowed them for there farther stay in the Countrey more then was expected.

1601
6 Julie.

A Gen^{r}all Court holden the 6. of Julie 1601.
Present.

Mr Ald^n Wattes Gou^r Mr Ald^n Bannyng ⎫
Mr Wm Rumney Deputy   Mr Ald^n Holliday ⎬ thrẽrs
Sr John spencer knight   Mr Tho Cordell   ⎭

Mʳ fra : Chery　　　　　　Mʳ Nich : lynge.　　　　1601
Mʳ Roger Howe　　　　　Mʳ Rich : Wyseman.　　6 Julie.
Mʳ Wᵐ Chamber.　　　　　Mʳ Jo Eldred.
　　　　　Mʳ Rich ; Staper.
　　wᵗʰ the greatest pt of the geñalitie.

T is ordered that all thes psons heervnder named　freemen
whose names are [heer] Left out of the pattent and
yet have pᵈ their adventures sett downe and ther supplies of 4ˢ the pound shall be admitted into the priviledges of
this felowship to enioy the same and all freedome thereof in as
Large and ample manner as yf they were Pattentees and [ther]
as yf ther names had bene conteyned in the pattent.

Richard Bowdeler　　　　Peter Helyn
Henry Butler　　　　　　Thomas Bramley
Tho Hayes　　　　　　　Thomas Ball　　　　Certen per-
Rich Humble　　　　　　Edmond Scott　　　sons made
　　　　　　　　　　　　　　　　　　　　free whose
Antho Moseley　　　　　　John Clenche　　　names are
John Westwray　　　　　　Jerom Davers　　　not in yᵉ
　　　　　　　　　　　　　　　　　　　　　Pattent.
Hughe Hamersley　　　　　xp̄ofer Nicholles
Wᵐ Kellett　　　　　　　　John Leaman
Wᵐ Albany　　　　　　　　Wᵐ Allyn mercer.

At this Court ffrauncis Dent on of the adventuroʳˢ of this　Georg
felowship whose name is conteyned in the Pattent did present　Bennett
to this Assemblie one George Bennett and praied that he might　in the place
be admitted in his place beinge willing to assigne vnto him both　of fraunces
his freedome and his adventure wᶜʰ is Two hundred and ffowrtie
poundes *in his* adventure sett downe and supplies wᶜʰ this Court
Assented vnto and in place of the said ffrauncis Dent have reᵈ
the said George Bennett and admitted him in to this ffreedome
as freelie as yf he had bene noiated in the Pattent.

It is moved by the auditors of the geñ̃all [Court] Accoumptes　The Erle of
of the Company that whereas the Erle of Cumberland hath as-　Cumber-
signed vᶜˡⁱ *lxxˡⁱ* of his adventure to mʳ Aldⁿ Bannyng wᶜʰ doeth *owe*　plies.
supplies at the rate of 4ˢ the ℔. that some order may be taken
therin that ether the same may be aunswered by the one or the
other Whervppon mʳ Aldⁿ Bannyng doeth consent voluntaryly

A A

1601
6 Julie.

that yf the said Erle be moved for the said Supplies and do not assent to pay it and charge it vppon m^r Aldⁿ willing him to pay it that then he will aunswer the same otherwyse he thinketh he can not be iustlie charged wth thes supplies nether did the Court at this tyme resolve to charge him vntill the said Erle hath bene moved herein.

that the supplies & adventures may be called for & psecuted

It is ordered that all suche of the brethren of the Companie as are behinde wth ther adventures or supplies shalbe prosecuted wth all expedition by Complaint vnto the LL : to thende that the voyage may be cleared of all debte and imputation.

Certen of the Pattentees disfrainchesed

Sr Edw: Michelborn Robt: Towerson Georg Vtley

At this court accordinge to the condicion or proviso in the Pattent of the Companies priviledges for suche as are noiated in the Pattent and do not bringe in ther adventures sett downe thes severall psons videlt . Sr Edward Michelborne Robt Towerson and George Vtley whose names are conteyned in the said Pattent and have not brought in ther somes of money by them sett downe for ther severall adventures. are by the geñall Consent of this Assemblie disfraunchesied out of the ffreedome and priviledges of this felowship and vtterlie disabled from takinge anie benifite or proffit therby.

        Sr Edward Michelborne   ⎫
        Robert Towerson   ⎬ disfraunchesed.
        George Vtley.   ⎭

The Election of the Governo^r Deputy & Comitties of the Company.

The priviledges of this felowship appointing the Eleccõn of the governo^r Deputie & comitties of this [ffelowship] Companie vppon the first day of Julie or wthin six daies followinge This Court proceaded to the Eleccõn of the said severall officers and by scruteny and geñall consent did make choice of thes severall psons to the severall offices following and havinge chosen them did before they were severally placed and admitted to ther severall places minister vnto them respectively the severall othes ordeyned and agreed vppon by [the] this geñall assembly and [herein] at this Court inregestred to stand for [a] standing thes to be ministred [hereafter] to the governo^r his deputie and Comitties hereafter from tyme to tyme to be chosen for the governing of the affaires of this felowship.

THE EAST INDIA COMPANY

Mr John Wattes Aldeman Elected governo^r for to governe y^e affaires of the Companie for one whole yere.
Mr William Rumney Elected Deputie Governo^r to governe the affaires of the Companie for one whole yere.

1601
6 Julie.
Governo^r
Deputy
gove^r.

Comitties
Sr John spencer knight
Mr Ald^n Bannyng Ju$\tilde{r}$
Mr Ald^n Hollyday
Mr Ald^n Cambell
Mr Richard Staper. Ju$\tilde{r}$
Mr Thomas Cordell Ju$\tilde{r}$
Mr Wm Garway
Mr Rich: Wyseman Ju$\tilde{r}$
Mr John Harby Ju$\tilde{r}$
Mr John Newman
Mr Thomas Symondes
Mr Thomas Allabaster.

Comitties
Mr Roger Howe Ju$\tilde{r}$
Mr Wm Chamber Ju$\tilde{r}$
Mr John Eldred J
Mr Rich : Wyche
Mr John Highelord
Mr Wm Harryson Ju$\tilde{r}$
Mr Nich: lynge Ju$\tilde{r}$
M^r W^m freeman Ju$\tilde{r}$
Mr Nich: leat Ju$\tilde{r}$
Mr Nich: Salter
Mr Thomas farrington Ju$\tilde{r}$
Mr Wm Greenwell.

Comitties

The oathe of the Governo^r of the Companie
and of his Deputie.

Yo^u shall swere that yo^u shalbe trewe Liegeman to o^r Soveraigne Ladie the Queenes Ma^{ie} and to her heires & successors Kinges & Queenes of Engiand and yo^u shalbe faithefull and trewe to the fellowship or Companie of the merchaunt^s of London tradinge into the East Indies and to their successors, the good state of the said Companie yo^u shall favou^r & affecte and ye priviledge of ye same to yo^u power endevo^r to maintayne & preserve. yo^u shalbe carefull to see & provide y^t an equall and indyfferent hand be car̃yed in the Goverm^t of this fellowshipp and in the affayres thereof to all the adventurers that shall adventure or putt in stocke in anie of the voiages sett owte or to be sett owte. by this fellowshipp that wthowte favo^r affection or partialitye all chardges may indyfferently be rated and all paym^{tes} groweinge to the adventure^{rs} maie indifferently be answered soe farre as yor knowledge in the state of the affaires of this fellowshipp may directe yo^u or the aucthoritie of yor place may conveniently beare yo^u soe helpe yo^u god.

180   THE COURT RECORDS OF

1601
6 Julie.

The oathe of Comitties for direction of the trade.

Yo^u shall swere that yo^u shallbe trewe Liedgmen to o^r Soveraigne Ladie the Queenes Ma^{ie} and to her heires and Successors King℮ and Queenes of Englande And yo^u shalbe faithfull and trewe to the Governo^r & Companie of m̃chaunt℮ of London tradinge into the Easte Indies and to their successors yo^u shall wth yor best advise and Councell assiste m^r Governo^r of this fellowship and his deputie from tyme to tyme in the affayres of this Companye that an equall and indyfferent hand be carried in the Goverm^t of this fellowshipp and in the busines thereof yo^u shall deale faithfully and equally in the orderinge & disposinge of the adventures stocke trade & merchandize of this fellowshipp Comitted to yor direction or truste in all voiadges wherein yo^u shalbe ymployed as a Comittie. and that wthowte favo^r or affection to anie man haveinge no singler respecte to yor self to the preiudice of the said fellowshipp or anie the said adventurers thereof, yo^u *shall* indifferently *to* knowledge rate & apportion all chardges & burthens of this fellowshipp according to the proporc̃on of e℘ye mans stocke or adventure & yo^u shall alsoe order & appointe wth like indifferency and ,pportion to yor best Skyll & knowledge all payment℮ groweinge dewe to the said adventurers vppon their stockes or adventures So helpe yo^u God.

1601
20 Julye.

The xxth of Julye 1601.

Mr Aldⁿ Wattes Go^r :   Mr Nicĥas Lynge
Mr Wm Rumney Dep :   M^r w^m freman
Mr Ricĥ : Staper   M^r w^m Grenewell
Mr Ric : Wyseman   M^r w^m Harison
M^r Jo : Highlorde   Mr Thomas farrington.
Mr Nicĥas Leate   Mr Thomas Symondes.

Wm Brett
16.16.11^d
for timber.

RDER is geiven to Aldⁿ Bannynge Thr̃er to paye vnto William Brett in full for timber & other ,pvisiones delivered to the Assention the some of sixtene pound℮ sixtene shilling℮ and eleven pence as p̃ bill of pticlers may appeare.

THE EAST INDIA COMPANY

It is ordered at this assemblie that ther shalbe allowed to m^r Wm Burrell. for his paines takeñ in the provisioñ of timber for the shipping of the voyage and for the Surveying of the worke of the same shippes the someñ of xv^{li}.

<small>1601 20 Julye. 15^{li}. o^s. o^d to Mr Wm Burrell for his travell about ye shippes.</small>

Whereas Mr John Ellicot of Exceto^r beinge an adventero^r of CC^{li} doeth owe 20^{li} for his supplies and being imployed by the Company to provide Spanishe Ryalles in the West Cuntrey hath geaven in a geñall accoumpte to ye Company of all his provision wherby he resteth debto^r to the voyage 32 11 8. It is ordered that a l^re shall be written vnto him [for the] from the geñalyty to sende vp his supply and a more pticler accoumpt of his imployments that this Reckoning may be cleared.

<small>Johñ Ellycott of Exceto^r.</small>

❧

Gen^rall Court.   The 24 of Julie 1601.

<small>1601 24 Julie.</small>

Mr Aldⁿ Wattes Go^r   Mr Tho Farrington
Mr Aldⁿ Cambell   Mr Wm Harryson
Mr Rumñey dep.   Mr Nich : Leete
Mr Rich : Staper   Sr *John Spenser*
Mr Tho Cordell   M^r W^m freeman
Mr Roger Howe   Mr Nich : Lynge
Mr Wm Grenewell   Mr Rich Wyche

wth the most part of the geñalyty.

AT this Co^rte one Mr Robt Bayly one that hath sett downe his adventure of CC^{li} and p^{tle} the same to [the] this felowship. and being vnwilling to [supply] bring in any supplie is wylling to assigne over his said CC^{li} and to relinquishe his fredome [vnto Sr John Spencer knight] surrendring vp the sum [to] in to the handes of this Sosciety Wheruppon Sr John Spenser [was] being present in Court doeth vndertake to accepte of his said adventure and offreth him Ciiij^{xxli} for the same wch m^r Bayly [doe] is content to accepte. and doeth in open Court Renownce his fredome and theruppon this Court doth accepte his surrender. and doe assent and agree that Sr John Spencer shall have the nōiatīon of a freeman to be

<small>Robt Bayly.</small>

<small>S^r Jo Spenser.</small>

1601
24 Julie.

made free of this felowship and to enioy the priviledg℮ thereof in as ample manner as anie *other* brother of this felowship Soe as the said Sr John Spencer do bring in to one of the the^rs: of this Company the some of xl^{li} for the supplies wch the said Mr Baylie was to pay/ The wch the said Sr John doeth presentlie promyse and vndertake to pay.

discovery of the north west passage to ye East Indies.

At this Court motion is made to the gen̄alyty by occasion of a l̃re written by one George Waymoth a navigato^r touching his attempte to be made for the discovery of the north west passage to the Est Indies whether the gen̄alyty be willing℮ to vndertake the said discovery and to supply the provision of 2 or 3 pinaces fytt for suche an enterprise yea or [noe]. And yf not vppon the gen̄all charge then whether the gen̄alyty wilbe content that private men shall deale therein. geaving them the benefite of the said discovery [yf they finde yt] *by the sole trade thereof* for certein yeres [and sole trade therof] wthout impechem^t *yf they discover the passage*. But this matter requiring further deliberation then [present] this present assembly can stand vppon It is agreed that the [matter] *resolution hereof* shalbe respited vntill the next gen̄all Court and then to be further considered vppon and in the meane tyme to be disgested by every pticler man howe he can enclyne him self to the enterprise And it is also moved that this gen̄all assembly would be thinke them selfes of anewe supply of shipping℮ to seconde the former shippes sent out to the Est Indies *by the cape of Bona Speransa* wth a Convenient adventure to be [sent] provided for this yeres voyage whether it be the half [of] or a thirde part of the valewe of the last adventure . and lyke order was taken therin as in the former motion that eche man do advyse him self herein betwene this and the next gen̄all Court.

1601
7 Aug.

A generall Court holden the 7th of August 1601.

Mr Aldⁿ Watts governo^r   Mr Wiseman
Mr William Rumny Dep℮   Mr Highlorde
Mr Thomas Cordell   Mr Howe.
Mr Richard Stapers   Mr Greenewell

THE EAST INDIA COMPANY

Mr Leate Mr Linge
Mr Harrison M^r farringeton
wth the most pte of ye geñality.

1601
7 Aug.

UESTION beinge made for the findinge out of the Northwest passage whether itt shalbe a vyage to seeke itt, or not. beinge put to handes it was consented vnto for a vyage.

Norwest passage.

And beinge put to the question whether the mony shouldbe levyed by the powle or by the pound it was by erectinge of hands ordered that the mony should bee levyed by the pound accordinge to ye first adventures sett downe in the booke for ye first East India vyage wthout supplie *none* to bee enforced, but every man to adventure y^t will, and to allowe xii^d the lⁱ. And all those that doe not subscribe his name to his Adventure [betwene this and   ] shalbe exempted from this trade of the north-west. And every man to bringe in thone haulfe by Michellmas & the rest by Christmas next.

These psones vndernamed are appointed Comittees to sett downe the chardge of this vyage for 3 pinyces & to make report vnto the next Court.

   Comitties for ye Northwest passage
  Mr Governor   Mr Stapers
  Mr Deputy   Mr Greenewell
  Mr Cordall   Mr Howe
     Mr Wiseman.

All this aforesaid notwthstandinge it was in the end concluded that Mr Governor should [prvse our] *pvse y^e* Charters betwene this and the next Court to see whether [wee] have authority to compell any of the Company to paye his mony towards this vyage or the next vyage by the straights of [Magelano] *Bona Speransa*.

   The first of [August] *September* 1601.
Mr Aldⁿ Wattes go^r Mr Thomas Cordell
Mr Wm Rumey dep. Mr Wm Greenewell
Mr Rich: Staper. Mr Tho : farrington
Mr Rich: Wyseman. Mr Georg Waymouthe
M^r Adⁿ Bunnyng. Mr Highelord.

1601
1 Sept.

1601
1 Sept.
North west passage.

HE said Comittees being met in conference wth Capten Waimouth for the necessarie preparation of shipping for the Northwest passage doe resolue that 2. Pinnaces wilbe sufficient shipping for the same discoverie the one of 50 and the other of 40 tuns. To be manned wth 30 men videlt the one wth 16 the other wth 14 men. The charge of all wch by estimation will amount to the valewe of 3000^{li} or therabout₵.

Georg Waymouth.

These Comitties haveing conferred wth the said m^r waymouth touching his enterteynment in the said voyage [It is] *he is* agreed wthall to goe for the some of one hundred pound₵ to be deliuered him to prepare his instruments and other necessaries: and yf he discover the passage then vppon his retorne to share by way of Contracte for this discovery the some of v^{cli} [more] referring him self to the favo^r of the Companie for suche further gratification as they shall thinke he deserveth wth this that yf he retorne and do not pforme the discovery he will aske nothing for his paines and travell.

George Waymouth.

1601
2 Sept.

A Gen^rall Courte the 2 of September 1601.
Present.

Mr Aldⁿ Wattes gouer^r   Mr Nich: lynge
Mr Wm Rumney dep: Mr Wm Garway
Mr Tho: Cordell   Mr John Highelorde
Mr Rich: Staper   Mr Tho farrington
Mr Rich: Wyseman   Mr Wm Grenewell.

wth the greatest part of the gen̅alyty.

16^{li}, 10^s, 0 to Symon furno^r for Gunpowder.

ARRAUNT is geaven to m^r Ald^r Bannynge to pay vnto Symon Furno^r vppon a rest of accoumpte for powder by him deliu̅ed to the shippes in full Clearing of all Reckoninges the some of sixtene poundes tenn shilling₵.

The Northe west passage.

At this Court the Comitties appointed at the last generall Courte made report of ther conference wth Captein Waymouth

THE EAST INDIA COMPANY

touching the Discoverie of the Northwest Passage and of ther   1601
opinions of the Charge of the preparation of 2 pinaces w^ch   2 Sept.
they thinke will come to the Charge of three thowsand poundes
as appeared by the pticlers of the same estimated by the said
Comitties and read to the generalitie W^ch being conceaved by
the generalyty they did well allowe thereof and did agree
that the said pinaces and all preparation and furniture therto
belonging shalbe taken in hand and a booke sent abroade to
the adventure^rs to sett downe ther somes vnder ther handes
at the rate of xij^d the pound according to the agreem^t of the
last generall Court.

At this Courte Nathaniell Martin on that had sett downe   Nath:
for his adventure the some of two hundred poundes and never   Martin. John Mo-
brought in the same but desired that a nother should take his   rice made
place was by erecting of handes dyscharged and dismyssed of   free.
the freedome of this fellowship. And in his place Mr John
Morice Clotheworker was receaved and by erection of handes
admitted vnto the said freedome in as large and beneficyall manñ
as any other freeman of the Company.

A Geñ'all Courte holden the 13 of September 1601.   1601
               Present.   13 Sept.
Mr Ald^n Wattes gouerno^r   M^r Jo: Highelord
Mr Wm Rumney deputy   Mr Wm Greenewell
Mr Rich: Staper   Mr Wm Harryson
Mr Rich Wyseman   Mr Nich: lynge
   wth the greatest part of ye geñalyty.

WHEREAS ther is some question made or doubte
conceaved that the Muskovia Companie may by   Moskovia
vertue of ther previledges claime the interest of   Company
the North west passage. the wch this Companie
are in hand to discover. the wch yf it shuld be discovered at
the charge of this soscyetie may be [claymed] *stode vppon* by
the said [Courte] Companie of Moskovia merchaunt^s by ther
priorytie of graunt for the clearing of wch doubte it is thought

B B

1601
13 Sept.

convenient that certen psons of this felowship shall conferre wth the governo^r and others principall merchaunt^s of the said Companie to knowe whether they will pmitt this felowship to enter into the discoverie of the said passage and wholie relinquishe all Claime of previledg therunto duringe the Contynuance of the pattent graunted vnto vs And to that ende [it is resolved by this Courte that] the psons herevnder named are apointed to require the [Consent] answer and Consent of the said Muskovia Companie in this behaulf and thereof to make report to the Generalytie at the next generall Court.

  Mr Gouerno^r   M^r ferro^r
  Mr Deputy   M^r [w] Grenewell
  Mr Wyseman   Mr Harryson
    Or anie 4 of them.

A seconde voyage by the Cape of bona esperanza.

And it is agreed by the geñall consent of this Court that ther shalbe presently sett out a seconde voyag^e to the East Indies by the Cape of bona speranca and [to that end] all expedition to be vsed to see what will be contributed to [that end] furnishe the same. to wch end a booke is to be prepared for the adventur^rs to sett downe their sommes of adventure vnder their handes to see howe the Contribuc̃on will arise But it is resolved by the generall Consent of this Co^rte that none shalbe received to adventure vnder the valew of one hundred poundes sterlinge but as muche above that valewe as anie man shalbe pleased to adventure and it is further agreed that none shalbe vrged to beare or bringe in anie further supply above his adventure sett downe.

⛊

1601
14 Sept.

xiiij September 1601.

  Mr Ald^n Watts go^r   M^r Jo: Highlord
  Mr Wm Rumney dep :   Mr Wm Grenewell
  Mr Ald : Holliday   Mr Wm Harrison
  Mr Wm Garway   Mr Nic͠has Linge
    M^r W^m freeman.

THE EAST INDIA COMPANY

AT this Co᷂te assemblyd the Comitties abovenamed did agree vppon a title or preface to the booke of Contribuc͠on to be sent abroad wch beinge sett downe some of them bargaine to sett downe vnder their handes their owne voluntary Contribuc͠ons and havinge so donne deliverd the Booke to the officer to be Carried to All the severall freemen of this fellowship to sett downe their severall adventures in this second voyage.

1601
14 Sept.

A Booke of
the adven-
tures in y^e
seconde
voyage.

A Generall Court holden the xiij^{th} of October 1601.
Present.

1601
13 Oct.

Mr Ald: Wattes Go^r: M^r W^m grenewell
Mr Wm Rumney dep: Mr Wm Harrison
S^r Jo: Spencer knight Mr Thomas Cordell
Mr Richard Staper Mr Tho: farrington
Mr Nic͠has Leet
wth the greatest part of the Gene^ralitie.

RDER is geaven to Mr Ald^rman Bañinge Thr̃er to pay vnto Beniamyn Decro Agent of the Muskovia Companie for the full rest of Cordage bought of the same Companie and in full payment of all debt͠s owinge to the same Companie the som̃e of fifty seven poundes sixteene shilling͠s and eight pence.

li s d.
57 16. 8.
to ye Mos-
kovia Com-
pany for y^e
restCordage

At this Co^rte Sr John Spencer Knight accordinge to the lib͠tie geaven vnto him at a generall Co^rte the 24th of July last. for the makinge of a ffreeman whensoever he shall present him *to* [of] this societye dothe in ꝑformaunce of the said Lib^rtie geaven him present vnto this Court one Joseph Jackson Clothewo^rker to receave the said freedome vppon whose presentm^t this Courte do accept him into the freedome of this fellowshipp to enioy the same in as ample [manner] and beneficiall manner as any other brother of this Companie doeth or ought to enioy the said ffreedome.

Joseph
Jackson's
admission.

At this Co te Mr Deputie doeth make reporte to this assemblie that accordinge to the order geaven at the Last generall

1601
13 Oct.

Touching the Northwest passage.

Courte touchinge the Northwest passage to move the Muscovia Companie to relinquishe their Claime into the said passage for the tearme of xv yeares to the end this Company may proceade therein. he the saide m^r Deputie accompanied wth m^r Grenwell did since the said Last Courte reporte to the Governo^r and divers of the said Muskouia Companie assembled togeather and propounded vnto *them* the moc̃on of this fellowshipp touchinge the said passage who gave them this aunswer that they havinge an inheritaunce in the same [said passage] would not by any meanes relinquishe their owne interest therein. for any tearme but yf this Companie would be willinge to joyne wth them in the discoverye of the said passage they would receive as manie of this Companie as will venture wth them and geave them the freedome of the said passage and all plac$\wp$ discovered therby in ppetuity wch aunswer beinge Considered of at this Court It is supposed that vnder this offer the Muskovia Companie may be at libertie to venture what they list, and so will supply them selves litle or nothinge and the whole or the greatest pte of the adventure will lye vppon this Companie and the discoverye beinge made at their Charge a trade shalbe putt into the other Companies handes for litle or nothinge disboursed or adventured by them for avoidinge of wch doubt It was propounded to the generalitie whether they would be willinge to adventure wth the Muskovia Companie suche sommes as they had already sett downe yf the Muskovia Companie wilbe Content to seclude *for the terme of xv yeres* all suche of ther owne felowship as will not joine in adventure wth the brethren of this Companie in the discoverie or findinge out of the said passage. Whervnto this Companie do agree and vppon that condition do yelde that all suche som̃es of money as they have already sett downe towardes the furnishing of the voyage for the said Northwest shall be ioyned wth the adventurors of the Muskovia Companie that will proceade together wth them in the said voyage and do require that the booke may be carried abroade amongest the residewe of the Companie that have not yet sett downe ther contributions . And it is ordered that the meane While m^r Deputie and the residewe of the Comitties appointed at the last generall Court shall repaire to ye Govern^{or} and Companie of the Muskovia merchaunt^s at ther generall Court to conferre wth them and to agree that ther shall noe more of that Companie claime the benyfyte of the freedome of the said passage yf it be discovered duringe the terme of xv yeres. then suche as shall ioine wth this Companie in the contribution And that all suche of this felowship as shall adventure in the said voyage the some of x^{li} shall have the freedome of the said discovery to them and ther posteritie vnder the Comõ seale of the said Muskovia Companie for ever.

1601
13 Oct.

This Companie havinge alsoe heretofore resolved to sett out a seconde supply to the East Indies [of one] by the cape of bona Esperansa, and the booke having bene carried abroade amongest the breethren of this Companie to sett downe the Contributions it appeareth that the Whole adventure already sett downe doeth not exceade the valewe of Eleven thowsand poundes. wch carrieth noe convenient proportion to sett out any voyage at all. And it *is* Notyfied to this Co^{rt} by Mr Govern^{or} that he beinge of late wth my L Admirall and Mr Secretary at the Court they enquired of him what was the cause that the Companie were so slacke in secondinge ther former voyage consideringe that the Duche nation had soe honorably gone throughe wth ther voyage and retorned againe wth soe good successe notinge vnto them that this Companie were not soe respective of her ma^{es} hono^r and the hono^r of ther owne Cuntrey as were fytt they shuld be. Wherevppon it was aunswered by some of the Companie that one especiall hinderaunce of the [slacke] proceadinge of this voyage is that it is doubted that for some private respectes the Comitties may be drawen in the preparation of the shippinge for the voyage [to fall in to] to preferre suche shippes as shall not be so serviceable as were convenient. Ffor the avoidinge of wch inconvenience. and to geave furtheraunce to the speady preparation of the voyage It is ordered that Noe ship shalbe prepared or enterteyned for the said voyage vntill the name of suche ship be notyfied to the generalitie at a generall Court and the gen^rall consent of the Companie geaven to certen Comitties to contract for [the] everie or

A seconde suply to ye East Indies.

1601
13 Oct.

anie suche ship soe p̃sented and offered to ther considerations. And it is also ordered that the booke shalbe carried abroade to the breetheren of this felowship by some men apointed that shalbe able to pswade and encorage them to proceade in the said adventure.

xpofer Cletherowe made free.

At this Court xp̃ofer Cletherow was admitted into the freedome of this ffelowship in the place of Rob̃t Bowyer supplyinḡ in his default. the som̃e of Two hundred and ffourtie poundes. wch he had sett downe in the booke of adventures. And for that the said Rob̃t Bowyer did not bring in his money according to the pattent and the ordenaunces of the Companie. he the said Rob̃t Bowyer is [disfranchesed] *excluded* and the said xp̃ofer Clethero admitted in to the said freedome in as large and ample manner as any brother of this felowship and holden a Contributo^r of the som̃e of CC and Fourtie poundes in Principall and supply.

Robt Bowyerdisfraunchised or excluded.

1601
5 Nov.

A Gen^rall Courte *the 5 of November* 1601.
Present

Mr Ald^n Wattes Govr   Mr Rich: Stapers
Mr Wm Rumney dep.   Mr Tho: farrington
Mr Ald^n Cambell   Mr Wm Grenewell
Mr Wm Carway   Mr Nich: lynge
Mr Nich: leete
And the greatest part of the geñalyty.

The North west Passage.

T this Court m^r Deputie maketh report [to this Court] that since ther last geñall assemblie the muskovia Companie have mett together aboute the motion. [to enter into] *of* the discovery of the Northwest passage and do finde that the said Companie seme to have no liking to Joine wth this Companie in the said discoverie. but rather will deale in the same them selves. yet they assigne noe tyme for the doing thereof nor for anie thinge that appeareth doe goe aboute to deale therin wth anie expedition. Whervppon this Companie thinking *it* not fitt that [suche] an enterprise of suche importaunce shuld be staked doe resolve to vrge the expedition of the same voyage (beinge of soe great a consequence to the Comon wealthe) [and therefore do resolve] ether to be pformed by that Companie or *by* this Companie And to that ende this Companie do entreat the psons herevnder named as Comitties for this felowship to offer Conference wth sixe of the Muskovia Company to enter into [the] a Course howe this passage may be proceaded in. and yf it shall appeare vppon the conference that the Muskovia Companie will vndertake this discoverie them selfes and enter into it to leave them to ther proceadinge therin yf otherwyse to prove them whether they will ioyne wth this felowship according to the former conditions ppounded and yf they will do nether then that a relation may be made to the LL. of her ma^{es} most honorable privy [the] Councell of ther refusall and ther hinderingof this company in the said discovery entended by them. And to thende the cause may not receave any delay that the muskovia Company may be required to geave ther directe aunswer *in writing* to this motion propounded.

1601
5 Nov.

Comitties.

Mr Governo^r Mr Cordell
Mr Deputy Mr Grenewell
Mr Ald^n Cambell Mr Bell
M^r olyver style Mr Nich: leat.

At this Co^{r}te was rec͠ed a l͠re from the LLp of the Councell notyfyingp her Ma^{es} mislike of the slacknes of the Companie in the secondinge of ther former viage to the East Indies by the Cape of Bona Speransa propoundinge vnto them thexample of the duche who doe prosecute ther viages wth a more honorable resolution But forasmuche as the Assemblie at this Court was not soe ample as the importaunce of the matter requireth it was thought fitt another Court shuld be called vppon Munday in the after noone to consider more deliberatly vppon ther honors l͠res and the same co^{r}t to be warned vppon a paine of xx^s vppon everie one that maketh default.

The Councelles lre for ye seconding of the first voyag to the East Indies.

192   THE COURT RECORDS OF

1601
9 Nov.

A Genʳall Court [1601] holden the 9 of November 1601.
Present.

Mʳ Aldⁿ Wattes goʳ   Mʳ Jo: Highelord
Mʳ Aldⁿ Hollyday   Mʳ Roger Howe
Mʳ Aldⁿ Cambell   Mʳ Rich: Wiche
Mʳ Tho. Cordell   Mʳ Nich: leate
Mʳ Rich: Stapers   Mʳ John Eldred
Mʳ Rich: Wyseman   Mʳ Wᵐ Harryson
            Mʳ Wᵐ freeman.
Wᵗʰ the greater nomber of the genʳalyty.

The Northe west passage.

T this Court the Northwest passage being againe brought in question vppon occasion of some speeche had wᵗʰ some of the muskovia Company since the last Court   And vppon some occasion of better opinion conceaved of the strengeth of oʳ owne previledgℯ then formly wee had touching oʳ interest in the same previledgℯ   It is resolved by this Geñʳall Court that the same vyage shalbe attempted and those [that] of the Companie that have not already written be solicited to wryte to thende the contribution may be made full. and yf anie of the Companie will deny to [for] adventure in this discovery according to the former ordinaunces that they shalbe secluded from anie benyfite of trade by the said passage, during the terme of the pattent of the previledgℯ. and the trade to be wholie in them that do adventure in the same   And it *is* further ordered that yf the said passage be discovered that then *the* trade made that way shalbe carried and handled from tyme to tyme during the [previledges] *contynuaunce of oʳ pattent* in a proportionall sorte. videlt according to yᵉ proportion of every mans adventure . to thende that every adventuroʳ may have that advancemᵗ or previledg of *his* adventure in every viage according to the rate or quantety of his [adventure] *stocke ventured* in this viage of dyscovery and not otherwise.

Clement Moseley his stocke assigned to

Whereas Clement Moseley Citizen and mercer of loⁿ one of the adventurors of this felowship is nowe deceased. havinge adventured in this first voyage sett out by the Companie by

THE EAST INDIA COMPANY. 193

the cape of bona speransa the some of 220^{li} in stocke and suply. did in his lief tyme assigne over the one moytie of his said adventure vnto Edmund Helmes of Burford in the Countie of oxon gent. in consideration of the some of one hundred poundes [by] him owing[by] *to* the said Edmund as by the said assignement shewed forthe and testified vnto the governo^{rs} deputie and others, of the Companie bearing date the 20th of may last appereth And whereas also the said Clement Moseley did alsoe assigne and sett over the other moitie of his said adventure vnto John Moseley gent in consideration of a certen debt owing by the said Clement vnto the said John. as by the said assignment done the day and yere abovesaid appeareth lykewyse testyfied to the said governo^r deputie and others. The interest of both wch assignments is by the said severall Assignees passed over vnto Elizabeth Moseley late the Wief of the said Clement Moseley in consideration of the some of Cij^{li} x^s by her paid to the said Edmund Helmes . and in consideration of Cij^{li} by her p^d to the said John Moseley as by the severall conveyhaunces thereof appeareth. Therfore the said Elizabeth is to be made Credito^r of the some of 240^{li} of Stocke and supplie When soever she shall have p^d the some of xx^{li} wch is behinde of the supply wch was to have bene brought in by the said Clement Moseley.

1601 9 Nov. Eliz Moseley.

The 20th of Novemb^r 1601.

THIS day by order of Mr Governo^r a warraunt was made to Mr Ald^n Bannynge Thrër to pay to Mr Abraham Campion for the rest of Accoumpte and debt Dewe by the Companie to him for beare for ye voyage the somme of Thirtie nyne poundes ij^s iiij^d.

1601 20 Nov.

Mr Campion forbeare. 39. 2. 4.

The 4 of December 1601.

Mr Ald^n Wattes go^r Mr Tho: farrington
Mr Rich: Stapers   Mr Wm Grenewell
Mr John Highelord   Mr Rich: Wyche
       Mr Wm Harrison

1601 4 Dec.

c c

1601
4 Dec.

An Englisheman brought home out of the East Indies in the Duche shippes.

PPON advyse written to Mr Ald^n Wattes from Midleboroughe touching the arryvall of 2 Dutche shippes retorned from the East Indies *full laden* wth Pepper wch have brought home from the Est Indies 13 men [w^{ch}] *who* have bene deteyned prysoners ther for the space of 4 yeres amongest wch ther is one Englysheman [w^{ch}] *who* hath the Language of Sumatra. and thexperience of the trade of divers Ilandes therabout? It is thought meet by thes Comitties that Mr Alderman take some private and secret course by writing to procure the said Englyshman to come over that some conference may be had wth him touching the state of the trade of those partes.

1601
22 Dec.

A Generall Court the 22th of December 1601.

Mr Ald^n Wattes gov^r Mr Rich Staper
Mr Ald^n Cambell   Mr Wm Chamber
Mr Wm Rumney   Mr Wm Harryson
    Mr Tho: farrington
wth a great Companye of the generalyty.

Touching ye question of the North west passage betwene this Comp. & the Muskovia Company.

HIS generall Court were at this assemblie made acquainted that since the last geñall Court Mr Governo^r [and the] Mr Ald^n Cambell and Mr Rumney and others having acquainted the LL: of the Councell that by reason of the difference betwene the Muskovia Companie and this Companie for the interest of the Northwest passage the preparation of the discoverie of the same passage wch this Companie were in hand wth all was staied It pleased ther LL: therfore for the Clearing of the said difference and the furthering of the said voyage to wryte ther lr̃es to the muskovia Companie. ether to joine wth this Companie in the said discovery or els to bring ther pattente to the Counsell board and to shewe ther Clayme *vnto the said priviledges*. vppon wch lr̃es the Muskovia Companie Soñoned them selfes together and conferred vppon the same Lr̃es and of the Worthines of the said enterpryse and thervppoñ resolved to joine wth this Companie

in the same discoverie, and to conferre vppon as manie of this 1601
Companie as would adventure therein jointlie wth them all beny- 22 Dec.
fyte of priviledge that lyeth in them to impart vnto [them]
the said adventurers. By wch consent of the Muskovia Companie all the former question and difference being cleared It
is nowe Resolved that all expedition possible shalbe vsed by
this Companie to goe on wth the said discovery, and the booke
to be carried abroade, that men may sett downe ther adventures
according to former orders and agreem^{ts}, viz at the rate of xij^d
the pound of ther [last] *first* contribution *sett downe* in the
viage by the Cape of bona Esperansa. or els to be pemptoryly
exempted out of all benyfyte that may growe by the discovery
of the said north west passage, not only during the Contynuance
of [the] o^r priviledges to the East Indies but for ever hereafter
And to thende that noe man shall excuse him self hereafter that
he hath not bene offered the Libertie of adventures in the said
discovery It is ordered that every adventure shall ether sett
downe vnder his owne hand his adventure. or els vnder his owne
hand sett downe his voluntary refusall to adventure therein.
And it is further ordered that all the Contributions *of the breeth-*
ren of this Company for this Discovery [*disbursed by the bretheren*
of this Company and wch are not fre of the Musko : Company] shalbe
brought in to m^r Rumney Deputy governo^r of this Company by
the xxth of January next. and that from tyme to tyme both in
the meane tyme and afterwardes the Comitties appointed for [the]
both the Companies to meete together. and to capitulate and
agree in the proceading of the said [preparation] voyage and of
the Conditions therto belong as shalbe convenient for all the
adventuro^{rs}. But forasmuche as ther is a doubte conceaved
whether ther can be be vnytinge out of two companies *of* divers
selected persons free of them bothe to [holde a priviledg] *become*
a Company to enioy a trade wch shalbe but a part of a priviledge
drawen out of the graunt of one of the said Companies therfore
it is ordered that the opinion of some lerned Counsell shall be
taken whether this voyage may be in this sort proceeded in as
hathe bene purposed and enioyed by vertue of suche an agreem^t
as shalbe made by Consent of the adventuro^{rs} amongest them

1601
22 Dec.

selves or by any Warraunt that can be deryved from other of the said former Companies.

1601
5 Jan.

A Gen^ral Courte holden the 5th of January 1601.

Mr Wm Rumney dep gov^r   Mr Tho : Farrington
Mr Aldⁿ Cambell   Mr Wm Garway
Mr Rich : Staper   Mr Wm Greenewell
Mr Tho : Cordell   Mr Wm Harryson

wth the greatest part of the gen^ralyty.

The opinion of lawe geaven y^t this Company have the right of the North west passage.

SINCE the last Courte, according to the Direction and resolution then holden for the satisfaction of the Companie touching the interest and previledge of the Northwest passage wch hath bene in Dispute and question betwene this Companie and the Moskovia Companie, ther hath bene a [course taken] the opinion of lerned Councell had touchinge the same. and it resolved for lawe that the interest of the same passage is expresselie in this Companie. And it is alsoe resolved [that One Company cannot graunt] touching the doubte that hathe bene formerlie propounded whether that a geñall Company out of ther geñall previledges thereof might graunt a part of ther previledges ether to a nother Companie or to anie private persons [and yet the psons to whom suche graunt is made] that a Companie cannot divide [the] and dismember ther previledg reteyning part

Comitties apointed to expedite the Northwest passage & to devyse ordinaunces to further ye same & other busines of the Company.

of them, and letting one other part So as nowe the doubte and questions formerlie a foote being Cleared and the interest thereof appearing to be in this Companie It is finallie resolved that the said viage shall wth all expedition be prepared aswell for that the shortenes of the tyme requireth expedition as that the Companie are ingaged in ther Credite to the lords to enter into it [soe as] as sone as it shall appeare that they have sufficient interest in the said previledge by ther pattent And to thende that [the] bothe the said voiages may be the better expedited and that the geñall governm^t of this felowship may be the better directed thes persons herevnder named are apointed by the geñalyty to [travell both in the said preparation and also in the] con-

THE EAST INDIA COMPANY.

ceav[ing] of suche reasonable lawes and ordinaunces [for the] as may both further the said acc̃on and better guide all other occasions that may concerne the priviledges of the Companie W^ch lawes and ordinaunces being soe conceaved and prepared the same to be brought to the next geñall Court to receave ther allowance and confirmation [therof at] by the consent of the geñalyty wch shalbe at a geñall Court vppon tuesday in the after noone.

_{1601
5 Jan.}

Comitties.

Mr Rumney deputy   Mr Chery
Mt Ald^n Cambell   Mr Grenwell
Mr Rich : Stapers   M^r farrington
Mr Garway   Mr Harrison
Mr Cordall   Mr Clerke

Or anie 4 of them.

At this Court was read a l̃re or [warraunt] *Certificat* vnder the hand and seale of the right ho : the Earle of Cumbland wherby it appeareth that he hath assigned over the som̃e of two hundred and thirtie poundes to m^r Alderman Holliday out of his hono^rs adventure wth the Companie and therby requireth that the same may be putt of from his Lp^s Accompte and Mr Ald^n Hollyday made Credito^r for so muche vppon wch Certificat this Court hath agreed that the Bookeap shall geave credite vnto Mr Ald^n Holliday for the same money.

_{230^li of the Earle of Cumblands [debte] adventure assigned to Ald^r Hollyday.}

A Gen^rall Court holden the xj^th of Januarie 1601.

Mr Wm Rumney Deputy   Mr Rich : Wyche
Mr Ald^n Cambell   Mr Tho : farrington
Mr Richard Staper   Mr Wm Harryson
Mr Wm Greenewell   M^r Jo : Eldred
Mr Nich̃as leet   M^t Jo : Highelord

wth ye greater part of the gen^ralyty.

_{1601
11 Jan.}

[T this Court] According to the geñall order taken at the [geñall] last geñall Courte touching the devys-ing and conceaving of lawes and ordinaunces for the better governm^t of the state of the trade, [and] the

_{Lawes and ordinaunces presented to be Confirmed.}

1601
11 Jan.

Comitties then appointed did at this Court present [certen] ther opinions by certen ordinaunces [already] by them devysed and offered the same to the Consideration of the Geñ'alytie wch severall ordinaunces being *divers tymes* distinctly read and waighed *and in some pointes reformed* by this Court in ample number assembled and throwghly digested and severally putt to Scruteny and erection of handes the same severall lawes are agreed vppon establyshed and confirmed for standing lawes and ordinaunces to be holden and observed by this Soscyety vppon the *severall* paines and penalties therin severally Limited the teno^r of wch Lawes Do followe in thes wordes videlt :

Whereas the Queenes most excellent Ma^{ie} by her graces l'res Patent vnder ye great seale of England bearinge date ye xxxith day of December in ye xliijth yeare of her ma^{tes} raigne hath incorporated this society by ye name of y^e [Company] goũno^r and company of the ñchaunt of Loⁿ tradinge into ye East Indies and hath geven them ye sole trade of ye said Indies by all such waies and passages as they shall thinke meete to visit those part eyther by ye way and passage already found out wch is by ye cape of bona Esperansa or by such waies and passages as shalbe hearafter found out by ye part of America to enioy ye said trade for ye terme of xv^{en} yeares from ye feast of ye nativity of o^r Lord god 1600 And wheras this society in ye settinge forth of their late viage by ye Cape of Bona esperansa toward ye Iland of Sumat' Java and other ye part therabout entendinge to trade those Iland and places for Pepper Spices gould and other ñchandizes wch are likest yeald ye most profitable returne for ye Adventuro^{rs} in ye same viage have sett forth ye greatest pte of theire adventure in English money Coyned of purpose for ye said voyage and other forreine coine Currant in those Ilands wch moneyes and coyne they could not p^rpare but wth great difficultie and trouble and not wthout some mislike of ye transportacõn of treasure out of land They therfore beinge desirous to vse ye priviledges to them graunted rather for ye good of ye Cõenweale of theire Countrie then for theire private benefite and to maintayne the trade of ye East Indies if it be possible by ye transportacõn and vent of Cloth and other y^e

native Commodities of this Realme wthout any money at all or eles soe litle as may be conveniently tollerated Do resolve to attempt ye discofiy of a Passage by seas into ye said East Indies by ye Northwest thorough some pte of America wch if they shall fynd navigable Then shall they by that passage arrive in ye Countries of Cataia & China beinge the Eeast pt(e) of Asia and Africa Climat(e) of that Temperature wthin all likelihood will aforth a most liberall vent of English clothes and kersies to ye generall advancement of ye trafficke of m̃chandize of this realme of England And to thend to putt in execuc͠on as well this theire resoluc͠on of ye discofiy of ye said passage as otherwise to bringe them selues and theire trade generally to a conformitie and order They do accordinge to ye libertie to them geven by ye said l̃res Pattent(e) for ye makinge of lawes constituc͠ons orders & ordinances for ye better advancement and continuance of theire trade and traffique make ordeine and constitute these seũall lawes constituc͠ons orders and ordinances followinge vizt.

1601
11 Jan.

First it is ordered and decreed by and wth ye generall consent of this Co^rte for standinge and vnchangeable decree that wth all convenient expedic͠on there shalbe preparac͠on made for ye attemptinge of ye discofiy of ye Northwest passage to ye East Indies wherin shalbe vsed two shippes or pinnaces of such burthen and makinge as shalbe hearafter considered of and resolved to be fitt for ye said voyage and manned victualled [and] furnished and provided wth such numbers of men munic͠on furniture victuall m̃chandize and other thing(e) as ye Com̃ittees hearafter nominated and appointed for ye prouision therof shall thinke meete And for ye levyinge of such [moyties] *moneis* as shall defray ye charges of the preparac͠on of ye said shippes or pinaces and all other thing(e) incident to ye said voyage And for ye bringinge of ye said moneys It is ordered that eũy brother of this felowshippe that hath contributed and adventured in ye former voyage to ye East Indies by ye Cape of Bona esperansa shall contribute to the settinge furth of this p^rsent voyage after the rate of xij^d at ye least for eũy pound of his former adventure by him adventured or wherin he is intereressed wthout supplie.

The voyag to the Northwest finally determined to be sett forthe.

1601
11 Jan.

And if any brother of this felowshipp shalbe willinge voluntarily to bringe in a greater contribuc̄on then after y̌e said rate of xij^d in ye pound of his said adventure in ye former voyage it shalbe at his pleasure And to thend to stirre vp men ye rather to enlarge theire said Contribuc̄ons to this enterprise It is alsoe ordered and agreed that after what rate or proporc̄on soeũ any man shall contribute in this discoũy Yf the passage be found out that he shall in all voyages hearafter to be made by ye said passage be aportioned or stinted in his adventures accordinge

the bringing in of ye money.

to ye same proporc̄on or rate and noe otherwise. And It is alsoe ordered that the said Contribuc̄on shalbe brought in by eũy ye Contributors in this manner vizt The one halfe before ye xxth day of January next comminge And ye residue or soe much therof as shalbe found necessary at ye goinge away of ye shippes to be paid to ye handẽ of Mr Ald Cambell appointed Thr̃er for ye same voyage Prouided allwaies that if any brother of this felowshippe shall deny to bringe in his said contribuc̄on at ye rate of xij^d ye pound of his former adventure *or do not bring in the same* at or before the daies and tymes before limited that then he or they that shall make default on that behalfe shall

forfeit v tymes the valew.

satisfy and pay for a fyne by way of deducc̄on out of his stocke adventured in ye last voyage fyve tymes ye valewe of ye Contribuc̄on by him payable by vertue of this act The same to be imployed to ye full furnishinge of ye said discoũy And if there remaine an oũplus to ye vse of ye adventurors in this intended voyage proportionably accordinge to theire seũall adventures.

It is alsoe ordered and decreed by ye generall consent of this Co^{r}te concerninge ye generall trade of this Society and ye preparac̄on of all Viages Contribuc̄ons and generall adventures of this felowshippe hearafter to be sett forth That if any daies or tymes be limited and appointed by order of any generall

To pay contribucons &c, at the tymes limited. Or to be fined in the dis-

Co^{r}te for ye bringinge in of any Contribuc̄ons adventures or supplies and that default be made in ye pforminge of those payments Contribuc̄ons and supplies at ye daies limited by any of ye adventurors or Contributo^{rs} of such voyages that ye stockẽ or adventures of such Contributors shalbe taxed and charged to answeare to ye cōen treasure or vse of this society such damages charges and allowances for not performinge of such payment℮ at ye daies limited as ye Audito^rs of ye Company for ye tyme beinge appointed to audit ye generall accompt℮ shall fynd to be equall and y^t the goūno^r Deputy and Comittes or ye most of them shall censure to be fitt to be paid w^thout any abatement.

₁₆₀₁
_{11 Jan.}
_{cretion of the Companie or of the Audito^rs appointed.}

It is alsoe ordered and agreed by like generall consent of this Society that if any brother of this Company shalbe sumoned or warned by ye officer of this felowshippe therto appointed To appeare at any generall Co^rte of this Society or at any other meetinge of m^r Goūno^r his Deputy and ye Comittees and ye said sumons or warninge geven to ye ptie himselfe or left at his house Yf then such person shall make default and not appeare at all or not appeare at ye howre assigned he shall forfeite for eū'y default of non apparance xij^d and for eū'y default of com- minge late vj^d vnlesse he can give a sufficient reason of his absence or late comminge and ye same to be allowed by ye generall consent of ye assembly or ye more part of them p^rsent eyther at a generall Co^rte or meetinge of Comitties.

_{For absence 12^d & late coming to courtes vj^d.}
_{12. 9 in the third waste booke.}

For ye better and more orderly proceedinge in ye deliberacōn of matters propounded in genall Co^rtes eyther for ye establish- inge of any act℮ or ordinances or in any other matters concer- ninge ye Company Is ordered y^t it shall not be lawfull for any brother of this Company to speake to any one matter pro- pounded aboue three sundry tymes vppon peine of forfeiture of iij^s iiij^d for eū'y such excesse in speach.

_{Not to speake in any mat- ter propoun- ded aboue 3 tymes pena lij^s iiij^d.}

It is alsoe ordered by late consent of a generall Co^rte that if any brother of this Company shall in any Contencōn or argu- ment houlden wth any other pson eyther in generall Co^rte or meetinge of Comittees vse any vnciville or intemperate speaches or behavio^r and soe censured by ye genall Co^rte or ye persons assembled in Comitte he shall forfeite for eū'y such offence x^s.

_{No vncivill speaches or behauio^r in Courtes pena x^s.}

And for ye avoydinge of confusion of speach or disco^rse in ye deliberacōn of matters to be handled in any genall Co^rte or meetinge of Comitties concerninge ye affaires of ye Company It is ordered that noe brother of this felowshippe shall interrupt any other in his declaracōn or disco^rse of any matter declared

_{That none do interrupt an other in his speaches in Courtes pena ij^s vj^d.}

D D

1601
11 Jan.

or disco^rsed to ye Company nor duringe such declaraĉon or disco^rse hold p^uate whisperinge speach or talke wth any other to ye disturbance of him that speaketh But if he be disposed to answear or reply to ye speaches propounded then to direct his answear or reply to m^r Goũno^r or his Deputy vpon peine of forfeyture for eũy such offence ij^s vj^d.

That eu'y one keepe silence being comanded by Mr Gou'no^r or deputie by the stroke of the Hammer pena vj^d.

It is alsoe ordered for ye pacificaĉon of contenĉon in argument in geñall Co^rtes and other meetingℓ and of lowde or confused speaches that when m^r Goũno^r or his Deputy commandeth scilence by ye stroake of ye hammer that then eũy eũy person keepe scilence vpon peine of forfeiture of vj^d for eũy offence.

For refusall of paym^t of fines ymprisonm^t.

And It is alsoe ordered that if any brother of this felowshippe shall vppon commandment or demaund of m^r Goũno^r o^r his Deputy refuse to pay such fynes or forfeytures as he shall have fallen into by ye breach of any of ye ordinances or actℓ of this felowshippe or do not pay them beinge required that then such person shalbe comĩtted to prison there to remaine duringe ye pleasure of Y^e generaltie.

Not to depte Courte but by licence pena xij^d.

And It is further agreed that if any brother of this society shall at any geñall Co^rte or meeting of Comĩtties depart out of ye Co^rte or meetinge before ye Co^rte shall breake vp or ye busines be ended except it be by licence asked of m^r Goũno^r or Deputy and by theire licence graunted that he shall forfeite for eũy default departinge w^thout licence xij^d.

All fines to be ymploied to the genall vse of the Companie.

And It is lastly ordered y^t all fynes and forfeytures forfeyted and lost by any brother of this felowshippe by ye breach of any ordinance now heretofore or hearafter to be made shalbe paid and geven to ye generall and cõen vse of this Society and to be imployed to ye bearinge of ye cõen charges of ye same and to ye releefe of ye poore To dispose accordinge to order from tyme to tyme to be geven in that behalfe.

At this Courte the psons heervnder named are apointed and elected to be Comitties to further the expediĉon of the voyagℓ of the Northwest passage and to prepare the shippinge and all other provisions belonging to the voyage at the best and easiest rates and prises that they can and whatsoever they shall doe

therin the Companie to allowe thereof and the thẽr to defray 1601
suche Charges as [They sh] the said Comitties or anie 4 of   11 Jan.
them vnder ther [warr] handes shall geave him warrant to pay.

Comitties for yᵉ Nortweast passage.

Mʳ Wᵐ Rumney deputy	Mʳ olyver Style
Mʳ Rich: Staper	Mʳ Wᵐ Harryson
Mʳ Thoᵐ Cordell	Mʳ Wᵐ Grenewell
Mʳ Rich: Wyseman	Mʳ Nich: Leat.

The 25 of January 1601.
Present.

1601
25 Jan.

Mʳ Aldⁿ Wattes goʳ	Mʳ Roger Howe
Mʳ Rumney deputie	Mʳ Rich: Wyseman
Mʳ Aldⁿ Cambell	Mʳ Wᵐ Chamber
Mʳ Tho Cordell	Mʳ Nich: lynge
Mʳ Rich: Staper	Mʳ Tho Farrington
Mʳ John Harby	Mʳ Wᵐ Harrison

Mʳ Nich: Leat.

WARRAUNT is geaven to Aldⁿ Hollyday oñ of the Thẽrs of the voyage sett out by the cape of Bona Speransa to pay to Mʳ Robᵗ Bell the somme of xiijˡⁱ iijˢ ijᵈ to him owing by the Companie for charges [of] *by him disbursed for* wharfage at Wiggens key and for Cutting of leade as appeareth by the pticlers thereof.

Like warraunt is geaven to the said Alderman to pay vnto mʳ Aldⁿ Bannyng the other thẽr of the said voyage the somẽ of iiijˡⁱ vijˢ vᵈ for so muche money by him disbursed above his receiptes for the affaires of the Companie.

The Comitties assembled have at this tyme geaven vnto 200 mkes to
Richard Wright Secretarie of this felowship for and in respecte the Secre-
of his great travell taken in the begininge of the [the settling of tarie.
the] procuringe of the previledges of this fellowship and in all
thinges concerning the viage and the trade the somẽ of two
hundred markes.

1601
25 Jan.
x^li p annū
to the Bedle
agmented to
xij^li p annū
thr.

At this meeting the said Comitties have agreed to geave vnto Thoms Evettsett the Bedell of this felowship for his service to the Companie the yerelie salarye of Tenn poundes [the] his tyme to begynn at xpm̃s last.

Ther is graunted vnto m^r Waymouthe towardes the provision of instrumentſ for the northwest passage the som̃e of thertie poundes to be p^d him by m^r Ald^n Cambell.

[Ther is] Warraunt is geaven to m^r Ald^n Holliday Thrēr to pay vnto Beniamyn Deycro Agent of the Muskovia Companie . the somme of One hundred and Nyne poundſ sixteene shillinges Eight pence in full paiment of Cordage deliv̄ed by him for the furnishinge of the shippes sett out by the Cape of Bona Esperansa to ye East Indies.

1601
17 Feb.
30 paid
Mr Weymouthe.

17 of Febr : 1601.

WARRAUNT was geaven by the psons heervnder named to m^r Ald^r Cambell Thrēr for the voyage by the Northwest passage to pay to George Waymouth for provisions for the same voyage the som̃e of thertie poundſ.

The Comitties who signed the warraunt were

1601
17 Mar.

The xvij^th of March 1601.

m^r Cordell
m^r Jo^n Eldred

m^r Ald Wattſ govern^or   m^r Wych
m^r Rumney deputy   m^r Chambers
m^r Ric^d Staper   m^r Ffreeman
m^r Oliver Style   m^r Waymouth
m^r Leat   m^r Barrell

20^li paid
George Weymouthe
to buy Instrumentes.

T this Co^rte warrant is geaven to m^r Ald^r Cambell Thrēr for ye Northwest Passage to pay to m^r Waymouth the som̃e of xx^li towardſ ye provision of Instrumentſ needfull for this intended viage.

A generall Co^rte houlden the xviij^th of March 1601.

m^r Ald Watt℈ governo^r
m^r Rumney dep :
m^r Ric^d Staper
m^r Tho : Cordell
m^r Ric Leat
m^r Ffarrington
m^r Wyche
m^r Ffreeman
m^r Lynge
wth y^e most pt of y^e generality.

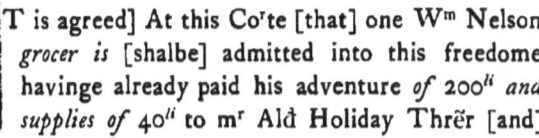[T is agreed] At this Co^rte [that] one Wm Nelson *grocer is* [shalbe] admitted into this freedome havinge already paid his adventure *of* 200^li *and supplies of* 40^li to m^r Ald Holiday Thrēr [and] who is received into ye said freedome wth ye full consent of both Assistant℈ and generalty. . . . And it is to be noted and Remembred for the Charging of the Accomptes of the Company that the said Wm Nelson gave to this Companie the somē of xxx^li sterlin℈ for ther consent to admitt him to *be an* adventuro^r wth them [and in] and to have the freedom of this felowship.

This Co^rte do [likewise] *apoint and* entreat m^r Leat and m^r Lynge to take paines to [warne ye persons that] *move all suche brethren of the Companie as* have not already [dis]contributed their full alottm^t *of xij^d in the lb* toward℈ ye discovery of the Northwest Passage vppon peine of forfeiture of ye penalty *mencōed* in an act of Co^rte [afore mencōed] ·*of the xj^th of January last.* That they beinge in their *said rate* [allottm^t] of xij^d vpon ye pound To m^r Ald Cambell Thrēr, before ye last of this p̄sent moneth.

Thomas Yerworth is enterteyned to be Purser of one of the shippes apointed for this viage to be made for ye discoūy of ye Northwest Passage and is content to accept of [ix^lb] *v^lb* in hand part of his wages to beginn from this [Co^rte and] *day at the rate of* forty shilling℈ [to be paid him for every] *a* moneth [imploym^t] yf ye discovery be [found] *made and if not then at the rate of* xx^s a moneth *duringe his imploym^t in the voyage* And ye said Yerworth is to give security for his [imploym^t] *good behavio^r in the execution of his Charge of Purser in this imploym^t* in a bond of [C markes] one hundred pound℈.

25th of March 1602.

1602
25 Mar.

WARRANT was geaven by the Persons herevnder named to m^r Aldⁿ Cambell Thrēr for ye viage by ye Northwest Passage *to pay to John Drewe enterteyned to goe as m^r of a ship for discoũy of ye said Passage* the some of fyve pound₷ wch is to be delivered him by way of Imp̃st in part of paym^t of his wages agreed vppon for ye viage.

The Comittes who signed the warrant were

27th of March 1602.

1602
27 Mar.

WARRANT was geaven by ye Persons herevnder named to m^r Ald Cambell Thrēr for ye viage by ye Northwest Passage To pay to Thomas Yerworth Purser of [y^e] y^e *a* shipp appointed to goe for discovery of the said Passage the some of fowreskore pound₷ wch is to be paid for clearinge of ye carpenters wages who were lately imployed about y^e [p̃parac̃on] *worke* of the said shipps.

The Comittees who signed the warrant were

John Watt₷ governo^r	Ric Staper.	Nic Leat
Wm Rumney Deputy	Tho: Cordell	Wm Harison.

A Gen^rall Court holden the 29th of Marche 1602.

1602
29 Mar.

Mr Aldⁿ Wattes governo^r	Mr John Eldred
Mr Wm Rumney deputy	Mr Tho: farrington
Mr Aldⁿ Cambell thēr	Mr Nic̃las Leete
Mr Rich: Staper	Mr Tho: Cordell.

wth ye greatest part of the geñalyty.

Touching the suply for the north-west passage.

HIS Co^rte was warned vpon occasion of ye want of bringinge in of the rate of xij^d ye pound by former Co^rtes agreed vpon to furnish ye viage *by* ye Northwest Passage wch want beinge signified to this Assembly and an accompt made vnto them how far ye Company are engaged in their provision already wch appeareth to be above ye some of 700^{li} all wch or ye most part therof would be lost yf they should not proceade and ye Company discredited in their not proceadinge in their discovery the same beinge made soe publique aswell to o^r owne Country as to Strangers in forrein part℮ Therfore this Co^rte do agree for ye better furtheringe of this viage wch for ye hono^r of o^r Country may not be left of And for ye better encoraginge of those that have already supplyed their xij^d in ye pound accordinge to former orders that whatsoever hath bene sett downe and brought in by any brother of ye Company [or shalbe brought] *or* shalbe sett downe and brought in by any brother of this Company toward℮ ye furnishinge of ye said viage to ye Northwest Passage shalbe demed part of ye adventure and stock by him or them adventured and contributed in ye viage already made by ye Cape of BONA ESPERANSA and that every adventuro^r or supplyer shall receave vpon such adventure as he shall bringe in for to be imployed in this discovery such benefite and profitt proporc͠onably wth ye rest of his adventure already brought in to ye viage to ye East Indies as though he had put in soe much stock and supply in ye former viage And to thend the Act of ye xjth of January *last* for ye forfeture of fyve for one to be forfeted by such as shall not pay their rate of xij^d the li. to this discovery shalbe ye better confirmed and *fortified* [forfeted] It is ordered that suite shalbe made to ye LL: of the Councell acquayntinge them wth ye necessity of this Co^rse entreatinge their hono^{rs} to give vs an order vnder their hand℮ menc͠oninge their likinge of this Co^rse taken by the Company and promisinge vs their readines to aid vs in ye execuc͠on of o^r said act sith ye same is intended for ye com͠on benefite and hono^r of ye realme And to thend ye consent of all such as were p^rsent at this Co^rte may appeare to ye Generalety of ye Company wch are absent every of ye said persons now p^rsent have vnder their hand℮ sett downe such som͠es as they will Contribute in this discovery willinge y^t ye same beinge brought in and received by ye Thr̃er of this viage may be indorsed vppon their bills of adventure wch are already geaven them vnder ye com͠on seale of ye Company wch is alsoe agreed vpon And yet notwthstandinge It is agreed y^t

1602
29 Mar.

208   THE COURT RECORDS OF

1602
29 Mar.
day shalbe continued accordinge to ye order of ye last Co^rte to such as yet have not brought in their Contribuc̃on of xij^d ye pound that they shall have that tyme vizt the last of this moneth to bringe in their mony to the Thr̃er and after y^t day the said Thr̃er shall not receive ye said xij^d ye li. of any man that hath not already paid it wthout Consent of a generall Co^rte.

1602
1 Aprill.
1 of Aprill 1602.

 WARRANT was granted to *ye Thr̃er to pay to* Austyn Bandicott Butche^r for 45^C 3 qters of Porke beinge 49 hogſ bought of him at xxiiij^s the hundred the som̃e of fyftie fowre poundſ eighteene shillings.

An other warrant was granted the day abouesaid to [Thomas Yerworth] m^r Ald Cambell Thr̃er to pay to Thomas Yerworth the som̃e of thirtie poundſ wch is to be paid to certen workemen at Ratcliffe and Lymehouse and for salt and mariners board wages where they lye.

An other warrant was granted the same day to the said Thr̃er to pay to m^r Richard Staper the som̃e of xxviij^{li} xviij^s wch the said m^r Staper hath disbursed for lxiiij hydes to make ye marino^{rs} Cassockſ Breaches and gownes

1602
2 Aprill.
The seconde of Aprill 1602.

Mr Aldⁿ Wattes governo^r   Mr Wm Chambers
Mr Wm Rum̃ey deputy   Mr Wm Harryson
Mr Rich: Staper   Mr Capten Waymouthe
Mr Nic̃as Leet   Mr Aldⁿ Cambell
M^r W^m farrington

xiij^{li} xix^s 6^d
p^d to M^r W^m
Rumey.
ARRAUNT is geaven to Mr Aldⁿ Cambell thr̃r to pay vnto m^r Wm Rumney deputy the somme of xiij^{li} xix^s vj^d for so muche delivered [him] *by his servauntſ to m^r Burrell* in gilderns lying wynd bound at Holland after the preparinḡ of the 2 shippes for the northwest passage.

THE EAST INDIA COMPANY

Another Warraunt is geaven to the said Ther to pay vnto [Captein Waymouth] Mʳ Roḃt Sandy merchaunte the sõme of threescore pound₠ sterlin₠ for so muche taken vp by exchaung by Captein Waymouthe at Excetoʳ of one Mʳ Newcombe to be pᵈ here in London to Mʳ Roḃt Sandye wᶜʰ money was taken vp for the hirin₠ of marinors.

1602 2 Apr. lxˡⁱ to Mʳ Sandy by exchaunge.

At this Assemblie the victualling and preparation of thing₠ necessarie for the 2 shippes was agreed vppon to be devyded amongest the severall Comitties herevnder named assigning them to ther severall charge in preparin₠ of the pticulers and severall kindes of Vittualls and other thinges as followeth viz

Provision of Victualles & other necessaries.

Sacke & Cassalia Wyne Vinegar Candelles Lanthornes	to	Mʳ Aldⁿ Wattes Mʳ Wᵐ Harryson Mʳ Wᵐ Chambers Mʳ Greenwell
Pease Butter Holland Ling Stockfishe Cheese Otemeale Oyle Iroñ Stoves Wood Baysalte Musterseede	to	Mʳ Aldⁿ Cambell Mʳ Wᵐ Rumney Mʳ Nich: Leat Mʳ Nich: Lynge
Bread Beare Aquavite Porke Beef Rice Water Caske Baricos Meale	to	Mʳ Cordall Mʳ Staper Mʳ farrington Mʳ Wiseman

E E

1602
2 Apr.

At this Assemblie Thomas Stephens is agreed wth all to take the charge of the keeping of the bookes of Accompte of the Companie and to have for his salarye yearely for the same the some of thirtie poundes to be p^d him quarterly.

1602
5 Apr.

The vth of Aprill 1602.

THIS day a warraunt was made to Mr Aldⁿ Cambell threr of the voyage throughe the Northwest passage to pay vnto Thomas Yarworth Purser of the Discovery. the somme of one hundred poundes. to pay for ancors and other necessaries for the same ship for wch he is to geave an accoumpte.

The Comittees who signed ye warraunt were

Aldⁿ Watt^s governo^r   Mr Nic. Leat
Mr Ric. Staper   Mr Harison
         M^r ffarrington.

1602
10 Apr.

The 10th of Aprill 1602.

THIS day a warrant was [granted] geaven to m^r Ald Cambell Thrēr for the viage by ye Northwest passage to pay to Joⁿ Drewe enterteyned to goe as m^r of the Godspeede in this intended viage ye some of ten pound^s in part of his wages.

1602
11 Apr.

Pleno robore per assensu curiæ tamen fore.

[The 11th of Aprill 1602.

[THIS day a warrant was made to m^r Ald Cambell Thrēr for ye viage by ye Northwest Passage to pay to Thomas Yerworth appointed to goo as Purser in one of ye ships for this intended viage the some of one hundred pounds [wch some is] to be paid for Sea Coales, wood, lead, and dyvers other necessaries And the said Yerworth to be accomptable.]

[An other Warrant was granted to the said Threr the same day for one hundred pound͡ȝ to be paid to Capten Waymouth by p͡cells as he shall have occasion to call for it beinge for dyvers mens wages who are to be answeared therwth.]

1602
11 Apr.

The   day of   1602.
Anno Rn° Elizabethe xliiij^{to}.

1602
April.

Articles of Agreement Indented made betweene the governo^r and company of the merchant͡ȝ of London tradinge into ye East Indies on ye one ptie and George Waymouth of   in the County of   marino^r on the other party . .
the   day of Aprill 1602.

HERAS the said governo^r and company of the merchant͡ȝ of London tradinge into ye East Indies vpon great deliberac͡on had and taken of the longe and tedious course wch hath benne hetherto houlden by all such as do trade or sayle from these part͡ȝ of the world in to ye East Indies alonge the coast of Europe and Africa by ye Cape of BONA ESPERANSA and of the great adventures wch are borne in soe longe a viage by many kinds of daungers offered therin and beinge moved wth great hope that ther is a possibility of discovery of a neerer Passage into ye said East Indies by seas by ye way of the Northwest yf the same were vndertaken by a man of knowledge in Navigac͡on and of a resoluc͡on to put in execuc͡on all possibility of Industrie and valo^r of the attayninge of soe inestimable benefite to his native cuntry and his *owne* perpetuall [fame] *bono^r* Have to that end [made] enterteinned the said George Waymouth a man in their opinion qualified and fitt to vndertake and attempt the performance of this discovery vnto whom they have d̃d before hand the some of one hundred pounds to furnish himselfe wth convenient instrument͡ȝ of navigac͡on accordinge to his owne choice and vnto whose direcc͡on they have com̃itted two ships [*sufficientlie manned*] the one called the Discovery the other the Godspeede beinge manned victualled

1602
April.

p̄pared and furnished wth all thinge̊s necessary and convenient for such a viage and therin bestowed and supplyed all kinde̊s of provisions accordinge to his owne desire wherby both the said George Waymouth and his company are provided of victualle̊s apparell and furniture for the space of [two yeares] 16 *monethes* and [hath] *have* alsoe laden aboard the said ships a convenient proporc̃on of severall kindes of merchandize   In considerac̃on wherof it is agreed between the said parties to these p^rsents in manner and forme followinge vizt.

The said George Waymouth doth promise covenant and agree to and wth the said governo^r and company of the merchante̊s of London tradinge into the East Indies that he and his Company shall and wilbe ready by the   day of next ensuinge the date hereof to depart from ye Port of London and as wynd and weather will permitt shall and will directly sayle towarde̊s the coast of Groynland into that part of the open Seas wch is described in sundry generall mappe̊s by ye name of FRETUM DAUIES and shall passe on forward in those Seas by ye northwest or as he shall fynd the Passage best to lye towarde̊s the parte̊s or kingedomes of Cataya or China *or ye backside of America* w^thout geavinge over the proceadinge on his Co^rse soe longe as he shall fynd those seas or any pte therof navigable and any possibility to make way or passage through them   And shall not himselfe returne or voluntarily suffer any of his company to returne back againe vnto or towarde̊s the Coast of England for any lett or impediment whatsoever vntill he and they have bestowed one yeare at ye least from the tyme of their departinge hence in goinge forward seekinge [and] soundinge and attemptinge the performinge of this intended viage.

And further the said George Waymouth doth promise grant and agree to and wth the said governo^r and company that he the said George Waymouth shall and will *not onlie well enterteyne and entreat but also* quietly permitt [and] suffer [*well entertaine and entreat*] such merchante̊s or pursers as the said governo^r and Company shall place or appoint to goe in the said ships or eyther of them to keepe a Register and accompt of all such goode̊s wares merchandizes provision & furniture as are shipped and laden in any yᵉ said shipꝭ how the same is bestowed bartered changed spent or otherwise disposed and alsoe to keepe an accompt of all other thingꝭ that shalbe bought bartered exchanged or receaved in liewe of any thinge that shalbe sould or made away and alsoe to make notes jornallꝭ and observacõns in wrytinge of their continuall proceedingꝭ in the said viage vntill their returne for England for yᵉ direccõn and helpe of posterity that shalbe occasioned or willinge hearafter to make a newe attempt vpon the same discovery [*and that he shall conceale what he hath discoũed therin from all other persons*] And further that he the said George Waymouth shall wᵗʰin [twenty] 10 daies after his returne in to England [*wᵗʰout concelemᵗ*] whether he do performe the said discovery or not *wᵗʰout concelement of anie thinge wᶜʰ he hath discovered in the voyage* deliver a declaracõn in wrytinge vnder his hand vnto yᵉ governoʳ of the said Company or his deputy conteyninge a report of all and every his proceedingꝭ in yᵉ viage worthie of note or memory for yᵉ good of yᵉ Company and for yᵉ helpe of such as shalbe disposed hearafter to proceade in the same passage and shalbe ready from tyme to tyme duringe yᵉ space of 40 daies after his arrivall & returne to London *vppon warninge or Somõns geaven him in that behaulf* to come before yᵉ governoʳ & deputy of yᵉ said Company for yᵉ tyme beinge and [x persons of the greatest adventure of yᵉ said Company] *the Comitties and such others of yᵉ Company as it shall please yᵉ governoʳ* [and the Comittees or ten at yᵉ least] *to call vnto them* in [this intended viage] & *will* truly relate vnto them such thingꝭ as passed in yᵉ said viage wherof they or any of them shall desire to be enformed wᵗʰout denyall or refusall in that behalfe *and shall not discover the secretꝭ or course of his proceading in the voyage to anie other ṗson or ṗsons whatsoever then to the said Governor deputie and Comitties.*

And the said governoʳ and company of the merchantꝭ of London tradinge into yᵉ East Indies for them and their successoʳˢ do in consideracõn of the ṗmises promise covenant and agree to and wᵗʰ the said George Waymouth to satisfy and pay vnto the said George Waymouth or his assignes wᵗʰin fortye daies after his returne in to England and after sufficient prooſe

1602
April.

and testimonial by him made that he hath passed thorough the Northwest passage into y̅e̅ East Indies and arrived at any Port w̅t̅h̅in the dominions of the kingedomes [and] *or* Empires of Cataya [or] China *or Japan* the some of fyve hundred pound℔ of lawfull English mony w̅t̅h̅out fraude or Covyn.

And lastly the said George Waymouth doth promise and agree that vnlesse in this intended viage he shall discover and passe through the same Northwest Passage and shal make sufficient proofe and give good testimoniall that he hath passed through the same passage and arrived in some part of the said East Indies in y̅e̅ dominions or kingedomes of Cathayia and China or one of them that then nether he the said George Waymouth nor his assignes shall or will demand or require of the said governo̅r̅ or company or any of them any Salary wages or reward for his viage or travell in y̅e̅ discovery of y̅e̅ said Passage in regard the said viage was vndertaken by y̅e̅ said governo̅r̅ and company ptly by his perswasion and vpon his resolucõn to adventure his travell and life therin for y̅e̅ good of his Cuntrey to w̅c̅h̅ his resolucõn the said Company were content to add the adventure of y̅e̅ settinge furth of ye viage to their great charge.

In witnes &c.

1602
14 Apr.

A generall Co̅r̅te houlden the xiiij̅t̅h̅ of Aprill 1602.

m̅r̅ A̅t̅d Watt℔ Governo̅r̅   m̅r̅ Wiseman
m̅r̅ Rumney deputy   m̅r̅ Harison
m̅r̅ Ric Staper   m̅r̅ Leat
m̅r̅ Farrington   m̅r̅ Lynge
m̅r̅ [Harison] Chambers   m̅r̅ Burrell.

AT this Co̅r̅te warrant was made to m̅r̅ A̅t̅d Cambell Thr̅e̅r for y̅e̅ viage by y̅e̅ Northwest Passage to pay to William Russell Butcher the some of one hundred eleven pound℔ 5ˢ for beefe and Porke bought of him to furnish the occasion in this intended viage.

M̅r̅ Wiseman and m̅r̅ Lynge be entreated to audit the accompt℔ of Tho: Yerworth for 210ˡⁱ w̅c̅h̅ he hath disbursed [for].

THE EAST INDIA COMPANY

Another warrant was made to the said Thrēr for one hundred and fyfty poundℓ to be paid to m^r Wm Chambers beinge for provisions of clothe and dyvers other necessaries.

*1602
14 Apr.*

Another warrant to the said Thrēr for to pay to m^r Nicholas Leat the some of 150^{li} for provision of [lyke] further necessaries. And he to be accomptable.

Another warrant was made to ye said Thrēr for payment of 150^{li} to m^r Staper to be disbursed to dyvers persons *for their wages* as they shall call for it. *And he to be accompt.*

[By this Court [*assembly*] it is *alsoe* ordered that the Pursers of the ships shall deliver the bills of *all* their provisions to m^r Burrell to receive allowance : and noe man to make provision for the store of the shipℓ but to have [direction from him] *allowance therof* vnder his hand.

The 20th of Aprill 1602.

*1602
20 Apr.*

Mr Aldⁿ Wattes governo^r   Mr Nich: Leat
Mr Wm Rumey deputy   Mr Tho: farrington
Mr Tho Cordell   Mr Wm Harrison
Mr Rich: Staper   Mr Wm Freeman
Mr Wm Chamber   Mr Roger Howe.

WARRANT is geaven to Mr Aldⁿ Cambell thēr of the North West passage, to pay vnto Josephe Page Baker [for] vppon an accompte of Biskett [deliuered and] to be delivered for the provision of the voyage the somme of three score poundes.

*Joseph
Page Baker
60^l*

22th : of Aprill 1602.

*1602
22 Apr.*

WARRANT geaven to the said Thrēr to pay vnto Thomas Yerworth 100^{li} to be vsed and disbursed vpon necessary provisions for this intended viage And the said Yerworth to give accompt therof.

1602
24 Apr.

The 24th of Aprill 1602.

[Mr Ald{n} watt{e} governo{r} Mr ffarrington
Mr Rumney deputy   Mr Leat
Mr Ald Cambell   Mr Harison
Mr Howe   Mr Stapers
Mr Chambers   Mr Wiseman

IT is agreed at this Co{r}te *by* [that] John Cartwright of London Preacher wth ye governo{r} deputy and company of merchant{es} of London tradinge into ye East Indies to sayle and goe wth Cap: George Waymouth vpon a viage for ye discovery of ye Northwest Passage for ye wch ye said Cartwright is to have *of* the said company 3{lb} p̱ moneth. beginninge his sallary from ye depture of ye ship{ps} appointed for ye said discovery from Gravesend And if it happen that discovery be not made wherby ye said ship{ps} or one of them may returne from ye kingedome of China or ye kingedomes of Cataya then ye said Jo{n} Cartwright is only to have for his sallary the one halfe wch is xxx{s} p̱ moneth to be paid him at his returne But over and above ye said governo{r} and company hath paid him the some of fyfteene pound{es} of lawfull mony of England the wch ye said company doth give him for his p̱parac̄on and furnishinge of *him selfe for* the said viage and in testimony of his agreement faithfully to be performed on both pts wherin the said Jo{n} Cartwright doth promise the said Comp: to do his best endevo{r} in all thing{es} [And further the] *The* said Cartw: is contented to enter into such covenant{es} for his imployment in ye said viage as by ye said company shalbe thought good to be devised.

Edward Pullison is enterteyned to goe in this p̱sent viage as Purser of *one of* the Pynnaces [for this intended viage] for ye discovery of ye north west Passage and is content to accept of v{li} in hand part of his wages to beginne from this day at y{e} rate of forty shilling{es} a moneth if y{e} discovery be made and if not then at y{e} rate of xx{s} p̱ moneth duringe his imployment in y{e} viage And the said Pullison is to give security for his good behavio^r in y^e *execuĉon of y^e* charge of Purser and otherwise if he be further imployed in a bond of C^{li}. 1602 24 Apr.

Warrant is geaven to m^r Ald Cambell Thrēr for ye viage by ye northwest Passage to pay to m^r Wm Chambers ye soīne of one hundred poundℓ wch is to be disbursed vppon necessary provisions [in] *to furnish* this [intended] viage and the said m^r Chambers [wil] *to* be accomptable therfore.

Warrant is geaven to y^e said Thrēr to pay to m^r Ric^d Stapers the soīne of two hundred poundℓ most part *of soe much* disbursed by y^e said m^r Stapers vpon necessaries and the residue to be disbursed as occasion shall serve for wch n̄$\tilde{}$he Stapers wil be accomptable.

A Geñall Court the last of Aprill 1602.   1602 Last of Apr.

Mr Ald^n Wattes governo^r Mr Rich: Wyseman
Mr Wm Rumney deputy   Mr Wm Chambers
Mr Tho: Cordell   Mr Nich: Leat
Mr Rich: Staper   Mr Nich: Lynge
   Mr Wm Harryson
The greatest part of the gen^{r}alyty.

AT this Co^{r}t the preparation of the viage for the North west passage being made and the shippes ready to dept certen articles of agreem^t [were] made betwene the Companie and Capten Waymouth were read, and ther were also read the Queenes l$\tilde{r}$e written to the Empero^r of China and Kathia wch being above the Court were made acquainted that divers of the Company that had not brought in ther moneys for the [said provision] provision of the said discovery allotted vppon ther adventures viz. ther xij^d in the pounde wherevppon it was ordered that [the] auditors should be chosen and the accompte of the charge of the voyage [shuld] brought vnto them to be audited, [and] wch done reporte of the said accompte *to be made* at the next geñall Court and therwthall the names of suche as have not brought in ther moneys to be [do] published [as] *to* that geñallyty, to thend the Company may [not onlie geave]

Articles of agreement wth Georg Weymouth read.

F F

218   THE COURT RECORDS OF

<small>1602
Last of Apr.</small>

take order what further supply shalbe brought in to pforme the whole charge of the voyage and what further course shalbe taken wth those that have not brought in ther supplies according to order and thes psons heervnder named [may] *or any 4 of them* were apointed to be auditors for the said accompte. [viz.]

Auditors

M^r fra Chery	Mr Rob̃t Bell
M^r olyver Style	Mr Nich. pierd
Mr Humfrey Basse	Mr Aug: skynner
M^r fra: Tayler	Mr Morice Abbott
Mr Hughe Hamersley	Mr Rob̃t Carrell
M^r Jo: fletcher	M^r Jo: Combes

or any 4 of them.

Warrant geaven to ye Threr̃ to pay to Capten George Waymouth the som̃e of fyfty pound℄ sterlinge wch is allowed by ye company for ye bearinge of the charges and dyett of him and his servant℄ attendinge ye p̃paracõn of ye viage before the goinge forth of the ship℄ [Takinge his acquittance.]

The 3 of May 1602.

<small>1602
3 May.</small>

Mr Rum̃ey deputy	Mr Nic̃has Leet
Mr Rich: Staper	M^r Jo: Newman
Mr Wm Harryson	Mr Tho: farrington
Mr Rich: Wyseman.	

<small>Watches compasses and other Instrumentes cost 30 li.</small>

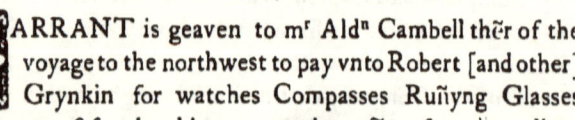ARRANT is geaven to m^r Aldⁿ Cambell ther̃ of the voyage to the northwest to pay vnto Robert [and other] Grynkin for watches Compasses Run̄yng Glasses and instrument℄ for the shippes vses the som̃e of xxx^{li} sterling.

Warrant is geaven to The Threr̃ to pay to m^r Leat the som̃e of xx^{li} to disgage the mariners cloathes.

Warrant is geaven to the said Threr̃ to-pay to Joⁿ Davies a couper *for caskes &c.* 50^{li} 11^s 8^d and to take his acquittance.

Warrant to the said Threr̃ to pay to Adam Wood vij^{li} 8^s for deales ores and other provisions &c Takinge his acquittance.

THE EAST INDIA COMPANY

Warrant to yᵉ Thrēr for payment of vi^li x^s to w^m wood- field Smith for [Iron] settinge on of Iron hoopes and such like worke takinge his acquittance.
1602 3 May.

Warrant to the Thrēr to pay to Tho: Robinson for three cables and Skeytes 29^li 18 Takinge his acquittance.

Warrant to the Thrēr for payment of 92^li 10^s *the 3. of June next* to m^r Skelton Chaundlo^r for butter candles Powder and such like provisions [the] Takinge his acquittance.

Post meridiem eiusd diei.

m^r Rumney deputy	m^r ffarrington
m^r Stap	m^r Harison
m^r Cordell	m^r newman
m^r Leat	m^r Greenwell
m^r Chambers	m^r Burrell

^r DEPUTY reported vnto *this assembly* [these cõ- mittees] beinge [spoken of] enformed by m^r Cham- bers [of] *how* some dislike *was* taken against yᵉ Purser Tho: Yerworth notw^thstandinge after some further dispute it was [concluded] *agreed* he should be continued.

It [is by these comittees likewise] *was alsoe* thought con- venient [that] and [fully] *therfore* agreed [was] *vpon in respect of* some difference dependinge [betwe] about yᵉ other Purser Pullison that if by the Captaine [ther] *it* shalbe thought needfull to imploy him then the agreem^t wth him yᵉ 24th of Aprill 1602 to stand in force otherwise to be discontinued.

Warrant granted to Mr Ald. Cambell Thrēr for yᵉ viage by yᵉ Northwest Passage to pay to m^r Johnson the some of xi^li vj^s and viij^d for bay Salt vsed in this p̄sent viage and to take his acquittance therfore.

A Geñ'al Court holden the 18th of May 1602.
1602 18 May.

Mr Ald^n Wattes governo^r	Mr Rich: Stapers
Mr Ald^n Cambell thrēr	Mr Wm Chamber
Mr Tho: Cordell	Mr Nich: Lynge
Mr Nich: leat	

1602
18 May.

WHEREAS Mr Aldn Cambell thẽr for the voyage by the Northwest passage is bounde by coveñnt vnder his hand and seale to John Drewe marinor for the payment of his wages xx nobles a moneth so longe as he shalbe in the voyage yf the passage be discovered and yf he discover not the said passage v marke a moneth and xvli moreover to be pd.

Vppon the xvth of marche   This court doeth agree that a bonde vnder the Comon seale of the Companie shalbe made to mr James Cambell sonne to mr Tho : Cambell *in the penaltie of CCli* to save the said mr Thoñs Cambell harmeles from the said Coveñnte.

Supplies to be brought in. Newe billes of adventure conteyning every mans stock and all supplies in one grosse some.

At this Court day is geaven to all the voluntarie suppliers for the setting forthe of the voyage *by the north west passage* wch have supplied above the rate of xijd the ℔. to bring in ther voluntary contribution by the [last] *xxth* of this moneth. And it is also ordered by this Cort that all the ratable supplies of xijd the ℔. for the northwest voyage and the voluntary supplies of encrease shalbe endorsed vppon everie adventurors bill of adventure by the ther *or otherwyse noted vnder his hand* And that bill to be [being] brought to the Secretorie and newe billes to be made vnder the coñon seale *for every suche adventuror* wch shall conteyne in one grosse soñe the severall adventures and the severall Supplies of everie brother of the Companie [ether] brought in and pd ether *for* the voyage by the Cape of bona Speransa. or [by] for the voyage by the Northwest passage wch bill being sealed wth the comon seale shall be a testimony to every adventuror what he is interest in the voyage sett forthe by the Cape of Bona Speransa according to the ordenaunces of the Company.

Fryday come sennight is apointed for the Auditors to meete together and that day to finishe the Accomptes of the northwest voyage to thende the Company may be informed at the next geñ'all court what is the whole charge of the same voyage.

Warraunt is geaven to [the] Mr Cambell thẽr to pay vnto Thoñs Barbor for canvesse [and] provided for to make sayles for the 2 flyboat(s) of the northwest voyage the soñe of 143li.

The lyke warraunt is geaven him to pay to Robert Hewghes saylemaker for making of sayles the some of thirtie and two poundes tenn shillinges.

1602
18 May.

Another warraunt is geaven to the said ther to pay to Arnold mabancke for pullies for the two fflye boates the some of [tenn] Nyne poundes and tenn shillings.

Another warraunt is geaven to the ther to pay vnto Thoms Tyler painter the some of thirteene poundes six shillinges and eight pence for worke done by him about the two pinaces.

Another warraunt is geaven to the said threr to pay vnto Roger ffrythe Smythe for yron worke for store for the said shippes the some of xix^{li}.

Another Warraunt geaven to the said ther to pay to Richard Hall Blacksmith for yron worke for the two flyboates the some of $xxvj^{li}$.

Another Warraunt geaven to the said ther to pay to George Gryce carriage maker iij^{li} $viij^{s}$.

Warrant to the Threr for payment of two and twenty pound^{es} six shilling^{es} to x͞pofer Tompson Smith for *Iron* worke &c. [done by him] about the Pynnaces.

Warrant to the Threr for payment of 12^{lli} to w^{m} Denham for Pullies &c.

Warraunt for payment of 120^{lli} 3^{s} to Abraham Campion for provisions of Beare.

Warrant for payment to Nic. Symonson carpinter for worke vpon the discovery the some of 58^{lli} 13^{s} and for tymber and a boat 13^{lli} in all 71^{lli} 13^{s}.

Warrant for payment of 7^{lli} 11^{s}. to Mr Skelton for powder sent in to the downes for the further provision of the Pynnaces.

20th of May 1602.

1602.
20 May

EALED vnder the common seale of the Companie a bonde *of* CC^{li} *penaltie* to James Cambell sonne of m^{r} Ald^{n} Cambell thre^{r} made in trust to save Mr Ald^{n} Cambell harmeles for a coveñnte by him sealed to John Drew marine^{r} for his wages in the voyage by the Northwest passage.

1602
20 May.

Warrant geaven to m^r Ald Cambell Thrēr for y^e viage by y^e Northw. to pay to m^r Ric: Wright Secretary to this felowship for charges by him disbursed about y^e procuringe of y^u queenes lres the soñe of 4^{lli} 15^s.

1602
21 May.
To the
Threr for
\ iage by
y^e northw:

21th of may 1602.

WARRANT to *pay to* Xp̄ofer and Thomas nicolls the soñe of thirtie fowre poundẽ seaven shillingẽ and ten pence for provisions of [ropes] cordage.

An other for m^r Savage to receive the soñe of three poundẽ for spare maystẽ.

1602
23 May.

23th of may 1602.

WARRANT to pay to m^r Richard Stapers the soñe of 40^{lli} 15^s 8^d for soe much restinge due vnto him as appeareth by accompt audited.

Warrant to pay to Wm Deyns Iremonger for provisions of spittẽ and such like necessaries received of him for the Pynnaces vse the soñe of 30^s 8^d.

1602
26 May.

26th of may 1602.

WARRANT to pay to Joⁿ Makesfield Brasier for corkẽ and pottẽ of brasse copper kettles and other *like* necessaries the soñe of 17^{lli} 17^s.

Warrant to pay to Joseph Page Baker for biskett for both shipẽ and for biskett bagẽ ye soñe of 41^{lli} 8^s.

Warrant to *pay to* Mr Ald Wattẽ governo^r the soñe of forty two poundẽ for 30^c of Iron hoopes at 28^s p centũ.

Warrant to pay to Tristram Eldrich the soñe of 4^{li} 7^s wch is by him to be repaid to severall psons poore men for lodginge *& other* charges the mariners heretofore *have put them vnto*.

THE EAST INDIA COMPANY 223

2 of June 1602.

1602
2 June.

WARRANT to pay to Peter Wright the some of forty three shilling$ for lanthornes and other thing$ for the Pynnaces.

Warrant to pay to Wm Thomas the some of twenty six shilling$ for lanthornes for the vse aforesaid.

Warrant to pay to   Smalwood a locksmith for lock$ staples & other thing$ the some of thirtie seaven shilling$.

Warrant to pay to Joseph Pett Shipwright for [sheathinge] worke vpon the Godspeede the some of fyfty two pound$.

3 of June 1602.

1602
3 June.

WARRANT to pay to m^r Ric Staps the some of 7^li 8^s 8^d beinge already disbursed by him to Jo^n ffranklyn for [his] charges in caryinge of a l{'r}e to Capten George Waymouth in to the Downes 28^s and 8^d and for the hyre of one Stace a Pylott to goe wth the Capten to Newcastle the some of 6^lli wch both amount to y^e s^d some of 7^lli 8^s 8^d.

8th of June 1602.

1602
8 June.

WARRANT to pay to w^m Hedger of wappinge for a boate made for y^e discovery wth rudder Irons and ringe bolt$ the some of five pound$ ten shilling$ *in full payment* agreed wth all by m^r Burrell [in full satisfa{c}on therof].

18th of June 1602.

1602
18 June.

WARRANT to pay to m^r nic Leat the some of fyfty one pound$ 3^s 3^d and is for *monyes* [merchandize & soe much he hath] laid out more then he hath rec^d for *provisions of* merchandize [and other provisions] sent in y^e two ship$ for discovery wch he is to give accompt of to the Audito^rs.

To the Three of the viage by y^e northwest.

1602
18 June.

129ˡⁱ 9ᵈ

Warrant to pay to John Fletcher for cordage the some of 129ˡⁱ 9ᵈ in full paymᵗ.

Warrant to pay to wᵐ Kymber for wharfage the some of 3ˡⁱⁱ.

1602
28 June.

A Coʳte the 28ᵗʰ of June 1602.
mʳ Rumney deputy   mʳ Wiseman
mʳ Eldred   mʳ Harison
mʳ Lynge.

IT is geaven in charge to the officer to warne a generall Coʳte to be at ffounders hall the sixt of July *next* to give their consents to the Eleccōn of governor dep: and comittees accordinge to certen clauses conteyned in yᵉ Pattent limitinge a tyme of this said eleccōn.

Order geaven to the bookekp̃ to finish the accomptẽ for the northwest *passage* and to charge every pticuler mans adventure last supplyed for discovery of yᵉ said northwest Passage together wᵗʰ his former adventures by yᵉ Cape of Bona Spe : [Speransa and to be entered in yᵉ bookes creditors for one entire some] *creditoʳ to yᵉ stock in one entire some in yᵉ bookes therfore appointed.*

1602
2 July.

A. Coʳte the 2. July 1602.
Mʳ Governor   Mʳ deputy
Mʳ farrington.

To the Threr of the viage by the Northwest.

WARRAUNT to pay to ffaithe may wief to John May one of the vj mʳ matẽ the some of xxxˢ in pte of his wagẽ he beinge in the Suzan.

A Warraunt to pay to Xp̃er Thompson for plates for the 2. pinckẽ thirteene shillingẽ tenn pence.

A Warraunt to pay to Wᵐ Edward Plumer for Lead and sodar for the Pinckẽ the somme of eight pound eight shillingẽ.

A Warraunt to pay mʳ John Wattẽ Governoʳ for thirty hundred of Iron hoopes at xxviijˢ p C. forty two poundẽ.

A Warraunt to pay Mʳ Rumney deputy for boate hier and other charges forty six shillingẽ eight pence.

THE EAST INDIA COMPANY

A Generall Court holden the vj July 1602.

1602
6 July.

Mr Alderman
  Wattℓ Gouernor.
Mr Rumney deputy
mr Richard Staper
Mr Richard Wisemam
Mr Robte Chamberlaine
Mr Frauncis Cherrie

Mr Thomas farrington
Mr Nicħas Leate
Mr Wm Harrison
Mr John Higelord
Mr Wm Chambers
Mr Rich : Wiche
Mr Nihas Leate.

Mr Nihas Linge
wth the most pte of the Generalitie.

HE preveledges of this fellowshipp appointinge the Eleccõn of the Governor Deputie and Comitties of this Companie vppon the first day of July or wthin sixe daies followinge *was reade.* This Cote proceeded to the Eleccõn of the said severall officers and by scruteny and generall consent did make choice of these severall psons to the severall officℓ followinge and havinge chosen them did before they were severallie placed and admitted to their severall placℓ minister vnto [them] *so many of them as were then present* respectively the severall othes ordeyned at the last Generall Cort of Eleccõn.

Sr [Ald] *John* Harte Alderman Elected Governor for to governe the affaires of the Companie for one whole yeare.

Mr William Rumney reelected Deputie Governor to governe the affaires of the Companie for one whole yeare.

Committies
Mr Aldn Wattℓ Juř
Mr Aldn Cambell Juř
Mr Thomas Cordell [Juř.]
Mr Wm Garrway Juř
Mr Rc Wiseman Juř
Mr Stapers Juř
Mr Jo : Coombe Juř
Mr Jo : Harby
Mr Wm Chambers Juř
Mr Jo : Eldred Juř

Committies
Mr Rich : Wiche Juř
Mr Jo : Higelord Juř
Mr Wm Harrison Juř
Mr Wm dale Juř
Mr George Booles Juř
Mr Tho : Horton Juř
Mr Nihas Linge Juř
Mr Tho : farrington Juř
Mr Wm Greenwell Juř
Mr Geo : Smithes Juř

1602
6 July.

Mr Humfrey Basse Ju̅r   Mr Giles Parsloe Ju̅r
Mr Humfrey Walcott Ju̅r   M^r W^m ferrers Ju̅r
Mr Robte Chamberlaine elected Thr̃er for the Companie.

Mr Richard Wrighte readmitted and contynued in the place of Secretary for the Companie for this yeare ensuinge.

Thomas Stephens admitted bookekeap for keepinge their generall accompt℥ for this yeare ensuinge demeaninge him selfe honestlye and faithfullie in his place.

Thomas Euesett readmitted to the place of Beadle for this yeare ensuinge.

Oathes.

A Warrant to pay to Tristrum Eldred Purser of the 2 Pinck℥ for paines taken in the Companies affaires the some of vj^{li} xiij^s iiij^d.

1602
28 July.

A Generall Courte holden the xxviijth of July 1602.

Mr Rumey deputy   Conmitties
Mr Alder : Cambell   Mr Wm Grenewell
Mr Aldⁿ Holliday   Mr Rob^{te} Chamberlaine Thr̃er
    Conmittees.   Mr Humfrey Basse
Mr Wm Harrison   M^r W^m dale.
Mr George Booles
    wth ye most pte of the Generalitie.

Mr Alderman Cambell new elected Gouernor.

AT the Last General Co'te Sr John Harte beinge by a generall consent elected Governo^r of this Companie desired since to be excused alleadginge his age weakenes of body and many other important business℥ of his owne. This Court therefore now proceaded to a new elecc̃on of a Governo^r and by scruteny and generall consent did make choice of Mr Alder : Cambell to guide the affaires of the Companie this ensuinge yeare who [respectively] tooke his oathe before his admission.

At this Court one Peter Wellington humbly desired to be admitted a freeman of this Companie in place of one Peter Helms lately deceased the rather for that the widowe of the said Peter had assigned over to him the stock and profitt℥

THE EAST INDIA COMPANY

thereof, the *stocke and* proffitt℥ arysinge by the said stocke is graunted to him. but his freedome altogether denied him.

1602
28 July.

Thomas Stephens likewyse humblie desired his freedome of this Companie but his sewte is defferred till further triall be made of his sufficiency and faithfull dischardge of that trust reposed in him about the Companies affaires.

Att this Court the Cassiers of the late Thrērs of this Company complained they had susteyned Losse by receavinge and painge out the Companies moneis some more some lesse And it was ordered they should be aunswered whatsoever they could iustly say they had Lost.

Warrant is geaven to [John Bowen] Mr *Chamblen thre^r* to pay vnto John Bowen six [five] q^r℥ rent [of] for the Companies meeting℥ at the founders Hall *to be* ended at [Midsommer last] *Michās next* the somme of vj^{li}.

The 16th of September 1602.
Present.

1602
16 Sept.

m^r Ald^n Cambell Gover^r	m^r Chambers
m^r Rumney dep :	m^r Harison.
m^r Cordell	m^r Bolles
m^r Stap	m^r Leate
m^r Chamblen Thrēr	m^r Toomes
m^r Wiseman	m^r Dale

M^r ffarrington.

HE Company after readinge of the Jornall sent from Capten Waymouth and] *At this Court a Journall sent [directed] from Capten Waymouth was was read* w^{ch} *gave* Intelligence *beinge* [geaven] *to this assembly* [of the said] *how* ye 2 Pinnaces [were] sent *forth for Discovery of a passage to the Est Indies by the Norw :* *are returned* & arrived at Dartmouth. *It is therfore* agreed by scruteny the [y] *said Pinnaces* shalbe brought about to London wthout sale of any of their provisions And thervpon ordered comission should be sent to Capten Waymouth for ye bringinge of the said Pynnaces about signifyinge

1602
16 Sept.

to him such thingȩ as remaine therin may serve for a seacond discovery   And further if the said Capten himselfe be sick he cannott fulfill the contentȩ of the said Comission then to [be further] *give order* as in the discrecōn of yᵉ said Capten shalbe thought most fitt for the speedy bringinge of them about.

Order lr̃es should be writt to the 2. Pursers *to this effect* That sith it hath pleased god to [crosse them] *send them noe better successe* in this their [viage] intended discovery they would *the rather therfore* be carefull for yᵉ preservinge of such thingȩ as remaine in the Pynnaces to serve for a seacond [di] adventure And to vse what industry they may in the speedy bringinge of them about.

Order geaven to Thomas Evesett to warne a generall Court at founders hall to morowe by two of the in yᵉ afternoone.

1602
17 Sept.

A Gen'all Court The 17ᵗʰ September 1602.
Present.

mʳ Rumney Dep :   mʳ ffarrington
[mʳ Ofield] mʳ Wiche   [mʳ Mosley]
[mʳ Wright] mʳ Lynge   mʳ Greenewell
And the most pt of the Generalty.

AT this generall court mʳ Cartwright *Preacher* beinge called to satisfy the Company of their returne soe suddenly did [in breefe referr that their] refer them to the readinge of Captein Waymouth's Journall wᶜʰ he had delivered vnto the Governoʳ and beinge demaunded further whether he could give intelligence of any thinge more then the said Capten in his Journall had signified alleadged in answear his ignorance in navigacōn by reason wherof he could not further satisfy them.

Mʳ Deputy gave intelligence to the Company how the Comittees at the last Court thought meete to send downe comission to Capten Waymouth for the speedy bringinge of the Pynnaces about to London wᵗʰout breakinge of bulke as alsoe to direct lr̃es to the 2. purse'rs for the safe p̃servacōn [as] of such thing ȩas

did belonge to the place they were appointed in wch course 1602
beinge liked of by the said Company l̃es to to that end were 17 Sept.
sealed vnder the com̃on seale and sent to Dartmouth where
the said Pynnaces are now at anker.

A Comittie the 29 of September 1602. 1602
                                        29 Sept.
Mr Ald^n Cambell gouerno^r   Mr John Eldred
Mr Wm Rumney deputie   Mr Wm Harryson
Mr George Bowles   Mr Nic̃has Lyng

HES Com̃itties have assembled them selfes together
vppon occasion of the longe stay of the cōming
aboute of Captein Waymouth and doe thinke it convenient that yf they do not heare from him w^{th}in thes 3 or 4
daies that then ther shall care be taken of a fitt man to goe
downe to take for ther com̃ing away.

The xiij^th of [September] *october* 1602. 1602
                                            13 Oct.
m^r Rumney deputy   m^r Dale
m^r Chamb̃len Thrẽr   m^r Lynge
m^r Combes   m^r Walcott
m^r Harison   m^r Smith
              m^r Horton.

[MR COMBES m^r Harison m^r Farrarr m^r Wiche
m^r Lynge are entreated to take the paines to see the
discharge of the two [shippẽ] Pynnaces [lately] sett
forth for a discovery to the East Indies by the northwest Passage
lately arrived at Dartmouth and now [retorned againe into] the
Port of London.]
  The two Pynnaces lately arrived at Dartmouth beinge now
come into the river of Thames accordinge to direcc̃on [of] from
the Company It is [now] thought meete for the discharge and safe
preservac̃on of all provisions remayninge therin that some of
the Com̃ittees should survey the discharge of both the said
Pynnaces And to that end m^r Coombes m^r Harison m^r Lynge

230 THE COURT RECORDS OF

1602
13 Oct.

m^r Wiche and m^r ffarrar beinge thervnto entreated have assented accordingly.

1602
18 Oct.

A Generall Court houlden the 18th of October 1602.

Present

m^r Governor   m^r ffarrington
m^r Boules   m^r Eldred
m^r Dale   m^r Lynge
m^r Harison   m^r Smithers

wth the most pt of the Generalty.

HIS Court beinge assembled vppon occasion that the two Pynnaces or barkes were neere discharged accordinge to order geaven by the last assembly of comittees Mr Governor thought meete to propound severall questions to the generalty [about] *touchinge* the sale of the barkes and all other provisions therin and about; wch wth assent of the said Generaltie are agreed vppon as hearafter followeth on the other side.

1. Imprimis The stronge beere to be sould after the rate of fowre pound^s p tonne to such of the Company as will buy it yf not to them to others at the same rate.
2. Itm they who have the caske in wch the beere is shall pay for the same caske at the rate of 20^s p tonne.
3. All those wch will have the said beere shall fetch it from thence by to morowe night oreles by Wednesday night at the furthest.
4. Their Sack^s to be laid vp in a seller for some [foure] 6. daies the caske beinge filled *wth ye same wine* [vp] and after that tyme sale to be made therof.
5. That there be a dry warehouse provided for their beefe and Porke and therof sale to be made.
6. It is in conclusion agreed that these provisions aforenamed the two barkes and all other thing^s whatsoever in or about the said barkes shalbe sould. and for the pformance therof the Generaltie doe refer the sale of all to m^r Governo^r

dep: and Comittees to do therin as in their opinions shall seeme best for the vse and behoofe of the Company.

Mr Ald Holiday havinge in his handẽ of the Companies money to the valewe of 38^{li} 6^s 9^d [as appeareth by account] would stay in his handẽ some [sixe] 8 or [seaven] 9 poundẽ *therof* wch was alledged to be [laid out by] *geaven away by* his wife but this Court not assentinge thereto have generally agreed that he shall bringe in the said some of 38^{li} 6^s 9^d to the Thrẽr.

The said Alderman Holiday beinge in arrerages for monies wch he should have supplyed towardes the discovery by the northwest It is agreed that he and all others who have not supplyed towardẽ the said discovery accordinge to the ordenances of the Company in that behaulfe provided shall have *such somes* defaulted out of their adventures *into ye East Indies* by the Cape of Bona Esperansa as by an order of the xjth of January 1601 was sett downe for such as did [incurre] offend contrary to the tenor of that lawe and to be put to accompt.

A Court 23th of October 1602.

m^r Ald Cambell go^r m^r Coombes
m^r Rumney dep :   m^r ffarrington
m^r Wiseman   m^r Parsloe
m^r Bowles   m^r Stapers
          m^r Lynge.

WARRANT granted to m^r Robert Chamblen Thrẽr to pay to such marinors as were hyred from Dartmouth to London to bringe the Pynnaces about such severall somes as shouldbe subscribed by m^r Governor or m^r Deputy vnder the said warrant.

Mr Wiseman havinge assented vppon request made for the sparinge of some convenient place to bestowe the chestẽ wherein the merchandizes were put at the sendinge out of the two Pynnaces It is thought convenient that the said chestẽ shalbe caried to m^r Wiseman's house & there to be vewed by the Comittees whether any of the quantety hath beene dimishhed.

THE COURT RECORDS OF

1602
25 Oct.

The 25th of October 1602.

Mr Aldⁿ Cambell go^r Mr Tho: farrington.
Mr Wm Rumey deputy M^r [Giles] *Humfrey* Walcott
Mr Robt Chambleyn Mr Wm Harryson
Mr John Harby Mr Rich: Wyche
Mr Gorg Bowles Mr Gyles Parslowe.
M^r Jo: Eldred. Mr Tho: Horton
Mr Rich: Wyseman Mr Wm Greenewell
M^r Jo: Combe.

OHN DREWE m^r of the Godspede being before the Comitties and exāied of the cause of the retorne of [the] Capten Waymouthe and his companie from ther voyage of the north west passage wthout anie discovery performed doeth confesse that Cartwright the minister was the principall pswader [defrauder] of the Companie n the ship called the discovery for ther retorne for England and geaving over of the voyage, and that [the] Capten Waymouth being the governo^r and generall of the voyage retorning homewardes he the said drewe and his companie were to followe ther geñall, and for the more certen proof that the said Cartwright was the pswader of the Companies retorne he saieth that the Boteson the Guñer and the Carpenter and others of the Companie of the discovery did signifie soe muche to the said Drewe, and as he thinketh will averr soe muche before the Company.

It is agreed that a demaund shalbe made [to] *at the handes* of the said Cartwright for the gowne and apparell delivered him to have bene vsed yf the voyage had bene made to the partes of Cathaia or China and yf he shall deny to deliver them then the opinion and direction some lerned counsell what acc̃on will best lye against him for the recovering thereof.

John Lane m^r mate of the Godspede beinge demaunded of the cause of the retorne of Captein Waymouth and his Companie from the northwest voyage doeth alledge that Mr Cartwright the minister as he him self did confesse and Justifie *to this John Lane* that he was the pswader and mover *of* the Company to retorne for England and to geave over the voyage.

A Gen^rall Courte the 24 of November 1602.

Mr Aldⁿ Cambell [Th͠er] Go^r   Mr Humfrey Walcott
Mr Wm Rumney deputy   Mr Thomas farrington
                               Mr George Bowles
    Comitties   Mr Nichas Lynge
Mr Wm Chamber   Mr Wm Harryson
    wth a greate part of the Gen^ralyty.

GENERALL order was geaven to the Bookeaper of this Companie to charge all suche brethren of this ffelowship as are anie way indebted to the Company in the accomptes of the Company as debtors for suche som͠es as they are in arrerages to thende yf the said money be not aunswered before the shippes returne. ther said debtes may be defaulted vppon ther severall stockes.

At this Co^rte the generalyty were informed by the relation of m^r Governo^r and m^r deputie of ther proceading against Capten Waymouth before the LL: of the Counsayll touching his retorne from the voyage of the northwest soe sone wthout *anie* discoverie. and what order was taken by ther handes in that cause. and doe further relate what was done by the commis͠sion's apointed by the LL: before whom the said Captein Waymouth was called. and demaunded vppon interr̃. whose aunswere was taken to those interr̃. and sett downe in wrytinĝ wch aunswere was read at this gen͠all courte wherin he gave the reason of his retorne and did expresse in writinge the [hope of] possibylyty [of] and hope of [the] divers Inlettes that treat [to the] throughe the coast of America [to] in to the Southseas or the East Indies vppon wch disco^rse and consideration of the great benyfyte that might growe to this com͠on wealth yf possybly a discovery may be made this Court were resolved that a newe attempte shalbe made wth [and] both ships [at the least] to see what can be done by the said Inlett͠e and to imploy the said Captein againe [therin] *in one of ye said ships* the rather for that he is very confident that ther will a passage be founde throughe some of [them] said Inlettes And because the Company having entred thus farre to finde and discover a passage

1602
24 Nov.

they meane to make this present attempte a finall proof whether ther be any passage or not. And therfore they doe agree by genᵃll consent to place another sufficyent man or captein to take charge of the second ship and to sett them forthe bothe to proceade in this discovery leavingͤ them to proceade therin ether Jointly together or severally apart eche of them taking ther severall coʳses according as [they shall thinke meet] *shall hearafter be agreed vppon* And for the preparation of the said shippes and all necessaries for the said voyage and for the calculation of the charge the better to informe the genᵃlyty at ther next meetingͤ the persons heervnder named are appointed and entreated to take paines herein viz.

Mʳ Gouʳ	Mʳ Chambers
Mʳ Deputy	Mʳ Harryson
Mʳ [Ald.] Will. Bannyng	Mʳ Greenewell
Mʳ Cordell	Mʳ Combe
Mʳ Garway	Mʳ Lynge.
Mʳ Staper	or any 4 of them.

Warrant granted to mʳ Robert Chamḃlen Thrͤr to pay to Thomas Smith for keepinge of the two Pynnaces at the rate of twelve shillingͤ p moneth the soṁe of xxiiijˢ the one halfe therof beinge dewe to him vppon Sᵃttrday last and thother halfe is for a moneth next ensuinge.

1602
29 Nov.

29 pʳd mensis.

Warrant granted to mʳ Robert Chamḃlen *Thrͤr* to pay to John Drewe mʳ of the Godspeede 5ˡⁱ John Lane xxxˢ Thomas Boarne iijˡⁱ and John Branskom xlvjˢ viijᵈ [They] ffor their imployment in the late intended discovery all amountinge to the soṁe of xjˡⁱ xvjˢ viijᵈ They acknowledginge the same in full of all demaundͤ.

4th of [August] december a° prd

1602
4 Dec.

ARRANT to the Thrēr aforesaid for payment of 6ˡⁱ 13ˢ 4ᵈ to Thomas Yerworth beinge in full for his imployment as purser of thone of the two Pynnaces sett out for discovery of the northwest Passage and [alsoe] for his dyet and attendance about the discharge of them.

A Court at founderę Hall xiijᵗʰ December 1602.

1602
13 Dec.

Mʳ Gouernoʳ   Mʳ Deputy   Mʳ Chamberlaine Thrēr

Comitties

Mʳ Staper   Mʳ Wiche

Mʳ Higlorde

Comitties

Mʳ Farrington

Mʳ Geo: Booles   Mʳ Linge.

R CHAMBERLAINE informethe this Assemblie that mʳ Stephen Hodsonn one of the Brethren of this Company had paide vnto him xˡⁱ for his supply towardę the discovery of the Northwest passadge and desired the Company to have him excused for non payment thereof till now for that he haith bene in the cuntry all this Sūmer and never hard thereof.

Order is geaven to Thomas Euesett to warne a Court vppon Weddnesday mornīge next. this Court not concluding of any thinge for want of a greater Assembly.

21ᵗʰ of December 1602.

1602
21 Dec.

ARRANT granted to mʳ Robᵗ Chamblen Thrēr to pay to Thomas Stevens Accompt keep for the Company for his Sallary dewe to him accordinge to the Companies agreement wᵗʰ him beinge vnpaid for 3. quarters [rent beginninge] *wᶜʰ is since* the 17ᵗʰ of March last amounteth to the somē of 23ˡⁱ 6ˢ 8ᵈ.

[A generall Coʳte holden the 4ᵗʰ of Januarie 1602.

1602
4 Jan.

Mʳ Aldⁿ Cambell governoʳ   Mʳ Aldⁿ Rumney deputy]

236   THE COURT RECORDS OF

1602
30 Dec.

30. of December 1602.

Mr [Governor] Aldn Cambell governor
Mr Aldn Romney deputy

Comitties

Mr Rich : Staper   Mr Nichas Lynge
Mr Jo : Combe   Mr Edw : Harryson
Mr Wm Garway

T is thought fitt by mr Governor mr deputy and the [said] comitties above mencōed that one of the companies barkes shalbe sett forth againe for the Northwest. So as they shall lyke well of [the] a newe conference wth Captein George Waymouth or some others.

1602
4 Jan.

A Genral Court holden the 4th of January 1602.

Mr Aldn Cambell governor   Mr George Bowles
Mr Aldn Rumney deputy   Mr Wm ferror
Mr Robt Chamberlayn ther   Mr John Combe
Mr Rich: Wyche.   Mr Parslowe
Mr Wm Garway   Mr Wm Harryson
Mr John Eldred   Mr Wm Greenwell.

wth an ample nomber of the genralyty.

T this Corte vppon relation made by mr Governor and [his deputie] *Mr Aldn Rumney* and vppon conference had in this Assemblie vppon the greatnes of the charge that the entended voyage by the Northwest will bring vppon the Company yf both ther barkes [of the Companie] shuld be set forth [in] and furnished for that discovery. It is resolved for the avoydinge of the excessive charge [that] of the double p̄paration of both the shippes that a computation shalbe made vppon the preparation and furnishing of on of them and to see how the victualles and furniture of them both [will] beinge laid together will sett forthe and defray a voyage by one of them wthout further charging of the Companie wth anie other suply And to

THE EAST INDIA COMPANY

that ende this Co^rte [*being aboute to make*] *have made againe* [have made] choice of the persons heervnder named as well to consider of the state and valewe of the p̄paration [of] and furnishinge of oñ ship to this enterprise and of the meanes already provided to defray the charge thereof as to confer wth Capten Waymouth and to see what resolution he holdeth to proceade in the said discovery, or wth some other fytt for the Enterprise who having [entered] advysed thervpon are intreated at the next geñall Co^rt to reporte ther opinions [and the] what they [fynde] conceave and fynde fytt and possyble to be done in this voyage according to the meaning of this Co^rt.

1602
4 Jan.

Comitties.

Mr Governo^r	Mr Grenwell
Mr Deputy	Mr Harryson
Mr Garway	Mr Hamersley
Mr Cordell	Mr Jennynges
Mr Staper	Mr Clerke

or any 4 of them.

An Assembly the 7th of January 1602.

1602
7 Jan.

m^r Governo^r	m^r Stap
m^r Ald. Rumney dep:	m^r Greenewell
m^r Garwey	m^r Hamersley
m^r Cordall	m^r Jennyngē
Mr Clarke.	

ACCORDINGE to the order of the last generall Court the Comittees abovenamed beinge mett together have thought meete in the proceadinge for the settinge out of one vessell for a discovery by the northwest *first* to sett downe the provisions for the two Pynnaces formerly sent forth and to make an estimate of the p̄ticulers therof aswell in respect they may take of the said provisions soe much as shalbe found fitt for the furnishinge of one as alsoe by sale of the residewe not found fitt to supply all other necessaries for the settinge out of the said vessell And to that end an estimacōn

1602
7 Jan.

beinge made both of the *said 2* Pynnaces and all provisions therfore they do resolve for the supplyinge of all necessary provisions as men and victuallę &c for setting out and furnishinge of one vessell to the northwest as shalbe reported to the next generall Court.

21 Jan.
1602

xxjth of January 1602.

WARRANT to Mr Chamƀlen Thrĕr for payment of certen porters for landinge and housinge of all the provisions out of the 2 Pynnaces the discovery and Godspeede the somĕ of fowre poundę.

Porters.

Thomas
Evesed
xxv^s vij^d

Another Warrant to the said Thrĕr for payment of 25^s vij^d to *Thomas Evesed* beinge disbursed by him heretofore to m^r Popes man as appeareth by y^e ꝑticulers sent wth the warrant to the Thrĕr.

26 Jan.
1602

A General Court [of] the 26th of January 1602.
Present.

Mr Ald^n Cambell gov^{er}
Mr Ald^n Rumney dep^{ie}
  Comitties
Mr Rich: Staper
Mr John highelord
Mr Wm Dale
Mr Wm Chambers

Mr Rich. Wyche
Mr John Combe
Mr Nich. Lynge
Mr Humfrey Baese
Mr Wm Harryson
M^r W^m ferro^r
Mr Humfrey Walcott

The greater part of ye Gen^{r}alyty.

THIS Court beinge called together to receave the opinion of the Comitties appointed for [the] consultation of the setting forthe of one of the barkes latelie retorned from the Northwest passage the said Comitties do report that they finde some impediment that moveth them to stay the proceading in the said enterprise and [rather] thinke it rather for the good of the Companie that a carefull course be taken for the sale of bothe the barkes wth ther furnyture and other ꝑparation and mchaundize, and that the same be converted into money wch may ryse to a convenient some fytt to defray other necessarie charges vppon the retorne of the fleet sent out by the Cape of Bona Speranza, according to whose opinions the matter being putt to the consideration of this geñall Co^rte and a question made whether one of the barkes shalbe sett forthe againe [or not] or the viage vtterlie geaven over It appered by scruteny and the consent of the most part of the geñality that the voyage shall vtterlie be left of and [all] the preparation [both of] as well shipping victualling and other furniture as merchaundize *or so moche thereof as the Comitties shall thinke meet* putt to sale and made away in as prevalent a sorte as may be and to [thende] that ende the Comitties apointed at the last geñall Courte [are] for the setting forthe of one of the said barkes having acquainted them selves wth the kindes and particlaryties of the said goodes are intreated to make sale of them for the good of the Companye or of so muche thereof as they shall thinke meet. the names of wch Comittees do followe hearafter vizt.

26 Jan. 1602

Comitties.

m^r Governor	m^r Greenewell
m^r Thomas Bramley dep :	m^r Harison
m^r Ald Rumney	m^r Hamersley
m^r Garwey	m^r Jennynge
m^r Cordall	m^r Clarke
m^r Stap	or any 4 of them.

Forasmuche as m^r Ald^n Rumney having executed the place of deputie [of] to ye governo^r of this Company and is nowe chosen *an* Alderman and cannot attende the busines of this Company therfore this Court did proceade to the Election of a newe deputy to contynue vntill the next day of Election and divers persons being noïated and putt in election the choice of the place of the said deputie is fallen vppon Mr Thomas Bramley.

Mr Tho: Bramley chosen deputy.

At this Co^rte Thomas Stephens the bookekeap of this Company is admitted to the freedome of this felowship in as ample manner as anie brother of the Companie [and hathe taken his othe accordinglie] hath and injoyeth the same by vertue of thes previledges.

1602
28 Jan.

28th January 1602.

ARRANT to the Thrēr for payment of xxiiij^s to Thomas Smith for keepinge of the Two pynnaces at the rate of xij^s p moneth for Two monethes The one halfe therof beinge dewe the 20th of this present moneth and thother halfe is to the 20th of the next moneth.

17 Feb.
1602

The 17. of february 1602.

Mr Aldⁿ Cambell Go^r	M^r w^m ferrers.
Mr Tho: Bramley deputy	Mr Rich: Wyche
Mr Wm Chambers	Mr Humfrey Walcott
Mr Nich: Lynge	Mr Georg Smythes
Mr Dale	Mr Tho: [Houghton] Horton.

Capten
Waymouthe.

HES Comitties being mett together to confer of some co^rse to be taken wth Captein Waymouth who maketh demaundes of the Companie for charges and other moneys [by the] by him expended or otherwyse dewe as he pretendeth [wch Capten Waymouth] and is contented to reserve him self and his demaundes to be arbitrably ended by 4. indifferent persons. forasmuche as he offreth his [action to be] demaundes to be arbitrably ended this assembly thinke it not fytt to refuse that co^rse and therfore do agree that whensoever he shall make choice of his arbitrators the Company will choose other arbitrators of like qualety: and for the better information of the [Comitties] Arbitrators thes persons are intreated to geave ther furtheraunce to solicite the state of the cause on the Companies behaulf.

Mr Governo^r	Mr Chambers
Mr Ald: Rumey	Mr Harrison
Mr Deputy	Mr Wyche.

Edwd:
Pullyson
6^{li}. o. o.

Warrant is geaven to M^r Thēr to pay vnto Edward Pullyson Purser of the Discouery in full discharge of his accompte and in full paym^t of all wages and demaundes the some of sixe poundes.

Warrant is geaven to m^r Thrēr to pay vnto the Wyef of Thom^s Bowrne steward of the Godspede in full satisfaction of all demaundes the some of } xx^s

A Comittee 29th of March 1603.

Mr Ald. Cambell go^r
Mr Bramley dep:
m^r Walcot
m^r fferris
m^r Lynge
m^r Wyseman

m^r Clarke
m^r Boules
m^r Harison
m^r Harby
m^r Wiche
m^r Greenewell.

HESE Comittees above menc̃oned havinge debated whether the two barkes shalbe presently sould or [to] stay *made of* the sale therof till the fyue of Aprill next do resolve *by their execc̃on of handƐ* that the said Barkes shalbe kept till that [said] tyme And that a carpinter shall viewe them and do *therto* what is necessary for the keepinge tite of their orelopƐ.

The said Com̃ittees do alsoe resolve to make sale aswell of [all] ye merchandize as all other thingƐ that are decayed or may decay at such prizes as shalbe thought convenient And wheras it is reported that cordage is *now* at a highe rate And *thought* we may be provided hearafter [at yf] *when* we shall have occasion for ye vse of any at *a* more easy rate then we can now make sale of the companies cordage It is therfore agreed if such prizes may be had as is reported sale shalbe made of the said cordage accordingly.

Warrant was granted at this assembly by order from m^r Governo^r That m^r Cham̃blen Thrēr shall pay to Tho: Smith for keepinge of the two pynnaces for two monethes at the rate of xij^s p moneth the som̃e of xxiiij^s The one halfe therof beinge dewe the xxth of this present moneth and the other halfe is to the xxth of the next moneth.

A Com̃ittee the xxiiijth of May 1603.
Present.

m^r Governo^r
m^r Harison
m^r JennyngƐ

m^r Wiseman
m^r lynge
m^r fferris

Mr Burrell.

242   THE COURT RECORDS OF

1603
24 May.

WHERAS an order was taken by certen Comittees the xxixth of March last that the Two barkes should be sould after the fyue of May It is concluded that if the some of 600^{li} may be had for them vizt 300^{li} for one vessell wth his Inventorie and the like for the other It shalbe accepted of and not vnder but by the consent of the Governo^r and 4 Comittees.

1603
4 June.

4th of June 1603.

WARRANT to the Thr͞er for payment of xxiiij^s to Tho: Smith for keepinge of the Two pynnaces at the rate of xij^s p̄ moneth for Two Monethes The one halfe therof dewe the xxth of the last moneth And thother halfe is to the xxth of this present moneth.

1603
6 June.

A Gen^rall Courte holden the vjth of June 1603.

Present	Comittes
Mr Aldⁿ Cambell governo^r	M^r olyuer Style
Comittees	Mr John Harby
Sr John Harte knight	Mr Robt Chamblayn
Mr Tho: Cordell	Mr Humfrey Basse
Mr George Bowles	Mr Wm Greenwell
Mr Rich: Staper	Mr Nich: lynge
Mr Rich: Wyseman	Mr Georg Smythes

Mr Tho: Horton
wth the greatest nūber of the gen^ralyty.

THIS generall Co^rte being̃ called together vppon occasion of the receipt of lr͞es re^d by a frencheman wch latelie departed at sea from one of o^r fleet the ship Assention wch lr͞es were written the one [from Ed. Highlord purser of the Assention and the other] from Roger Style Cape Merchant of the Assention. and the other from Ed: Highelord Purser of the same ship. bothe discoursing̃ the state of the voyage bothe concerning̃ the partes wch have bene visited for trade and howe [they] many of [the] o^r men are dead in the voyage. By wch discourses [in] this gen̄all Assemblie doe conceave good hope that the voyage will fall out suche as may minister incoragem^t to sett out another voyage for the further discovery of the partes of the East Indies.

1603
6 June

A Com̄ittee the ixth of June 1603.

1603
9 June

m^r Ald Cambell Go^r
m^r Bramley dep:
m^r Garwey
m^r Wiseman
m^r Smithies
m^r Clarke.
Mr Harrison.

m^r fferris
m^r Stile
m^r Lynge
Mr Bowles
Mr Giles Paslowe
Mr Rich: Wyche

IT is resolved that lr̃es shalbe written to the ffacto^{rs} & *Company* of the Assention and sent downe to the west cuntrey geving them to vnderstand the whole Companie here in care of the relief and comfort of all suche as are sicke in the ship and [for the] supply of anie wantes that they [or anie of ther Comp] stande fitt to be supplied [by] wth all the Companie here have written ther lr̃es of credite to some of the principall merchant^e of the Towne of Plymouth Dertmouthe and other the port^e therabout^e to take suche sicke and weake men on shore wch are desirous to leave the shippes. And to require the said ffactors and other officers of the shippes that forasmuche as this care is taken to furnishe ther wantes by the credite of the Companie here that they forbeare by anie pretence or want to breake bulke or make sale of anie thinge that doeth belonge to the *generall* adventure.

And it is alsoe ordered that according^{ly} to the said lr̃es soe to be written to the said factors and other officers in the ship Mr Rob̄t Mydleton Mr Bateman and Mr Howe shalbe moved to make choice of suche m̄chaunt^e in the said Townes of Plymouth Dartmouth &c. wth whom they are best acquainted to th ende that m^r Governou^{rs} lr̃e may be directed to them subscribed

1603
9 June.

also wth ther handes entreating them to geave to the facto{r} Captein or principall in charge in the said ship credite for any suche moneys as he shall want for the vse of the ship. and to take in to ther townes suche sicke men as shall come on shore and to see them supplied wth suche relief as ther wantes require and the Companie vppon ther billes or advyse of the charges disbursed directed to m{r} Robt Chambleyn will see them satysfied.

1603
16 June.

A General Court the 16th of June 1603.

Present.

Mr Ald Cambell gov{r}	Mr John Combe
Mr Tho: Bramley deputy	[Mr Humfrey Basse]
Sr John Spencer	Mr Geo: Smithes
Mr Ald{n} Wattes	Mr Humfrey Basse.
Mr Ald{n} Hollyday	Mr Wm Chamber
Mr Ald{n} Swynerton	Mr Rich: Wyche
Mr Ald{n} Hampson	Mr Wm Harryson
	Mr Jo: Highelord
Comitties	Mr Gyles Paslowe
Mr Wm Garway	Mr Humfrey Walcott
Mr Tho: Cordell	Mr Wm Dale
Mr Robt Chambleyn	Mr W{m} ferrys
Mr Rich: Wyseman	Mr Nich: lynge
Mr [olyuer] George Bowles	Mr Wm Greenewell

wth an ample nūber of the gen{er}alyty.

The assention returned from the East Indies.

HER is propounded to this gen{er}alyty the choice of a convenient place of receipte of the goodes retorned in the Assention wch is nowe come in to the Ryuer. and for ther better direction what places are likelie to be hired for that p̄pose ther is nominated thes severall places or houses hereafter following [viz] out of which the comitties may make ther choice vppon the viewe of the fittest.

Warehouses
{ The vault vnder thexchaunge
Sr John Spencers warehouse
The great house in Sething lane
Sr Edward osbornes house
The La : Barnes her house.
Mr Cartwrightes house.

1603
16 June.

At this Cou^{r}te the geñ'alyty have agreed that the comÿytties according to the geñall trust wch is reposed in them for the managinge of the [trade of] merchaundize brought home in this voyage, shall appoint suche men as they shall thinke meet to goe aboarde the assention. and to attende ther from tyme to tyme vntyll the ship be vnladen.

Men to attende aboarde.

The generall Co^{r}te beinge broke vp the comitties did stay together in conference to geave order for the disposing̃ of the m̃chandize aboard the ship : and ther vppon did resolve for the present that of these comitties the persons herevnder nõīated shall p̃sently goe downe to the ship and ther take order that noe marino^r or anie other shall presume to deliuer and carry from the ship anie thinge whatsoever vnlesse it be visited vppon paine of deteyning̃ in the Companies handes the wages of everye suche marino^r or other Officer :

Mr Bramley deputy Mr Chambers
Mr Highelord Mr Harryson.

And besides the comitties who are to take ther tornes as occasion shall serue to goe aboard the ship. these p̃sons of the geñalyty herevnder named are appointed to goe downe and to take ther tornes of warding̃ aboarde when they shall be appointed.

Mr Wm Jennyns Mr Anth : Gibson
Mr Rich : Clerke Mr Whyte
Mr Rich : Browne Mr Tho : Southewyke
Mr Taylby Mr Geo : Bennett
Mr Barth : Haggett Mr Ald^n Hollydaies man
Mr Roger Hemyng Mr Ald^n Bannynges man
Mr Wm Nelson [cowcheman] Robt Bar-
Mr Edm Nicholson ker.

246   THE COURT RECORDS OF

1603   Mʳ Lytleford   Mʳ Wᵐ Wastall
16 June.
                    Ambrose Wheeler
             dc̅o̅ xvj° Junij 1603
        An Assembly of yᵉ Comitties above named.
These 4 persons vndernamed are apointed to goe aboard the Assention to morrowe morning the xvij*ᵗʰ* June at 6 of the clocke and to contynewe ther vntill the next day the same howre viz :

    Edmund Nicholson   [Rich. Taylby]
    Ambrose Wheler.   [Roḃt Barker for]
    [Roger Hemmynge]   [Mʳ Paull Bannynge]

for *Satherday* the 18ᵗʰ of June are apointed these p̃sons vdlt.

    Roger Hemmyng   [Mʳ Rich : Taylby]
    Roḃt Barker for   [Mʳ Wᵐ Wastall]
    Mʳ P. Bannyng   [Mʳ James Turnoʳ]
    [Mʳ Antho Gibson]   [Mʳ Aldⁿ Hollydaies mañ]

For Sunday yᵉ 19 of June are appointed to awaite aboarde these persons viz.

    Antho : Gibson   Rich : Taylby

For Monday the 20ᵗʰ of June are appointed to goe aboarde the ship. and to attende the from sixe in the morning vntill vj of the clocke the next day.

    Mʳ Ja : Turnoʳ   Mʳ Rich : Clerk
    Mʳ Wᵐ Jennyns   [Mʳ Wᵐ Wastall]
    Mʳ Aldⁿ Hollydaies man   [Mʳ   ]

For Tuesday yᵉ 21ᵗʰ of June 1603 are apointed these persons viz.

    Mʳ Wᵐ Wastall   Mʳ Barth : Haggett
    Mʳ Rich : Broun   Mʳ Wᵐ Nelson

It is ordered that Mʳ Style and the Purser doe attende aboard vntill the [that] shipp be discharged.

touching my L. Admiralles tythes.   It is thought meet by the Comitties above menc̃oed touchinge the tenthes belonging to my L. Admirall for the prise wᶜʰ the Companies shippes have taken in the East Indies. that his Lp̃ shalbe made acquainted wᵗʰ the advyse wᶜʰ Captein Lancaster

hath written in that behaulf wherin it may appere that the   1603
comodities taken are not vendable here but more fitter to be   16 June.
solde in the Indies.

    Mr Ferrers and Mr Lynge are entreated by this assembly   Canvas
to provide 50 or 60 peeces of Polldavies for the makinge of   bagges.
bagg℔ for the bagginge of the pepper brought home in the
shippes And to putt them out to makinge. And alsoe to provide 6 sewtes of canves dublett and hose w^thout pockett℔ for
6. porters to be imploied in the fillinge of the pepp.

    It is ordered that an entrie shalbe made in the custome house
of the goodes in the Assention consisting of the pticlers viz.

        Pepper loose in the ship xxj m^li   CCxm^li
        Cloves 16 small bagg℔ cñ^ts   xj C^li
        Synamoñ 87 Cannasters cñ^ts   vj mxxx^li
        Gum lacre 67 bagg℔ cñ^ts   iiij miiij*xx*^li.

    Warrant is geaven to m^r Thr℥r to pay vnto Mr Midleton of   Mr Midle-
Plymouth for his paines ryding hether wth the first report of the   ton v^li for ryding post
coming of the Assention out of the East Indies the some of v^li.   from Plymouth.

                A Comittee the 21th of June 1603   1603
                                                           21 June.
    Mr Ald^n Cambell governo^r   Mr John Eldred
    Mr Tho: Bramley deputy   M^r W^m ferrers
    Mr Wm Garway   Mr Tho: Horton
    Mr George Bowles   Mr Wm Harryson
    Mr Humfrey Basse   Mr Wm Greenewell
                Mr Richard Wyche.

R Governo^r is moved by this Assemblie to take
some other of the Companie to be bounde wth him to
the Customers for the Subsedye due to the kinge for
the goodes brought home in the Assention . and for ther Indempnity they shall have an order of geñall co^rte and the
companies comon seale to save them harmeles whervnto the
said Mr Governo^r [is] doeth geave his assent and m^r Eldred
doeth agree to be bound wth him.

    Mr Bowles and M^r [Harryson] *Grenewell* are appointed and

1603
21 June

intreated to [goe] see the seullerage or vautes [in] *vnder* the exchaunge prepared and fytted to receave the said goodes . and to see the floores plancked and boarded for that purpose.

Mʳ Wᵐ Grenewell and Mʳ wyche *and mʳ Harryson mʳ Horton* are appointed to be at the waterfall vppon Wensday and Thursday to see the goodes taken vp and sent to the [Exchaunge] Warehouses at the Exchaunge and the bookeap to be present wᵗʰ them to make tickettℯ for the carrmen.

Mʳ Bowles [and] Mʳ Eldred *Mʳ Lynge Mʳ Ferrers* are apointed to attende at the warehowses at thexchaung the same daies [and] to receave in the goodes and to waighe them and to vse the helpe of Tho: White to keepe a note of the waight.

for pilotage vjˡⁱ to the wief of John May purser in the Susan 56ˢ.

Warrant is geaven to [Mʳ Thĕr] *Tho: Stephens* to pay to the wyef of John May one of the mʳᵉ Mates of the Susan for her relief in her husbandes absence a monthes wages coming to lvjˢ *And to pay for pilotage for bringing vp the Assention into yᵉ ryver vjˡⁱ.*

1603
23 June

A Genʳall Courte the 23ᵗʰ of June 1603.

Present

Mʳ Aldⁿ Cambell Governoʳ   Mʳ Wᵐ Chambers
Mʳ Tho Bramley deputy   [MʳRobt.Chambleyn Th.]
Mʳ Rob̄t Chamberleyn   Mʳ Aldⁿ Hollyday
    Comitties   Mʳ John highelorde
Mʳ Paull Bannyng   Mʳ Giles Parslowe
Mʳ Aldⁿ Wattes   Mʳ Wᵐ Ferrers
Mʳ John Harby   Mʳ George Bowles

wᵗʰ the greatest part of the geñality.

WHEREAS ther is dewe to the kinge for custome ixᶜ and xvijˡⁱ poundes *or theraboutes* for the wᶜʰ Mʳ Aldⁿ Cambell and Mʳ Eldred stande bounde by obligation in double the valewe by way of penaltie Therfore it is ordered for the indempnitie of the said Mʳ Aldⁿ Cambell and Mʳ Eldred that they shall have the com̃on seale of the company to save them harmeles ether made to them selfes or to suche as they shall noīate to have bondes made vnto. wch bondes this geñalyty will alway mainteyne for a good securitie vnto them.

1603
23 June

It is ordered at this geñall Courte for the payment of the marino^rs wch are come home in the Assention that moneis shalbe taken vp at interest [and vppō] and that the geñalytie shall save them harmeles that shalbe bounde for it. and geave *them* the companies bonde vnder the cōen seale, vppoñ wch order soe taken by the geñalyty thes persons herevnder named being present are entreated to geave ther bondes for the taking vp of two thowsand poundes viz.

Sr John Harte and Mr Chamberleyñ for 1000^li Mr Paull Baning Esquier and m^r Ald^n Wattes for 1000^li to be contynued at interest for 3 monethes, [this Co^rte] the geñalytie entendinge hereafter to take a co^rse to levie by the pole and vppon the rates of the pticler adventures, all suche soñies of money as the Companie shall have occasion to vse hereafter.

This Courte doe geave order and geñall coñission to the Comitties from tyme to tyme to proceade in sales of the goodes nowe brought home and to take the best opportunety in ther discretions for that purpose and geñaly to pforme all thinges incydent to the ordering and venting of the same coñiodities And for the further helpe of the geñall busines It shalbe lawfull for m^r Governo^r and m^r Deputy or ether of them from tyme to tyme to apointe any one or two of the adventurors to pforme anie pticler office or service wch the geñall busines requireth.

The 28th of June.   Present
Mr Bramley deputy   Mr Wm Dale
Mr George Bowles   Mr Wm Harryson
Ry Wright secretary

1603
28 June

Fowre obligations vnder coñon seale of the Company sealed in the presence of the psons above named videlt.

Two obligations of the penalties of 3000^li a peece the one to m^r [John] James Cambell the other to m^r John Eldred being

1603
28 June.

made to save them harmeles for 900^{li} and seventeene poundes w^{ch} *the* are bounde for to the kinge for the custome of the goodes brought in the Assention the one half the xxth of decemb̃ next the other the xxth June followinge.

Two other obligations of the penaltie of 1000 markes a pece the one to [m^r] Sr John Hart and the other to Mr Robt Chamberlayñ for the payment of 500 12^{li} 10^s a peece to ether of them vppon the xxvijth of September next at ther severall dwelling houses.

Billes of aduenture sealed.

	li.	s.	d.
21th of March 1600. To Stephen Hodgeson a bill of aduenture & supply at ij^s the li.	240	0	0
10 June 1601. To Wm Angell a Bill of adventure & supplies	240	0	0
13 June 1601. To Roger Hemyng a bill of adventure & supplies	240	0	0
17 June 1601. To John Eldred a Bill of adventure & supplies	600	0	0
To Humfrey Myllward a bill of adventure & supplies	240	0	0
To Richard Hearne a bill of adventure & supplies	240	0	0
14 August 1601. To [Richard] *Robert* Pennington a bill of adventure & supplies	240	0	0
17 June 1601. To Thomas Talbutt a bill of adventure & supplies	240	0	0
18 June 1601. To Roger Ofeilde a bill of adventure & supplies	360	0	0
To John Stoackly a bill of adventure & supplies	240	0	0
To William Megges a bill of adventure & supplies	240	0	0

		li.	s.	d.
18 June 1601. To John Coucheman a bill of adventure & supplies		240	0	0
To William Adderly a bill of adventure & supplies		240	0	0
To Bartholmew Holland a bill of adventure & supplies		240	0	0
[To Richard Gosson a bill of adventure & supplies		240	0	0]
To Richard Humble a bill of adventure & supplies		240	0	0
To Thomas Bootheby a bill of adventure & supplies		240	0	0
[To William Jennyns a bill of adventure and supplies		240	0	0]
To Andrewe Chamberlin a bill of adventure and supplies		240	0	0
To Robte Offeley a bill of adventure & supplies		240	0	0
To Clement Mosely a bill of adventure & supplies. *This bill is made to Eliz Moseley widowe*		240	0	0
To Thomas Southacke a bill of adventure & supplies		240	0	0
To William Quarles a bill of adventure and supplies		240	0	0
19 June 1601. To Reynolde Greene a bill of adventure & supplies		240	0	0
To Lawrence Waldoe a bill of adventure & supplies		240	0	0
To Raphe Buzby a bill of adventure & supplies		240	0	0
To William fferrers a bill of adventure & supplies		240	0	0
To William Bonham a bill of adventure and supplies		240	0	0
To Thomas Juxon a bill of adventure & supplies		240	0	0

THE COURT RECORDS OF

		li.	s.	d.
19 June 1601. To Thomas Shipton a bill of adventure & supplies		240	0	0
To Edward Barker a bill of adventure & supplies		300	0	0
23 June 1601. To George Whitmore a bill of adventure & supplies		240	0	0
To Thomas Bramby a bill of adventure & supplies		240	0	0
To Henrie Poulsteede a bill of adventure & supplies		240	0	0
To ffrauncys Barker a bill of adventure & supplies		240	0	0
To Richard Washer a bill of adventure & supplies		240	0	0
To John Hodgson a bill of adventure & supplies		240	0	0
To Humfrey Basse a bill of adventure & supplies		240	0	0
To Wm Wollastone a bill of adventure & supplies		240	0	0
To Humfrey Wallcott a bill of adventure & supplies		240	0	0
To John Newman a bill of adventure & supplies		240	0	0
To Samuell Armitage a bill of adventure & supplies		240	0	0
To Henrie Bridgeman a bill of adventure & supplies		240	0	0
To Wm Bond a bill of adventure & supplies		240	0	0
To Thomas Horton a bill of adventure & supplies		240	0	0
To John Swinerton a bill of adventure & supplies		360	0	0
To Robte Waldoe a bill of adventure & supplies		240	0	0
To Humfrie Style a bill of adventure & supplies		240	0	0

		li.	s.	d.
23 June 1601.	To Thomas Farrington a bill of adventur & supplies	240	0	0
	To Wᵐ Cotton a bill of adventure & supplies	240	0	0
	To Edmond Nicholson a bill of adventure & supplies	240	0	0
	To Raphe Gore a bill of adventure & supplies	360	0	0
	To Oliver Stile a bill of adventure & supplies	560	0	0
	To Richard Bell a bill of adventure & supplies	240	0	0
	To Richard Piott a bill of adventure & supplies	240	0	0
	To Robte Myldmay a bill of adventure & supplies	240	0	0
	To John Buzbridge a bill of adventure & supplies	240	0	0
	To Robte Coxe a bill of adventure & supplies	240	0	0
	To Richard Peierce a bill of adventure & supplies	240	0	0
	To Richard Ball a bill of adventure & supplies	240	0	0
	To Robte Cobbe a bill of adventure & supplies	240	0	0
	To George Coles a bill of adventure & supplies	240	0	0
	To Robte Bucke a bill of adventure and supplies	240	0	0
	To Richard Hale a bill of adventure & supplies	240	0	0
	To Wᵐ Hale a bill of adventure & supplies	240	0	0
	To Wᵐ Greewell a bill of adventure & supplies	240	0	0
	To Robte Johnson a bill of adventure & supplies	240	0	0

	li.	s.	d.
23 June 1601. To Andrewe Banninge a bill of adventure & supplies	240	0	0
To Thomas Hewitt a bill of adventure & supplies	240	0	0
To Robte Mydleton a bill of adventure & supplies	240	0	0
To Wm Stoane a bill of adventure & supplies	600	0	0
To Wm Cavendishe a bill of adventure & supplies	240	0	0
To Samuell Hare a bill of adventure & supplies	240	0	0
To Edmund Spencer a bill of adventure & supplies	240	0	0
To Morrice Luellen a bill of adventure & supplies	240	0	0
To Niclīas Barmesly a bill of adventure & supplies	240	0	0
To John Hewitt a bill of adventure & supplies	240	0	0
To Jno Cornelius a bill of adventure & supplies	240	0	0
To James Turner a bill of adventure & supplies	240	0	0
To Thomas Barbar a bill of adventure & supplies	240	0	0
To Richard Poyntell a bill of adventure & supplies	240	0	0
To James Deane a bill of adventure & supplies	360	0	0
To Thomas Westrow a bill of adventure & supplies	240	0	0
To Rowland Backhowse a bill of adventure & supp̃.	240	0	0
To Bartholmew Barnes a bill of adventure & supplies	240	0	0
To Ellis Crispe a bill of adventure & supplies	240	0	0

THE EAST INDIA COMPANY

	li.	s.	d.
23 June 1601. To Richard Clarke a bill of adventure & supplies	240	0	0
To Raphe Hamer a bill of adventure & supplies	240	0	0
To Jnº Hawkyns a bill of adventure & supplies	240	0	0
To Thomas Henshawe a bill of adventure & supplies	240	0	0
To Thomas Garway a bill of adventure & supplies	240	0	0
To Thomas White a bill of adventure & supplies	240	0	0
To George Candler a bill of adventure & supplies	240	0	0
To Robte Bateman a bill of adventure & supplies	240	0	0
30 June 1601. To Thomas Bostocke a bill of adventure & supplies	240	0	0
1 July 1601. To John Clinche a bill of adventure & supplies	240	0	0
2 July 1601. To Nicholas Leate a bill of adventure & supplies	240	0	0
To Robte Sandy a bill of adventure & supplies	260	0	0
To Richard Wyseman a bill of adventure & supplies	600	0	0
4 July 1601. To Hughe Crompton a bill of adventure & supplies	240	0	0
6 July 1601. To John Wollstenham a bill of adventure & supplies	240	0	0
To Robte Gore a bill of adventure & supplies	240	0	0
To John Leman a bill of adventure & supplies	240	0	0
7 July 1601. To Allphonsus ffowle a bill of adventure & supplies	240	0	0
9 July 1601. To Wm Romney a bill of adventure & supplies	240	0	0

THE COURT RECORDS OF

	li.	s.	d.
10 July 1601. To John ffletcher a bill of adventure & supplies	240	0	0
To Morrice Abbott a bill of adventure & supplies	240	0	0
14 July 1601. To Richard Tailbye a bill of adventure & supplies	240	0	0
21 July 1601. To John Cason a bill of adventure & supplies	240	0	0
To Thomas Allabaster a bill of adventure & supplies	240	0	0
To *Nichas Pierde a Bill of adventure & supplies*	240	0	0
22 July 1601. To Thomas Smithe a bill of adventure & supplies	360	0	0
To Roger Howe a bill of adventure & supplies	360	0	0
To John Westwraye a bill of adventure & supplies	360	0	0
To Edward Leeninge a bill of adventure & supplies	360	0	0
To Thomas Cambell Ald^n a bill of adventure & supplies	360	0	0
To John Wattes Ald^n a bill of adventure & supplies	600	0	0
To George Bowles a bill of adventure & supplies	300	0	0
To John Hart Knight a bill of adventure & supplies	600	0	0
To Edward Holmeden Ald^n a bill of adventure & supplies	1200	0	0
To John Spencer Knight a bill of adventure & supplies	360	0	0
To Robte Sampson Ald^n a bill of adventure & supplies	360	0	0
To Wm Offeley a bill of adventure *without* supplies	300	0	0
To John Middleton a bill of adventure & supplies	240	0	0

THE EAST INDIA COMPANY

	li.	s.	d.
22 July 1601. To Nicħas Peird a bill of adventure and supplies	240	0	0
To Giles Parsloe a bill of adventure and supplies	240	0	0
To Edmnd Scott a bill of adventure & supplies	240	0	0
To Edward Barkham a bill of adventure & supplies	240	0	0
To Anthonie Stratford a bill of adventure & supples	240	0	0
To Augustine Sknñ a bill of adventure & supplies	240	0	0
To Ambrose Wheler a bill of adventure & supplies	240	0	0
To Anthonie Moseley a bill of adventure & supplies	240	0	0
To Thomas Richardson a bill of adventure & supplies	240	0	0
To Wm Burrell a bill of adventure & supplies	240	0	0
To Thomas Lydall a bill of adventure & supplies	240	0	0
To Samuell Backhowse a bill of adventure and supp^{ls}	240	0	0
To Richard Barrett a bill of adventure & supplies	240	0	0
To Peter Helinge a bill of adventure & supplies	240	0	0
To Nicħas Lynge a bill of adventure & supplies	240	0	0
To James Lancaster a bill of adventure & supplies	240	0	0
To Wm Hynde a bill of adventure and supplies	240	0	0
To James Donkon a bill of adventure & supplies	240	0	0
To George Bennett a bill of adventure & supplies	240	0	0

258   THE COURT RECORDS OF

	li.	s.	d.
22 July 1601. To Edward Walker a bill of adventure & supplies	240	0	0
To Robert Stratford a bill of adventure & supplies	240	0	0
To Gregorie Allen a bill of adventure & supplies	240	0	0
To Edward Harrison a bill of adventure & suppl:	240	0	0
To Wm Turner a bill of adventure & supplies	240	0	0
To Thoms Ball a bill of adventure & supplies	240	0	0
To Edward Latterfeild a bill of adventure & supplies	240	0	0
To Anthony Gibson a bill of adventure & supplies	240	0	0
To Robte Bell a bill of adventure & supplies	240	0	0
To Ric^d Ironsyde a bill of adventure & supplies	240	0	0
To Niclias Manley a bill of adventure & supplies	240	0	0
To Wm Chambers a bill of adventure & supplies	240	0	0
To Wm Millett a bill of adventure & supplies	240	0	0
To Wm Freeman a bill of adventure & supplies	240	0	0
To Wm Albany a bill of adventure & supplies	240	0	0
To Jefferie Kerby a bill of adventure & supplies	240	0	0·
To Robte Key a bill of adventure and supplies	240	0	0
To Tho: Symonde a bill of adventure & supplies	240	0	0·
To Simon Lawrence a bill of adventure & supplies	240	0	0
To Niclias Crispe a bill of adventure & supplies	240	0	0
To Barthol: Haggett a bill of adventure & supplies	240	0	0

THE EAST INDIA COMPANY

		li.	s.	d.
22 July 1601. To Wm Smithe a bill of adventure and supplies		240	0	0
To Lewis Pope a bill of adventure & supplies		240	0	0
To Ric^d Bowdler a bill of adventure & supplies		240	0	0
To Rob̃te Ducy a bill of adventure and supplies		240	0	0
To Rob̃te Brocke a bill of adventure & suppł.		240	0	0
To Rob̃te Carrell a bill of adventure & supl		240	0	0
To Richard Deane a bill of adventure & suppł.		240	0	0
To Richard Cokes a bill of adventure and supplies		240	0	0
To Nicħas ffarrar a bill of aduenture and supplies		240	0	0
To James Cullymore a bill of adventure & suppł.		240	0	0
To John Harby a bill of adventure and supplies		240	0	0
To Roger Cotton a bill of adventure & supplies		240	0	0
To Rob̃te Baylie a bill of adventure & supplies		240	0	0
To George Cater a bill of adventure & supplies		240	0	0
To Ric^d. Wiche a bill of adventure & supplies		240	0	0
To Wm Dale a bill of adventure & supplies		240	0	0
To Richard Burrell a bill of adventure & supplies		240	0	0
To Leonard White a bill of adventure & supplies		240	0	0
To George Hollman a bill of adventure & suppł.		240	0	0
To Henrie Archer a bill of adventure & suppl :		240	0	0

	li.	s.	d.
22 July 1601. To Stephen Harvy a bill of adventure & suppl:	240	0	0
To Josephe Salbancke a bill of adventure & suppl:	240	0	0
To John ffryer a bill of adventure & supplies	240	0	0
To Wm Wastell a bill of adventure and supplies	240	0	0
To Humfrie Handford a bill of adventure & supplies	240	0	0
To W^m ffysher a bill of adventure & supplies	240	0	0
To Henrie Robinson a bill of adventure & supplies	240	0	0
22 Febr: 1600. To Humfrie Robinson a bill of adventure & suppt.	240	0	0
22 July 1601. To Wm Harrison a bill of adventure & supplies	240	0	0
To John Greenewood a bill of adventure & supplies	240	0	0
To John Humfrey a bill of adventure & supplies	240	0	0
To Humfrey Smithe a bill of adventure & supplies	240	0	0
To Roger Die a bill of adventure & supplies	240	0	0
To Wm Cater a bill of adventure and supplies	240	0	0
To ffrauncys Taylor a bill of adventure & sup:	240	0	0
To John Combe a bill of adventure & supplies	240	0	0
To Wm Palmer a bill of adventure & suppl:	240	0	0
To John Highlorde a bill of adventure & supt:	240	0	0
23 July 1601. To Rob̃te Ducy a bill of adventure & supplies	240	0	0
To Henrie Butler a bill of adventure [and supp^l.]	200	0	0
To Jeremie Davers a bill of adventure &c	200	0	0
To Wm Allen a bill of adventure &c	200	0	0

THE EAST INDIA COMPANY

	li.	s.	d.
23 July 1601. To Thomas Heyes a bill of adventure &c	200	0	0
To Wm Palmer a bill of adventure &c	200	0	0
To Wm Starkye a bill of adventure &c	200	0	0
To Thomas Marshe a bill of adventure &c	200	0	0
To Raphe Allen a bill of adventure &c	200	0	0
14 August 1601. To Richard Chamberleyn a bill of adventure &c.	240	0	0
To Richard Champion a bill of adventure &c	240	0	0
To Robt Chamberleiñ a bill of adventure &c	240	0	0
To George Chamberleiñ a bill of adventure &c.	240	0	0
To Frauncis Evington a bill of adventure &c.	240	0	0
To John Morrice a bill of adventure &c	240	0	0
28 August 1601. To Richard Stap a bill of adventure &c	800	0	0
To John Jackson a bill of adventure &c	240	0	0
To William Kellett a bill of adventure &c	240	0	0
9 October 1601. To Robte Robinson a bill of adventure &c	240	0	0
To John Watt^e a bill of adventure &c	240	0	0
To Xpofer Cletherowe a bill of adventure &c	240	0	0
7 November 1601. To Hugh Hamersley a bill of adventure &c	240	0	0
19 November. To Eliz Moseley Widowe a bill of adventure	240	0	0
xxvijth of January 1601. To George Dorrington a bill of adventure & supplies &c	240	0	0
To Nic. Salter a bill of adventure and supplyes &c	240	0	0
To Richard Wragge a bill of adventure & supplies &c	240	0	0
John Wragge a bill of adventure & supplyes &c	240	0	0
To Willm Jennyng^e a bill of adventure and supplyes &c	240	0	0
To Richard Gosson a bill of adventure & supplyes &c	240	0	0

		li.	s.	d.
17th of February 1601. Leonard Holiday Ald a bill of adventure and supp : &c		1440	0	0
xxvjth of February 1600. Roger Style facto^r a bill of adventure		40	0	0
2 of March 1601. Erle of Cumberland a bill of adventure		500	0	0
Countesse of Cumberland a bill of adventure		50	0	0
Ric Persons a bill of adventure		200	0	0
xth of March 1601. To Mr Leonard Holiday Ald a bill *of* adventure of ccxxx^{li} assigned to him by Therle of Cumberland		230	0	0
xxvjth of Apirill 1602. To Mr Ald Moore a bill of adventure & supp :		480	0	0
To Xp̄ofer Nicholl℮ a bill of adventure and supp		240	0	0

THE EAST INDIA COMPANY

[Memoranda on the fly leaves at the end of the volume.]

The 10th daie of August 1603.

A Comittie or Meeting of

M^r [P] Thomas Bramlye deputie   Mr Wittm Chambers
Mr Pawle Banninge   Mr Hughe Hamerslye

THEIS Comitties have thought good to entertaine into their s^rvice Elias Bradshawe for *the* consideracõn of tenne poundes for the yeare to be imployed in the busines of the East India company as they shall thincke good.

WHEREAS ther is a viage preparing to the Est Indies sett forthe by certen merchantes the preparation whereof requireth much expedition to be vsed in Shipwrightȩ and ship carpenters wch viage her ma^ie doeth favor   *A warraunt to take vp carpenters.*

The names of such as have p̃sented themselues to bee employed as ffacto^rs in this voyadg :—

    Wm Garway   Wm Skidmore
    Robt Chambleyn   Robt Rickman

The Carnation of Colchester M^r Jo. Thurston bound from Lo^n. to Colchester. bouyed vpon an Anker belonging to the Scourge. owner Stephen Johnes.

names of shipȩ.	men	tonnag	state of the adventure	tonnage
Red Dragon	180	600	68373^li besidȩ the charge of the northwest.	State of the Adventure number of men in every ship
Hector	100	300		
Assencõn	80	260		
Suzan	80	240		
		440		

[Guift sent *cast* out] Guift sent out wth victualſ and soe thought she was cast off at sea afterwardſ.

Humfrey Robinson bound in for Tho. Yermouth

Tho. Yermouth to Humfrey Robinson

$$160 \underline{\quad - \quad - \quad 500} \quad - \quad -$$
$$350 \quad - \quad -$$

Tho Yerworth.

LETTERS.

To yᵉ Ambassdʳ Mʳ Lyllo resident at Constantynople.   1599
Marche.

. HONORABLE. wee reᵈ yʳ *Lo:* Lr̃ẽ: of the 17 of November 99, wherbie it appeareth that the Graund signior hath Roially graunted all caputulations, saving the consulage of foresteers wherin his redines *of assent* also appeared but that yoᵘ were crossed by the Frenche Ambassadʳ, of whose proceadin͠g besides the advyse wᶜʰ yoᵘ wrote vs and [*of*] [wch] *whereof* mʳ Coltherst did in lyke sorte advertyse vs [in the said conten] *touching yoʳ crossinge and* contention for the [said] *said* foresteers. wee were made acquainted by [Mʳ Secretary] *Sʳ Rob̃t.* Cycill. by occasion of a complaint wᶜʰ the frenche ambassadʳˢ lieges heer had made to her maⁱᵉ and wee were required to write vnto yoᵘ as by order from her maⁱᵉ to desist all contention [for ye] wᵗʰ the frenche [for] in that behaulf leaving the dutche and others to ther owne election to patronize them selfes [as] wher they seemed best [affection] affected wᵗʰout vrging or compelling them by comaundemᵗˢ procured. of wᶜʰ order geaven vs yoʳ [weare] *L.* hath bene ptelie advertysed [since] by a private Lr̃ẽ written yoᵘ by Mʳ Stap. But forasmuch as wee do collecte by the cowrse yoᵘ [purpose] take in sendin͠g hether [Gʳ] *signiʳ* Paull Pinder to her maⁱᵉ to acquainte her highnes wᵗʰ the proceadin͠g of the frenche that ther [is] hathe bene some further and more indirecte workin͠g in this matter then yoᵘ do [comitt to] *mencon* in yoʳ Lr̃es sent to vs and for that wee do observe by the ernest solicitin͠g of the cause heer to her maⁱᵉ that the

1599
Marche.
ffrench [leaveth] omitteth [noe] no meanes or oportunety [omitted] to prevaile in the obteyning his purpose. The matter being both an hono[r] and a benifite to [w[ch]] *that* side *or part wch* [soever] prevaileth *in the contention* [wee thinke it.] And albeit we are willed to signefie to your Lordsh[s] it is her ma[tes] pleasure that yo[u] shuld take no course to enforce the dutche or other fforesteers to come vnder yo[r] consulage, yet wee thinke it wysdome not to loose anie advauntage, but to reserve the cause in equall termes vntill yo[u] receave a more absolute order in Comission ymediatlie from her ma[ie] and therfore referre o[r] selfes to yo[r] L. approved care of the cause w[ch] being entred in to so farre as it is would not be remisselie lost or lett [passe] pas.

And touching the accomptes and other pticlers *by* yo[r] *L*. mencōned to be sent by *Signior* Paull Pinder wee hope wee shall receave them at his cōming whereof wee will wryte yo[u] o[r] [conceiptes] opinions as oportunety shall pmitt. the meane *tyme* wee propounde vnto yo[r] L. [for] *in the name of the gen[er]alyty* the accepting of o[r] former motion wch is the allowaunce of 3000 cheskeens to begynne from m[r] Bartons decease *for y[e] defraying of yo[r] charges and expences* because the companie would gladlie stande vppon a certenty of ther charge as well for yo[r] L as for *Mr. Coltherste* the Consull at Aleppo wherto wee *have* [found] *heretofore found* him inclynable. And wee move yo[u] againe the rather for that yt appereth the graund signio[rs] allowaunce is nowe aunswered and is lyke to be contynued w[th]out stay or question and also for that divers of yo[r] frendes here did [not only] vndertake in yo[r] behaulfe that ye choice of you [beinge chosen] that [behaulfe yo[r] enterteynment] for her ma[tes] ambassador should not only be a saving co[r]se to the comp. but that yo[u] would willingly accept [therof] of the allowaunce of 3000 c[ns] w[ch] was supposed to be more then yo[u] [could well expend] neade to expende but only in respecte of the first yeres charge vppon w[ch] it was considered that yo[u] shuld have it allowed yo[u] from m[r] Bartons death. Our care to avoide the *sending* [question vse] of Billes of exchaung made vppon vs [as] *ether for* venice [and here in] *or for*

THE EAST INDIA COMPANY 267

England; and also all question of accepting the same, *when* 1599
they come vppon vs vnexpected and wee vnprovided hath moved vs Marche.
to charge all o^r goodes. comīng to Constantynople and Aleppo
besides ther consulage wth ½ doller by way of lone vppon every
kersey every Cth of tynn and every Cth of dry skynes *to be aunswered here at v^t vj^d the doller* and *to* contynue the charge *thereof* for
the supporting of bothe yor allowaunces because [wee] wee would
be loth yo^u shuld seeke further of, for yor *necessary and convenient*
supplies then the places of yor residences or neare thervnto.
And wee doubt not but the said consulage and Lone together
wth suche forestere consulage as shall occurre will liberally wth
an ouerplus support [the needfull] yor nedefull and convenient
expense. *wch said allowaunce of* 3000 *c^{us} p ann yf it please yo^u to
accepte shalbe from tyme to tyme aunswerd yo^u by the Consull of
Aleppo or soe much thereof as shall make vp the consulage and
Lone money collected at Constantynople to ryse to the said* [some]
sōme of 3000 *c^{us}*.

Another motive that hath drawen vs in to ye takinḡ of this
course of a sett and standynḡ charge is some trowbles that
hathe happened vs of late by reason of a demaunde made by M^r
John Bate to her ma^{ies} *privy* Counsull for the paym^t of v^{cli} by a
bill of exchaunge sent by Mr Barton vppon the late L Ther^r for
soe muche pretended by [him] *the said Bate* to be taken [vp vppon
m^r Bates fact^r] *at Constantynople* [*vppon his*] *from his factor violently
by cold of her ma^{ies} comission* [to serve his turne to] *to serve the
ambassadors turne to* goe wth the graund signio^r in to *the* Hun-
garia *warres*, [wch demaunde] vppon wch wee were convented
before ther hono^{rs} divers tymes and required to take some
course to see him contented because *as they affirmed* m^r Barton
was placed ambassador by o^r mediation. [and of w] and for the
protection of o^r trade of whose service *ther honours alledged* her
ma^{ie} had no vse, but wee [examyning the the wee] lokinge into
the *manner of the* growinḡ of the debt founde that the greatest
part of the said v^{cli} grewe vppon an accoumpte betwene the
said m^r Barton and m^r Bate and that only 400 Cheskeens was
taken vp by cōmaundem^t [whereof] *wherein* [three] *divers* others
besides Mr Bate were interessted [but] [yet] in conclusion

1599
Marche.

wee [have absolutely] *absolutelie* denyed to pay anie part of the said v^{Cli} because the Bill came not vppon the companie, and also because ther are other billes of like kinde wch the said m^r Barton gave to other pticler men for divers great somes of money that would be required to be p^d by vs yf we shuld pay m^r Bates. [But of this matter] *Of wch proceading before the Counsell* wee doe the rather geave you a tast, because vppon o^r deniall [m^r Bate] to geave satisfacc̃on. [he seemeth] *Mr Bate seemeth* to [have a] *depend vppon some course or* meane to recover his debt in Turky ether vppon Peter Gallaunt *or* John Saunderson who deliuered the money or els by some other [meanes] *extraordinarie course* wch is doubted *by some* may concerne the companie or [preiudice] touche her ma^{ie} in hono^r whereof we pray yor L. have a care and to observe that ther be noe indirecte dealinge geaven way vnto no^r [wee] her ma^{ie} or the companie touched ether in damage or reputation by [defaulte] anie default or neglecte of the cause.

Wee do verie well allowe of yor L course taken fo^r the satisfaction of the dragoman, and do thanke yo^u for yor care in the prevention of his coming hether and for all other yor carefull and painefull offices done for the good of the Companie wch wee pray yor Lo. contynue.

[*It was vndertaken be shuld accepte of.*]

[For anie other speciall Other] For anie other speciall or pticler matter we have *not* at this tyme further to inlarge vnto yor L. other then [th] onlie this main and principall point wth wch wee of purpose *reserve for a conclusion* [conclude *wch is* for the better y^r L. better remembring thereof] which is this, that *it* hath bene moved both by yor frendes and others that wee shuld geave y^r L. this frendlie note (wch to yor modest disposition *and tractable nature* is thought to be sufficient) to have a care that the hono^r of y^r place doe not carry you *into the erro^r of y^r predecess^r. to deale in thinges imptinent to y^r imploym^t* [place] *nor that yo^u* [or   move yo^u to carrie soe highe a course to] *beare yor selfe aloft in so highe a course as that o^r people seeme to be despised by yor L.* [and] *Nether that the authorytie of yor commission be extended or stretched to the c̃omaundinge of any mans goodes further then for yor necesfarie supplie* *according to our actes and ordenaunces [and contracte] and according to yᵉ meanes wᶜʰ shalbe apointed by vs for the aunswering of yʳ allowaunce agreable wᵗʰ [the] oʳ contracte made to her maⁱᵉ or by agreemᵗ made betwene yoᵘ and vs* [too farre *too* farre into excessive expence for that the charge therof is to be borne by vs that are m̃chauntℲ who have bene reproved and for pmitting *some* of oʳ Ambassadʳˢ to ruñe into suche insolent coʳses of [ryott] excesse and ryot *as they have done* and have not in tyme acquainted suche of her maⁱᵗˢ counseill as might have repressed the extremyty thereof and for yᵗ wee have *not* taken good securyty for ther better carriage and behavioʳ of ther place.]

1599
Marche.

The exceading of wᶜʰ Limites by mʳ Barton was imputed vnto vs by the Ll. of the Counseill as oʳ fault for that wee [for that wee] had not taken good securyty for him for his conteyninge him self wᵗʰin some reasonable *boundes* [LimitƐ] Thus not doubting of yʳ L care both of yoʳ owne honoʳ and of that dewe regarde wᶜʰ is to be had of vs who are willing to beare all reasonable charge that may conveniently be required to support the same wee comitt yoʳ [and] Lordship and the direction of yoʳ affaires to God. London this   day of Marche 1599

Yoʳ L. loving frendes.

<small>More in the seconde Leafe following in the B. side of the leafe.</small>

These being kepte vntill the   of marche. 99 we add for further advyse to yʳ L. touching the obteyning of foresteers, that wee were [certefyed] required by mʳ Secretary that excepte ther were the like course taken wᵗʰ the frenche ambassadʳ at Constantynople to restraine him from *vsing of any meanes by procuring or inviting* [forcyble vrging] the Dutche and other nations foresteers to come vnder his protection that yoᵘ shuld not *neade to* geave way [to yoʳ pre] or forbeare *any* [*lawfull*] *reasonable* [anie meanes] *course* to procure them to come vnder yoʳ protection. and wee do not heare of any [course] *order* that hath bene taken to restraine the frenche ambassadoʳ yoʳ competitoʳ therfore oʳ advyse is that you geave him no advauntage but wee leaue yoᵘ to yoʳ owne wysdome and discretion to *proceade* [prevaile] therin [as yoᵘ cañ best] by the best meanes yoᵘ can devyse to prevayle in yoʳ purpose Wee send yoᵘ here [in] inclosed the copies of oʳ

1599 Marche.

severall actes of court vnder the hande or fyrme of o^r secretary concerning the Lone of ¼ doller vppon a kersy, C of tynn, C of cony skins &c to thende that yf anie fact^r for any of the Company shall ether deny or delay [to satisfie] to pforme o^r order *therin, or in the payment of consulage* that you may sease ther goodes and levy the sommes thervppon dewe by o^r orders. And otherwyse proceade wth them for their contempte of o^r actes [as shall stande wth good discretion] and the aucthoryty of yor place as [is] shall stande wth good discretion. And so as before we comytt yo^{ur} L. to the tuytion of the most highest.

London the   of marche/

To ye Wo: m^r Richard Colthurst Consull for ye Right Wo. Companie of the Levant merchaunt℮.

^R o^r hartie cōmendacōns premysed &c : yor last of the 29th of September wth [th] yor former therin recyted *we have rec^d* And wher yo^u seeme discoraged [by] to accepte of a certen allowaunce *from the companie* to bearg yor charge *in Aleppo* [*of consulage*] according to the offer made yo^u of the ¼ Consulage w^{ch} *discoragem^t groweth as yo^u alledge* by reason of the Dutches ther discoverie of the East Indies. Wee see not [cause] anie reason whie that shuld be any iust discoragem^t *or cause* to *move yo^u to* chaunge yor *former* opinion for that wee o^r selfes whom the care of o^r trade concerneth more then this [pticler contracte] pticler contracte may concerne you are noe way doubtfull of anie preiudice that cañ [growe] spedelie growe vnto vs by ther discoverie for ther are manie impediment℮ that may hinder [a trade of soe] ther voiages of soe longe [and great] courses and great adventures, and may move the dutche m^rchaunt℮ rather to frequent a knowen and peaceable trade in Turkey then hassard the daunger of Seas and enemyes of soe longe a circuite and infestious clymates. [And besides] *Nether it is* o^r intention [is not] to tye yo^u to any inconvenience but for o^r better satisfaction in mainteyning a knowen charge. wee wishe yo^u to

accepte of it for a yere or too or so longe as yo^u shall finde yo^u may frugallie handle the matter for yor owne good and o^r [benefites] *ease bothe* wch wee wishe to concurre or els wee would be loth to move yo^u therto. Wee rather incyte yo^u [heretofore] *to this course* for that wee doubt not but the Ambassado^r will accepte of a sett allowaunce for ye defraying *of* his charges at Constantynople. to w^{ch} [ende] *effecte* wee have written him. And to thende that both a competent and convenient maintenance may be levied to defray both *his and* yor charges wee have ordered by acte of Courte that all shippes that come for [ye Aleppo] Allexandretta Constantynople or other the portes of Turkey besides ther consulage shall by ther goodes contynue the Lone of ½ doller vppon a kersy and the like of every C of Tynn cony skines &c. returning *for* the somes lent [by] *billes of* exchaung̃ at *vs* [iiij] vj^d the doller. wch consulage and Lones together wth the helpe of the consulage of foresteers, we doubte not but the same wyll defray [all] bothe yor *severall* charges wth an overplus. and wee have geaven order to ye said ambassado^r to make over vnto yo^u *his* billes [of exchaunge] for 3000 c^{ns} yerelie. *or for so much as together wth his receipts of consulage and Lone at Consta: shall make vp* 3000 *ch^{ens}* whereof we pray yo^u see him supplied. The vncertenty of his paiments and acceptation of his billes at venice besides, the repaiment of those billes by exchaung̃ here cōming many tymes vnseasonably to ye Company when *wee* [they] were vnprouided hath moved vs to take order for the bearing̃ of o^r charge w'hin the compas of the places of o^r trade or chiefest residence.

1599 Marche.

Touching *the* envyous and violent courses taken by the frenche ambassad^r. for the obteyning̃ of the dutche foresteers besydes the advyse wch wee re^d both from [yo^u and] [*Mr Lello the Ambassad^r*] the Ambassador and from yor self wee [founde] *hadd* some *notice* [*and*] [experience] heer, for the frenche ambassad^r Liedges in London [being therein instructed] *by order and instruc̃cons* from the ffrenche king. had made a great complainte to her Ma^{ie} against her *highenes* Ambassado^r at Constantynople and by his [importunety] complaint soe farre prevayled wth her Ma^{ie} that her highnes gave order to vs *by m^r*

1599
Marche.

Secretaries appointem to wryte to [the Ambass] Mr Lyllo that he shuld noe further contend for the said forresteers but to leave everie foresteer nation to ther owne voluntarie choice what [consull] protection they would *accept of* ether Englishe or ffrenche. but notw^thstanding for asmuche *as* to prevaile in the obteyning of these foresteers is not onlie honorable considering the contention had therabout but alsoe profitable wee have written to ye Ambassado^r *to* preserve the cawse in equall termes. w^thout preiudice vntill it shall appeare what further cowrse her ma^ie will directe vppon information brought over by *Signio^r* Paull Pynder [by] whom [the] Mr Lyllo sendeth over [over] of purpose to acquainte her Ma^ie with his proceadinges, and because yor [travell] favor wth the Bashawe may make muche to the obteyning the dutche consulage. wee pray yo^u vse all reasonable and fitt meanes to effecte the same or to pserve the state of the cawse w^thout preiudice vntill her Ma^ies pleasure be knowen. and yo^u further thereof advysed.

We pray you contynue yor care to discouer and prevent the privie traffique of o^r facto^rs to Marcelles. *and to all other places* vppon frenche shippes or otherwyse *whereof yo^u have re^d any suspition by any report or other probable presumption* and yf yo^u shall finde any ground of suche practyses *we desire you to* take suche a cowrse therin as yo^u shall finde expedient, for the best prevention of suche mischiefes is to stay ther begynninges wherin wee doubt not yor [discretion and] good and discreete care.

For the matters written vnto you *out of percia* concerning Sr Anthony Shurley and his proceadinges. Wee concurre wth yo^u in opinion *therein* expecting little good of ther event wishing them better successe then wee [have looke for therin] by anie probabylyty cann hitherto coniecture. wee sende you here inclosed the copie of o^r severall actes of Court [wherin wee] wherby wee have contynued the Lone of ½ doller vppon o^r goodes firmed vnder the hand of o^r Secretery. Not doubting but the same being well executed. All necessarie [supplies for] charge and disbursement(will by this meanes and by the consulage largely be supplied. And thus having no other occasion to

inlarge further at this tyme wee cõmitt you to god. London 1599
this   of marche 1599.   Marche.

To o{^{r}} verie Lovinge frend m{^{r}} John Saunderson..
merchaunt [at] resident at Constantynople.

Per le exchaunge.

AFTER o{^{r}} verie hartie cõmendacions wee have re{^{d}} yo{^{r}} Lr̃es of the 17 November [p the   ] w{th} yo{^{r}} former therin related and touching yo{^{r}} opinion of o{^{r}} tolleration of the dutche for ther peaceable traffique in Turkey wee concurre w{th} you and hold it fitt to enterteyne them kindelie. [wherby] *to thend* wee might receave benefite by ther consulage, but as yo{^{u}} have had some experience of the frenche Ambassado{^{r}} his opposition against ther cõminge vnder o{^{r}} Consullage, soe hathe it appeared here by complaint made to her ma{^{ie}} oy the frenche Ambassado{^{rs}} liedges [hee] howe they take to hart the obteyninğ of the dutche nation vnder [them] ther Ambassado{^{r}} in Turkey wherfore vntill [S{^{r}}] *Signio{^{r}}* Paull Pinder hath bene heer and that her ma{^{ie}} hath bene made acquainted w{th} all proceadinges   Wee knowe not what corse to advyse therein.

Yo{^{r}} care of the supplyinge the provision *and wantes* of M{^{r}} Lyllo her ma{^{ies}} Ambassad{^{r}} wee can not but take in verie thankefull part and think [o{^{r}} sel] the Companie beholdinge to yo{^{u}} therein and for firme and sufficient *order* to be geaven yo{^{u}} for his furnishinğ according as is fitt wee [have] are also carefull yet do wee not see what *other* [*more*] *or* [firmer] or better cowrse wee can take therein then by geñ'all consent and order of Court to agree [vppon a course] to charge o{^{r}} goodes [beinge vnder his aucthoritie and comaund] *comÿng into Turkey ether to Constantinople Alexandretta or els wher* to beare suche a levie as wee by our consent have imposed vppon them, and howsoever some wilfull and vnbrideled yonge heddes have for some other respectes shewed their stomakes yet the order in it self is both firme and verie sufficient to [releve] afforthe suche [meanes of

1599 Marche.

supplie] [*the suche*] *payments* as therby wee intended, and noe doubt vppon better [considered] consideration of the matter wilbe so accepted and obeyed by those who haue most hotly opposed them selfes against it.

Wee resolving vppon all good and ready meanes to supply his L. accordinge to agreem^t do finde none soe apte as the contynuaunce of the Lone of $\frac{1}{4}$ doller vppon everie kersye, every Cth of Tynn and Cth of Cony skins, that come into Turkey together wth the consulage of the same goodes. And therfore have ordered that the same Lone shalbe contynued and rep^d here againe by exchaunge at [iiij^s] v^t vj^d the doller. vntyll the companie shall vppon further consideration otherwyse advyse. and to that ende wee have written to his L. to make his billes [by exchaung] vppon the consull at Aleppo for the payment of *so much as wth the receipts at Consta:* shall make vp 3000 c^{ns} ꝑ an฿ as his occasions shall [move him] *nedefully import him* not doubting̊ but the same together wth the graund signio^r his allowaunce (the contynuaunce whereof we nothing̊ doubt) will very lyberally defray his expences. to ye contynuaunce of wch course of chardging o^r goodes wee were the rather induced to avoyde[th] bothe yor and the ambassado^{r}ȩ trowble in seeking credite to supplie his occasions.

As touchinge the disposing of the Galata house wherin yo^u depende vppon o^r order wee [are of] wee thinke it fytt to be sold and made away to the best comoditie and advauntage. *And* wee wishe *the same* to be done yf it might be wthout bestowing anie further chardge thervppon, but yf yo^u thinke the Ruynes thereof being not in some sorte repaired would hinder vs more *in* the sale theñ. [some small charge the forbearing of] a matter of some small charg thervppon bestowed would amount vnto wee referre vs to yor good consideration [therin and leave it who doe] to take suche course therein as yo^u shall thinke may best advaunce *the* [o^r] sale still holding it for o^r full resolution that the same [is] shalbe sold away.

a secretery.

And wher yo^u write that the Ambassado^r is credito^r to the Company 1000 ch^{ns} when the accoumptes are come to o^r handes and wee see howe the same doeth ryse wee shall god willing geave his L. satisfačon.

THE EAST INDIA COMPANY

Wee have considered of yor motion for allowaunce [of] for yor paines in the collecting of the consulage and Lone money. and have agreed *to* allow yo^u *fyve* vppon the 1000 of all moneys by yo^u collected according to o^r orders *praying you to accepte thereof in good part* and for yor better warraunt for the collection of the lone money wee sende yo^u herewth the copie of o^r severall actes contynued for the [collection] *levyinge* thereof firmed vnder the hande of o^r secretary. ^{1599 Marche. 5 p m^l for the allow- aunce 30 ye ambassador^s purchase.}

This being kepte vntill the   of marche 99 [and] wee vppon further consideration of the disposing of the gallata howse do chang o^r former opinion touching the sale of the same. and do pray yo^u [to] carefully to consider of the necessarie wantes of repacons thereof, and to supplie the same as frugallie and carefully as yo^u can, and then to lett out the same for the most advauntage and benefite that it may reasonably make *by yerelie rent to suche of the company as shall neade it* bothe for the discharge of the Rent *wch we pay* and the benefyte of the company *by the overplus of the Rent that it may yeld*. Reteyninge the same still in the companies handes for that [may] many of vs are of opinion that ther may [may] be vse of the same howse bothe for the company in generall and for the^r factors in pticler in respecte whereof the sale of the same is altogether to be [respected] forborne. Thus having not at this tyme any further cause to inlarge, we comit yo^u to god London this [of]   of Marche 1599. Y^r loving frends.

To my very lovinge frend Mr Byddell preacher [preacher] at Aleppo.

^r Since I was chosen to the place of the Governo^r of the Companie I re^d a lre from yo^u directed to the generaltie wch I publyshed at a generall Courte and the same being read [to the genalyty] *the company have* [they have] according to yor desire [they have] agreed that what money soever shall fall out dewe vnto you besides that wch yo^u have re^d shall be aunswered to m^r Cockes after the rate of 50^{li} p

276 THE COURT RECORDS OF

1599
Marche.

anſi according to ye Agreement betweene the Companie and yo^u and yor wages to begynne at Micħas 1598 and that money wch y^{ou} have *already* re^d *to* be rated vnto yo^u at v^s the doller. And touching the money impresed vnto you wch was x^{li}. albeit the same was entended by the Company to be only lent *to supply yor neceessarie provision and to be* [and] discoumpted vppon y^r wages yet for yor better incoragem^t and comforte in y^r charge they are content freely to bestowe it vppon yo^u as [a g]ther guift and gratuyty besides y^r enterteynment agreed vppon. Not doubting but [that] according to the good opinion they have conceaved of yo^u and the good report they heare of yo^u hetherto yo^u will contyneue and proceade in yor charge both [to] *in* the instrucčon of o^r people [and in the repr] in knowledg of Religyon and in reprovinğ and rebukinğ whatsoeuer y^u shall *ether* see or be dewly informed of to [be] deserve reproof or [admonis] admonition And soe cõmendinğ yo^u and yor charge [to god] *to almightie god* wth my harty cõmendačōns I conclude for this tyme.

   London this   of Marche 1599.
          Y^r Loving frende/

1599
10 Marche.

AFTER our hartie commendacons, [yo^u shall receave] wee sende yo^u *by* this ship the Exchaunge the pticlers of all the goodes laden in her for the companie as *the same are* [appereth by] *collected & [the notes] taken out of the* cockettℯ *and* thentries in the Custome Howse wch wee pray yo^u to compare wth the goodes discharged [in above] and yf yo^u shall finde any more then are pticlerly [entred] herein noted they goe wthout warraunt or assent of the Companie [Saving only wee have graunted to Mr Aldⁿ Hollyday part owner of the said exchaunğ for his part of the shippes stocke licence to ship to ballettℯ of 24 kersers] Soe as what soever shalbe founde above the [said] same pticlers before menčōned [and above the Invoice herewith to *you* sent and inclosed] wee wishe yo^u to sease it to the Companies vse reteyning the one half of the valewe to [yor self] the vse of the company and the other half betweene the

Consull and y^r self [whereof and thereof also to geave vs advyse] geaving vs advyse what yo^u finde soe shipped contrarie to order We are further to lett yo^u vnderstande that divers of the Companie vppon the viewe of yor invoices sent vs do averre that yo^u do not carrie an equall course therin and therfore wishe that you shuld be admonished to beare an [equall] *even* hande in the generall service of the Companie that no man have cause to charge yo^u wth partiall dealingᵉ hereafter it shall suffice that we note vnto yo^u this erro^r founde hoping yo^u wilbe more carefull to avoide the like hereafter. You complaine that the mariners denie to bringe the goodes from the shippes to the magasine. and wishe vs to take some co^rse to binde them therto. It appeareth by ther chartre ptie that they are to bring the goodes in to the magasine, and that is much as wee can tye them to doe [by chr̃e partie] for anie further helpe for the stowingᵉ of [them] *the goodes being brought in* that yo^u would require *of them* We doubt not but vppon well intreating of them or some small gratification geaven them they will not refuse to pforme *you* anie resonable [helpe wherin yo^u are] labo^r therin [wch is] wch is to be drawen from them by kinde vsage. You shall receave according to y^r desire 2 lanternes wch wee haue sent by this ship. further we have not at this tyme to enlarge but conclude with this note of remembraunce that yo^u do certenlie and at large certefie vs from tyme to tyme by the shippes what yo^u receave from hence or otherwyse brought in to Scanderona and what yo^u ship from thence respecting noe man wth affection. but equally expressing althinges according to the Trueth and so bidd yo^u hartely farewell.

London this 10th of marche 1599

To the right honorable the LL. and others her ma^{ies}
most honorable priuy Counsellers.

IGHT hl. yor late suppliauntᵉ the m̃chauntᵉ trading the Seignorie of venice whose shippes were arrested for *restitution of* the late prise taken by Englishe men of warre [do] having re^d newe advyse from venice [that sentence is geaven ther] that the arrest not only contynueth but is senten[sed]*ced* to stand *excepte pledg or securyty be geaven w*th*in viij daies for restitution of so muche of the goodes taken as shall be proved to belonge to venetians,* [*and in default hereof*] and besides this sentence the englishe fact^{ors} ther resident do feare the arrest both of ther persons and all the goodes vnder ther handes [vntill order be taken. Do most humblie renewe ther humble sewte to yor LL. to have consideration of the great damage and all o^r Englyshe merchauntes and ther goodes further threatened to be imprisoned and seased vntill securyty *or pledge* be geaven for the restitution of soe muche of the goodes as *shalbe proved to belong to* Venetians] In tender consideration whereof and for the avoyding͡ [of further daunger] bothe of the present and further daunger threatened It may please y^r LL. to graunt a sequestration of the said *ship* spoiles and debtes thereof proceading͡ to be deposited in some indifferent hand vntill [the] triall be made to whom the [goodes] prise *ship and* goodes belong vppon advyse [whereof] *of w*^{ch} *yo͞r honors order sent to venice* y^r Suppliaunt͡e doubt not but [some] a discharge of [thes] said shippes may be procured and yor said suppliauntes shalbe bounde to y^r ho. for y^r ho: favo^r extended to them herein.

To the wo^r. or verie Loving frend m^r Richard Colthurst Consull for the English nation resident at Alleppo.

1600 Sept.

A l͡re in the behaulf of Ryland administrato^r to Ed Rose late facto^r Maryne.

AFTER our verie hartie comendacons. Vppon notice of the deathe of o^r late facto^r Edwarde Rose L͠res of administrac͠on were graunted out of the prerogative court of Canterbury to [one] Humfrey Rylaunce who maried the said Rose his Sister in the behaulf of her and other two Sisters wch Rylance hath ernestlie solicited vs for o^r L͠res to yo^u for yor assistaunce in the Collection and recovery of the state of the said Edward Rose remayning in those ptes. to thende his freindes and kindred who are by nature and the Lawes of this Realme interested therin may receave that wch belongeth vnto them. Wee therfore beinge desirous to further

THE EAST INDIA COMPANY 279

so equall and iust a motion Doe hereby verie hartelie pray yo^u and entreat yo^u by all the best meanes yo^u can [ether] *both* by yor [advyse] aucthority and [or] advyse to be ayding and assysting to the said humfrey [Rylandes] Rylance or his assigne deputy or attorney wch shall solicite yo^u in his behaulf to deliver in to [the] his or her handes all suche goodes moneys and merchandizes as yo^u shall [know] finde [and] *or* knowe [to knowe] to belonge to the said estate. wch yo^u may by some meanes come by. together wth all suche *private* bookes of the said Edw Rose as do conteyne anie Remembraunces of his private debtes or accoumptes *beinge severed from the Accomptes of the Companie*. And yf in [o^r] the bookes of o^r shippinge belonging to o^r trade ther appeare anie thinge that may further the receaving or recovery *of any debte* wch is iustlie dew vnto him wee pray yo^u [further] *assist* him therin by suche notes. sending vnto vs the said Bookes by the next convenient meanes And thus [wth] wee cōmitt yo^u to god
        London this   of September 1600
                  Y^r verie Loving frendℓ/

1600 Sept.

To my *very* Loving frend m^r Jo Saunderson.

1600
12 Sept.

AFTER my verie harty cōmendacōns. I re^d [of] yo^{rs} of the 25 of may, wth a post script of the seventh of June wherin yo^u make relation that yo^u had written divers L<del>r</del>es. whereof yo^u have re^d noe aunswere. and as touching *the* [the] ambassado^{rs} provision supplied by yor [meanes] meanes and credite, and his terme therein served wee toke knowledge thereof by o^r L<del>r</del>es sent by thexchaunge and therin noted the Companies *acceptation* [*of*] [acknowledgment] of yor good service. And ther resolution of the meanes howe [the said] his Lp̄ shuld be supplied hereafter videlt by the Lone of ¼ doller vppon [a kersey] every kersy, every Cth of tynne &c. together wth the Consulage money. to wch L<del>r</del>es I referre myself [because wee have advyse of the aryvall] presumyng that longe since the

1600
12 Sept.

same are come to yor handes and o^r order [touching] in that behalf *beinge* written not only in the l̃res directed to yo^u but in his Lp^s l̃re and alsoe in [the] o^r L̃re directed to the Consull of Alleppo. And as touching the outrages rapyns and robberies of o^r englishe men of warre in the straightes wee have very ernestly enforced the complaint thereof *not onlie* to [y^e] the L. admirall but also to all the residewe of the LL. of the Councell: so as wee doubt not but that order wilbe taken hereafter for the prevention [thereof] of those mischiefes.

The Billes of exchaunge made vppon the Company for moneys [del] taken vp for his Lp^s vse in the factors of m^r Leet and m^r Salter are accepted [to yor Likinge] and shalbe [discharged] *satisfyed* as conveniently *as* they may. The late troubles offered to ye company to supplant vs out of o^r trade by others who were ready to vndertake to pay to her ma^{ie} an imposition of v^s vj^d vppon every Cth of curraunce vj duckettes vppon every but of [wyne] *muskadell* v^s vppon every barrell of oyle whereof I make no doubt [yo^u have had ..dvyse] *advyse hath come to Constantynople divers waies* hath bene the cause why yor expectation hath not bene aunswered by L̃res from hence for that whiles these troubles held the Company were so disturbed [that they could] and so distracted that they could not resolve [whose] howe to directe ther owne *busines* nor assure them selfes of the having of the trade. But these [troubles] stormes being overblowen. wee hope wee shalbe able to hold a better corespondency [in the] not only in the enterco^rse of o^r L̃res and advyses but in all other thinges concerning the trade and government of the Company. The said troubles hath driven vs to vndertake the trade at the yerelie ferme of 4000^{li} [₽ anñ and] to be freed of all the said impositions and to have o^r priveledges renewed, wch priviledges are not yet vnder the great seale. by reason whereof we can not proceade to order o^r government as wee hereafter entende. and therfore I am to pray yo^u to have patience touching yor demaunde of increase of consideration vntill o^r estate be setled [and] *and* a course resolved howe the Queenes ferme and all other o^r needful charges shalbe supported And thus for this tyme [I cease cōmitting w^th] I cease cōmytting yo" to god. London the 12 of September, 1600.

Yo^r loving frende
T. Smythe Go^r.

To Mr May at Constantynople.

[S^r I cōmende me verie hartely vnto yo" yo"]

r. After my verie harty cōmendaĉŏns. Whereas yo" were enterteyned by the company to goe for Aleppo and ther to preache the worde and minister the sacramentℓ to o^r nation ther resident [in] *the exercyse whereof* [in wch ministery ther] toke not soe good effecte as I for my part and the residewe of the company could have wished it had. Soe as by the discontentem^t and disagreement betwene o^r facto^rs and yo" wee were occasioned to sende m^r Beddle [to minister at Aleppo] to supply yor place entendinge that yo" shuld have come directly for England not w^thstanding contrary to o^r expectation and order yo" have gone vp to Constantynople, and ther remained ever since. the company still expecting yor returne for England wch at length they pceaving yo" entended not hath moved them at a Generall court to geave order for yor coming home. Therfore thes are to [pray and] require yo" that [yo"] vppon the receipte of thys my Lr̃e by order of the Companie to yo" directed in that behaulf [to] *you do* prepare yor self to come for England by the next and spediest meanes that shalbe offered yo" by shipping or other [meanes] *wyse* by land soe that the Company be not occasioned by yor stay [ther] contrary to ther order to *growe into further* [encrease] myslyke towardes yo" And soe [wishing y] as one vnaquainted wth yo" yet wishing yo" well I cōmytt yo" to god

London this 11 of September.

1600
11 Sept.

To y̓ᵉ L. Ambassado⁻ at Constantynople.

IT may please y⁻ [hono⁻] L to be aduertysed that I re^cd y⁻ generall l̃re of the 21 June together wth the [inclosed] copies of the frenche Ambassadors proceadingꝭ against y⁻ self and o⁻ nation [generally] wch proceadinges wee have exhibited to m⁻ *secretary and the residewe of* the Ll. of her ma^es Councell who do alledge that the frenche king [in the] doeth greatly wronge her ma^ie in the translation of her l̃re written vnto him concerning the [plane speeche] motion of peace wth Spaine and the appointing of the place of the Comissioners meeting, alledging that the l̃re is not to that purpose but muche falsefyed, as we doubt not but yo⁻ L shalbe better advertysed by m⁻ Secretary hereafter whom we meane to solicyte to wryte [to y⁻ L.] vnto *you* the trueth of that matter, Of the outrages of o⁻ meñ of warre in the Levant seas wee had informed both the L. Admirall and the residew of the Ll. before the frenche information came to o⁻ handes having re^cd severall advyses thereof [by both] from Aleppo and other places in the Levant, wherin wee hope ther wilbe some redresse vsed. and wee are sewters and are in hope to obteyne some warraunt of redresse of these peines to be graunted vnto vs in o⁻ priviledges, wch are nowe to be renewed Whereof and of the trowbles we have lately had touching the payment of impositions vppon curraunce wyne and oyles. and howe we are drawen to pay a ferme of 4000^li p anñ to the Queene because I presume you are certefyed thereof by other meanes I forbeare to enlarge herein. [only] Only observing this to yo⁻ L. that the great trouble charge and heavy ferme nowe being laid vppon o⁻ trade will drive vs assone as we have o⁻ priviledges confermed a newe to devyse the best remidies wee may to governe the same in good order. Whereof wee will hereafter more at large acquainte *you* [yo⁻ L.] And so for this tyme I take my leave of yo⁻ L.

London this 11 of [M] September.

To Mr Colthurst Consull at Alleppo.

1600
11 Sept.

^r Yo^r Last of the 22th of January written to Mr. Staper hath bene [publyshed to the Company] *considered of and deliuered over to me* wherby you seeme contented to be lymited to a certen allowaunce to begynne [for a yere] the seconde of ffebruary for a yere. wch we doubt not vppon the proof of one yere yo^u shall haue cause to accept for a longer tyme The charges of o^r trade by reason of the late disturbaunce offered vs and the great demaunde of impositions endevored to be raysed vppon vs, wch is nowe brought to a ferme of 4000^{li} p ann̄ whereof (because I knowe yo^u have bene advysed and certefyed [thereof] by other meanes I refrayne to make discourse) will necessaryly vrge vs to loke to o^r meanes [wh] howe this great charg and burthen wilbe supported and therfore we are to entreat [the] *yor* best advyse and likewyse the advyse of others of best experience in the trade [howe] for o^r better direction therein. The outrages rcd by englishe men of warre in the Levant seas [hathe] *have* bene related by vs *both to my L. admirall and* to the LL. of the Councell wherin wee are promysed a course of redresse. Our priviledges being to be renewed vnder the Great Seale [and] wch is not yet done [maketh vs] will geave vs occasion and good warraunt when they are confirmed to advyse of some good courses of government howe o^r trade shalbe better guided *both heare and in Turkye* [and o^r great payment and charges defrayed] vntyll wch tyme we can *not* resolve of such advyse and directions as shalbe necessary for vs to consider of and to putt in execution. Therfore I will forbeare to enlarge any further at this tyme [but] *vntill some better opportunety* and so wth my very harty cōmendacōns cōmytt yo^u to god. London this 11th of September.

INDEX.

BBOTT, Maurice, assembly, 59; will bring in his money, 63; creditor, £100, p. 127: auditor, 218; bill of adventure sealed, £240, p. 256.
Accounts, *see also Bookkeeper, Auditors, Warrants.* Mr. Allabaster or Julinus Beamish appointed accountant, 25; Mr. Allabaster will supervise the accounts, 41; order for all pursers to bring in accounts, 97; several committees to clear accounts with creditors, 127; treasurer's accounts to be made up and audited, 156; all creditors to make up their accounts, 159; Mr. Howe and Mr. Combe to bring in their West Country accounts, 172; the general accounts to be audited, 172; arbitrators to settle Mr. Adye's timber account, 173; Thomas Stephens, book-keeper, 210; pursers in the North West voyage to keep accounts of all goods laden and how disposed of, 212-3.
Acts of Court of the Levant Co. for levies on goods entering Turkish ports to support the charges of the ambassador and consuls, 270, 272, 275.
Adderley, } William, adventurer with Thomas
Adderly,   } Henshawe, £300, p.2; Mr. Hen-
Addersley, } shaw will pay, 63; bill of adventure sealed, £240, p. 251.
Admiral, *term as applied to the principal ship,* "*The Red Dragon,*" 136.
Admiral, *see Lord Admiral.*
Admiralty, Court of, damage done by the anchor of the Red Dragon, 128.
Admiralty, Sergeant of the, 141.
Adventures,   } *see also East India Co.*
Adventurers,
List of, and amounts subscribed, 1-4; ship or commodities to be received as portions of adventures, 6; factors and officers to be elected by a general assembly, 6; adventures to be paid in two instalments; not less than £200 admitted; levy of 12d. per £100 for petty expenses, 7; directors chosen with power to use the help of any adventurer when required, 12; order for adventure money to be brought in by the end of September, 1600, 15; the venture proves larger than expected, 27; probable withdrawal of many adventurers if gentlemen are employed, 26; no one to

be refused who will adventure £200 until £55,000 is reached, 45; instructions for persons in the West Country desiring to adventure, 53-4; delay in bringing in adventure money, 60; adventurers attempting to withdraw to be certified to the Privy Council, 61; those in arrears to answer before the Privy Council, 62; names of persons wishing to withdraw, and their reasons, 62; names of those in arrears who promise to pay, 63; Robert Cobbe in arrears deposits security of bonds, 67; every mariner to receive two months' pay in adventures as his stock, 70; the amount of adventure given to the factors, 81; persons who refuse to pay to be called on for their reasons, that some course may be taken before engrossing the patent, 85; arrears to be paid in a week and defaulters to be held chargeable for damage, 93; committee to audit the treasurer's accounts in view of an increase of the general adventure if necessary, 107; adventurers not mentioned in the patent to be deemed equally as free as those named, 109; their names to be presented at the next court and then confirmed as freemen, 110; the adventure subscribed falls short £4,000 or £5,000 of what is necessary considering the great preparations of the Dutch; but as some have not paid and others will not pay as much as at first subscribed, the total falls short eight or nine thousand pounds of what is necessary to "make a good voyage;" deliberations to supply this want; levy of 2s. in the £ on all adventures agreed to; if the amount be raised by voluntary increase of stock the overplus of the levy to be proportionately restored; complaint to be made to the Privy Council of all who have disappointed the preparation of the voyage by their default, 110; the levy to be paid in six days on pain of forfeiture of double the value, but all those voluntarily increasing their stock to be exempt from the levy, 111; committee to wait on the Privy Council with complaint of the defaulters, 111; order in council for the defaulters to pay at once on pain of imprisonment, 112-3; the levy of 2s. in the £ confirmed, 113; every adventurer to have a bill of adventure under the common seal of the company, 113; committee to go to the Court with list of defaulters, &c., 115; an act touching the pay-

Adventurers, *continued.*
ment of the supplies of 2s. in the £ and penalties for default, 137-8; two forms of bills of adventure read, 144-6; bills of adventure sealed, 152, &c., *see Bills of Adventure;* the state of the adventure on March 6, 1600, showing the amount not yet brought in, 156; order for a new supply of 2s. in the £ with penalties by reduction of stock in default, 160-1; £9,000 set down not yet brought in, 160; Earl Cumberland assigns £200 stock to William Beerblock, 161; Mr. Megges's adventure in arrears, 162; order in council touching the adventures in arrears and ordering all defaulters to appear and be punished for contempt, 165; warrant for the summoning of those who have not paid, 169-70; list of defaulters, 170; defaulters committed, 170-1; John Bate assigns to John Jackson, 174; William Smyth refused his freedom for £105 and ordered to pay up the balance, 174; Mr. Hamersley and Mr. Milward bring in their adventures, 175; Mr. Dent named in the patent desiring to assign, is referred to a general court, 175; his assignment allowed, 177; bills of adventure to be delivered to all who have paid up in full, and 6d. to be paid for the same, 175; Richard Tailby agrees to pay £73 6s. 8d. to Mr. Atye, and £100 to the Muscovia Co. in part of his adventure, 176; the liability for the supplies due on Earl Cumberland's assigned stock, 177; all those in arrears to be prosecuted, 178; certain defaulters disfranchised, 178; John Ellicott ordered to pay up his supplies, 181; Robert Bayly assigns £200 stock to Sir John Spencer for £180, and Sir John to nominate a freeman, 181; voluntary levy of 12d. in the £ for the North West voyage, and when to be paid, 183; Mr. Governor to peruse the charter to see if power is given to enforce payments for the North West voyage or a second voyage by the Cape, 183; a book to be sent round for adventurers to subscribe for the North West voyage at 12d. in the £ on their original stock, 185; Nathaniel Martin disfranchised, and John Morice made free in his place, 185; a second voyage by the Cape resolved on, adventure not less than £100, 186; a book to be sent round for the freemen to subscribe, 187; Joseph Jackson made free on the nomination of Sir John Spencer, 187 *(see* 181); deliberations with the Muscovia Co. as to the respective rights to discover and use the North West Passage, 187-9, *see North West Passage;* adventure subscribed for the second Cape voyage insufficient (£11,000), 189; the book sent round again by men able to persuade and encourage the brethren to adventure, 190; Xpofer Cletherow disfranchised and Robert Bowyer admitted in his place, 190; stock of Clement Moseley deceased to be assigned to his wife on payment of £20 supplies in arrears, 193; £230 stock assigned to Mr. Holliday by Earl Cumberland, 197; dislike to the transportation of coin out of the country, 198; hopes of obviating this by the discovery of a North West passage, 198-9; laws and ordinances for general business and for the proposed voyage to the North West, showing amount of adventure to be raised, &c., &c., 198-202, *see East India Co.;* William Nelson admitted a freeman on paying £240 and £30 premium, 205; committee to persuade those who have not done so to pay their contributions for the North West voyage, 205; state of the North West voyage, and steps taken to encourage adventures by making every man's contributions become part of his original stock for the Cape voyage, and to bear profit accordingly, 206-8, *see East India Co.;* auditors appointed to ascertain the state of the North West adventure that further supplies may be called up and some course taken with defaulters, 217-8; day appointed for payment of voluntary supplies for the North West voyage ; the rateable and voluntary supplies to be endorsed on the bills of adventure, and new bills made out shewing in one sum what is each man's interest in the voyage by the Cape, 220 *(see* 206-8); the book-keeper to enter up each adventurer's credits in a lump sum, 224; Mr. Holliday and others being in arrears with supplies for the North West voyage, it is ordered that the sums be defaulted from their stock for the voyage by the Cape, 231 *(see* 200 and 207); the book-keeper to charge up the accounts of all brethren debtors to the Co. that the amounts due may be defaulted on their stock if not paid before the return of the ships, 233; Stephen Hodson pays up £10 supplies, 235; the governor and deputy empowered to appoint any adventurer to perform any service which general business requireth, 249; list of bills of adventure sealed, with their dates and amounts, 250, *see also Bills of Adventure;* the state of the adventure, 263.

Ady } John, delay with timber at Woolwich,
Adye } 46; warrant £100 for timber, 114; committee to determine the reckoning for timber, 155; the account referred to arbitration, 173.

Africa, coast of, route to the East Indies by the Cape, 211.

Agreements, with Captain Davis, 37; with Captain Waymouth for the North West voyage, 211-4, 217; with John Cartwright, preacher, for the North West voyage, 216.

Albany, William, made free though not named in the patent, 177; bill of adventure sealed, £240, p. 258.

Aldermen adventurers, *see* Nicholas Mosley; Paul Bannyng; Leonard Holliday; Richard Goddard; John Moore; Edward Holmden; Robarte Hampson; Robarte Lee; Thomas Cambell; John Swinerton; John Wattes.

Aldeworth } Richard, adventurer, £200, p. 2;
Aldworth } assembly, 4.

Aleppo, Mr. Colthurst, consul, 265, *see Colthurst;* levy on certain goods entering, to support consuls' allowance, 267; letter of instructions to Mr. Colthurst, 270-2, *see Company of Levant merchants;* letter to Mr. Byddell, preacher, 275-6, *see Company of Levant merchants.*

Alexandretta, levy on certain goods entering, to maintain the charges of ambassador and consuls, 271, 273.

Allabaster, Thomas, assemblies, 22, 31, 39, 66, 77, 78, 80, 88; committees, 12, 26, 28, 32, 40, 58, 71, 72, 73, 77, 91, 124; general committee or directors, 63, 179; appointed accountant, 25; respecting the accounts, 41; order to provide moneys at Calais, 41; do. at Calais and Rouen, 58; warrant £500 for royals, 68; do. £500, p. 82; do. £500, p. 91; do. £500, p. 95; do. £700, p. 106; the conveyance of bullion from Calais, 84; commission

INDEX 287

Allabaster, Thomas, *continued.*
for the provision of royals continued, 91; order to provide no more royals, 102; several warrants entered, 111; receives Norromborough ware, 138; bill of adventure sealed, £240, p. 256.
Allen, Gregorie; bill of adventure sealed, £240, p. 258.
Allen, Raphe; bill of adventure with William Starkey, £400, sealed, 149; bill of adventure £200, sealed, 261.
Allen, William, *mercer*, adventurer with Richard Barrett, £200, p. 3; bill of adventure sealed, £200, p. 149; made free, though not named in the patent, 177; bill of adventure sealed, £200, p. 260.
Allom, William, *lighterman*, order to be paid £10 for lighterage, 173.
Allyn, George, admitted as an extra factor, 102.
Allyn, William, *see Allen.*
Altham, Mr., reads draft of the patent, 25.
Ambassadors, *see also Company of Levant merchants*; letters from the Levant Co., to Mr. Lyllo, English ambassador at Constantinople, 265, 282; rivalry with the French ambassador as to consulage, &c., 265-6, 269, 271-2; Mr Lyllo's allowance, 266-7, 271; the late Mr. Barton was placed ambassador at the request of the Levant Co., 267; credit supplied to Mr. Lyllo by Mr. Saunderson, 273, 279.
America, *see also North West Passage*; the objects of the attempt to discover a North West Passage through some part of America, 198, 199; the North West Passage supposed to lead to "Cataya or China or ye backside of America," 212; Captain George Waymouth's confidence in the discovery of a passage to the South seas by divers inlets that treat through the coast of America, 233.
Amounts of original adventures and names, 1-4; total, 4.
Anchors, damage done to a ship by the anchor of the " Scourge," 125, 128; warrant, £30 10*s.*, for two for the " Hector," 151; left behind, 159; for the " Discovery," 210.
Ancients, streamers and flags ordered, 108, 149.
Aneys, Henry, *see Annis.*
Angell, William, assembly, 59; warrant, £50, for fish, 92; to clear accounts with Mr. Holliday, 127; to bring in his account, 159; Bill of adventure sealed £240, p. 250.
Angells, *coin*, 106.
Annis, Henry, nominated factor, 77; recommended by the Lord Treasurer to be employed, 85.
Anthonie, Charles, order to be paid £29 10*s.* for stamps for the East India money, 174.
Anys, *see Annis.*
Apsome, a place recommended for the purchase of bisket, 48; do. cider, 49.
Aquavitae, 3½ tonne of caske required for, 30; quantity for each ship, 35; committee to provide, 75; do. caske, 76; warrant £96 8*s.* for 482 gallons at 4*s.*, p. 107; do. £30, p. 143; committee to provide for the North West voyage, 209.
Arbitration, price of the "Mare Scourge," 32; Mr. Adye's account for timber, 173; Waymouth's demands for charges, &c. referred, 240.
Archbishop of Canterbury, *Privy Council*; order in council, 164.

Archer, Henry, assembly, 60; bill of adventure sealed, £240, p. 259.
Armitage, Samuel, assembly, 59; bill of adventure sealed, £240, p. 252.
Arms of the Company assigned by the king of heralds, 171.
Assention, ship, tonnage, 260; 80 men; Roger Hankin, *master*; William Brand, *principal factor*; Edward Highlord, *purser*; Christopher Newchurch, *surgeon*; Thomas Salterne, *second factor*; Roger Style, *third factor*; Phillip Winchecomb, *fourth factor.* Viewed, 13; surveyors appointed, 14; inventory, 16, 22; William Leake, *purser*, guaranteed by Mr. Garway, 33; rated 80 men, tonnage 260, 34; aquavitae, 35; warrant 100 markes on account of repairs, 57; to be manned with 80 men, 72; warrant £200 on account of preparations, 85; the nnmber of carpenters, caulkers, gunners, stewards, cooks, surgeons and barbers to be employed, 89-90; warrant £100 for her provision, 91; William Brund to sail as a principal factor, 94; ballast, 97; warrant £20 to Christopher Newchurch, surgeon, for furnishing his medicine chest, 98; warrant £100 for repairs and preparations, 99; officers appointed, 100; factors appointed, 101; warrant £100 for smithery, 104; do. £100 to Mr. Garway, 105; do. £100 for timber, 114; do. £150 towards repairs, 114; warrant to Robert Rickman, £133 6*s.* 8*d.*, in full payment of his 6th part of the ship, 115; do. £333 6*s.* 8*d.* to William Skidmore, in full of his sixth part, 117; committee to provide stores, 117; warrant £150 to William Leake for men's wages, 117; the amount of new and Spanish money apportioned to be carried and how packed, 122; warrant £100 to the purser for necessaries, 126; do. £100 to Mr. Garway for her provision, 140; do. £50 for clearing away, 144; list of presents carried, 151; warrant £100 for wages and clearing away, 154; do. £161 13*s.* 1*d.* for nails and iron work, 157; do. £6 10*s.* for porterage and lading, 158; ship's boat at Blackwall ordered to be sold, 159; warrant £42 15*s.* for canvas, 168; do. £22 4*s.* for chaundler's provisions, 169; do. £16 16*s.* 11*d.* for timber, &c., 180; letters from Roger Style, *factor*, and Edward Highlord, *purser*, brought home by a Frenchman, 242; letters sent to the West Country to the factors and officers, saying the merchants of Plymouth and Dartmouth have been instructed to attend to the sick and give credit for the use of the ship; orders not to break bulk or make sale of anything belonging to the general adventure, 243; arrival in the river, 243; warehouses suitable for the receipt of goods, 244-5; several committees to attend on board in turns whilst unloading, 245-6; no mariner or other person to carry anything from the ship "unless it be visited," on pain of detention of wages, 245; Mr. Style and the purser to attend on board till ship is discharged, 246; tithes due to the Lord Admiral for a prize taken, 246-7; bags to be made for the pepper, also suits without pockets for the porters employed, 247; entry to be made at the Custom House and list of goods, 247; warrant £5 to Mr. Midleton for riding with the first report of the return, 247; Mr. Governor and Mr. Eldred give bond for the customs due to the king, 247; warrant £6 for pilotage into the river, 248; the customs amount to £917 and Mr. Cambell

INDEX

Assention, *continued*.
and Mr. Eldred to be indemnified for their bonds given for payment of the same, 248; money to be taken up at interest for payment of mariners' wages, 249; memorandum, tonnage, 260; men, 80, p. 263.

Assignments of adventures and stock, Earl of Cumberland to Mr. Beerblock, 161; John Bate to John Jackson, 174; Francis Dent to George Bennet, 174, 177; Earl of Cumberland to Mr. Bannyng, 177; Robert Bayly to Sir John Spencer, 181; Nathaniel Martin to John Morice, 185; Xpofer Cletherow to Robert Bowyer, 190; Clement Moseley to Edward Helmes and John Moseley, and re-assignment to Elizabeth Moseley at a premium, 193; Earl of Cumberland to Alderman Holliday, 197.

Attorney, the Queen's; the patent of the Co., 88, 91; warrant £71 13s. 4d. for charges in drawing and engrossing the patent, 96.

Atye, John, *see Ady*.

Auditors, ⎫ Purser's accounts, 99; treasurer's
Audits, ⎭ accounts, 107, 156, 166; various trade accounts, 127, 146, 147, 148; accounts of the purser of the "Red Dragon," 147; Mr. Howe's and Mr. Combe's West Country accounts, 172; the general accounts, 172; power to inflict fines for delay in the payment of adventures, 201; Thomas Verworth's accounts, 214; the accounts of the North West voyage, 217, 220.

Axmouth, a fit place to buy cider, 49.

Babbington, Vrye, adventurer, £200, p. 3; assembly, 5.
Babington, Edwyn, warrant £100 for Canary wine, 95; do. £160, p. 103.
Babington, Richard, recommended as a purser, 39.
Backhouse, Rowland, adventurer with Bartholomew and Edward Barnes, £400, p. 3; bill of adventure sealed, £240, p. 254.
Backhouse, Samuel, bill of adventure sealed £240, p. 257.
Backhouse, Thomas, assembly, 5.
Bacon, William, warrant £16 0s. 10d. for masts, 157.
Baese, *see Basse*.
Bags, Polldavies to be bought and made up in the West Country, 86; biskett bags, 222; for pepper brought home, 247.
Baker, Captain Thomas; committee, 68; sent to join Captain Davis in the West Country to purchase provisions, &c., 29; commission for the provision of victuals, 38, 41; ordered to send up the ship's boat of the "Malice Scurge" from Plymouth, 40; commission for provisions altered, 46; commission for provisions, &c., 48-54; second commission, 54; money at Plymouth, 64; letter of advice as to money, &c., 64; letter sent to, 66; bills of exchange, 47, 68, 69, 80; letter from, 74; order to provide no more bread, &c., 88.
Bakers, *see Joseph Page*.
Ball, Richard, assembly, 59; bill of adventure sealed, £240, p. 253.
Ball, Thomas, made free though not named in the patent, 177; bill of adventure sealed, £240, p. 258.
Ballast, warrant £36 0s. 4d. for ballast and freight of two hoyes, 97; warrant £6 13s. 4d. for ballast, 121.
Bandicott, Austyn, *butcher*; warrant £44 18s. for pork, 208.

Baning, ⎫
Baninge, ⎬ *see Bannyng*.
Banninge, ⎭
Bannyng, Andrew, assembly, 60; warrant £213 6s. 8d. for oil, 111; bill of adventure sealed, £240, p. 254.
Bannyng, Paul, Alderman, adventurer £1,000, p. 1; assemblies, 4, 14, 20, 22, 26, 27, 28, 31, 33, 37, 39, 44, 45, 46, 47, 56, 57, 58, 64, 65, 67, 68, 69, 71, 73, 74, 76, 78, 79, 80, 82, 91, 107, 109, 113, 119, 121, 122, 123, 125, 128, 167, 168, 170, 171, 172, 175, 176, 183, 248; committees, 12, 26, 31, 37, 38, 40, 57, 58, 63, 67, 68, 71, 72, 73, 75, 76, 77, 80, 99, 114, 234; committees, per his coachman, Robert Barker, 245, 246; warrants paid as treasurer, *see warrants*; views ships, 13; sells the "Susan" on certain terms, 13; surveyor for the "Susan," 14; to treat for the "Cherubim," 15; guarantees Joseph Salmon as purser of the "Susan," 33; compounds for iron, 41; bills from the West Country, 50; signature to West Country commissions, 52, 54, 55; letter respecting Spanish money, 66; a mast for the "Hector," 71; to buy ling, 75; to buy oatmeal, 75; sale of the "Susan" made absolute, 120; required to pay £200 set down for Jeffrey Kerby, 126; entreated to raise £1,500 with Alderman Holliday on their credits, 146; to render accounts, 156; to be called on to bring in his account, 139; to be indemnified for the £1,500 raised at interest, 161; to deliver bills of adventure to all adventurers and to receive 6d. for each for the secretary, 175; the supplies due on £570 stock assigned to him by Earl Cumberland, 177; general committee and sworn, 179; order to be paid £4 7s. 5d. for disbursements, 203; requested to give his bond with Mr. Wattes for £1,000 as security for money to be raised at interest on the return of the "Assention," 249.
Barbar ⎫ Thomas, warrants for canvas £200,
Barber ⎬ p. 114; £100, p. 163; £200, p. 167; £309, p. 172; £143, p. 220; bill of adventure £240, p. 254.
Barbers, one to be carried in each ship, 90.
Barbor, George, warrant £27 5s. 0d. for sails for the "Susan," 167.
Barbor, Thomas, *see Barbar*.
Baricoes ⎫ eight dozen iron hooped required,
Baricos ⎬ 30; committee to provide, 76; do. for the North West Voyage, 239.
Barker, Edward, bill of adventure sealed, £300, p. 252.
Barker, Frauncis, assembly, 60; bill of adventure sealed, £240, p. 252.
Barker, Robert, *Alderman Bannyng's coachman*, committees, 245, 246.
Barkham, Edward, bill of adventure sealed, £240, 257.
Barks for the North West Voyage, *see ships, pinnaces, also "Godspeed" and "Discovery."*
Barley, Robert, adventurer with Thomas Haies and Mathew Hamond, £300, p. 3.
Barme, Francis, elected one of the principal factors, 81.
Barmesley, *see Barnesley*.
Barnes, Bartholomew, adventurer with Rowland Backhouse and Edward Barnes, £400, p. 3; bill of adventure sealed, £240, p. 254.
Barnes, Edward, adventurer with Rowland Backhouse and Bartholomew Barnes, £400, p. 3.
Barnes, Francis, nominated factor, 77.

Barnes, The Lady, her house nominated as a suitable warehouse for goods brought home in the Assention, 245.
Barnesley, Nicholas, *grocer*, adventurer, £150, p. 2; assembly, 60; bill of adventure sealed, £240, p. 254.
Barrell, William, adventurer with Walter Porter, £400, p. 4; warrant to bring in his adventure at once, 170.
Barrels, *see Casks*.
Barrett, Richard, adventurer with William Allen, £200, p. 3; bill of adventure sealed, £240, p. 257.
Barrett, William, *see Barrell*.
Barrey, Gyles, bill of exchange, £40, p. 104.
Barrycods, *see Baricoes*.
Barton, Mr., late ambassador at Constantinople, 265; his bills of exchange on the Levant Co. in favour of Mr. Bate repudiated, and the accounts investigated, 267; appointed ambassador at the Levant Company's request, 267; remarks on his conduct, 269.
Bashaw of Turkey, 272.
Basse, Humfrey, assemblies, 226, 238, 242, 244, 247; auditor, 218; general committee and sworn, 226; bill of adventure sealed, £240, p. 252.
Bate, John, assemblies, 24, 31, 37, 39, 59; committee, 12; views ships, 13; signature to West Country commission, 52; declines to adventure and reason why, 62; warrant to bring in his adventure at once, 170; commitment warrant for non payment, 171; disfranchised and John Jackson admitted in his place, 174; bills of exchange drawn on the Levant Co. in his favour by Mr. Barton, repudiated, 267; the accounts investigated, 267; proposed course to recover his money, 268.
Bateman, Robert, adventurer with Thomas and Robert Midleton, £500, p. 2; assembly, 59; committee, 243; bill of adventure sealed, £240, p. 255.
Baylie } Robert, ? see Barley; assigns his £200
Bayly } adventure to Sir John Spencer for £180, p. 181; bill of adventure sealed, £240, p. 259.
Baysalt, 209, 219.
Beadle of the company, *see Thomas Evettsett*, salary £10, augmented to £12, p. 204; reappointed, 226.
Beale, Richard, assembly, 60.
Beamish, Julinus, appointed accountant, 25.
Beans, 50 quarters required, 29; 30 tonne of dry caske required, 30; 20 quarters to be bought, 33; estimate of quantity and price, 34; price in the West Country to be ascertained, 49; 30 quarters ordered, 65; Lord Treasurer's warrant for the provision of peas and beans and transport from Cambridge and Norfolk, 66; committee to provide, 75; do. caske for, 76; warrant £100 for peas and beans, 82; do. £100, p. 96.
Beare, Mr., to be conferred with as one of the chief masters, 90.
Beddle, Mr., *see Byddell*.
Beef, 26; 30 tonne of caske (hogsheads) required, 30; estimate of quantity and price, 34; committee for ordering, 68, 75; do. caske, 76; 120 oxen to be provided for making salt meat, 114; committee to provide for the North West voyage, 209; warrant £111 5s. for beef and pork for the North West voyage, 214; order for the sale of beef brought back from the North West voyage, 230.

Beer, 26; 170 tonne of caske (pipes) required, 30; estimate of quantity and price, 34; a barrel a day allowed to the workmen on the "Mare Scourge" to prevent their running from their work to the alehouse, 40; 240 tuns of beer ordered, 67; committee to provide, 75; do. caske; warrant £15 7s. for 59 barrels for the "Scourge," 154; [do. £200 on account], 155; do. £500, p. 171; do. £39 2s. 4d., 193; committee to provide for the North West voyage, 209; warrant £120 3s., 221; beer brought back from the North West voyage to be sold, 230.
Beerilock, William, *Goldsmith*; £200 stock assigned to him by Earl Cumberland, 161; increases his adventure to £250, 162.
Beeston, Hughe, mortgagee of land belonging to Mr. Brodebent, Master of the "Red Dragon," 128.
Bell, Richard, bill of adventure sealed, £240, p. 253.
Bell, Robarte, adventurer with John Potter, £200, p. 3; assemblies, 5, 59, 64, 65, 67, 68, 78, 79, 80, 82, 83, 85, 89, 92, 93, 94, 95, 107, 108, 117, 118, 123, 125, 127, 139, 144, 168, 170, 175; committees, 67, 75, 76, 79, 86, 147, 191; surveyor of the "Mare Scourge," 33; General committee, 63; buys meal, 90; warrant £90 10s. for paper, 126; buys pewter, 12); warrant £13 3s. 2d. for wharfage, &c., 203; auditor, 218; bill of adventure sealed, £240, p. 258.
Bennett, George, *Salter*; desires to become adventurer in lieu of Francis Dent, 175; the assignment assented to, 177; committee, 245; bill of adventure sealed, £240, p. 257.
Bennett, Widow Elizabeth, warrant £100 for iron, 119; do. £90 for nails, &c., 172.
Billett, Thomas, of Poole, bill of exchange, £200, p. 129.
Bills of Adventure, *see also Adventures*. Every adventurer to have a bill under the common seal, 113; Philip Grove to have a bill for the composition made with him, 139; two forms of bills read for factors and adventurers, 144-6; bills of adventure sealed, 148, 149, 150, 152, 153, 159, 250-262; bills to be delivered to all who have cleared accounts and 6d. each to be charged for the Secretary, 173; the contributions for the North West voyage to be endorsed on the bills, 207; new bills to be made out in a lump sum, 224.
Bills of exchange, *see Warrants*, instructions for drawing, &c., 50, 53; the Levant Co.'s desire to avoid bills from the ambassador at Constantinople, 266-7, 271; the trouble growing out of the bills drawn by the late Mr. Barton, 267-8; Mr. Saunderson's bills accepted, 280.
Biskett, *see Bread*, the provision of in the West Country, 21.
Biskett bags, 222.
Black Jacks, 105.
Blacksmiths, *see also Smiths*, Lewys Tyght, Lewis Tate, Richard Hall.
Blackwall, 159.
Boales, George, *see Bowles*.
Boarne, Thomas, *Steward of the "Godspeed,"* warrant £3 for wages for the North West voyage, 234; do. 20s. to his wife in full of all demands, 240.
Boats, *see also Ships, Pinnaces, Barks*; the boat of the "Mare Scourge" ordered up from Plymouth, 40; new boat ordered, 46; the boat at

Boats, *continued*.
Plymouth to be inspected, 51; warrant, £100 for boats, &c., 115; the "Assention's" boat lying at Blackwall to be sold, 159; the two vessels for the North West voyage described as "flyboats," 220; warrant £13 for timber and a boat, 221; warrant £5 10s. for a boat for the "Discovery," 223; do. 46s. 8d. for boat hire, 224.
Bolles, George, *see Bowles*.
Bolton, appointed sailmaker to the "Mare Scourge," 40.
Bona Speransa, cape of, *see Cape*.
Bond ╲ William, *merchant taylor*, adventurer
Bonde ╱ with William Harrison, £200, p. 3; assembly, 59; bill of adventure sealed, £240, p. 252.
Bonds, *see also Guarantees, Security*; all factors to give bonds for their good behaviour, 105; amounts of the bonds for the factors, 105; Mr. Bannyng and Mr. Holliday indemnified for £1,500 borrowed on their credit, 161 (*see* 146); Richard Tailbey, adventurer in arrears, gives bond for £200 to the agent of the Muscovia Co., 176; Thomas Yerworth, purser, to give bond in 100 marks for his good behaviour, 205; Edward Pullison, do. do. 216-17; general bond to James Cambell in £200 to hold his father harmless against his covenant to pay the wages of John Drew, a master in the North West voyage, 220; the bond sealed, 221; Mr. Cambell and Mr. Eldred give their bonds for the payment of customs dues, 247; money to be taken up at interest on the bonds of Sir John Harte and others, 249; Mr. Cambell and Mr. Eldred to be indemnified by general bonds under the common seal, 248-9 (*see* 247); obligations of £3,000 each sealed to them, 249-50; obligations of 1,000 marks each, to Sir John Hart and Mr. Chamberlain, 250.
Bonham, William, bill of adventure sealed, £240, p. 251.
Bookkeeper, Thomas Stephens, *see also Accounts*; to charge all defaults in supplies against the stock, 161; to draw up the West Country accounts, 173; Thomas Stephens appointed, salary £30, p. 210; order to enter up each adventurer's credits in a lump sum, 224; Thomas Stephens re-appointed, 226; order to charge up the accounts of all brethren who are debtors to the Co., that such amounts may be defaulted from their stock if not paid before the return of the ship, 233; warrant for salary, 235; admitted a freeman, 239; to make tickets for the carmen removing the "Assention's" goods from the Exchange, 248.
Book of the adventurers in the North West voyage, 185.
Book of the adventurers in the second voyage by the Cape, 186-7, 190.
Book of the "Flemyng's" voyage, 125.
Booles, George, *see Bowles*.
Bootheby, Thomas, bill of adventure sealed, £240, p. 251.
Bostocke, Thomas, adventurer with John Ramridge, £200, p. 3; assembly, 5; surveyor for the "Assention," 14; bill of adventure sealed, £240, p. 255.
Boules, George, *see Bowles*.
Bover, James, warrant £24 19s. for spectacles, &c., 155.
Bowdeler, Richard, appointed auditor, 166; made free, though not named in the patent, 177; bill of adventure sealed, £240, p. 259.

Bowden, John, warrant £40 for sails, 168.
Bowen, John, warrant £6 for rent of Founder's Hall for the Company's meetings, 227.
Bowles, George, assemblies, 226, 227, 229, 230, 231, 232, 233, 235, 236, 241, 242, 244, 247, 248, 249; committees, 247, 248; warrant £46 17s. for Curraunce, 168; general committee and sworn, 225; bill of adventure sealed, £300, p. 256.
Bowles, Thomas, warrant to be paid £30 on a bill of exchange, 69.
Bowne, Thomas, *see Boarne*.
Bowyer, Robert, warrant to bring in his adventure at once, 170; commitment warrant for non payment, 171; disfranchised, and Christopher Cletherow admitted in his place, £240, p. 190.
Bradbanck, William, *see Brodebent*.
Bradbury, Robert, warrant £86 15s. 4d. for sails, 168.
Bradley, —, warrant £6 13s. 4d. for ballast, 121.
Bradshawe, Elias, employed at £10 a year, 263.
Bramley, Thomas, assemblies, 240, 241, 244, 247, 248, 249; elected Deputy Governor, 239; committee, 245; bill of adventure sealed, £240, p. 252.
Brand, William, *see Brunde*.
Branding iron for the shipping mark, 107.
Branskom, John, warrant 46s. 8d. for wages in the North West voyage, 234.
Brasiers; John Maxfield, 164.
Brass pots, 222.
Bread and biskett, estimate to be drawn up, 26; to be bought at Dartmouth and Plymouth, 29; estimate of quantity and price, 34; revised estimate, 46, 54-5; quantity to be bought in the West Country, 41, 52; quality, and how to be packed, 48; bakers to guarantee bread to keep sweet two years, 51; quantity ordered to carry the ships to the West Country, 67; committee to provide in London, 75; order for no more to be bought, 88; warrant £50, p. 157; do. £45 10s. 11d. p. 167; committee to provide for the North West voyage, 209; warrant £60, p. 215; do. £41 8s., p. 222.
Breeches, 118, 208.
Brende, William, *see Brunde*.
Brett, William, warrant £16 16s. 11d. for timber, 180.
Brewers, ╲ Abraham Campion.
╱ Anthonie Duffeilde.
Bridgehouse, 89.
Bridgeman, Henrye, *leatherseller*, adventurer, £200, p. 4; assembly, 59; bill of adventure, sealed, £240, p. 252.
Bridgewater, 73.
Brimstone, 142.
Broadbent, *see Brodebent*.
Brocke, *see Brooke*.
Brodebent, William, *Master of the "Red Dragon,"* a fit man to take charge in the voyage, 44; appointed to sail in the "Mare Scourge," 90, 100; order to be paid £100 on account, 104; is lent £100 on mortgage, 128; bill of adventure sealed in special terms, 153; repayment of his mortgage, 153.
Brooke, Roberte, adventurer with Augustine Skynner and Thomas Westray, £300, p. 3; bill of adventure sealed, £240, p. 259.
Broun, *see Browne*.
Browne and Co., order to supply cordage, pitch, tar, &c., 121.
Browne and Co., Richard, adventurers, £500, p. 3; assembly, 5; committees, 245, 246.

INDEX

Brunde, William, nominated factor, 77; elected factor of the second sort, 82; will not accept as second factor, 93; chosen as a principal factor and nominated to the "Assention," 94, 100; warrant £100 for his provision to sea, 125; commission to take chief command in the event of deaths of Captains Lancaster and Middleton, 135; bill of adventure sealed, £200, p. 150.

Buck } Robert, assembly, 60; bill of adventure
Bucke } sealed, £240, p. 253.

Buckhurst, T., *see Lord Treasurer.*

Bullion, *see Coin.*

Burde, Mr., assembly, 30.

Burford in the County of Oxon, 193.

Burrage, William, confirmed as boatswain of the "Mare Scourge," 33.

Burrell, Richarde, adventurer, £200, p. 3; bill of adventure sealed, £240, p. 259.

Burrell, William, assemblies, 20, 22, 26, 27, 29, 30, 31, 39, 46, 59, 99, 156, 158, 167, 204, 214, 241; committees, 27, 155; surveyor for the "Hector," 14; general surveyor, 21; to provide timber, 21; warrant to take up carpenters and shipwrights, 40; nominates sail makers, 40; order for timber, 46; warrant £100 for timber, 47; order to take men from the "Susan" to finish the "Mare Scourge," 56; warrant £200 for timber, 65; order to see the ships "symented vppon ther sheething" before leaving dock, 69; order to use a mast for the "Hector," 71; warrant £200 on account of the shipping, 74; do. £100, p. 85; order for timber, 89; warrant £80 for timber, 92; do. £100, p. 104; do. £100 for boats, &c., 115; to settle accounts with Mr. Wiseman, 127; warrant £100 on account, 157; to sell the "Assention's" boat, 159; to gather together in a warehouse all stores left behind, 159; to be called on for his account, 159; to enquire into Mr. Adye's account for timber, 173; order to be paid £15 for his pains in the provision of timber, &c., 181; all pursers to deliver him their bills to receive allowance, 215; agrees with William Hedger on the price of a boat for the "Discovery," 223; bill of adventure sealed, £240, p. 257.

Busbridge, *see Buzbridge.*

Busby, *see Buzbie.*

Bushea, a fit place to buy cider, 49.

Butchers } Austyn Bandicott, 208.
} William Russell, 214.

Butler, Henry, made free though not named in the patent, 177; bill of adventure sealed, £200, p. 260.

Butter, estimate of quantity and price, 35; committee to provide, 75; do. for the North West voyage, 209; warrant, £14 5s., p. 125; do., £61 5s. 9d. for butter and cheese, 142; do., £92 10s. for butter, candles, powder, &c., for the North West voyage, 219.

Buzbie, Ralfe, *grocer*, adventurer, £200, p. 4; assembly, 59; bill of adventure sealed, £240, p. 251.

Buzbridge, John, *linendraper*, adventurer with James Turner, £200, p. 3; assemblies, 5, 59; compounds for iron, 41; warrant, £125 10s. for linen cloth, 97; do. £150 on account of iron, 104; do. £300, p. 111; bill of adventure, sealed £240, p. 253.

Buzby, *see Buzbie.*

Byddell, Mr., *preacher at Aleppo*, letter from the Levant Company, 275-6; *see Company of Levant merchants*; successor to Mr. May, 281.

Cables, 219.

Calais } £3,000 worth of royals to be taken up
Callis } there, 41; £5,000 do., 58, £500, p.
Callyce } 68; Mr. Allabaster commissioned to
Cadys } convey the bullion from thence, 84.

Cambell, James, bond of indemnity, £200, pp. 220, 221. *See Bonds.*

Cambell, Thomas, *alderman*, adventurer with Miles Huberd, £200, p. 2; assemblies, 5, 7, 9, 10, 181, 190, 192, 194, 196, 197, 203, 206, 208, 216, 219, 226, 227, 229, 230, 232, 233, 235, 236, 237, 238, 240, 241, 242, 244, 247, 248; appointed director, 6; committee, 8; general committee, 179; treasurer for the North West Passage voyage, 200; warrants as treasurer, *see warrants per Mr. Cambell*; all contributions for the North West voyage to be paid in to him by the end of March, 1601, p. 205; bound by covenant to pay the wages of John Drewe, 220; a bond of indemnity, £200, given to his son, 220; the bond sealed, 221; general committee and sworn, 225; elected governor, 226; Mr. Cartwright delivers to him Captain Waymouth's journal, 228; resolutions for the sale of stores from the two pinnaces, 230; warrant for payment of mariners hired from Dartmouth to London, 231; relates the result of proceedings against Captain Weymouth before the Lords of the Council, 233; thinks only one ship should go in the second North West voyage, 238; warrant to the Treasurer to pay 24s. for keeping the two pinnaces returned from the North West, 241; the pinnaces not to be sold under £300 each without his consent, 242; bound with Mr. Eldred as security for the payment of customs dues on the goods brought home in the "Assention," 247; is indemnified by a general bond of £3,000 under the common seal, 249; the bond sealed, 249; bill of adventure sealed, £360, p. 256, *see also Governors.*

Campion, Abraham, *brewer*, warrant, £200 for beer, 155; do. £300, p. 171; do. £39 2s. 4d., p. 193; do. £120 2s., p. 221.

Canary wine, *see Wine.*

Candell, Francis, *painter*, warrant, £30 for painting the "Red Dragon," 157; do £48, p. 172.

Candish, William, warrant, £150 for lead, 105; do. £49, p. 143.

Candishe, Captain, 72.

Candler, George, bill of adventure sealed, £240, p. 255.

Candler, Richard, recommends Thomas Wasse as a factor, 56.

Candles, *wax and ordinary*, estimate of quantity and price, 35; committee to provide, 76; do., for the North West voyage, 209; warrant, £200, p. 104; do. £86, p. 142; do. £92 10s. for candles, butter, powder, &c., for the North West voyage, 219.

Candyshe, *see Candish.*

Cannons, 159.

Canterbury, 278.

Canvas, warrants, £200, p. 114; do. £100, p. 163; do. £42 15s., p. 164; do. £200, p. 167; do. £300, p. 172; do. £143, p. 220.

Canynge, George, adventurer with William Paule, £300, p. 2.

Cape of Bona Speransa, 182, 183, 186, 191, 198, 199, 203, 204, 207, 211, 220, 224, 239.

Captains, *see also Masters*, Thomas Baker, John Davies, Captain Candishe, James Lancaster, John Middleton, George Waymouth.

INDEX

"Carnation," ship of Colchester, 263.
Carpenters, *see also Shipwrights, see Edward Stephens, Nicholas Symonds*, 14, 27; warrant by the Lord Treasurer for taking up carpenters, 40, 263; number to be employed in each ship, 89; to be hired by Mr. Burrell and their wages agreed on, 89; committee to provide stores, 117; masts overcharged, 121, 157; committee to agree on disputed prices of timber, 124; Adam Wood, 168, &c.; Nicholas Symonson, 172, &c.; warrant £80 for wages for work on the ships for the North West Passage voyage, 206.
Carrell, Robert, *auditor*, 218; bill of adventure sealed, £240, p. 259.
Carriages, ? trucks, 163, 221.
Carriage Makers, John Hedland, 163; George Gryce, 221.
Carter, Richard, adventurer with Sir Stephen Soame, £400, p. 1.
Cartwright, John, *preacher, see also North West Passage and Waymouth*, engaged for the North West Passage voyage, 216; his salary contingent on the discovery of the passage, 216; his return and delivery of Captain Waymouth's Journal to the Governor, 228; can give no other particulars of the voyage, 228; accused of persuading Captain Waymouth to return and abandon the voyage, 232; ordered to give up the gown and apparel delivered to him to be used if the voyage had reached China, 232.
Cason, John, assembly, 60; bill of adventure sealed, £240, p. 256.
Cassalia Wine, 209.
Cashiers ordered to be repaid their losses in receiving and disbursing moneys, 227.
Cask, Caske, committee to provide and quantity required, 30; warrant £200, p. 41; do. £100, p. 92; the supply in the West Country to be ascertained, 49; warrant £100, p. 104; shipping mark, 107; warrant, £78 10s. 4d., p. 143; do. £61, p. 146; do. £57 15s., p. 147; do. £40 12s., £19 16s., and £36 10s., p. 148; do. £3 15s., p. 172; do. £50 11s. 8d., p. 218.
Cassocks, 138, 208.
Castle Soap ordered, 107. ? Castile.
Cataia ⎫ Proposed trade by the North West
Cataya ⎭ Passage if discovered, 199; supposed destination of the voyage if the passage is discovered, 212; Captain Waymouth to have £500 if he arrive at any port in Cataia, &c., 214; the salary of Mr. Cartwright, preacher, contingent on reaching Cataia, 216; Queen's letters to the Emperor, 217; Cartwright's gown for use in Cataia if reached, 232.
Cater, George, bill of adventure sealed, £240, p. 250.
Cater, William, assembly, 59; warrant, £28 14s. for Roan cloth, 97; bill of adventure sealed, £240, p. 260.
Caudell, *see Candell.*
Caulkers (Cawkers, number to be employed in each ship, 89; to be hired by Mr. Burrell and wages agreed on, 89.
Cavendishe, William, bill of adventure sealed, £240, 254.
Cecyle, *see Cycill.*
Cellarage under the Exchange used as a warehouse, 245, 248.
Chamberlain
Chamberlaine
Chamberlayn ⎬ *see Chamberleyn.*
Chamberlayne

Chamberlein ⎫ George, assembly, 59; bill of
Chamberleyn ⎭ adventure sealed, £240, p. 261.
Chamberleyn, Richard, bill of adventure sealed, £240, p. 261.
Chamberleyn, Robert, assemblies, 225, 226, 227, 229, 232, 235, 236, 242, 244, 248; warrants as treasurer, *see warrants per Mr. Chamberleyn;* nominated factor, 77; elected treasurer, 226; Stephen Hodson's supplies, 235; ordered to pay bills drawn by Plymouth merchants for expenses on the return of the "Assention," 244; requested to give his bond with Sir John Harte for £1,000 as security for money to be raised at interest for expenses on the return of the "Assention," 249; indemnified by a general bond under the common seal, 250; bill of adventure sealed, £240, p. 261.
Chamberlin, Andrewe, bill of adventure sealed, £240, p. 251.
Chambers, William, adventurer with William Stoane, £500, p. 2; assemblies, 4, 14, 20, 22, 24, 26, 27, 29, 31, 33, 37, 39, 46, 56, 58, 64, 66, 67, 68, 69, 71, 73, 76, 78, 80, 82, 83, 85, 86, 88, 89, 90, 91, 92, 93, 94, 95, 96, 98, 99, 100, 102, 103, 106, 107, 112, 113, 119, 121, 122, 124, 125, 128, 138, 139, 140, 142, 158, 170, 172, 174, 176, 177, 194, 203, 204, 208, 214, 215, 216, 217, 219, 225, 227, 233, 238, 240, 244, 248; committees, 12, 13, 22, 27, 30, 67, 69, 70, 76, 79, 120, 127, 128, 143, 209, 234, 240, 245; views ships, 13; feoffee in trust for ships bought, 32; warrant, £100 for casks, 33; to provide cider, 38; warrant £200 for casks and iron work, 41; the purchase of the "Mare Scourge," 45; signature to the West Country commission, 52; warrant, £100 for casks and hoops, 56; general committee, 63; warrant, £100 for casks, 92; recommends Walter Poyner as a factor, 97; warrant, £100 for casks, 104; warrant to pay 34s. 3d. to Captain Middleton, 142; auditor, 147; general committee and sworn, 179; do. 225; warrant, £150 for cloth, &c, 215; do. £100 for disbursement for the North West Passage voyage, 217; the dislike to Thomas Yerworth, *purser,* 219; bill of adventure sealed, £240, p. 251.
Chamlettes, sixty pieces shipped without warrant, 123.
Champion, Richard, warrant to bring in his adventure at once, 170; bill of adventure sealed, £240, p. 261.
Chapman, George, warrant, £36 19s. for casks, 148.
Charters of the company, *see also Patent*, the charters to be perused to see if power is given to compel payments towards the North West Passage voyage or a second voyage by the Cape, 183.
Chaundler, Georg, assembly, 59.
Chaundlers, *see Francis Covell, Mr. Skelten, Simon Yomans.*
Cheese, estimate of quantity and price, 35; committee to provide, 75; do. for the North West voyage, 209; warrant, £37 15s. 6d. p. 125; do. £61 5s. 9d. for cheese and butter, 142.
Cherie, Francis, *vintner,* adventurer, £200, 2; assemblies, 4, 10, 22, 68, 82, 86, 88, 94, 98, 100, 104, 109, 112, 119, 128, 144, 168, 177, 225; committees, 9, 10, 12, 69, 70, 115, 197; views ships, 13; general committees, 63; orders silver plate, 116; sells the ship "Guift" for £300, p. 147; auditor, 218.
"Cherubim," *ship,* 15.
Chery, *see Cherie.*

INDEX

Cheskeens (Sequins), Turkish money, 266, 267, 271, 274.
Chests, for cloth, 118; Warrant, £11 1s., 138.
Chief command in the voyage; commission to Captain Lancaster, and others in succession, 132-7.
China, proposed trade by the North-West Passage, if discovered, 199; supposed destination of the voyage if the passage is discovered, 212; Captain Waymouth to receive £500 if he arrive at any port in China, &c., 214; the salary of Mr. Cartwright, *Preacher*, contingent on reaching China, 216; the Queen's letters to the Emperor, 217; Mr. Cartwright's gown to be used in China, if reached, 232.
Cicell, *see Cycill.*
Cider, the provision of in the West Country, 21; estimate of quantity and price, 34; Mr. Chambers to purchase what he can, 38; revised estimate, 46, 54-5; 100 tons to be bought in the West Country, 41, 52; instructions as to quality and preparation for shipment, 48; best places for buying, 49; 40 tons to be provided, 67; 60 tons to be provided in the West Country, 68; committee to provide casks, 76; £5 allowed to Mr. Fletcher for racking, 176.
Cinnamon, estimate of quantity and price, 35; quantity ordered and committee to purchase, 75; quantity brought home by the "Assention" and entered at the Custom House, 247.
Clarck, Walter, warrant, £105 12s. 4d. on Bill of Exchange, 102.
Clarke, *see Clerke.*
Claret wine, 169.
Clenche, John, brought in as an adventurer of £200 by Mr. Megges, 162; made free, though not named in the patent, 177; bill of adventure, £240, sealed, 255.
Clerke, Richard, assemblies, 237, 241; Committees, 197, 237, 239, 245, 246; bill of adventure sealed, £240, p. 255.
Cletherow, Christopher, admitted adventurer and freeman in lieu of Robert Bowyer, 190; bill of adventure sealed, £240, p. 261.
Clinche, *see Clenche.*
Cloth, } *see also Cassocks, Gowns, Breeches.*
Clothes, }
Committee to provide, 31; quantity to be sent out as merchandise with description and price, 36; warrant £19 6s. 3d. for chests for cloth, 118; do. £12 8s. 6d. for cloth work done, 159; proposed trade with China and Cataia by the North West Passage if discovered, 199; warrant £150, p. 215; do. £20 for mariner's clothes, 218; suits without pockets to be made for the porters employed to fill bags of pepper, 247.
Clothworkers, *see John Jackson, Joseph Jackson, John Morice, Nicholas Pearde, Edwarde Collins.*
Cloves, estimate of quantity and price, 35; quantity ordered and committee to provide, 75; quantity brought home by the "Assention" and entered at the Custom House, 247.
Coals, sea coals for the North West Passage voyage, 210.
Cobbe, Robert, being behind with his adventure, offers security of bonds, 67; bill of adventure sealed £240, p. 253.
Cockain, Richard and Co., adventurers £3,000, p. 2.
Cockein, Richard, assembly, 4.
Cockes, Mr., touching the salary of Mr. Byddell, *preacher* at Aleppo, 275.

Cockes, Richard, *grocer*, adventurer £200, p. 2; assemblies, 4, 5, 59; bill of adventure sealed £240, p. 259.
Cockes, Robarte, *see Coxe.*
Cockeyn, } William, assemblies, 4, 7, 10; di-
Cockin, } rector, 6; committee, 8.
Coghill, John, adventurer with Henrye Parkehurste, £200, p. 3.
Coin, *see also Money*; petition to the Privy Council for leave to send out foreign money and to coin more in the mint when required, 8; petition to carry 5 ml. weight of bullion without charge, 10; warrant solicited to coin £5,000 in the Tower, 78; committee to provide £5,000 of bullion for coining, 80; Mr. Allabaster commissioned to convey bullion from Calais, 84; Lord Treasurer solicited for £3,000 bullion in the Tower, 87; order to coin £20 additional to be distributed to the lords and others, 114; respecting the £6,000 coining in the Tower, 120; mislike to the transportation of treasure out of the country, 198.
Cokes, *see Cockes.*
Colchester, 263.
Cole, Elkana, nominated factor, 77.
Coles, Mr., warrant £200 ou Bill of Exchange, 57.
Coles, George, assembly, 60; bill of adventure sealed £240, p. 253.
Colles, John, warrant £100 on Bill of Exchange, 88; do., £40, p. 104.
Colletton, fit place to buy cider, 49.
Collimore, Richard, nominated factor, 77; Roger Style appointed to take his place, 105.
Collins, Edwarde, *clothworker*, adventurer, £200, p. 2; assembly, 4.
Cothurst, Richard, *consul at Aleppo*; advices respecting the differences between the French and English ambassadors at Constantinople, 265; as to a fixed salary, 266; letters of instructions from the company of Levant Merchants, 270-2, 278-9, 283; *see Company, &c.*
Combe, } John, *see Coombe.*
Combes, }
Commissions, *see also Committees*; for the provision of victuals in the West Country, 28; Captain Baker's commission to buy victuals, &c., 38, 40; do. read and signed, 41; do. full copy, 47-52; to Mr. Allabaster's servant to take up royals at Calais, 41; West Country commission altered, 46; to Captain Davies to provide victuals, &c., in the West Country, 52; to various committees for the provision of victuals, 77; to Mr. Allabaster to convey bullion from Calais, 84; to Captain Lancaster as chief in command of the voyage, and others in succession, viz. : power to correct offences; penalties for private trade; ships to be searched for private merchandise; penalties for deceit and fraud; instructions for leaving resident factors in the Indies; instructions for the devolving of the chief command in case of death, &c., 132-7; to Mr. Howe and Mr. Combe to go into the West Country to attend the discharge of the ships, 147, *see* 149; four commissions for the factors in succession, 153; to Captain Waymouth to bring his ships returned from the North West Voyage round to London from Dartmouth, 227-8; for the sale of the goods brought home in the "Assention," 249.
Committees, for the direction of the voyage generally, also to make suit to the Queen for sole privilege and for immunities from Customs and other favours, 6; to solicit the

Committees, *continued*.
Lords of the Council with a petition for privilege, &c., 8; to seek for ships, 8; to solicit the Lords of the Council for an answer to the petition, 9; to solicit the Lords of the Council for further favours, &c., 10; for the preparation and business of the voyage with power to use the help of any adventurer in any employment requiring the same, 12; to inspect the ships at Woolwich and Deptford, 13; to request the use of the docks at Woolwich and Deptford, 13; surveyors for the ships "Hector," "Assention," and "Susan," 14; for the provision of victuals and dollars in the West Country, 21; to find pinnaces in the river fit for the voyage, 22; to consider the estimate of victuals for the voyage, 26; to consider what merchandise is suitable to be shipped, 26; to survey the ship "Mare Scourge," 27, 33; to prepare a commission for the provision of victuals, &c., 28; to provide casks, 30; to provide clothes and kersies, 31; to arbitrate on the price of the "Mare Scourge," 32; to act as feoffees in trust for the ships bought, 32; to buy beans and mustard-seed, 33, 65; to compound with Captain Davies for the voyage, 37; to compound with Peter Francis, a native of Portugal, 38; to watch the preparation of the "Mare Scourge," 39; to act as remembrancer and in some sort prepare the business for the general committee, 40; to choose and appoint masters and mariners, 57; to treat with Captain Lancaster for taking chief command, 58, 66, 71, 73; general committee of 24 as mentioned in the patent, 63; to purchase biskett to carry the ships to the West Country, 67; to purchase beer, 67; to purchase cider, 68; to provide beef and pork, 68; to compound with Roger Hankin, *Master Mariner*, 69, 70; to review the estimate of victuals and the progress of the victualling, 72; several committees to purchase various kinds of provisions, &c., 75-6; to agree with Captain Middleton for the voyage, 77, 90; to solicit the Lord Treasurer's warrant for coining £5,000 in the Tower, and for providing bullion for the same; also to finish the patent; also to solicit the Lord Treasurer's warrant to transport provisions in the West Country, 78; to order small merchandise—knives, glasses, &c., 79; to provide lead and tin, 79; to provide £5,000 of bullion, 80; to buy Spanish meal taken prize by Lord Willoughby's ship, 86; to hire and compound with a master and officers, 87; to solicit the Lord Treasurer for £3,000 bullion in the Tower, 87; to confer with Mr. Beare to be one of the four chief masters, 90; to confer with Henry Napper as to his employment, 94; to confer touching letters to Potentates in the East to be solicited from the Queen, 91; to set down all names to be mentioned in the patent, 91; to audit the accounts of the pursers, 99; to audit the accounts of the treasurers, 107, 156, 166; to make complaint at Court against defaulting adventurers, 111; to purchase 120 oxen for making salt beef, 114; to go to Court with the names of defaulting adventurers, also to answer their petitions, 115; to provide silver plate, 117; to provide gunners, stewards', cooks', and carpenters' stores, 117; to enter all goods, pay customs, and make a cargazon of the whole, 118; to provide prunes, currants, and raisins, 118; to attend to the shipping of the money and victuals in the West Country, 120; to seal the bargain of sale of the "Susan" at £1,600, p. 120; to agree with the carpenters on disputed prices of timber, 124; to devise orders for the prevention of private trade, 124; to confer as to the damage done to a ship by the anchor of the "Scourge," 125; to take an inventory of all the furniture of the ships, 125; to agree with Captain Middleton, 127; several committees to settle accounts with various creditors, 127; to see to the discharge of the ships from the West Country, 128, 140; to wait on Lord Cumberland respecting the damage done to a ship by the anchor of the "Red Dragon," 128; to receive a mortgage from William Brodebent as security for £100 loan, 128; to entreat a warrant from the Lord Treasurer and Mr. Secretary for the removal of the plate and other presents from Mr. Governor's house, 141; to see the moneys entered in the Custom House, and waterborne to Gravesend and stowed in the ships, 142; to find a small ship to stow provisions and accompany the voyage part way, 143, 147; to audit the accounts of the purser of the "Red Dragon," 147; to go to Gravesend to see to the discharge of the ships, 147; to go to the West Country to see to the discharge of the ships, 147 (*see* 140); to settle disputed accounts for timber with Mr. Ady and other shipwrights, 155; to audit the accounts of the treasurer's, 156, 166; the general committee, 179; to set down the charge for three pinnaces, &c., for a voyage to find the North West Passage, 183; to confer with the Muscovia Company as to their rights in the discovery of the North West Passage, if made, 186; to expedite the preparation of the North West Passage voyage, and to devise laws and ordinances for the guidance of general business, 196-7; to prepare the shipping, &c., and forward the preparation of the North West Voyage, 202-3; to persuade adventurers to bring in contributions for the North West Voyage, 205; three committees to provide victuals and other necessaries for the North West Voyage, 214; to audit and report on the accounts of the North West Voyage, 217; the general committee elected and sworn, 225; to see to the discharge of the ships returned from the North West Voyage, 229; to prepare a second voyage to the North West, and to calculate the charges, 234; to consider the cost of equipping one vessel, and to confer with Captain Waymouth, 237; to attend to the sale of the ships and stores returned from the North West Voyage, 239; to investigate the demands of Captain Waymouth, 240; to make choice of merchants in Plymouth, Dartmouth, &c., to be instructed to give credit to the "Assention" on her return, 243; several committees to watch in turns the unloading of the "Assention," 245-6; to buy polldavies and make bags for the pepper, also suits without pockets for the porters, 247; to see the cellarage and vaults under the Exchange prepared to receive goods, 247, 248; to see the goods sent to the warehouse, 248; to attend at the warehouse and receive and weigh the goods, 248.

Common Seal of the Company. Ordered, 113; references to, 132, 141, 145, 247, 248, 249, 250; the seal of the Muscovia Company, 189.

INDEX

Company of Levant Merchants.
Several drafts of letters in the East India Company's Record Book tending to show that the East India Company was partially an outgrowth of the Levant Company, as several persons mentioned appear to have been prominent members of both companies, notably, Sir Thomas Smith (*see* 62 and 281), who was governor of both companies, 265-83, *viz.* :—
Letter to Mr. Lyllo, ambassador at Constantinople : instructions as to the differences with the French respecting consulage, &c. ; orders to desist from all contention but to lose no advantage ; Signior Paul Pinder sent home to acquaint Her Majesty of the doings of the French ; complaints to the Queen by the French ambassador's lieges in London ; private advices sent by Mr. Staper ; accounts sent home by Signior Paul Pinder ; amount of salary offered and how to be provided for ; no bills of exchange to be drawn but a levy to be charged on all goods entering Constantinople and Aleppo to meet the charges of the ambassador and consul ; troubles arising out of bills drawn by the late ambassador Mr. Barton in favour of John Bate and payment refused by the company ; Mr. Bate's proposed course to recover his money ; instructions to preserve the honour and credit of Her Majesty and the company and to avoid the errors of Mr. Barton ; further instructions as to the rivalry with the French as to the Dutch consulage, &c. ; Acts of Court and instructions for enforcing the levy on goods, 265-70.
Letter to Mr. Colthurst, consul at Aleppo : he is dissatisfied with the offer of half the consulage, as he fears a falling off of trade on account of the discovery of the East Indies by the Dutch ; it is thought the Dutch will prefer peaceable trade in Turkey to the perils of the East India voyages ; duties to be levied on goods entering Turkish ports to maintain his charges and those of the ambassador at Constantinople and thus avoid bills of exchange on Venice ; instructions respecting the rivalry with the French as to Dutch consulage ; orders for the prevention of private trade to Marseilles (Marcelles) ; Sir Anthony Shurley's doings in Persia ; Acts of Court for the duties to be levied, 270-2.
Letter to John Saunderson, merchant at Constantinople : the toleration of the Dutch trade in Turkey ; the French rivalry as to the Dutch consulage, &c. ; Signior Pinder sent home to acquaint the Queen as to the proceedings of the French ; thanks for supplying the wants of the ambassador ; proposed course for meeting the ambassador's charges in future ; instructions for selling, repairing, or letting the Galata House ; the ambassador creditor for 1,000 cheskeens ; allowance for the collection of consulage, 273-75.
Letter to Mr. Byddell, preacher at Aleppo : his salary £50 per annum ; gratuity of £10 allowed ; his good character, 275-6.
Letter to ————, factor at Scanderona (?) : invoices sent of the goods shipped in the "Exchange ;" orders to seize all goods not invoiced ; complaints of impartial dealing ; trouble with mariners refusing to carry goods into the magazines ; all goods received or shipped to be certified to the Company, 276-7.
Petition to the Privy Council respecting the Company's ships seized at Venice as restitution for the late prize taken by the English men-of-war, 277-8.
Letter to Mr. Colthurst, Consul at Aleppo, to attend to the affairs of the late Mr. Edward Rose, factor there, 278-9.
Letter to John Saunderson : the ambassador's allowance and steps taken to support it ; the trouble arising out of the action of the English men-of-war in the Straits ; bills of exchange will be paid ; troubles arising through the opposition of parties offering to pay imposts on certain goods to the Queen ; the Company agree to pay £4,000 per annum to the Queen for a renewal of privileges and in lieu of imposts ; Saunderson's demand for increase of salary, 279-81.
Letter to Mr. May, ex-preacher at Aleppo, ordering him to come home at once, 281.
Letter to the ambassador at Constantinople : the Queen's letter respecting peace with Spain falsified in translation by the French king ; the outrages by the English men-of-war in the Levant ; the payment of £4,000 per annum to the Queen in lieu of imposts on wine, oil, &c. ; privileges to be confirmed, 282.
Letter to Mr. Colthurst : as to his allowance ; the payment of £4,000 per annum to the Queen ; privileges about to be renewed under the great seal ; the outrages by the men-of-war, 283.
Compasses, 218.
Comptroller, Mr. (Privy Council). Orders in council, 112, 164.
Constantinople. Letters to Mr. Lyllo, English ambassador, 265-70, 282, *see Company of Levant merchants*. Levies on goods entering Constantinople and Aleppo to support the ambassadors and consuls' charges, 267, 270, 271, 273-4 ; letters to John Saunderson, Merchant, 273, 279.
Consulage. Differences between the French and English ambassadors at Constantinople, 265-6, 269, 271-2, 273, *see Company of Levant merchants* ; consulage at Aleppo thought to be affected by the discovery of the East Indies by the Dutch, 270 ; allowance to Mr. Saunderson for collection of consulage, 275 ; Mr. Colthurst's allowance, 283.
Consuls. Mr. Richard Colthurst at Aleppo, 265, &c. ; *see Colthurst and Aleppo*.
Cony skins, 271, *see Skins*.
Cooks, the number to be employed in each ship, 90 ; committee to provide stores, 117.
Coombe, }
Coombes, } John, adventurer, £200, p. 4.
Assemblies, 59, 64, 65, 71, 73, 74, 77, 78, 80, 82, 83, 85, 86, 88, 89, 93, 95, 99, 100, 103, 107, 108, 115, 116, 117, 122, 124, 128, 140, 142, 143, 144, 148, 170, 172, 173, 176, 227, 229, 231, 232, 236, 238, 244 ; committees, 75, 76, 77, 128, 228, 234 ; general committee, 63 ; buys vinegar, 115 ; warrant £14 12s. for vinegar, 116 : warrant £20 for attending to business in the West Country, 140 ; commission to go into the West Country and see to the discharge of the ships, 147 (*see* 140) ; orders to bring in his West Country accounts, 172 ; presents his account, 173 ; allowed £18 7s. 2d. with Mr. Howe for expenses in the country,

INDEX

Coombes, John, *continued*.
176; appointed auditor, 218; general committee and sworn, 225; bill of adventure sealed, £240, p. 260.
Coopers. William Done, 139; John Davies, 218; John Spencer, 148.
Copper vessels, 164, 222.
Cordage ordered to be purchased of Browne and Co., 121; warrant £180 to John Lacy for cordage bought of the Muscovia Co., 126; bought of the Muscovia Co., 162, 170, 204; warrant £34 7s. 10d., p. 222; do. £129 9s., p. 224; the cordage returned from the North West voyage to be sold as current prices are high, 241.
Cordall, } Thomas, *mercer*, adventurer, £300,
Cordell, } p. 2.
Assemblies, 30, 37, 44, 46, 47, 56, 57, 58, 65, 67, 68, 69, 71, 76, 80. 82, 86, 88, 89, 90, 92, 93, 94, 96, 98, 99, 100, 102, 103, 104, 105, 107, 108, 109, 112, 113, 116, 118, 122, 128, 139, 140, 142, 143, 144, 148, 150, 151, 152, 154, 156, 158, 162, 163, 172, 176, 181, 182, 183, 184, 187, 192, 205, 206, 215, 217, 219, 227, 237, 242, 244; committees, 6, 8, 10, 12, 4", 57, 58, 67², 71, 73, 75, 77², 87², 90, 91, 99, 107, 124, 128², 147², 155, 166, 183, 191, 197, 203, 209, 234, 237; surveyor of the " Mare Scourge," 33; appointed adventurer £500 by the Earl of Cumberland, 45; signatures to West Country commissions, 54, 55; general committee, 63; reports purchase of the "Guift," 147; assigned by Mr. Brodebent to pay the balance of his mortgage, 154; auditor, 166; general committee and sworn, 179; signature to treasurers' warrant, 206; general committee and sworn, 225.
Cornelis,   } John, *goldsmith*, adventurer,
Cornelius, } £200, p. 3; assemblies, 5, 59;
Cornelys, } bill of adventure sealed, £240, p. 254.
Cornwall, *see Devon and Cornwall*.
Cotton, Roger; bill of adventure sealed, £240, p. 259.
Cotton, William; bill of adventure sealed, £240, p. 253.
Coucheman, John; bill of adventure sealed, £240, p. 251.
Council, Lords of the, *see Privy Council*.
Counsels' opinion as to the respective rights of the Muscovia and East India Cos. in the discovery of the North West Passage, if made, 196.
Court of Admiralty, 128.
Courts, *see General Courts*.
Covell, Francis, supplies peas, 31; beans and mustard seed, 33; peas and beans, 65, 66; oatmeal, 75; warrant, £100 on account, 82; do. £100, 96; do. £17 4s. 11d., 105; do. £22 4s., 164; do. £22 4s., 169.
Covenants, *see Bonds*.
Cowper, John, *notary*, adventurer, £200, p. 3.
Coxe, Robarte, *grocer*, adventurer, £250, p. 1; assembly, 59; bill of adventure sealed, £240, p. 253.
Crane, John, warrant £4 9s. 8d. for pullies, 167.
Credit order for £1,500 to be raised at interest on the credit of Mr. Bannyng and Mr. Holliday, 146.
Cressell, Robert, nominated factor, 77.
Creswell, Robert, recommended as a purser, 39.
Crispe, Ellis, warrant £200 on bill of exchange, 68; bill of adventure sealed, £240. p. 254.
Crispe, Nicholas, adventurer, £200, p. 3; assemblies, 5, 59; bill of adventure sealed, £240, p. 258.
Crompton, Hughe, bill of adventure sealed, £240, p. 255.
Crosse, —, *vintner*, warrant £14 10s. for Malaga wine, 169.
Cryse,   } *see Crispe*.
Cryspe, }
Cullymore, James, bill of adventure sealed, £240, p. 259.
Cumberland, Countess of, bill of adventure sealed, £50, p. 262.
Cumberland, Earl of, assemblies, 44, 47, 69, 87; offers the ship "Mare Scourge, 20; committee to survey and report on the ship, 27; declines £3,000 and offers her at £4,000, p. 29; will not take less than £4,000, but is offered £3,500, p. 30; accepts £3,700. p. 32; advises a chain pump for the ship, 44; seals bargain for the sale of the ship, 45; becomes an adventurer, 45; damage done by the anchor of the " Red Dragon," 128; assigns £200 of his adventure to Wm. Beerbloch, 161; the supplies due on £570 of adventure assigned to Mr. Bannyng, 177; assigns £230 adventure to Mr. Holliday, 197, 262; bill of adventure sealed, £500, p. 262.
Currants,   } 118, 168; impost offered to the
Curraunce, } Queen in opposition to the Le-
Currents,   } yant Company, 280.
Custom House, committee to see the monies entered, 142; goods brought home by the " Assention" entered, and list of the same, 247; the entries of goods shipped by the " Exchange" to Scanderona, 276.
Customs. Suit made to the Queen for immunities from Customs, 6; petition to the Privy Council, 8-9; freedom of the Dutch from Customs, 9; committee to pay custom, 118; bonds given for the payment of dues on the goods brought home by the "Assention," 247; duties amount to £917, p. 248.
Cutteler, Thomas, *grocer*, adventurer £200, p. 3.
Cycill, Sir Robert, *secretary*, letters from the Privy Council to the Company, 60, 61; orders in council, 112, 164; the complaints of the French as to consulage, 263.

Dale, William, adventurer, £100, p. 2; assemblies, 59, 226, 227, 229, 230, 238, 240, 244, 249; warrant £112 on Bill of Exchange, 88; general committee, 225; bill of adventure sealed, £240, p. 259.
Dartmouth, provisions at, 29; Mr. Sandy, 70; recommended for the purchase of biskett, 48; do. cider, 49; to be the place of assembly for all provisions bought, 49; return of the ships from the North West Passage Voyage, 227-9; mariners hired to bring ships to London, 231; letters to the principal merchants to give credit to the "Assention" on her return, 243.
Dassell, Thomas, nominated factor, 77; appointed third factor of the "Hector," 101; warrant £30 for wages, 104; bill of adventure £50 sealed, 153.
Davers, Jerom or Jeremie, made free though not named in the patent, 177; bill of adventure sealed, £200, p. 260.
Davies, Captain John, assemblies, 14, 22, 24, 26, 27, 31, 33, 47, 143; committees, 22, 26, 68, 72; view ships, 13; sent to the West Country for provisions, 21; ordered to draw out an estimate of victuals for 500 men, 22;

Davies, Captain John—*continued*.
letter to the Earl of Essex asking his approval of Captain Davies as Chief Director of the voyage, 25; presents his estimate of victuals, 26; compounds for his entertainment and profit in the voyage, 37 (*see also* 152); respecting the provision of seines, hooks, and lines, 49; do. victuals, &c., 51; commission for purchasing provisions, &c., in the West Country, 52, 54, 55; letter 10, 66; letter from, 74; to sail in the "Red Dragon" as pilot-major of the fleet, 100; warrant £360 for salary, 127; bill of adventure sealed with profit contingent on the success of voyage. 152.
Davies, John, *Cooper*, warrant £50 11s. 8d. for casks, 218.
Davies Straits, Captain Waymouth's sailing orders, 212.
Davis, Captain John, *see Davies*.
Davyes, George, warrant £19 6s. 3d. for chests for cloth, 118; do. £11 1s., p. 138.
Deals, 164, 169, 171, 218.
Deane, James, *Draper*, adventurer, £300, p. 3; assembly, 59; bill of adventure sealed £360, p. 254.
Deane, Richard, assembly, 60; bill of adventure sealed £240, p. 259.
Decro, Benjamin, *Agent of the Muscovia Co.*, warrant £57 16s. 8d. for cordage, 187; do. £109 16s. 8d., p. 204.
Denham, William, *Shipwright*, warrant £6, p. 169; do. £12 for pulleys, &c., 221.
Denman, Mr., *Master of the Bridgehouse*; order to deliver timber to Mr. Burrell, 89.
Dent, Fraunois, assembly, 59; desires to assign his adventure to George Bennet, 175; the assignment allowed, 177.
Deodands for the "Hector," 169.
Deptford, committee to inspect ships there, 13; use of the docks requested, 13.
Deputy governors, Mr. William Rumney elected, 111, *see Rumney*; the oath of office, 179; powers at general courts, 200-2; Mr. Rumney re-elected, 225; Mr. Thomas Bramley elected in place of Mr. Rumney, 239; power to depute adventurers to perform any services required, 249.
Devon and Cornwall, letter from the Lord Treasurer to her Majesty's Receivers authorising credit to be given to the Company's agents, 38.
Deycro, *see Decro*.
Deyns, William, *Ironmonger*; warrant £30 8s. for necessaries for the pinnaces, 222.
Dickson, *see Dixon*.
Die, Roger, bill of adventure, sealed, £240, p. 260.
Directors of the voyage and their duties, 6, 12, 63; Captain Davies principal director, 25.
Discovery, *one of the ships for the North West voyage; see also North West Passage, Pinnaces, Ships, Waymouth, Yerworth*; warrant £100 for anchors and other necessaries, 210; manned, victualled, and prepared according to Captain Waymouth's own desires, 211, 212; several warrants for the provision of stores and necessaries, 220-24, *see Warrants*; return to Dartmouth, 227-29; ordered to be sold with all stores, &c., 230; arrival in the Thames, 229; the boatswain, gunner and carpenter aver that Mr. Cartwright, the preacher, was the main mover for the return of the expedition, 232; warrant, £4, to the porters for landing and housing the stores, 238; warrant, £6, to Edward Pullyson, *purser*, in full of his account and for wages, 240; the sale of the ship deferred, 241; ordered to be sold if £300 can be obtained, 242.
Disfranchisement of certain defaulting adventurers, 178; of Nathaniel Martin, 185; of Xpofer Cletherow, 190.
Dixon, William, *purser of the "Red Dragon;"* warrant £50 for the use of the Dixson, gon;" ship, 105; do. £100, p. 108; do. Dixsy, £100, p. 111; do. £190 for the "Hector," 111; do. £150 for the "Red Dragon," 114; do. £250, p. 117; do. £250, p 120; do. £200, p 127; do. £200, p. 139; do. £100, p. 144; William Brodebent's account, 153; warrant £180 for mariners' wages, &c., 154.
Docks at Woolwich and Deptford; the use of requested, 13; the "Mare Scurge" at Woolwich, 27; dock charges to be paid, 80; ships ready to come out, 92.
Dollars, *see Spanish money, royals, &c.*; the provision of, in the West Country, 15; 1,000 dollars contracted for at 4s. 6d., p. 20; adventures received in dollars, 63; duties charged at Constantinople and Aleppo to be answered in London at 5s. 6d. the dollar, 267, 271; Mr. Byddell's salary to be rated at 5s. the dollar, 276.
Doncomb, Giles, adventurer with Richard Welbye £200, 4.
Done, William, *Cooper*, warrant £38 7s. 7d, p. 139.
Donkon, James, bill of adventure sealed £240, p. 257.
Dorrington, George, bill of adventure sealed £240, p. 261.
Downs, the, letter sent to Captain Waymouth, 223.
Dragon, *ship, see "Red Dragon."*
Drapers, *see Thomas Garwaye, William Garwaye, James Deane*.
Drewe, John, *master of the "Godspeed;"* appointed master of a ship for the North West voyage, 206; warrant £5 on account of wages, 206; do. £10, p. 210; Mr. Alderman Cambell, treasurer, bound by covenant for the payment of his wages, 220; bond of indemnity £200 sealed to James Cambell, 221; examined as to the causes of the return of the North West Expedition, 232; avers that Mr. Cartwright was the persuader for the return, 232; warrant £5 for wages, 234.
Drugs; Edmund Scott to go on the voyage in hope of his service in the choice of drugs, 109.
Duck, Thomas, warrant £29 for ancients and streamers, 149; do. £12, p. 163.
Duckett, John, adventurer with William Hallidaie, £200, p. 3.
Ducy, Robert, bill of adventure sealed £240, p. 259; do. 260.
Duffeilde, Anthonie, *Brewer*, warrant £15 7s. for beer, 154.
Dunkin, James, assembly, 60.
Dutch; their success in the East Indies; preparing for a new voyage; ships bought in England, 8; freedom from Customs, 9; their preparations, 110; return of their voyage with honour, 189; their example propounded to the East India Co. in a letter signifying Her Majesty's mislike to the delay in the second voyage, 191; an Englishman brought home out of the East Indies in the Dutch ships, 194; the rivalry between the English and French at Constantinople to obtain the

Dutch, *continued*.
Dutch consulage, 265, 266, 269, 271; the discovery of the East Indies by the Dutch as affecting the consulage at Aleppo, 270; trade in Turkey, 270, 273.

Dyckes, *see Dixon*.

East India Company: list of adventurers and the amounts subscribed, 1-4; formation of the company, royal assent, objects, rules to be made, 5; rules made, 6, *see Rules*; directors appointed, 6; suit to be made to the Queen for sole privilege and immunities and freedom from customs, 6; all officers or factors to be elected by a general assembly, 6; petition to the Privy Council for incorporation, privilege, &c., 8-10, *see Privy Council*; preparation of the voyage postponed by reason of the treaty of peace in hand with Spain, 10; the preparation resumed, 11, 12; general committee, 12; the adventure proves larger than expected, and hence more shipping required, 27; no gentlemen to be employed, 28; agreement with Captain Davies for his profit in the voyage, 37; remembrancers appointed to prepare the business for the general committee, 40; no adventure of £200 to be refused until £55,000 is reached, 45; general court summoned to take notice of a letter signifying Her Majesty's pleasure, 57; general court, 58-63, viz. the objects and proceeding of the company reviewed, 60; letter from the Privy Council confirming privileges, with assurances of no hindrances of the voyage, 61; adventurers in arrears to be certified to the Privy Council, 61; the patent drawn up, 62 (*see* 198); election of Sir Thomas Smyth as first governor, 62; election of the general committee of 24, pp. 62-3; all business committed to the care of the governor and committee, 63; election of four classes of factors, 81-3; deficiency in the adventure, and steps taken to supply it, 110-11; order in council for defaulting adventurers to bring their money at once on pain of imprisonment, 112-13; common seal ordered, 113; every adventurer to have a bill of adventure under the common seal, 113; coining in the Tower (? special coinage), 114; resolution respecting prizes and prize money, 118; ordinances, laws, and decrees for the guidance of trade, 129, 131 (*see also* 197, 202); everything to be managed as a joint stock, and no private trade to be practised, 130; all private goods shipped to be forfeited to the common stock, 130; ordinances against fraud, 130; proposed leaving of factors to trade in the East Indies, 131; the commission to the general or principal merchant and to others in succession, 132-37, *see Commissions*; two forms of bills of adventure for merchants and factors, 144-46; £1,500 to be borrowed on the credit of Mr. Bannyng and Mr. Holliday, 146; the treasurer's accounts on March 6, 1600, showing amount of debts also of adventures not yet brought in, 156; being £9,000 in arrears, a supply of 2s. in the £ is ordered, with penalties by reduction of stock in default of payment, 160-61; order in council touching the discredit likely to arise by the remissness of the company in paying their debts, and ordering defaulting adventurers to appear and be punished for contempt, 164-65; resolution that great care be taken to remove all discredit, and for the better ordering of business, Alderman Wattes elected governor in place of Sir Thomas Smyth in prison, 166; auditors chosen for the treasurers' accounts, 166; an estimate to be made of the money in the treasurers' hands, 167; warrant for the summoning of all defaulting adventurers, 169-70; arms assigned by the King of Heralds, 171; disfranchisement of certain defaulters, 177, 181; election of governor, deputy, and committee, 178-79; the oaths of office, 179-80; letter received from Captain George Waymouth touching his attempt to be made for the discovery of a North West Passage to the East Indies, asking whether the company will undertake the enterprise, and if not whether they will allow private men to deal therein, giving them the benefit of the discovery, if made, by the sole trade for certain years, 182, *see North West Passage* and *Waymouth*; a second voyage by the Cape proposed, 182; the charters to be perused to see if power is given to compel payments towards the North West Passage voyage, or the second voyage by the Cape, 183; second voyage by the Cape resolved on, the adventure to be not less than £100, p. 186; adventure subscribed for the second voyage amounts to £11,000 only, which is insufficient, 189; enquiries by the Lord Admiral and Mr. Secretary as to the great delay in furthering the voyages as compared with the Dutch, and complaining that the company were not so respective of Her Majesty's honor as they should be, 189; the causes of the delay, 189; to avoid delay no ship to be prepared until approved by a general court, 189; the subscription book to be carried round by men able to persuade and encourage the brethren to adventure, 190; letter from the Privy Council notifying Her Majesty's mislike to the delay in the second voyage, and propounding the example of the Dutch, 191; general court summoned to deal with the matter, with penalty of 20s. for non-attendance, 191; return of two Dutch ships laden with pepper, 194; an Englishman brought home by the Dutch after being detained a prisoner four years, and knowing the language of Sumatra; Mr. Wattes is desired to induce him to come over to confer as to trade, &c., 194; committee appointed to expedite the second voyage by the Cape and the North West voyage, and also to devise laws and ordinances for the better guidance of general business, 196-97; laws and ordinances for the government of trade, &c., as devised by the committee and revised and agreed on by the generality, viz., preamble; by the Queen's letters patent the company have the sole right to the trade with the East Indies for 15 years, either by the Cape or by such passages as shall be hereafter found out by the parts of America; in the late voyage by the Cape the greater part of the adventure was taken out in English and foreign coin prepared with great difficulty and not without mislike to the transportation of treasure out of the country; therefore for the good of the country, and in order to carry on the trade with the Indies with little or no money, it is resolved to attempt to discover a passage through some part of America, so that by reaching Cataia or China, countries of temperate climate, a

East India Company, *continued*.
market would be found for a liberal sale of clothes and kerseys to the general advancement of English trade; resolved therefore that the voyage to the North West be set forth with all convenient expedition; two ships or pinnaces to be employed; every adventurer to contribute at least 12*d*. in the £ on the amount of his adventure for the voyage by the Cape; if the discovery he made every man to participate in the benefit in proportion to his adventure, and in all future voyages in the same ratio only; dates for the payment of adventures; Mr. Cambell appointed treasurer; any one declining to adventure or being behind time in his payments to be fined 5 times the value of his levy at 12*d*. in the £ to be deducted from his original stock, such fines to be employed in the preparation of the voyage, and any surplus proportionately divided; all future contributions or levies for the general trade to be paid on the days appointed on pain of fines in the discretion of the company or of the auditors; penalty for absence from a general court, 12*d*; for being late, 6*d*.; no one to speak on any one matter more than three times, penalty, 3*s*. 4*d*.; penalty for uncivil speeches or behaviour, 10*s*.; no one to interrupt another in a speech or disturb by private whisperings, but all replies to be directed to the governor or deputy on pain of penalty, 2*s*. 6*d*.; silence to be kept at the stroke of the hammer, penalty, 6*d*.; penalty for non-payment of fines, imprisonment; no person to leave a general court without leave, penalty, 12*d*.; all fines to be employed to the general use of the company or to the relief of the poor, 197-202; committee for the preparation of the North West Voyage, 202-3; the tardiness of payment of contributions for the North West Voyage reported at a general court; the expenses already incurred amount to £700, all which would be lost, and the company discredited at home and abroad if the voyage did not proceed; resolved therefore for further encouragement that all sums brought in shall be deemed part of the adventure for the voyage to the Cape, and shall bear profit and benefit in that voyage in proportion with the original stock; the act for the forfeiture of five times the value of the levy by defaulters confirmed and fortified, and ordered that suit be made to the Privy Council to approve the same; those present set down their contributions in writing their consent may appear to those absent, and all contributions to be endorsed on the bills of adventure; all contributions to be brought in by the end of March, 1602, after which date no payments to be received without the consent of a general court, 206-8; committees appointed to provide victuals and other necessaries for the North West Voyage, 209; articles of agreement with Captain Waymouth with his orders and instructions, 211-14, viz., the company's desire to discover a nearer passage to the East Indies (*see* page 182, Waymouth's suggestions); Captain Waymouth considered a fit and proper person to attempt the discovery, and is allowed £100 to furnish his instruments to his own choice; two ships committed to his charge, the "Discovery" and the "Godspeed," manned, victualled, and furnished for 16 months to his own desires, and also laden with various merchandise; Waymouth agrees to be ready to sail by a certain date and to proceed towards the coast of Greenland into Davies Straits, thence to the north west "or as he shall fynd the Passage best to lye" towards the kingdoms of Cataya or China "*or ye backside of America*," without giving up the attempt as long as he shall find those seas navigable, or any possibility of finding a passage, and will not return or suffer voluntarily any of his company to return till a year has been bestowed on the attempt; agreed for merchants and pursers to go in the ships to keep a register of goods laden and how disposed of, also to make notes, journals, and observations for the direction and help of posterity; within 10 days of his return to deliver a report of all his proceedings, and within 40 days on a summons to appear before the company and relate such things as they desire to be informed of, and will not discover the secrets of the voyage to any person whatsoever; within 40 days of his return the company will on proof of his having arrived at any port in China, Cataya, or Japan by the North West Passage pay unto him £500, but if the passage be not discovered it is agreed that he is to make no claim for salary, wages, or reward, seeing that the expense of the voyage was undertaken at his persuasion and on his resolution to adventure his life for the good of his country, 214-14; agreement with John Cartwright to go as preacher in the North West Voyage with salary contingent on the discovery of the passage, 216; the agreement with Waymouth read to the generality, also the Queen's letters to the Emperor of China and Kathia, 217; auditors chosen to report on the state of the adventure, that further supplies may be called up and some course taken with the defaulters, 217-18; day appointed for the payment of supplies for the North West Voyage; the rateable and voluntary supplies to be endorsed on all bills of adventure, and the secretary then to make out new bills showing in one lump sum what is every man's interest in the voyage by the Cape, 220 (*see* 206-8); order to the bookkeeper to enter up each adventurer's credits in a lump sum, 224; election of treasurer, secretary, book-keeper, and beadle, 226; election of governor, deputy, and committees, 225-26; the return of the North West expedition, 227, *see North West Passage*; Mr. Holliday and others being in arrears with supplies for the North West Voyage, it is ordered that the same be deducted from their stock, 231 (*see* pages 200 and 207); the book-keeper ordered to charge up the accounts of all brethren debtors to the company, that the amounts may be defaulted on their stock if not paid before the return of the ships, 233; proceedings against Waymouth before the lords of the council; deliberations and preparations for a second voyage; the idea of a second voyage abandoned, and the ships and stores ordered to be sold off; dispute with Waymouth as to his demands for charges, and the same referred to arbitration, &c., &c., 232-42, *see North West Passage*; Mr. Thomas Bramley elected deputy-governor in place of Mr. Rumney, 239; letters from the "Assention" brought home by a Frenchman

East India Company, *continued*,
who lately departed at sea from that ship, by which good hope is conceived of a successful voyage and encouragement given to set forth another, 242-43; letters to be written to the factors and officers of the "Assention" and sent into the West Country saying that orders have been sent to the principal merchants in Plymouth, Dartmouth, &c., to take any sick men on shore and supply their wants and to give credit for money required for the use of the ship; orders not to break bulk or make sale of anything belonging to the general adventure; committee to make choice of the merchants in Plymouth, &c., to be written to, to supply the wants of the ship, and the same to be reimbursed by the treasurer, 243-44; arrival of the "Assention" in the river, 244; warehouses for the goods, 245; committees to attend in turns to the unloading, 245-46; no mariner to remove anything from the ship "unlesse it be visited" on pain of detention of wages, 245; the tithes due to the Lord Admiral for a prize taken in the East Indies, 246-47; bags to be made for the pepper, also suits for the porters *without pockets*, 247; list of goods brought home and entry to be made at the Custom House, 247; Mr. Governor and Mr. Eldred give bond for the payment of customs, 247; customs amount to £917, and Mr. Cambell and Mr. Eldred indemnified for their bonds given for the payment of the same, 248; £2,000 to be taken up at interest for the payment of mariners' wages, and Sir John Harte and others asked to give their bonds to secure the same, 249; future monies required, to be raised by a levy on the pole and upon the rates of particular adventures, 249; order for the sale of the goods brought home, 249; the governor and deputy empowered to appoint any adventurer to perform any service which the general business requireth, 249; two obligations of £3,000 each sealed to Mr. James Cambell and Mr. John Eldred, who gave their bonds for the payment of customs, 250; two obligations of 1,000 marks each to Sir John Harte and Robert Chamberlayne for money taken up at interest, 250; several drafts of letters of the Levant Company written in the East India Company's record book tending to show that the East India Company was partially an outgrowth of the Levant Company, several persons mentioned appearing to have been prominent members of both companies; notably Sir Thomas Smith (*see* 62 and 281), who was governor of both companies, 265-83, *see Company of Levant Merchants*.

East Indies: the objects of the East India Company, 5, 60; the Dutch voyages, 8; letters from the Queen to potentates in the East, 91, 131, 134; resident factors, 97, 102; Mr. Hacklett, historiographer, reads his notes and is desired to furnish a list of places where trade is, 124; orders and instructions respecting the leaving of resident factors, 131; warrant £13 7s. 8d. to William Segar, *Herald*, for writing the Queen's letters to the kings of the East Indies, 139; the presents for the kings and how distributed in the ships, 151; warrant £29 10s. for making stamps for the East India monies, 174; Captain George Waymouth's proposed voyage for the discovery of a North West Passage to the East Indies, 182, *see North West Passage*; an Englishman, a prisoner for four years, brought home from the East Indies by the Dutch, 194; two Dutch ships returned laden with pepper, 194; abstract of the objects and aims of the company in reference to trade in the East Indies, 198, *see East India Company*; Waymouth's confidence in the discovery of a passage by divers inlets that treat through the coast of America, 233; the return of the "Assention," 242, &c., *see East India Company and "Assention;"* the discovery of the East Indies by the Dutch as affecting the Consulage at Aleppo, 270.

Eaton, Thomas, adventurer with William Essington, £200, p. 3.

Edmondes, Thomas, *Clerk to the Privy Council*, signatures to orders in council, 113, 165.

Edmonds, Richard, adventurer with Humfrey Wymers, £200, p. 3.

Edward, William, *plumber*, warrant £8 8s. for lead and soda, 224.

Edwardes, Thomas, adventurer, £200, p. 2; assembly, 4.

Eldred, John, adventurer, £400, p. 1; assemblies, 4, 26, 27, 28, 31, 37, 44, 45, 46, 57, 58, 59, 64, 67, 71, 73, 76, 80, 82, 83, 92, 94, 95, 98, 102, 103, 104, 106, 108, 109, 113, 114, 119, 121, 122, 124, 125, 139, 144, 155, 156, 158, 160, 162, 164, 171, 175, 177, 192, 197, 206, 224, 229, 230, 232, 236, 247; committees, 12, 26, 31, 76, 120, 141, 155, 248; views ships, 13; feoffee in trust for ships bought, 32; purchase of the "Malice Scurge," 45; general committee, 63; recommends Thomas Eldred as a captain, 72; general committee and sworn, 179; ditto, 225; bound with Mr. Cambell as security for the payment of customs dues on the goods brought home in the "Assention," 247; indemnified by a general bond under the common seal, 248; the bond of indemnity in £3,000 sealed, 249; bill of adventure sealed, £600, p. 250.

Eldred, Thomas, *of Ipswich*, willing to be employed as a captain, 72.

Eldred, } Tristram, *purser of the two pinnaces*,
Eldrich, } warrant £4 7s. to be disbursed for mariners' lodgings, &c., 222; warrant £6 13s. for his pains taken in the company's affairs, 226.

Elections: of officers, 6, 8; of Sir Thomas Smyth as governor, 62; of three principal factors, 81; of four second class factors, 82; of third and fourth class factors, 83; of William Rumney as deputy governor, 111; of Mr. Alderman Wattes as governor, in place of Sir Thomas Smyth in prison, 166; of Mr. Wattes as governor, and Mr. Rumney as deputy, 179; of the general committee, 179, 225; of Sir John Harte as governor, and Mr. Rumney as deputy, 225; of Alderman Cambell as governor, in place of Sir John Harte, who declines, 226; of Thomas Bramley as deputy, in place of Mr. Rumney, 239.

Elington, Francis, warrant £600 for cloth, 45.

Elizabeth, Queen, *see Queen*.

Ellacott, } John, *of Exeter*, respecting money
Ellecott, } on the West Country, 50, 51, 53;
Ellecote, } 54, 56, 64; bills of exchange, 58,
Ellecott, } 65, 69, 83, 102, 108, 109, 115, 119;
Ellicott, } Spanish money, 66; warrant £500 for royals of plate, 105; to confer with Mr. Pope as to shipping the Spanish money, 119; as to Mr. Augustine Skinner's adven-

INDEX

Ellacott, John—*continued*.
ture of £200 being received in royals, 124; bill of adventure sealed, £220, p. 149; ordered to render his account and pay up his supplies, 181.

Emerson, James, order to be paid £30 for aquavitae, 143.

Essex, Earl of, letter to, on behalf of Captain Davies, 25.

Essington, William, adventurer with Thomas Eaton, £200, p. 3.

Evesed, } Thomas, *beadle of the Company*,
Evesett, } warrants for general courts, 57,
Evettsett, } 228, 235; salary fixed at £10 per annum, 204; re-appointed, 226; warrant for 25s. 7d. disbursed to Mr. Pope's man, 238.

Evington, Francis, adventurer; assembly, 59; warrant £120 on bill of exchange, 56; bill of adventure sealed, £240, p. 261.

Europe, Coast of, route to the East Indies, 211.

Exchange, *ship of the Levant Company*, letters sent, 273, 279; Mr. Holliday, part owner, 276; goods shipped and invoices sent, 276.

Exchange, the, warehouses under, 245; committee to prepare the vaults and receive goods, 248; committee to receive and weigh goods, 248.

Exeter, 56, 58, 66, 74, 81, 83, 84, 97, 102, 106, 119, 125, 181, 209.

Eydes, John, *of Exeter*, bill of exchange, £50, p. 83.

Factors, all to be elected by a general assembly, 6; Thomas Wasse recommended, 36; list of factors nominated, 77; the scale of remuneration fixed, 81; election of four sorts of factors, 81, 82, 83; to give security and to abstain from private trade, 86; Roger Style not being elected, offers to serve without salary, or to remain in the East Indies and learn the language, 86; the choice of factors to be discussed at a general court, 92; Mr. Brund recommended as a principal factor, 93; elected, 94; names of the principal factors appointed to each ship, 94; Walter Poyner recommended as an extra factor without salary to serve in case of death, or to be left resident in the Indies, 97; William Martin recommended and security offered as a resident factor in the Indies, 97; appointed to their respective ships, 100-1; bonus £50 to Robert Pope for his pains in the provision of victuals, &c., 101; list of extra factors to serve in case of death, or be left resident in the Indies, 102; Mr. Howe to answer letters from factors in West Country, 103; warrant £30 to William Wilford for salary, 103; Roger Style to take the place of Richard Collymore of the third class, 105; bonds to be given for truth and good behaviour, 105; amounts of bonds for the four classes, 105; warrant £30 to William Starky for his salary and preparation, 106; ditto £30 to Roger Style, 108; orders for the prevention of private traffic, 136; orders and instructions for factors left resident in the Indies, 131; form of bill of adventure read, 144-5; bills of adventure sealed, 148, 149, 150, 152, 153; four commissions sealed, 153; letters to the factors of the "Assention" on her return, 243; names of factors offering to be employed, 263; orders for the prevention of private trade from Aleppo to Marseilles,

272; difficulties at Venice by reason of prizes taken by English men-of-war, 278; orders to Mr. Colthurst to attend to the estate of Edward Rose, deceased, at Aleppo, 278-9; money taken up from Mr. Leet's and Mr. Salter's factors, for the use of the ambassador, 280.

Fans, 141.

Farrar, } Nicholas, *Skinner*, adventurer, £200,
Farrer, } p. 2; assemblies, 4, 59; committees, 186, 229, 230; bill of adventure sealed, £240, p. 259.

Farrington, Thomas, *Vintner*, adventurer, £200, 2; assemblies, 59, 180, 181, 183, 184, 187, 190, 193, 194, 196, 197, 203, 205, 206, 208, 214, 215, 216, 218, 224, 225, 227, 228, 230, 231, 232, 233, 235; committees, 197, 209; general committee and sworn, 179; do. 225; signatures to treasurer's warrants, 210; bill of adventure sealed £240, 253.

Feathers, 141, 151.

Fenton, Peter, *carpenter of the "Susan,"* deceit in the supply of masts, 121.

Ferries, } William, assemblies, 236, 238, 240,
Ferrers, } 241, 244, 247, 248; offers the ship
Ferris, } "Phenixe," 14; assembly, 59; general committee and sworn, 226; to provide bags for pepper and suits *without pockets* for the porters, 247; committee, 248; bill of adventure sealed £240, p. 251.

Ferror, Nicholas, *see Farrar*.

Ferror, } William, *see Ferries*.
Ferrys, }

Finchcomber, William, nominated factor, 77.

Fines, various fines or penalties for breach of rules, 200-2; all fines to be employed to the use of the Co. or to the relief of the poor, 200.

Fish, estimate of quantity and price, 34; quantity to be bought in the West Country, 41, 52; revised estimate, 46, 54-5; as to quality and packing, 49; 1000 ling to be bought to carry the ships to the West Country, 67; committee to provide, 75; warrant £50, p. 92; stockfish for the North West Voyage, 209.

Fisher, William, assembly, 59; warrant £80 for oil, 114; bill of adventure sealed £240, p. 260.

Fishing tackle, 52.

Fitche, Mr., committee for merchandise, 26.

Flags, streamers and ancients ordered, 108; do. for the "Hector," 151.

Fleming, } Giles, bill for iron, 128; balance
Flemyng, } due to Richard Hart, assigned to Mr. Flemyng, 147; warrant £29 1s. 4d., p. 172.

Flemyng's Voyage, the Book of the, dedicated to the Co., 125.

Fletcher, Mr. } provision of cider, 38, 68;
Fletcher and Co. } order to settle accounts, 127; allowed £5 for racking cider, 176.

Fletcher, John, auditor, 166, 218; warrant £129 9s. for cordage, 224; bill of adventure sealed £240, p. 256.

Fletcher, Walter, adventurer, £200, p. 2; assembly, 5.

"Flyboats" for the North West Voyage, 220, 221.

Formation of the Co. and objects, 5.

Fortescue, Sir John, *Privy Councillor;* letter from the Privy Council to the Co. favouring the voyage, 61; orders in council, 112, 164.

Founders Hall; used for the Company's meetings, 11; general court, 57; warrant £6 for six quarters rent, 227.

Fowle, Alphonsus, bill of adventure sealed £240, p. 255.
Franklyn, John, carries a letter to Captain Waymouth in the Downs, 223.
Frauncis, Peter, *of Bridgewater, a native of Portugal;* compounds for his entertainment in the voyage, 38; to sail in the "Susan" with Mr. John Havard, 117.
Free-brethren } of the Company, *see Freemen.*
Free-brothers }
Freeman, *see Freman.*
Freemen, *see also Disfranchisement;* adventurers not named in the patent to be deemed equally as free as those mentioned, 109; their names to be presented and then confirmed as free, 110; William Beerblock admitted by way of assignment of part of Earl Cumberland's stock, 161; John Jackson admitted in lieu of John Bate, 174; refusal to grant freedom for £105, p. 175; Francis Dent named in the patent desires to assign, and referred to a general court, 175; list of persons made free though not named in the patent, 177; disfranchisement of certain defaulting adventurers, 178; Robert Bayly assigns to Sir John Spencer, and renounces his freedom, 181; Sir John Spencer allowed to nominate a freeman, 181; John Morice made free in place of Nathaniel Martin disfranchised, 185; book sent round for all freemen to subscribe to the second voyage, 187; Joseph Jackson made free on the nomination of Sir John Spencer, 187 (*see* 181); Robert Bowyer made free in the place of Xpofer Clethrowe, 190; William Nelson admitted on paying £240 adventure and supplies and £30 premium, 205; freedom denied to Peter Wellington, 226-7; the freedom of Thomas Stephens deferred, 227; Thomas Stephens admitted, 239.
Freman, Ralfe, adventurer with William Freman, £300, p. 2; assembly, 4.
Freman, William, adventurer with Ralfe Freman, £300, p. 2; assemblies, 180, 181, 186, 192, 204, 205, 215; general committee and sworn, 179; bill of adventure sealed £240, p. 258.
French; letters brought home from the "Assention" by a Frenchman, 242; rivalry between English and French ambassadors at Constantinople as to consulage, 265, 266, 269, 271, 272; complaints to the queen by the French ambassador, 265, 271, 273; Signior Paul Pinder sent from Constantinople to acquaint the queen of the doings of the French, 265, 272, 273; instructions to the English ambassador, 266, 269; do. to the consul at Aleppo, 271-2; orders for the prevention of private trade by French ships from Aleppo to Marseilles, &c., 272.
Fretum, Davies, route to the North West Passage, 212.
Frier, } John, assembly, 59; bill of adventure
Fryer, } sealed £240, p. 260.
Frythe, Roger, *smith,* warrant £19 for iron work, 221.
Furner, Symon, warrant £326 13s. 4d. for powder, 122; do. £371 15s., p. 142; do. £16 10s., p. 184.
Fysher, *see Fisher.*

Gallata House, instructions to Mr. Saunderson for its sale or letting, 274-5.
Gallaunt, Peter, *merchant in Turkey,* 268.
Gamond, John, *surgeon of the "Susan,"* warrant £20 to provide remedies, 98.

Gamram, } Nathaniel, elected factor of the
Gamrym, } third sort, 83; to sail in the "Dragon," 101; warrant £30 for his entertainment, 139; bill of adventure sealed £50, p. 150.
Garrard, Samewell, adventurer with John Suzan, £200, p. 4.
Garroeway, *see Garway.*
Garway, Thomas, *Draper,* adventurer, £200, p. 1; bill of adventure sealed £240, p. 255.
Garwaye, William, *Draper,* adventurer, £500.
Garwey, } p. 2; assemblies, 7, 9, 10, 20, 24, 26, 27, 28, 31, 37, 46, 57, 58, 64, 68, 69, 73, 78, 80, 82, 85, 86, 88, 90, 93, 94, 98, 99, 102, 106, 107, 108, 114, 116, 118, 121, 138, 140, 142, 144, 148, 151, 152, 158, 164, 167, 184, 186, 190, 196, 236, 237, 244, 247; committees, 6, 8, 9, 12, 32, 58, 71, 76, 77, 87, 91, 106, 141, 147, 155, 197, 234, 237, 239; views ships, 13; surveyor for the "Assention," 14; to enquire price of peas, 26; desired to answer the Lord Treasurer's letter respecting the employment of Sir Edward Michelborne, 28; guarantees William Leake as purser of the "Assention," 33; warrant 100 markes towards repairs of the "Assention," 57; do. £200, p. 85; do. £100, p. 91; do. £100, p. 105; do. £150, p. 114; do. £100, p. 126; do. £100, p. 140; do. £50, p. 144; general committee, 63; warrant £194 5s. 6d. for oil, 114; buys steel, 138; assigned by Mr. Brodebent to pay balance of his mortgage to the company, 154; general committee, 179; do. and sworn, 225.
Gawldsmith, Mr., supplies meal, 90.
General Courts.
October 28, 1600. The objects and proceedings of the company reviewed, 60; letter from the privy council confirming privileges, &c., 61; adventurers in arrears to be certified to the privy council, 61; the patent drawn up, 62, (*see* 198); election of Sir Thomas Smyth as first governor, 62; election of the general committee of, 24, 62-3; all business committed to the care of the governor and committee, 63.
December 8, 1600. Order for the bringing in of adventures in arrears, 93; Mr. Brund elected a principal factor, 93.
January 9, 1600-1. The patent read, 109; deficiency in the adventure and steps taken to supply it, 111; Mr. Rumney elected deputy governor, 111.
January 14, 1600-1. Order in council for adventurers in arrears to bring in their money at once on pain of imprisonment, 112-13; order confirming a levy of 2s. in the £, 113; the common seal ordered, 113.
February 10, 1600-1. Laws and ordinances enacted, viz., all things to be managed as a joint stock and no private trade to be practised, 130; all private goods shipped to be forfeited to the common stock, 130; ordinances against fraud, 130; proposed leaving of factors to trade in the East Indies, 131; the commission to the general or principal merchant and to others in succession, 132-37 (*see Commissions*); an act touching the bringing in of the supply of 2s. in the £, 137-38.
April 1, 1601. A new supply of 2s. in the £ to pay the company's debts, 160; the £1,500 taken up at interest by the treasurer to be discharged by the company, 161; William Beerblock admitted an adventurer of £200 by way of assignment of so much of the

INDEX 303

General Courts, *continued*.
Earl of Cumberland's stock and also made free, 161.
April 11, 1601. Order in council touching the discredit likely to arise through the remissness of the company in paying their debts and ordering defaulting adventurers to appear and be punished for contempt, 164-65; resolution that great care be taken to remove all discredit, and for the better ordering of business Alderman Wattes elected governor in place of Sir Thomas Smyth in prison, 166; auditors chosen for the treasurers' accounts, 166.
May 29, 1601. John Hate disfranchised, and John Jackson admitted a freeman, 174; respecting other adventurers in arrears, 174-5.
July 6, 1601. Certain persons made free whose names are not in the patent, 177; touching the supplies due on the Earl of Cumberland's assigned stock, 177; adventurers in arrears to be prosecuted, 178; certain freemen disfranchised, 178; election of governor, deputy, and committees and the oath of office, 179-80.
July 24, 1601. Assignment of John Bayly's stock to Sir John Spencer, 182; letter received from Captain George Waymouth proposing that the company should undertake a voyage for the discovery of a North West Passage to the East Indies, 182.
August 7, 1601. A voyage to discover the North West Passage resolved on, 183; a levy of 12d. in the £ to support the expence of the same, 183; committee appointed to estimate the expense, 183; the governor to peruse the charters to see if authority is given to compel contributions for the North West Voyage, 183.
September 2, 1601. Two ships for the North West Voyage to be prepared forthwith and the subscription book to be sent round for adventurers to set down their sums at 12d. in the £, 185.
September 13, 1601. Differences with the Muscovia Co. as to the respective rights of the two companies to the North West Passage if discovered, 186; a second voyage by the Cape resolved on, and the adventure to be not less than £100, p. 186.
October 12, 1601. Respecting the differences with the Muscovia Co. as to the North West Passage, 187-89, *see North West Passage*; the second voyage by the Cape, complaints as to the delay, &c., &c., 189-90, *see East India Company*.
November 5, 1601. *See North West Passage*, 190-91; letter from the privy council respecting the delay in the second voyage by the Cape, and propounding the example of the Dutch, 191.
November 9, 1601. *See North West Passage*, 192; the assignment of the stock of Clement Moseley, deceased, 192-93.
December 22, 1601. *See North West Passage*, 194-96.
January 5, 1601-2. *See North West Passage*, 196-97.
January 11, 1601-2. Laws and ordinances for the government of trade, &c., agreed on, 197-202, *see East India Company*; committee to expedite the North West Voyage, 202-3.
March 17, 1601-2. William Nelson admitted an adventurer of £200 on paying £30 premium, 205; the supply for the North West Voyage to be brought in at once on pain of forfeiture, 205; Thomas Yerworth engaged as purser, 205.
March 29, 1602. Touching the supplies for the North West Voyage, *see East India Company*, 206-8.
April 14, 1602. Several warrants signed, 214-15.
April 30, 1602. Articles of agreement with Captain Waymouth read, also the Queen's letters to the Emperor of China, 217; auditors appointed to ascertain the state of the adventure that further supplies may be called up and some course taken with the defaulters, 217-18.
May 18, 1602. Bond of indemnity sealed to Alderman Cambell; supplies for the North West Passage to be brought in at once; new bills of adventure to be made out containing every man's stock and all supplies in one gross sum, 220; several warrants for necessaries for the North West Voyage, 221.
July 6, 1602. Election of governor, deputy, and committees, &c., 225-6.
July 28, 1602. Election of Mr. Cambell as governor, 226.
September 17, 1602. The return of Waymouth, 228-9, *see North West Passage*.
October 18, 1602. Certain stores, &c., returned from the North West Passage to be sold, 230; Alderman Holliday's payments being in arrears, ordered that the same be deducted from his stock, 231.
November 24, 1602. Proceedings respecting Waymouth's return, *see North West Passage*, 233-4.
January 4, 1602-3. Deliberations as to a second voyage for the discovery of a North West Passage, 237-8.
January 26, 1602-3. The North West Voyage abandoned and committee appointed to see to the sale of the ships and stores, 238-9; Mr. Thomas Bramley chosen deputy-governor, 239.
June 6, 1603. Letter received from the purser of the "Assention" homeward bound, 242-3.
June 16, 1603. Proceedings respecting the return of the "Assention," *see East India Company and "Assention,"* 244-7.
June 23, 1603. Customs Duties on the goods from the "Assention," 248; money raised to pay the mariners, 249; orders and commissions for the sale of the goods brought home, 249.

Georg, Giles, nominated factor, 77.
Gibbons, Roger, warrant £39 on bill of exchange, 79.
Gibson, Anthony, adventurer, committees, 245, 246; bill of adventure sealed £240, p. 258.
Gilderns, 208.
Ginger, quantity ordered and committee to provide, 75.
Girdeler, Francis Tailor, 169. (N.B. The Girdlers Company was incorporated in 1448.—*Bailey*.)
Glasses, to be ordered, 79; warrant £43 16s. 6d., p. 129.
Globe, *ship*, viewed, 13.
God, John, warrant £40 on bill of exchange, 82.
Goddard, ⎱ Richard, *Alderman*, adventurer,
Godderd, ⎰ £200, p. 1; assemblies, 4, 7, 9, 10; committees, 6, 8, 12.

Godspeede, one of the ships for the North West Passage Voyage, *see also Pinnaces, Ships,* " *Discovery,*" *North West Passage, Waymouth.* John Drewe, *master;* Edward Pullison, *purser;* Johu Lane, *master's mate;* Thomas Boarne, *steward.* Warrant £10 to John Drewe in part of his wages, 210 ; manned, victualled, and furnished to Waymouth's own desires, 211-12 ; covenant for the payment of John Drew's wages, 220, 221 ; several warrants for the provision of stores and necessaries, 220-1, *see Warrants;* return to Dartmouth, 227-9 ; arrival in the Thames, 229 ; ordered to be sold with all stores, &c., 230 ; Mr. Cartwright, *preacher,* accused of being the persuader of the return of the voyage, 232 ; various warrants for wages, 234-5 ; warrant £4 to the porters for landing and housing the stores, 238 ; warrant £20 to the wife of Thomas Bowrne, steward, in full of all demands, 240 ; sale of the ship deferred, 241 ; ordered to be sold if £300 can be had, 242.

Gelding, Robert, *of Radcliff, mariner;* order to be paid £300 for the " Guift," 154.

Goldsmiths, *see Richard Wiseman, John Cornelis, Richard Yonson, William Beerblock, George Smythes.*

Goods, *see Merchandise.*

Gore, John, adventurer with William Gore, £300, p. 3.

Gore, Raph, assembly, 59 ; bill of adventure sealed £360, p 253.

Gore, Robert, assembly, 59 ; bill of adventure sealed £240, p. 255.

Gore, William, adventurer with John Gore, £300, p. 3.

Gossen, { Richard, ordered to clear accounts Gosson, } with Mr. Holliday, 127 ; to bring in his account, 159 ; [bill of adventure sealed, £240, p. 251] ; do. £240, p. 261.

Gover, John, warrant £96 8s. for aquavitae, 107.

Governor and Company, *see East India Company, also Company of Levant Merchants.*

Governors of the East India Company, *see also Deputy Governors;* Mr. Thomas Smyth elected first governor, 62 ; Mr. William Rumney elected deputy, 111 ; Sir Thomas Smyth being in prison and Mr. Rumney ill, Mr. Alderman Wattes elected governor, 166 ; Mr. Wattes re-elected with Mr. Rumney as deputy, 179 ; the oaths of office, 179 ; powers at a general court, 201-2 ; Sir John Harte elected governor, 225 ; Sir John Harte declines to serve and Mr. Cambell elected in his stead. 226.

Gowns, 208.

Grand Signior (*Turkey*) ; grants all capitulations except as to consulage, 265.

Grants of Privilege, &c., *see Patent, also Privilege.*

Gratuities, £100 in gold to be given, 106 ; £20 (or 20s. ?) to William Walter who dedicated to the company the Book of the Flemyng's Voyage, 125.

Gravesend, 44, 153 ; ships to be surveyed there before sailing, 141 ; bullion to be shipped there, 142 ; Mr. Holliday to take down money for harbour wages and clearing expenses, 146 ; committee to see the discharge of the ships thence, 147 ; committee left there, 152 ; warrant to Mr. Rumney for travelling expenses, 158 ; Waymouth to sail from thence, 216.

Great Seal, warrant for expense of making, 107.

Greene, Lawrence, adventurer, £200, p. 2.

Greene, Reynold, adventurer with John Newman, £200, p. 2 ; assemblies, 4, 59 ; bill of adventure sealed £240, p. 251.

Greene, Robert, nominated factor, 77.

Greenewell, *see Grenewell.*

Greenewood, John, bill of adventure sealed, £240, p. 260.

Greenland, *Groynland,* 212.

Greenwell, William, assemblies, 180, 181, 182, 183, 184, 185, 186, 187, 190, 193, 196, 197, 226, 228, 232, 236, 237, 241, 242, 244, 247 ; committees, 183, 186, 191, 197, 203, 209. 234, 237, 239, 247, 248 ; surveyor of the " Malice Scurge," 33 ; auditor, 166 ; general committee, 179 ; do. and sworn, 225 ; bill of adventure sealed, £240, p. 253.

Greewell, *see Grenewell.*

Gregorie, Richard ; warrant £40 on bill of exchange, 84.

Grenewell, *see Greenwell.*

Grocers, *see Nicholas Barnesley ; George Bowles ; Richard Burrell ; Ralfe Buzbie ; Richard Cockes ; Robarte Coxe ; Thomas Cutteler ; George Holman ; Thomas Juxon ; William Nelson ; Edmond Nicholson ; Robarte Sandye ; Nicholas Style ; Oliver Style ;* warrant to pay the grocers' porters for loading the ships, 158.

Grove, Peter ; warrant £70 in full payment, 71.

Grove, Philip, *second pilot ;* assembly, 46 ; appointed pilot, 47 ; warrant £30 on account of wages, 56 ; committee on lead, 79 ; to sail in the " Hector " as second pilot of the fleet, 100 ; warrant £11 for boat hire, &c., 138 ; to have a bill of adventure for the composition made with him, 139 ; bill of adventure sealed £500, p. 148.

Groynland, Greenland, 212.

Gryce, George, *carriage maker,* warrant £3 8s. p. 221.

Grynkin, Robert, warrant £30 for watches, compasses. &c., 218.

Gryvell, Foulke, *treasurer of the navy,* asked for the use of the docks at Woolwich, 13.

Guarantees, Alderman Bannyng for Joseph Salaman, purser of the " Susan," 33 ; Mr. Stapers for George Parsons, purser of the " Hector," 33 ; Mr. Garwaye for William Leake, purser of the " Assention," 33.

Guift, *ship,* 120 *tons,* bought to accompany the fleet with victuals, 147-48 (*see* 143) ; warrant £300 in payment, 154 ; sent out with victuals and to be cast off afterwards, 264.

Gully Key, *wharf,* 158.

Gum Lacre, quantity brought home by the " Assention " entered at the Custom House, 247.

Gunners, number to be employed in each ship, 90 ; committee to provide stores, 117 ; warrant £30 12s. 4d. for stores, 157.

Gunpowder, 122, 142, 184, 219, 221.

Haberdashers, *see Hugh Hammersley ; Humfrey Milward ; Thomas Smithe ;* warrant to pay the haberdashers' porters for lading ships, 158.

Hackett, } [Richard], *historiographer ;* assembly, 10 ; requested to give information as to places of trade in the East Indies, 123-24 ; warrant £10 for his advice and 30s. for maps, 143.
Hacklett, }

Haggett, Bartholomew, assembly, 60 ; respecting the payment of his adventure, 126 ; war-

INDEX

Haggett, Bartholomew, *continued*.
rant to bring in his adventure at once, 170; committees, 245, 246; bill of adventure sealed £240, p. 258.
Haies, *see* Hayes.
Haiward, John, nominated factor, 77.
Hakluyt, Richard, *see Hacklett*.
Hale, Mr., *of the Bridgehouse;* order to deliver timber to Mr. Burrell, 89.
Hale, Richard, bill of adventure sealed, £240, p. 253.
Hale, Sergeaunt, *see Heale*.
Hale, William, bill of adventure sealed, £240, p. 253.
Hall, Richard, *blacksmith*, warrant, £30 10s. for anchors, 151; do. £26 for iron work, 221.
Halledaie, }
Halleday, } Leonard, *see Holliday*.
Hallidaie, }
Hallidaie, William, *Mercer*, adventurer with John Duckett, £200, p. 3.
Hallydaie, } Leonard, *see Holliday*.
Hallyday, }
Hulmeden, Edward, *see Holmeden*.
Hamer, Ralfe, *see Hamor*.
Hamersley, Hugh; assemblies, 59, 237; committees, 237, 239; surveyor for the "Assention," 14; declines to adventure, 62; warrant to bring in his adventure, 170; offers to make discharge of some account in lieu of adventure money, 170; pays his adventure £240, and admitted a freeman, 175; made free though not named in the patent, 177; appointed auditor, 218; bill of adventure sealed, £240, p. 261.
Hamond, Mathew, adventurer with others, £300, p. 3.
Hamor, Ralfe, *Merchant Tailor*, adventurer, £200, p. 2; assembly, 60; bill of adventure sealed, £240, p. 255.
Hampson, Robarte, Alderman, adventurer, £300, p. 1; assembly, 244.
Hanckey, *see Hankin*.
Handford, Humfrie, bill of adventure sealed, £240, p. 260.
Hangar, George, warrant £231 10s. for canary wine, 103.
Hankin, Roger, *Master of the "Assention;"* committee to treat with him, 69, 70; master of the "Assention," 97; warrant £36 0s. 4d. for ballast, &c., 97; to sail in the "Assention," 100; warrant £50 on account of wages, 104.
Harbie, John, *Skinner*, adventurer, £200, p. 4; assemblies, 203, 232, 241, 242, 248; general committee and sworn, 179; do. 225; bill of adventure sealed, £240, p. 259.
Harbour wages at Gravesend, 146.
Harby, *see Harbie*.
Hardway, John, warrant £57 15s. for casks, 147.
Hare, Samuel, bill of adventure sealed, £240, p. 254.
Harrison, Edward, assembly, 59; bill of adventure sealed, £240, p. 258.
Harrison, } William, adventurer with William
Harryson, } Bonde, £200, p. 3; assemblies, 20, 22, 24, 26, 27, 28, 33, 37, 39, 46, 56, 57, 58, 59, 64, 66, 67, 68, 73, 74, 77, 80, 82, 83, 85, 86, 88, 89, 90, 91, 93, 94, 95, 96, 98, 99, 103, 104, 106, 108, 113, 114, 117, 118, 119, 121, 122, 123, 124, 125, 128, 138, 139, 140, 144, 150, 151, 155, 156, 158, 160, 162, 163, 164, 167, 170, 171, 172, 174, 175, 176, 180, 183, 185, 208, 214, 215, 216, 217, 218, 224, 225, 226, 227, 229, 230, 232, 233, 236, 238, 241, 244, 247, 249; committees, 12, 22, 27, 30, 67, 75, 76,
99, 107, 124, 127, 143, 147, 156, 158, 186, 197, 203, 209, 229, 234, 237, 239, 240, 245, 248; views ships, 13, requested to provide peas and beans, 29; signature to West Country commission, 52; general committee, 63; warrant £378 for canary wine, 103; do. £70 for vinegar, 114; to provide ship's stores for the "Assention," 117; audits accounts, 147, 148[3], 158; to gather into a warehouse all stores left behind, 159; appointed auditor, 166; general committee and sworn, 179; do. 225; signatures to treasurer's warrants, 206, 210; bill of adventure sealed, £240, p. 260.
Hart, Richard, warrant £100 for snuffery, 104; balance of account to be paid to Mr. Flemyng, 147; warrant £161 13s. 1d. for iron work, 157.
Harte, Sir John, Knight, adventurer with George Boales, £1,000, p. 1; assemblies, 4, 58, 111, 159, 164, 242; elected governor, 225; declines to serve on account of age, 226; gives his bond as security for money to be raised at interest, 240; indemnified for the same by a general bond under the common seal, 250; bill of adventure sealed, £600, p. 256.
Harvy, John, appointed auditor, 166 (? Harby).
Harvy, Stephen, bill of adventure sealed, £240, p. 260.
Harvy, William, *of Bridgewater*, warrant £50 on bill of exchange, 73; do. £40, p. 74; do. £400, p. 141.
Haselton, Agnes, warrant 40s. to relieve her husband hurt in the "Hector." 173
Haselton, Richard, 173.
Havard, John, elected a principal factor, 81; appointed to the "Susan," 94, 100; to sail in the "Susan" with Peter Francis, 117; order to provide ship's stores for the "Susan," 117; warrant £230 for men's wages for the "Susan," 118; do. £100 for his entertainment in the voyage, 123; commission to take chief command in case of death of Captains Lancaster and Middleton, and Mr. Brund, 135; bill of adventure sealed, £200, p. 150.
Hawkyns, John, bill of adventure sealed, £240, p. 255.
Hayes, Thomas, adventurer with others, £300, p. 3; made free though not named in the patent, 177; bill of adventure sealed, £200, p. 261.
Heale, Sergeaunt, will provide money in the West Country, 45; draws bill on Warwick Heale (of Plymouth), £200, p. 47, 54; warrant £200 for do., 55; warrant £500 for so much paid to the company's agent at Exeter, 119.
Heale, Warwicke, *see Heale, Sergeaunt*.
Hearne, Richard, warrant to bring in his adventure at once, 170; bill of adventure sealed, £240, p. 250.
Heckes, *see Hick*.
Hector, *ship*, 300 tons; Captain Middleton, *first factor;* Henry Napper, *master;* Philip Grove, *second pilot of the fleet;* George Parsons, *purser;* James Lovering, *surgeon;* William Starkey, *second factor;* Thomas Dassell, *third factor;* Thomas Tudd, *fourth factor.* Surveyors appointed, 14; inventory, 15; warrant £100 for necessaries, 25; the purser guaranteed by Mr. Stapers, 33; rated 100 men, 300 tons, 34; the aquavitæ shipped, 35; warrant £100 for repairs and provisions, 65; a mast ordered, 71; to be manned with 100 men, 72; warrant £100 for her provision, 79; do. £100, p. 88; number of carpenters, caulkers, gunners, stewards, cooks, surgeons

R R

Hector, *continued.*
and barbers to be employed, 89-90; Captain Middleton to sail in the "Hector," 94; warrant £100 for preparations, 96; warrant £25 to James Lovering, *surgeon*, for his medicine chest, 98; warrant £100 for repairs and preparations, 99; Vice Admiral's ship, 100; list of officers appointed, 100; do. factors, 101; warrant £200 for wax candles, &c., 104; do. £50 for iron work, 105; do. £60 to Xpofer Thompson, a smith, 111; do. £100 to Mr. Wyseman, 111; do. £100 to William Dixon, 111; do., £100 for timber, 114; committee to provide stores, 117; warrant £250, 117; do. £100 for provisions, 121; the amount of new and Spanish money carried in each ship and how packed, 122; warrant £100 for wages, 139; do. £2 13s. to Mr. Pope, Sergeant of the Admiralty, on a bill of charges for the burial of those slain in the "Hector," 141; warrant £100 to the purser for charges, 142; do. £20 to Henry Napper, *master*, for his pains in the preparation of the ships, 143; warrant £30 10s. for anchors, 151; list of presents to be carried, 151; warrant £100 for wages and clearing expenses, 154; do. £8 4s. for porterage and lading, 158; do. £6 for a pinnace, 167; do. £86 15s. 4d. for sails, 168; do. £3 15s. for caske, 172; do. 40s. to relieve Richard Haseltion, hurt, 173; memorandum tonnage 300, men 100, p. 263.
Hedger, William, warrant £6 for a pinnace for the "Hector," 167; do. £5 10s. for a boat for the "Discovery," 223.
Hedland, John, warrant £16 1s. 8d. for carriages, 163.
Heighoo, Robert, warrant £42 15s. for canvas, 164, 168.
Helinge, Peter, warrant to bring in his adventure at once, 170; made free though not named in the patent, 177; bill of adventure sealed £240, p. 257.
Helle, *see Heale*.
Helmes, Edmund, *of Burford in Oxon;* Re the assignment of £100 adventure from Clement Moseley, deceased, 193.
Helms, Peter, deceased, 226; his stock assigned to Peter Wellington, 226.
Helyn, *see Helinge.*
Hemyng, } Roger, assembly, 59; committees, Hemmyng, } 245, 246; bill of adventure Hemmynge,} sealed £240, p. 250.
Henshaw, } Thomas, adventurer with William Henshawe,} Adderley, £300, p.2; assemblies, 5, 59; will bring in Mr. Addersley's adventure. 63; bill of adventure sealed, £240, p. 255.
Heralds, warrant £13 7s. 8d. to William Segar, *herald*, for writing the Queen's letters to the Kings of the East Indies, 139; warrant 20 merkes to the King of Heralds for assigning the company's arms, 171.
Herbert, Mr. Secretary, 9, *see Privy Council;* letters from the Privy Council to the company, 60, 61; orders in council, 112, 164; committee to solicit a warrant to remove the plate from the governor's house, 141.
Hercules, *ship*, 99.
Hertrowe, 74.
Hewett, John, adventurer, £333 6s. 8d., p. 3; bill of adventure sealed, £240, p. 254.
Hewett, William, assembly, 59.
Hewghes, *see Hughes.*
Hewitt, John, *see Hewett.*
Hewitt, Thomas, bill of adventure sealed, £240, p. 254.

Hewys, Thomas, *Clothworker*, warrant £12 8s. 6d., p. 159.
Heyes, *see Hayes.*
Hiccocke, Thomas, adventurer, £100, p. 1; assembly, 4.
Hick, Baptiste, *Mercer*, adventurer, £400, p. 2; assembly 4.
Hickes, Thomas, nominated factor, 77; elected factor of the third sort, 83.
Hickock, *see Hiccocke.*
Hides, warrant £28 18s. for hides to make the mariners cassocks, breeches, and gowns for the N. W. voyage, 208.
Higelord, *see Highlord.*
Highoe, } *see Heighoo.*
Highoo, }
Highelord, } Edward, *purser of the "Mare Highlord,*} *Scourge," afterwards of the "Assention,"* warrant £100 for repairs of the "Scourge," 87; do. £200 for her preparation, 106; do. £180 for mariners' wages, &c., 154; letter from him from the "Assention" brought home by a Frenchman, 243; order to attend on board the "Assention" until ship is discharged, 246.
Highlord John, adventurer with John Marris, £200, p. 3; assemblies, 4, 59, 64, 66, 68, 69, 71, 73, 77, 80, 82, 83, 85, 86, 88, 89, 92, 94, 98, 99, 100, 103, 104, 106, 109, 112, 115, 123, 127, 138, 140, 144, 154, 155, 156, 158, 160, 162, 164, 167, 168, 170, 171, 172, 173, 175, 176, 180, 182, 183, 184, 185, 186, 192, 193, 197, 225, 235, 238, 244, 248; committees, 158, 245; appointed treasurer, 7; surveyor for the "Susan," 14; general committee, 63; to wait on Lord Cumberland as to damage done by the anchor of the "Red Dragon," 128; warrant, £14 7s. 4d. for money laid out, 162; general committee, 179; do. and sworn, 225; bill of adventure sealed, £240, p. 260.
Hilles, Peter, warrant £3 15s. for casks, 172.
Hilliard, Mr., contracts for dollars at 4s. 6d., p. 20; committee, 79.
Historiographer, *see Hacklett.*
Hodgeson, John, assembly, 60; bill of adventure sealed, £240, p. 252.
Hodgeson, Stephen, bill of adventure sealed, £220, p. 159; pays £10 supplies for North West voyage with apologies for delay, 235; bill of adventure and supplies sealed, 240, p. 250.
Hodgson, } *see Hodgeson.*
Hodsonn, }
Hogsheads, *see Casks.*
Holiday, *see Holliday.*
Holland, Bartholomew, assembly, 59; bill of adventure sealed, £240, p. 251.
Holland, Ling, 209.
Hollidaie, } Leonarde, Alderman, adventurer Holliday, } £1,000, p. 1; assemblies, 4, 14, Hollyday,} 20, 22, 24, 26, 27, 28, 31, 33, 46, 47, 56, 57, 58, 64, 65, 67, 68, 69, 71, 76, 78, 80, 82, 83, 85, 86, 81, 89, 91, 92, 93, 94, 95, 99, 100, 102, 104, 106, 107, 109, 112, 115, 119, 124, 127, 128, 140, 144, 148, 150, 151, 158, 160, 167, 173, 176, 180, 192, 226, 244, 248; committees, 12, 32, 37, 38, 58, 68, 71, 73, 76, 77, 80, 91, 99, 141, 142; per his man, 245, 246; warrants for the payment of money as treasurer of the company, *see Warrants*; views ships, 13; bills from the West Country, 50; signature to West Country commissions, 52, 54, 55; general committee, 63; to buy fish, 75; as to the coining of £6,000 in the Tower, 120;

Hollyday, Leonarde, *continued.*
account of the new and Spanish money in his custody prepared for shipment, 127 ; to clear accounts with Mr. Angell and Mr. Gosson, 127 ; to carry to Gravesend money for the clearing of the ships, 146 ; order to raise £1,500 on his credit and Alderman Bannyng's, 146 ; to render accounts, 156 ; to be indemnified for the £1,500 raised at interest, 161 ; to deliver bills of adventure to every adventurer, 175 ; general committee, 179 ; £230 adventure assigned to him by Earl Cumberland, 197 ; receives £240 adventure from William Nelson with £30 premium, 205 ; ordered to bring in £38 6s. 9d. balance of his treasurer's accounts, 231 ; being in arrears with his adventure for the North West voyage, ordered that the same be defaulted out of his East India stock, 231 ; bill of adventure sealed, £1,440, p. 262 ; do. £230 assigned to him by the Earl of Cumberland, 262 ; part owner of the ship "Exchange," 276.
Hollywell,—nominated factor, 77.
Holman, George, *Grocer,* adventurer, £150, p. 1 ; assemblies, 4, 60 ; bill of adventure sealed, £240, p. 250.
Holmden, } Edward, *Alderman;* adventurer
Holmeden, } £500, p. 1 ; assemblies, 74, 78,
Holmenden, } 79, 80, 119 ; general committee, 63 ; bill of adventure sealed, £1,200, p. 256.
Holway, Nycholas, warrant £50 on bill of exchange, 58.
Honey, barrels required, 30 ; estimate of quantity and price, 35 ; committee to provide, 35 ; warrant £21 1s. for 32 jars, 125.
Horton, Thomas, assemblies, 59, 229, 232, 240, 242, 247 ; general committee and sworn, 225 ; committee, 248 ; bill of adventure sealed, £240, p. 252.
How,   } Roger, adventurer, £200, p. 3 ; assem-
Howe, } blies, 5, 7, 9, 10, 28, 31, 37, 39, 46, 47, 56, 57, 58, 64, 66, 67, 69, 73, 74, 79, 82, 85, 86, 88, 93, 98, 100, 102, 104, 109, 118, 122, 124, 140, 142, 170, 172, 173, 175, 176, 177, 181, 182, 192, 203, 215, 216 ; committees, 6, 8, 12, 28, 40, 41, 75, 76, 99, 120, 127, 183, 243 ; views ships, 13 ; sent to the West Country for dollars and victuals, 15, 21 ; warrant £500 for use in the West Country, 29 ; feoffee in trust for the ships bought, 32 ; provision of victuals, 38 ; purchase of the "Malice Scurge," 45 ; signature to West Country commissions, 52, 54, 55 ; warrant £200 to pay to Sergeaunt Heale for a bill of exchange on Plymouth, 55 ; do. £50 to pay to Laurence Waldo for a bill on Exeter, 55 ; general committee, 63 ; to answer letters from Plymouth, 64 ; letters to Captains Baker and Davies, &c., 66, 74 ; to see to the making of bags, 86 ; to write into the West Country to provide no more bread, &c., 88 ; warrant £60 on bill of exchange, 102 ; to answer letters from West Country factors, 103 ; buys vinegar, 115 ; to clear accounts with Mr. Sandy, 127 ; warrant £20 for attending to business in the West Country, 140 ; commission to go into the West Country, 147 ; to bring in his account, 159, 172 ; presents his West Country account, 173 ; allowed with Mr. Combe £18 7s. 2d. for expenses in the country, 176 ; general committee and sworn, 179 ; bill of adventure sealed, £360, p. 256.
Howse, Richarde, adventurer with Henry Robinson, £200, p. 3 ; assembly, 5.

Huberd, Miles, adventurer with Thomas Cambell, £200, p 2.
Hughes, Robert, appointed sailmaker of the "Mallyce Scurge," 40 ; warrant £49, p. 167 ; do. £32 10s. p. 221.
Hule, Hugh, admitted as an extra factor, 102.
Hull, peas and beans to be bought there, 29.
Humble, Richard, made free though not named in the patent, 177 ; bill of adventure sealed, £240, p. 251.
Humfrey, John, bill of adventure sealed, £240, p. 260.
Hurleston, Thomas, nominated factor, 77.
Huse, *see Hughes.*
Hylliard, Edward, appointed surveyor of the works on the "Malice Scurge," 40 ; to prevent the workmen from running to drink, 40.
Hynde, William, bill of adventure sealed, £240, p. 257.

Impositions on certain goods offered to the Queen by persons attempting to supplant the Levant Co., 280 ; £4,000 per annum agreed to be paid to the Queen by the Levant Co. in lieu of impositions, 280, 282.
Incorporation of the East India Co. ; petition to the Privy Council, &c., 8 ; *see East India Co. and Privy Council.*
Indemnities, *see Bonds.*
Instruments (naval), £30 granted to Captain Waymouth, 204 ; do. £20, p. 204 ; £100 allowed to Waymouth, 211 ; warrant £30, p. 218.
Interest, £1,500 to be borrowed, 146 ; £2,000 do. 249.
Inventories of the ships "Hector," 15 ; "Assention," 16, 22 ; "Susan," 17 ; "Malice Scurge," 42.
Ipswich canvas, 164.
Iron, 30 tons to be sent out in the ships, and price, 36 ; 20 tons purchased, 41 ; quantity increased to 50 tons, 99 ; warrant £150, p. 104 ; do. £100, p. 104 ; do. £300, p. 111 ; do. £100, p. 119.
Iron hoops, quantity and price in the West Country to be ascertained, 49 ; warrant £36, p. 129 ; do. £6 10s., p. 219 ; do. £42, p. 222 ; do. £42. p. 224.
Ironmongers, *see William Deyns, Nicholas Leatt, James Waters, John Woodwarde.*
Iron stoves for the North West voyage, 209.
Ironsyde, Richard, assembly, 60 ; bill of adventure sealed, £240, p. 258.
Ironsyde, Thomas, will bring in his money, 63.
Ironwork, *see also smiths, iron iron hoops, &c.*; warrant £200, p. 41 ; do. £50 for the "Hector," 105 ; payment of a smith's bill stopped because he hath not paid for his iron, 128, 147 ; warrant £100 for the "Red Dragon," 157 ; do., £161 13s. 1d. for the "Assention," 157 ; warrant £100, p. 163 ; do. £27, p. 168 ; do. £19 1s. 4d., p. 172 ; do. £227, p. 173 ; do. £19, p. 221 ; do. £26, 221 ; do. £22 6s., p. 221.

Jackson, John, *Clothworker,* admitted adventurer in lieu of John Bate, £200, p 174 ; bill of adventure sealed, £240, p. 261.
Jackson, Joseph, admitted a freeman on the nomination of Sir John Spencer, 187 (*see* 181).
Jamryn, *see Gamrym.*
Japan, Waymouth to receive £500 if he arrive

Japan, *continued*.
  at any port in Japan by a North West
  Passage, 214.
Java, 198.
Jaymes, Edward, adventurer, £200, p. 3.
Jennynges, (William, assemblies, 59, 237, 241 ;
Jennyns,   (committees, 237, 239, 245, 246 ;
  (bill of adventure sealed, £240, p. 251]; do.,
  261.
Jewels, Mr. Hacklett, *historiographer*, reads
  out of his notes and books divers instructions,
  124 ; instructions to the principal factor, 132,
  133.
Johnes, Stephen, owner of the ship "Carnation" of Colchester, 263.
Johnson, John, offers to serve as a master, 27.
Johnson, Patrick, warrant £38 for salt, 121 ;
  do. £12 6s. 8d., p. 219.
Johnson, Robert, bill of adventure sealed,
  £240, p. 253.
Johnson, Thomas, *runaway servant of the
  Earl of Oxford*, order not to be allowed to
  go in the voyage, 125.
Joint stock, *see East India Co., and Adventurers*, all things to be managed as a joint and
  common stock, and no private trade to be allowed, 130, 133.
Jones, Thomas, bill of exchange for £200 paid
  to the company at Plymouth, 68.
Journals, the pursers of the North West voyage
  to make notes, journals, and observations for
  the direction and help of posterity, 213 ;
  journal from Captain Waymouth, 227.
Juxon, Thomas, *grocer*, adventurer £200, p. 3 ;
  bill of adventure sealed, £240, p. 251.

Kathia, *see Cataia*.
Kellett, William, warrant to bring in his adventure at once, 170 ; made free though not
  named in the patent, 177 ; bill of adventure
  sealed, £240, p. 261.
Kempe, William, warrant £30 on bill of exchange from Plymouth, 80.
Kerby, *see Kirby*.
Kerseys, (Committee to provide, 31 ; quantity
Kessies, (to be sent out, description and
  price, 35 ; proposed trade with China and
  Cataia by the North West passage if discovered, 199 ; duties at Constantinople and
  Aleppo to support the ambassador's and consuls' charges, 267, 270, 271, 274, 279.
Key, Robert, bill of adventure sealed, £240,
  p. 258.
King James I., customs due on goods brought
  home in the "Assention," 247, 248, 250.
King of Heralds, *see Heralds*.
Kings of the East Indies, letters to, 91, 131, 134,
  139.
Kintalles, weight for bread, 41.
Kirby, Jeffrey, Mr. Bannyng required to pay
  the £200 set down for Jenrey Kirby, 126 ; bill
  of adventure sealed, £240, p. 258.
Knives, 79.
Knowles, Sir William, Privy Councillor, 60.
Kymber, Mr., *wharfinger*, warrant £34 16s. 8d.
  for lighterage and porterage, 158 ; do. £3,
  p. 224.

Lacy, John, warrant, £188 for cordage, 126.
Lacy, William, *of Hertrowe*, warrant £110 on
  bill of exchange, 128.
Lading of the ships, warrant to pay the porters,
  158.
Lambard, Henry, warrant £10 5s. 8d. for
  Black Jacks, 105.

Lamps, five dozen required, and price, 35.
Lancaster, Captain James, *chief commander in
  the voyage*, assemblies, 14, 22, 24, 26, 27, 28,
  31, 33, 39, 44, 45, 46, 47, 56, 57, 64, 71, 73,
  74, 76, 78, 80, 82, 83, 86, 88, 89, 90, 91, 92,
  94, 95, 96, 98, 99, 100, 102, 103, 104, 106, 107,
  109, 113, 114, 117, 118, 119, 142, 143, 144 ;
  committees, 12, 22, 26, 27, 28, 30, 37, 40, 57,
  67, 69, 72, 75, 87, 91, 94 ; views ships, 13 ;
  warrant £200 to buy iron work and caske,
  41 ; signature to West Country commission,
  52 ; committee to treat with him for taking the
  chief command, 58, 66, 71, 73 ; general committee, 63 ; warrant £100 on account for his
  entertainment, 89 ; order to agree with the
  carpenters, caulkers, and gunners, 90 ; nominated as principal factor to sail in the
  "Scourge," 94, 100 ; instructions as to the
  mariners' shares of reprisals, 119 ; motion for
  £100 to be paid to the purser of the "Hector"
  for provisions, 121 ; his commission and instructions for the voyage, 132 ; the Queen's
  approval of his appointment, 132 ; authority
  by letters patent to correct and chastise
  offenders, 132 ; private traffic not to be permitted, but all trade to be reckoned as a
  joint and common stock, 133 ; measures to
  prevent private trade, 133 ; penalties for embezzlement and fraud, 134 ; instructions for
  factors to be left resident in foreign parts,
  134 ; instructions for the devolving of the
  chief command in case of death, &c., 135 ;
  warrant £200 for his entertainment, 139 ; do.
  £11 7s. 8d. for money disbursed, 139 ; purchase of the ship "Guift," 147 ; bill of adventure sealed, £1,500, p. 150 ; bill of adventure sealed, £240, p. 257.
Lane, John, *master's mate of the "Godspeede,"*
  examined as to the cause of the return of
  Captain Waymouth, 232 ; warrant 30s. for
  wages, 234 (*see* 205).
Language of Sumatra. An Englishman knowing the language brought home by the
  Dutch, 194.
Lant, John, *of Exeter*, warrant £150 on bill of
  exchange, 81.
Lanternes, (157, 209, 223.
Lanthornes, (
Latterfield, Edward, bill of adventure sealed,
  £240, p. 258.
Launches, *see pinnaces*.
Lawrence, Simon, bill of adventure sealed,
  £240, p. 258.
Laws, decrees, and ordinances of the company,
  see also Rules and East India Company,
  129, 197-98, 198-202.
Lead, quantity to be sent out and price, 36 ;
  committee to provide, 79 ; warrant, £224 2s.,
  p. 95 ; do. £150, p. 105 ; do. £49, p. 143 ;
  warrant for payment of charges for cutting
  lead, 203 ; warrant for lead for the North
  West voyage, 210 ; do. £8 8s., p. 224.
Leake, William, purser of the "Assention,"
  33 ; warrant £150 for men's wages, 117 ; do.
  £100, p. 154.
Leaman, John, made free though not named in
  the patent, 177.
Leanyng, Edward, assembly, 59.
Leat,   (*see Leatt*.
Lente,   (
Leatherseller, *see Henrye Bridgeman*.
Leatt, Nicholas, *Ironmonger*, adventurer,
  £200, p. 1 ; assemblies, 4, 7, 9, 10, 59, 180,
  183, 187, 190, 192, 197, 203, 204, 205, 206, 208,
  214, 215, 216, 217, 218, 219, 225, 227 ;

INDEX

Leatt, Nicholas, *continued*.
committees, 6, 8, 10, 191, 203, 205, 209; surveyor for the "Hector," 14; appointed auditor, 166; general committee and sworn, 179; signatures to treasurer's warrants, 206, 210; warrant £150 for necessaries provided, 215; do. £20 for mariners' clothes, 218; do. £51 3s. 3d. for disbursements, 223; bill of adventure sealed, £240, p. 255; money taken up at Constantinople from his factor for the use of the ambassador, 280.
Lecheland, Mr., *of Culleton*. Price of peas, 54.
Lee, Robarte, *Alderman*, adventurer, £300, p. 3.
Leeninge, Edward, bill of adventure sealed, £360, p. 256.
Leet, *see Leatt*.
Leman, John, bill of adventure sealed, £240, p. 255.
Letters to the Earl of Essex asking his consent to Captain Davies being appointed chief director of the voyage, 25; from the lord treasurer recommending Sir Edward Michelborne to be employed, 28; from the Lord Treasurer to the receivers of Devon and Cornwall, authorizing credit to be given to the company's agent for purchasing provisions, 38; letters commending several men to be employed as pursers, 39; from Mr. Pope with advice of proceedings in the purchase of provisions, 64; do. from Captain Baker, 64; from Mr. Ellycot as to the provision of royals in the West Country, 64; replies to Captain Davis, Captain Baker, Robert Pope, Mr. Ellicott, and Mr. Sandy, 66; from the West Country as to the proceedings of the business, 74; from the Queen to potentates in the East Indies, 91, 131, 134, 151; warrant £13 7s. 3d. to William Segar, *herald*, for writing the Queen's letters, 139; from the Privy Council respecting adventurers in default, &c., 164-65, the Queen's letters to the Emperor of China, &c., for the North West voyage, 217; warrant £4 15s. for charges for the Queen's letters, 222; warrant 28s. 8d. to John Franklyn for carrying a letter to Captain Waymouth in the Downs, 223; to the pursers of the North West voyage to preserve all things suitable for a second voyage, 228; letters from and to the purser of the "Assention," respecting the return of that ship, 242-43; to the merchants of Dartmouth and Plymouth to give credit to the officers of the "Assention," 243-44, *see East India Company*; several drafts of letters in the East India Company's Record Book, tending to show that the East India Company was partially an outgrowth from the Levant Company, 265-83, *see Company of Levant merchants, viz.:* to Mr. Lyllo, English ambassador at Constantinople, 265-70, 282; to Richard Colthurst, consul at Aleppo, 270-72, 278-79, 283; to Mr. John Saunderson, merchant at Constantinople, 273-75, 279-80; to Mr. Byddell, preacher at Aleppo, 275-76; to Mr. ———, merchant at Scanderona (?), 276-77; to Mr. May, preacher at Constantinople, 281.
Letters Patent, *see Patent*.
Levant merchants, *see Company of*.
Levant seas. Outrages by English men-of-war, 280, 282, 283.
Levies of 2s. in the £ to make up deficiency in the total required, 110; to be brought in within 6 days on pain of forfeiture of double the value, 111; levy confirmed, 113; act touching the bringing in the 2s. in the £, 137; voluntary levy of 12d. in the £ for the North West adventure, 183; 12d. in the £ for the North West voyage and penalties for default, 199-200; proposed levy by the poll and upon the rates of particular adventures to raise money hereafter required, 249; levy on certain goods entering Constantinople and Aleppo to support the ambassador's and consuls' charges, 267, 270, 271, 272, 274, 279.
Lieth, Thomas, warrant £68 18s. for pewter, 129.
Lighterage, 158, 173.
Lighterman, William Allom, 173.
Limehouse, 208.
Linen cloth, warrant £125 10s. for, 97.
Linendrapers, *see John Buzbridge, see also Drapers*.
Ling, *see Fish*.
Ling, Holland Ling, 209.
Linge, *see Lynge*.
Lioness, *ship*, viewed, 13.
List, of adventurers and amounts subscribed, 4; of caske required, 30; of provisions required, 34-5; of merchandise to be carried, 36-7; of timber borrowed from Her Majesty's storehouse at Woolwich, 71-2; of factors nominated, 77, 101; of silver plate and presents, 141, 151; of provisions for the North West voyage, 209; of bills of adventure sealed, 250-62.
Locks, } Mr. Smalwood, 223.
Locksmith, }
Lodgings for mariners, warrant £4 7s., p. 222.
Lokar, Edward, nominated factor, 77.
Looking-glasses, to be provided as presents, 116, 141, 151.
Lord Admiral, letters from the Privy Council to the company, 60, 61, 164; wine given to him in lieu of deodand claimed for the "Hector," 169; touching the tithes due for the prize taken in the East Indies, 246; respecting the outrages by the men-of-war in the Levant seas, 282.
Lord Chief Justice, 61, 112.
Lord Keeper, 112, 164.
Lord Mayor of London, Sir Stephin Soame, 1.
Lords of the Council, *see Privy Council*.
Lord Treasurer (? T. Buckhurst, *see* p. 38), 9, 60, 61, 112, 164; *see Privy Council*; letter recommending Sir Edward Michelborne to be employed, 28; letters to the receivers of Devon and Cornwall to extend credit to the company's agents, 38; warrant for providing peas and beans in Cambridgeshire and Norfolk, 66; letter recommending Henry Aneys to be employed, 85; respecting bullion in the Tower, 87; committee to solicit warrant to deliver the silver plate out of Mr. Governor's house, 141.
Lovering, James, *surgeon of the "Hector;"* warrant £25 to provide remedies, 98.
Luellen, Morrice, bill of adventure sealed, £240, p. 254.
Lydall, Thomas, bill of adventure sealed, £240, p. 257.
Lyllo, *Mr.*, resident English ambassador at Constantinople, letter of instructions, 265, *see Company of Levant merchants*; his salary, 271; contentions with the French as to the Dutch consulage, 271-2; credit for his wants supplied by Mr. Saunderson, *merchant*, 273, 279; creditor of the company for 1,000 chiskeens, 274.
Lymehouse, *see Limehouse*, 208.

Lyng, ⎱ Nicholas, adventurer, £100, p. 2 ; as-
Lynge, ⎰ semblies, 4, 7, 9, 59, 64, 68, 77, 78, 79, 80, 82, 83, 88, 91, 92, 93, 94, 95, 96, 99, 100, 107, 108, 112, 118, 122, 124, 128, 129, 140, 142, 143, 155, 158, 162, 164, 167, 168, 170, 171, 175, 176, 177, 180, 181, 183, 184, 185, 166, 190, 203, 205, 214, 217, 219, 225, 228, 229, 230, 231, 233, 235, 236, 238, 240, 241, 242, 244 ; committees, 6, 8, 97, 128, 156, 158, 205, 209, 214, 229, 234, 248 ; surveyor for the "Assention," 14 ; general committee, 63 ; buys cloth, &c., 97 ; warrant £20 for charges, 111 ; general committee and sworn, 179 ; do. 225 ; requested to provide bags for the pepper brought home in the "Assention," and suits without pockets for the porters, 247 ; bill of adventure sealed, £240, p. 257.
Lypson, Derick, warrant £40 for steel, 138.
Lytleford, Mr., committee, 246.

Mabanck, Arnold, *pulleymaker* ; warrant £56 7s. 9d. for work done, 163 ; do. £9 10s. for pulleys, 221.
Macy, William, bill of exchange, £112, p. 88.
Magelano, Straits of, 183.
Makesfield, John, *brasier*, *see Maxfield*.
Malaga wine, 169.
Malice Scurge, ⎱
Mall E-courge, ⎰ *see* "*Mare Scurge*."
Mallett, Justice, *see Mullett*.
Mallett, William, warrant £70 on bill of exchange, 85.
Malyce Scurge, *see* "*Mare Scurge*."
Manley, Nicholas, bill of adventure sealed, £240, p. 258.
Maps, three maps supplied by Mr. Hacklett, 143 ; Fretum Davies and Greenland, 212.
Marche, *see Marsh*.
Mare Scurge, *ship*, afterwards re-named the "Red Dragon ;" 600 tons, Admiral ship of the fleet. Captain Lancaster, *General of the Fleet* ; Captain Davis, *Pilot Major of the Fleet* ; William Broadbent, *Master* ; Robert Pope, *Second Factor* ; Nathaniel Gamram, *Third Factor* ; Xpofer Stradling, *Fourth Factor* ; William Burrage, *Boatswain* ; Ralph Salter (?) *Surgeon*. Motion for buying her from the Earl of Cumberland, 20 ; her tonnage found to be too great, but recommended for the second voyage, 20-1 ; surveyed and price inquired, 27 ; £3,000 offered for her, but declined ; offered at £4,000 ; to be re-surveyed and price considered, 29 ; £3,500 offered and declined, 30 ; price settled at £3,700 by arbitration, 31-2 ; surveyors appointed, 33 ; William Burrage, boatswain, ordered to see to the preparation of the ship, 33 ; rated, 200 men, tonnage, 600, p. 34 ; quantity of aquavitæ, 35 ; committees to watch her preparation, 39 ; a barrel of beer a day allowed to the workmen to prevent their running from their work to the alehouse, 40 ; ship's boat lying at Plymouth to be sent up, 40 ; sailmakers appointed, 40 ; inventory of the ship, 42 ; a chain pump advised, 44 ; the bargain and sale sealed with the Earl of Cumberland, and manner of payment, 45 ; a new long boat ordered, 46 ; the boat lying at Plymouth to be inspected, 51 ; men required to complete the ship to be drawn from the "Susan," 56 ; warrant £1,000 for repairs, 65 ; do. £100, p. 70 ; quantity of timber borrowed from Her Majesty's storehouse at Woolwich, 71 ; to be manned with 180 men, 72 ; warrant £100 for timber, 74 ; do. £80

for preparations, 74 ; do. £100, p. 84 ; do. £50 for repairs, 87 ; do. £100, p. 87 ; do. £4 recompense to a poor man for the bulging of his crane, 88 ; number of carpenters, gunners, caulkers, stewards, cooks, surgeons, and barbers to be employed, 89-90 ; the Pilot-Major and Mr. Bradbanck, *Master*, to sail in the "Scurge," 90 ; Captain Lancaster appointed principal factor, 94 ; ordered to be launched and re-named the "Red Dragon," 96, *see henceforth* "*Red Dragon* ;" the "Carnation" of Colchester buoyed on an anchor belonging to the "Scurge," 263.
Margann, *see Morgan*.
Mariners, *see also Masters* ; William Tavernor engaged, 68 ; all mariners to be paid two months' wages in advance and two months' wages in adventure stock, 70 ; number of men in each ship, 72 ; to be engaged by the committee and masters, 78 ; as to prizes and prize money, 118 ; warrant for board wages, 208 ; hiring of mariners in the West Country, 209 ; warrant £28 18s. for hides to make mariners' cassocks, breeches, &c., for the North West Voyage, 208 ; warrant £20 for clothes, 218 ; warrant £4 7s. for mariners' lodgings, &c., 222 ; warrant to pay mariners hired at Dartmouth to bring to London the ships returned from the North West voyage, 231 ; penalty for removing goods without leave from the "Assention," 245 ; money to be raised at interest to pay mariners' wages, 249.
Marris, John, adventurer with John Highlord, £200, p. 3.
Marseilles (Marcelles), orders for the prevention of private trade from Aleppo, &c., 272.
Marshe, Daniel, assembly, 59 ; offers to bring in his money if he can be employed, 63 ; nominated factor, 77.
Marshe, James, warrant £9 15s. for deals, &c., 169 ; order to enquire into Mr. Adye's account for timber, 173.
Marshe, Thomas, bill of adventure sealed, £200, p. 261.
Masters, *see also Captains* ; John Johnson offers as a master, 27 ; William Brodebent thought suitable, 44 ; Roger Hankin to be compounded with, 69, 70 ; Thomas Eldred recommended, 72 ; no master to be employed till seen and spoken with, 72 ; to engage other officers and mariners, 78 ; committee to hire and compound with, 87 ; Mr. Bradbanck to sail in the "Scurge," 90 ; committee to treat with Mr. Beare, 90 ; the choice of masters to be discussed at a general court, 92 ; appointed to their respective ships, 100 ; Samuel Spencer of the "Susan," 116 ; the terms of Mr. Brodebent's bill of adventure, 153.
Masters' mates, John May, 224.
Martin, Nathaniel, assembly, 59 ; declines to adventure, 62 ; John Morice adventures £200 in his place, 185.
Martin, Roger, admitted as an extra factor, 102.
Martin, William, *of Exeter*, respecting money in the West Country, 51, 53, 54 ; his son recommended to be employed, 97.
Martyn, *see Martin*.
Masts for the ships : "Hector," 71 ; overcharge by the carpenter of the "Susan," 121, 157 ; warrant £16 0s. 10d., p. 157 ; do. £150, p. 164 ; do. £3, p. 222.
Maxfield, John, *brasier*, warrant £11 10s. for

Maxfield, John, *continued*.
copper vessels, 164 ; do. £17 17*s*. for brass pots and copper kettles, 222.
May, Faith, *wife of John May*.
May, John, *master's mate of the "Susan*," warrant 30*s*. to Faith May in part of his wages, 224 ; do. 56*s*., p. 248.
May, Mr., *preacher at Aleppo*, letter ordering him home, 281.
Mayflower, *ship*, viewed, 13
Meal : an estimate submitted, 26 ; estimate of quantity and price, 34 ; revised estimate, 46, 54-5 ; quantity to be bought in the West Country, 41, 52 ; instructions as to quality and packing, 48 : warrant to buy the Spanish meal taken prize in Lord Willoughby's ship, 86 ; no more to be bought, 88 ; committee to provide for the North West Voyage, 209.
Medicine, warrant £32 to Raphe Salter for furnishing his chest, 95 ; do £25 to James Lovering, surgeon of the "Hector," 98 ; do. £20 to Christopher Newchurch, surgeon of the "Assention," 98 ; do. £20 to John Gamond, surgeon of the "Susan," 98.
Megges, William, order to bring in £100 balance of his adventure, 162 ; bill of adventure sealed, 250.
Men-of-war, outrages by English, in the Levant, 280, 282, 283.
Mercers, *see William Allen, Thomas Cordell, William Halliday, Baptiste Hick, Clement Moseley.*
Merchandise : committee to consider what is suitable for the voyage, 26 ; quantity and description to be shipped, 36 ; total value, 37 ; committee to consider and order small merchandise, glasses, knives, &c., 79 ; shipping mark, 107 ; committee to enter and pay customs, &c., 118 ; sixty pieces of chamlettes shipped without warrant, 123 ; all merchandise to be accounted for as a joint and common stock, 130, 132 ; rules for the prevention of private trade, 130, 133 ; the kinds to be sought in the East Indies, 198 ; the object of the attempted discovery of the North West Passage was to create a market for English goods in the temperate climates of Cataia and China, 199 ; a convenient quantity laden in the two ships for the North West Voyage, 212 ; the pursers to keep an account of the same, 212-13 ; warrant £51 3*s*. 3*d*., p. 223 ; the merchandise returned from the North West Voyage to be carried to Mr. Wiseman's house and inspected, 231 ; ordered to be sold, and a committee appointed to attend to the sale, 239, 241 ; committee to attend to the unloading of the "Assention," 245 ; list of goods brought home in the "Assention," 247 ; committee to prepare the vaults under the Exchange to receive goods, 247-48 ; committee to see the goods sent to the Exchange, 248 ; committee to receive and weigh goods at the Exchange, 248 ; order and commission for the sale of the goods, 249.
Merchants, *see Factors, Adventurers* ; letters to merchants in Plymouth and Dartmouth to give credit to the "Assention" on her return, 243.
Merchant Tailors, *see William Bonde, Ralfe Hamor, John Robinson, senior*.
Michelborne, Sir Edward, recommended by the Lord Treasurer to be employed as a chief commander, 28 ; resolution of the committee to employ no gentlemen, 28 ; disfranchised, 178.

Middleton, *see Midleton*.
Midleboroughe, advice from thence of two Dutch ships returned laden with pepper, 194.
Midleton, Mr., *of Plymouth* ; warrant £5 for riding post from Plymouth with first report of the return of the "Assention," 247.
Midleton, Henry, recommended as a purser, 39 ; appointed surveyor of the works on the "Mallice Scurge," 39 ; order to prevent the workmen running to drink, 40 ; warrant £100 for charges for the "Mace Scurge," 56 ; nominated factor, 77 ; warrant £100 for the "Scurge," 78 ; elected factor of the third sort, 83 ; warrant £300 for the provision of the "Scourge," 95 ; appointed second factor in the "Susan," 101 ; warrant £100 as purser of the "Red Dragon," 104 ; warrant £50 for his entertainment, 141 ; bill of adventure sealed, £100, p. 152.
Midleton, Captain John ; assemblies, 33, 37, 39, 44, 57, 59, 64, 67, 68, 71, 74, 77, 78, 80, 83, 86, 8d, 89, 90, 92, 93, 94, 95, 96, 98, 100, 103, 104, 106, 107, 108, 109, 117, 118, 121, 122, 123, 139, 140, 142, 143, 144 ; committees, 30, 57, 72, 86, 94 ; surveyor for the "Susan," 14 ; do. "Mare Scourge," 27 ; commends Henry Midleton as a purser, 39 ; general committee, 63 ; committee to agree with him for going on the voyage, 77, 90 ; nominated factor, 77 ; elected a principal factor, 81 ; to sail in the "Hector," 94, 100 ; ordered to provide ship's stores for the "Hector," 117 ; his commission, 135 ; appointed to take chief command in the event of the death of Captain Lancaster, 135 ; warrant £100 for his entertainment, 140 ; do. £8 3*s*. 7*d*. for disbursements, 140 ; do. £34 3*s*., p. 142 ; directs £100 to be paid to the purser of the "Hector," 142 ; bills of adventure sealed, £400 and £220, p. 150 ; receives £38 10*s*. from Mr. Runney for mariners' wages, 158 ; bill of adventure sealed, £240, p. 256.
Midleton, Robert, adventurer with others, £500, p. 2 ; assemblies, 4, 59 ; warrant £27 6*s*. 6*d*. for sugar, 149 ; committee, 243 ; bill of adventure sealed, £240, p. 254.
Midleton, Thomas, adventurer with others, £500, p. 2 ; assemblies, 4, 9, 28 ; committees, 6, 8, 9 ; recommends Robert Creswell as a purser, 39.
Mildmay, Robert, assembly, 59 ; warrant to bring in his adventure at once, 170 ; bill of adventure sealed, £240, p 253.
Millett, William, bill of adventure sealed, £240, p. 257.
Milward, Humfrey, *haberdasher*, assents to bring in his supplies, 175 ; bill of adventure sealed, £240, p. 250.
Money. *See also Dollars, Bullion, Coin, Royals, Warrants, Adventurers* ; no sum above £10 to be disbursed by the treasurers without a warrant, 24 ; money in the West Country, 45 ; instructions for taking up money and giving bills of exchange, 50 ; money wanted to pay wages, 92 ; committee to attend to the shipping of money in the West Country, 120 ; £6,000 coined in the Tower, 120 ; amount of new and Spanish money apportioned to be carried in each ship and how packed, 122 ; to be entered at the Custom House and waterborne to Gravesend and stowed in the ships, 142 ; order for £1,500 to be taken up at interest, 146 ; warrant £29 10*s*. for stamps made for the East India monies, 174 ; the mislike to

312   INDEX

Money, *continued.*
  the transportation of so much coin out of the country, 198; money to be raised at interest for payment of mariners' wages returned in the "Assention," 249.
Moone, Richard, money supplied in Plymouth, 64.
Moore, John, *alderman,* adventurer, £300, p. 1; assemblies, 7, 9, 58, 65, 68, 71, 82, 87, 89, 90, 93, 94, 96, 98, 99, 100, 102, 103, 115, 118, 123, 140, 144, 148, 150, 151, 159, 176; committees, 8, 58, 71, 73, 77, 91, 115, 147; appointed director, 6; general committee, 63; bill of adventure sealed, £480, p. 262.
Morgan,   } Thomas, nominated factor, 77;
Morgann, } elected factor of the fourth sort, 83; to sail in the "Susan," 101; order to be paid £20 for his provision to sea, 126; bill of adventure sealed, £40, p. 152.
Morice, } John, adventures £200 in place of
Morrice, } Nathaniel Martin, 185; bill of adventure sealed, £240, p. 261.
Mort, royals to be procured there, 51.
Mortgage, £100 lent to William Brodelent, master of the "Red Dragon," 128; the same repaid, 153.
Moseley, Anthony, warrant to be paid £25 10s. for vinegar, 115; made free, though not named in the patent, 177; bill of adventure sealed, £240, p. 257.
Moseley, Clement, adventurer with Jerome Suger, £250, p. 2; assembly, 4, 59; deceased and assignment of stock, 192; bill of adventure, sealed, £240 to his widow, 251.
Moseley, Elizabeth, widow of Clement Moseley, 193; bill of adventure sealed, £240, p. 251; do. £240, p. 261.
Moseley, John, assignment of £100 of Clement Moseley's stock, 193; assembly, 228.
Moseley, Nicholas, *alderman,* adventurer, £300, p. 1; assembly, 4.
Moskova, } Company. See *Muscovia.*
Moskvy, }
Mosley, *see Moseley.*
Mullett, Justice, employed as a smith at Woolwich, 40; warrant £29 1s. 4d. for iron work, 172.
Muscatel wine (muskadell), impost offered in opposition to the Levant Company, 280.
Muscovia, } Company, warrant £180 for cordage,
Muskovia, } 126; do. £57 16s. 8d., p.
Muskovy, } 187; a target and headpiece, 141; respecting cordage, 162, 170, 204; £100 adventure in arrears from Richard Tailby assigned over for payment to the Muscovia Company, 176; touching the respective rights of the Muscovia and East India Companies to the benefit of the North West Passage if discovered, 185, 186, 188-89, 190-91, 194-96, see *North West Passage.*
Mustard seed, one tonne of dry caske required, 30; thirty bushels to be bought, 33; estimate of quantity and price, 35; committee to provide 30 bushels and caske, 76; committee to provide for the North West Voyage, 209.
Myddleton, } *see Midleton.*
Mydleton, }
Myldmay, *see Mildmay.*
Mylward, *see Milward.*

Nails, 157, 172.
Napper, Henry, "*master of the Hector;*" committee to confer with him touching his employment, 94; to sail as master in the "Hector," 100; warrant £20 for his pains and expenses in the preparation of the ships, 143.
Nelson, William, admitted an adventurer £240, and pays premium of £30, p. 205; committees, 245, 246.
Nets, fishing, to be bought in the West Country, 41.
Newcastle, 223.
Newcastleship, *ship,* viewed, 13.
Newchurche, Christopher, *surgeon of the* "*Assention;*" warrant £20 for providing surgeon's remedies, &c., 98.
Newcombe, Mr., bill of exchange £60 for money advanced to Captain Waymouth, 209.
Newman, John, adventurer with Reinold Greene, £200, p. 2; assembly, 218; general committee, 179; bill of adventure sealed, £240, p. 252.
Newton, a fit place to buy cider, 49.
Nicholles, Christopher, made free though not named in the patent, 177; bill of adventure sealed, £240, p. 262.
Nicolls, Xpofer and Thomas, warrant £34 7s. 10d. for cordage, 222.
Nicholson, Edmond, *Grocer,* adventurer, £200, p. 4; committee, 245, 246; bill of adventure sealed, £240, p. 253.
Nicholson, Edward, assembly, 59.
Norromborough. Ware, 79; warrant, £207, p. 138.
Northeover, Thomas, warrant £40 on bill of exchange, 80.
North West Passage, *see also Waymouth and East India Co.;* letter received from Captain George Waymouth suggesting an attempt be made for the discovery of a North West Passage to the East Indies, asking whether the company will undertake the expedition, &c., 182; the matter adjourned for further consideration, 182; the voyage resolved on, 183; the adventure to be voluntary at the rate of 12d. in the £ on the amounts of original adventures, 183; committee to set down and report the charge for three pinnaces for the voyage, 183; the charters to be perused to see if power is given to compel payments towards this voyage, 183; conference with Waymouth; two pinnaces resolved on of 50 and 40 tons with 16 and 14 men and the total charge estimated at about £3,000, p. 184; Waymouth agrees to undertake the voyage for £100 for his instruments and to receive £500 if he discover the passage but to claim nothing if unsuccessful, 184; Waymouth's agreement reported to a general court and approved and the preparation of the voyage to be taken in hand, 185; a book to be taken round for adventurers to subscribe at 12d. in the £, 185; doubts arising as to the rights of the Muscovia Co. and fearing they might claim the benefit of the discovery if made, a committee appointed to enquire whether that company will relinquish their privileges during the continuance of the patent, 187; deliberations with the Muscovia Co. who decline to give up their rights, but offer to admit as freeman all those of the East India Co. who will contribute to a joint adventure, 188; proposal that the Muscovia Co. shall exclude from all benefit in the discovery for 15 years all their own members who will not contribute, and such of the East India Co. as will contribute £10 to have the freedom of the discovery under the seal of the Muscovia Co., 188-89; the Muscovia Co. having no liking to

North West Passage, *continued*.
join with the East India Co. prefer to deal in the discovery by themselves, but will assign no time for so doing; the importance of the enterprise urged, and a committee appointed to confer again, to the end that if the Muscovia Co. will undertake the discovery, they may be left to proceed in it, but if otherwise then to request them to join with the East India Co. on conditions formerly propounded; and if they will do neither, a relation to be made to the Privy Council of their refusal and hindering of the East India Co. in the intended discovery, and the Muscovia Co. to be required to answer in writing, 191; in consequence of a better opinion conceived of the strength of their privileges, the East India Co. resolve to attempt the voyage alone; ordered that adventurers shall write their contributions at once, and any person refusing, to be excluded from all benefit during the term of the patent, and all profit in the discovery to rest proportionately in those who will adventure, 92; the Privy Council learning that by reason of the difference between the two companies the preparation of the voyage is delayed, wrote to the Muscovia Co. to either join with the East India Co., or else bring their patent before the Council to show their claim to their privileges, 194; the Muscovia Co. thereupon agree to act jointly with the East India Co., 195; the subscription book to be sent round that everyone may set down his adventure or else refuse, and those who refuse to be exempted from all benefit in the discovery for ever, 195; the amounts adventured to be brought in within a month, 195; the committees of both companies to meet from time to time to agree on the preparations of the voyage, &c., 195; doubts arising as to the powers of either Co. to subdivide themselves and unite partially with each other, it is ordered that counsel's opinion be taken thereon, 195; counsel's opinion that the interest in the discovery rests expressly with the East India Co. and that no company can divide their privileges or grant a portion of their rights to another company, 196; finally resolved that the voyage shall be prepared and a committee appointed to expedite the same and to devise laws and ordinances for the general guidance of business, 196-97; the laws and ordinances devised and the main object of the proposed discovery set forth together with the details for the preparation of the voyage, 198-202, *see East India Co.*; £30 allowed to Waymouth for his instruments, 204; warrant £30 to Waymouth for provisions, 204; do. £20 for instruments, 204; committee to persuade adventurers to pay their contributions on pain of the penalty enacted, 205 (see 200); Thomas Yerworth appointed a purser with wages contingent on the success of the voyage and to give bond for his good behaviour, 205; John Drewe appointed a master, 206; warrant £80 to Thomas Yerworth, purser, for carpenters' wages, 206; state of the preparation of the voyage and steps taken to encourage the adventure, &c., 206-8, *see East India Co.*; warrants for pork, mariners' wages, &c., 208; warrant £28 18s. for hides to make the mariners' cassocks, breeches, and gowns, 208; mariners hired at Exeter, 209; committee to provide victuals, &c., 209; warrant £100 for anchors and other necessaries, 210; warrant £10 to John Drewe, master of the "Godspeed," in part of his wages, 210; warrant £100 to Thomas Yerworth for sea coals, wood, lead, &c., 210; do. £100 to Waymouth for men's wages, 211; articles of agreement with Waymouth containing his orders and instructions for the voyage, 211-14, *see East India Co.*; agreement with John Cartwright, *preacher*, with salary contingent on the success of the voyage, 216; articles of agreement with Waymouth read to the generality, also the Queen's letters to the Emperor of China, &c., 217; auditors appointed to ascertain the state of the adventure, that further supplies may be called up and some course taken with the defaulters, 217-18; Waymouth allowed £50 for his expenses prior to sailing, 218; warrant £30 for watches, compasses, &c., 218; do. £20 for mariners' clothes, 218; do. £50 11s. 8d. for casks, 218; do. £7 8s. for deals, oars, &c., 218; do. £6 10s. for iron hoops, &c., 219; do. £29 18s. for cables and skeyts, 219; do. £92 10s. for butter, candles, powder, &c., 219; do. £11 6s. 8d. for bay salt, 219; dislike to Thomas Yerworth, purser, 219; differences with the other purser Pullison, 219; Mr. Cambell indemnified for his bond given for the payment of John Drew's wages, 220; day appointed for the payment of supplies and new bills of adventure to be made out, showing in a lump sum what is every man's interest in the voyage by the Cape, 220, (see resolutions on pages 206-8); day appointed for the auditors to complete the accounts that the whole charge may be made known, 220; warrant £143 for canvas for sails, 220; several warrants for sails, pullies, iron work, beer, timber, powder, &c., 221-24, *see Warrants*; the book-keeper to complete the accounts for the North West voyage and to enter up each adventurer's credit in a lump sum, 224; journal from Waymouth announcing return to Dartmouth; orders to bring the ships to London without sale of provisions; letters written to the pursers to preserve all things useful for a second voyage, and general court summoned, 227-28; Mr. Cartwright on being asked to state the reasons for the return, can give no further information than Waymouth's journal, 228; the ships ordered to London without breaking bulk, 228; Waymouth's delay in coming to London, 229; ships' arrival in London and committee appointed to see to their discharge, 229; certain provisions to be sold, also the two ships and their belongings, 230; Mr. Holliday and others being in arrears with their supplies it is ordered that the amount be defaulted from their stock, 231 (*see* page 200); the merchandise brought back to be taken to Mr. Wiseman's house and inspected, 231; John Drewe, master of the "Godspeed," and John Lane, master's mate, and others aver that Cartwright was the chief cause of the return, 231; ordered that demand be made of Cartwright for the gown and apparel delivered to him, 232; proceedings against Waymouth before the Privy Council; his hopes of the discovery of divers inlets that treat through the coast of America to the Southseas or East Indies; a new and final voyage resolved on and Waymouth reappointed chief in command; his confidence in the discovery of a passage; a

S S

INDEX

North West Passage, *continued.*
suitable captain to take charge of the second ship to proceed with Waymouth or separately as may be agreed; committee appointed to see to the preparation of the ships and calculate the charges, 233-34; various warrants for wages in the late voyage, 234-35; Stephen Hodsonn pays his supplies, 235; a new voyage with one ship only thought advisable, and conference to be had with Waymouth, 236; to save new expense it is suggested that the stores, &c., brought back by the two ships may be sufficient to equip one ship for a new voyage; committee to consider and confer with Waymouth or some other fit person, 236-37; the committee decide to use such old stores as are fit and by sale of the residue equip one ship for a new voyage, 237; at a general court the committee report against a second voyage and suggest it be abandoned and that the ships, &c., be sold, that money may be raised to defray the charges on the return of the fleet by the Cape, and by general consent the voyage is abandoned, and the ships, victuals, merchandise, &c., ordered to be sold and committee appointed to effect the sale, 239; demands by Waymouth for charges, moneys expended or otherwise due as he pretendeth, and the same agreed to be settled by arbitration, and committee appointed to investigate, 240; the sale of the ships deferred, but all perishable merchandise to be sold at once, and prices being high at present all cordage to be sold at once, 241; the ships to be sold if £300 each can be obtained, 242.
Norwich stuff, quantity to be shipped and price, 36.
Notary, *see John Cowper.*
Number of men and tonnage of ships, for the East India voyage, 34; for the North West voyage, 184.
Nutmegs, estimates of quantity and price, 35; quantity ordered and committee to purchase, 75.

Oars (ores), 218.
Oaths of office for the Governor, Deputy and committees, 179-80.
Oatmeal, 12 tonne of dry caske required for, 30; estimate of quantity and price, 35; committee to provide, 75; do. caske for, 76; committee to provide for the North West voyage, 209.
Objects of the East India Company, 4, 198.
Objects of the proposed attempt to discover a North West passage, 199.
Obligations, *see Bonds.*
Ofeilde, Roger, *see Owfield.*
Offeley, Robert, assembly, 59; declines to adventure, 62; bill of adventure sealed, £240, p. 251.
Offeley, William, the elder, adventurer, £200, p. 4; bill of adventure sealed, £300, p. 256.
Officers, all officers to be elected by a general assembly, 6, 8; committee to hire ships' officers, 87; list of officers appointed to each ship, 100; the officers to be called on for an account of the provisions supplied to each ship, 126.
Oil, estimate of quantity and price, 35; committee to provide sweet oil, 76; do. rape oil, 76; do. casks for, 76; warrant, £213 6s. 8d., p. 111; do. £80, p. 114; do. £194 5s. 6d., p. 114; a barrel allowed to Samuel Spencer, master of the "Susan," 123; committee to provide for the North West voyage, 209; impost offered to the Queen in opposition to the Levant Company, 280.
Onnyslowe, Leonard, warrant £40 12s. for casks, 148.
Orders for the payment of money, *see Warrants.*
Orders in Council, *see Privy Council.*
Ordinances, for the guidance of the traffic of the voyage, 129-31; for the guidance of general business, 197-202; *see East India Company.*
Ordnance, quantity carried in the "Mare Scurge," 43-4.
Osborne, Sir Edward; his house nominated as a convenient place for storage of goods brought home in the "Asstention," 245.
Osseley, *see Offeley.*
Owfield, Roger, adventurer, £300, p. 3; [assembly], 228; bill of adventure sealed, £360, p. 250.
Oxen, 120 to be bought for making salt beef, 114.

Page, Joseph, *baker;* warrant £80, p. 149; do. £50, p. 157; do. £45 10s. 11d., p. 167; do. £60, p. 215; do. £41 8s., p. 222.
Painter, John, *of Dartmouth,* bill of exchange £110, p. 70.
Painters, *see Francis Caudell, Thomas Tyler.*
Palmer, William, assembly, 59; warrant to bring in his adventure at once, 170; bill of adventure sealed, £240, p. 260; do. £200, p. 261.
Paper, warrant, £90 10s., p. 126.
Paragon, *ship,* viewed, 13.
Parkehurste, Henrye, adventurer with John Coghill, £200, p. 3.
Parkins, Thomas, warrant £20 1s. for honey, 125; do. £78 16s. 4d. for casks, 143.
Parrett, warrant £207 for Norromborough ware, 138.
Parsloe, assemblies, 231, 232, 236, 244, 248; Parslowe, general committee and sworn, 220; bill of adventure sealed, £240, p. 257.
Parsons, George, purser of the "Hector," 33; warrant £100 for provisions, 121; do. £100 for men's wages, 154.
Paslowe, *see Parsloe.*
Patent of the East India Company; petition to the Privy Council for leave to prepare a grant of privilege, &c., 10; Mr. Altham reads the draft of the patent, 25; the patent drawn, 62; committee to finish it, 78; adventurers in arrears to be dealt with before engrossing, 85; the patent read and the secretary ordered to solicit the Queen's attorney to make an end to the same, 88; committee to set down all names to be mentioned, 91; warrant £71 13s. 4d. to Mr. Attorney and clerks for drawing and engrossing the patent, &c., 96; warrant £50 for other charges in passing the patent, &c., 107; the patent read to the generality, 109; all adventurers not mentioned to be deemed equally as free as those named, 109; an adventurer named in the patent desiring to assign, is referred to a general court, 175; the assignment allowed, 177; list of persons made free though not named in the patent, 177; disfranchisement of certain defaulting adventurers, 178; reference to the patent as set forth in the preamble of the general laws and ordinances,

INDEX

Patent of the East India Company, *continued*—198; power to make laws and ordinances, 199; the charters to be perused to see if the Company have power to compel payments towards the North West voyage and the second voyage by the Cape, 183; conferences with the Muscovia Company in reference to the respective rights to the North West Passage if discovered, 189; counsel's opinion that the East India Company have the right to the North West Passage under their patent, 192; limited time for the election of governor, deputy, and committees, 224.
Paule, William, adventurer with George Canynge, £300, p. 2.
Payment of money, *see Warrants*.
Peace with Spain, 10.
Pearde, Nicholas, *see Pierd*.
Peas, to be provided, 26; one hundred quarters required, 29; 30 tonnes dry caske required for peas and beans, 30; 60 or 70 quarters ordered, 31, 65; estimate of quantity and price, 34; price in the West Country to be ascertained, 49; instructions for buying in the West Country, 54; Lord Treasurer's warrant for the provision and transport of peas and beans from Norfolk and Cambridge, 66; committee to provide, 75; ditto, for the North West voyage, 209; committee to provide casks, 76; warrant £100 for peas and beans, 82; do. £100, p. 96.
Peierce, Richard, bill of adventure sealed, £240, p. 253.
Peird, *see Pierd*.
Penalties, for private trading and fraud, 130, 132, 133; for breach of the general laws and ordinances, 200-2; for default in the payment of adventure or supplies, 200, 207.
Pennington, ⎱ Robert, warrant to bring in his
Pennyton, ⎰ adventure at once, 170; bill of adventure sealed £240, p. 230.
Pepper, estimate of quantity and price, 35; committee to provide 12 lbs., 75; two Dutch ships returned laden with pepper, 194; one of the articles to be traded in, 198; bags to be made and suits *without pockets* for the porters employed to fill in the pepper brought home in the "Assention," 247; quantity brought home in the "Assention" entered at the Custom House, 247.
Persia, Sir Anthony Shurley's doings in Persia, 272.
Persons, George, *see Parsons*.
Persons, Richard, bill of adventure sealed £200, p. 262.
Petitions of the East India Company to the Privy Council, *see Privy Council*.
Petition of the Levant Company to the Privy Council respecting their ships seized at Venice for restitution of the late prize taken by English men of war, 277-78 (*see also* 280, 282, 283).
Pett, Joseph, *shipwright*; warrant £42 for work on the "Godspeed," 223.
Pett, Peter, *shipwright*; warrant £17 12s. 6d., p. 169.
Pewter, warrant £68 18s., p. 129.
Phipps, Humfrey, warrant £20 for vinegar, 115.
Phœnix, *ship*, viewed, 13; offered for £1,400, and to be taken back for £700 after the voyage, or for £1,200 without return, 14; time taken to consider the matter, 21.
Piece, Nicholas (? Pierd), assembly, 59.
Pierd, ⎱ Nicholas, *clothworker*, adventurer,
Pierde, ⎰ £100, p. 1; assembly, 4; surveyor for the "Hector," 14; to clear accounts with Mr. Sandy, 127; ordered to bring in his bill, 159; appointed auditor, 218; bill of adventure sealed, £240, p. 256; do. £240, p. 257.
Pilotage, warrant £6 for bringing the "Assention" into the river, 248.
Pilot Major of the Fleet, *see Captain Davies*.
Pilots; Philip Grove appointed and his pay fixed, 47; the pilot-major to sail in the "Scurge," 90; pilots appointed to their ships, 100; warrant £300 for salary to John Davies, pilot-major, 127; bill of adventure sealed to Philip Grove, 148; do. to Captain Davies, 152; warrant £6 for the hire of one Stace, a pilot, to go with Captain Waymouth to Newcastle, 223.
Pinder, Signior Paull, sent home by Mr. Lyllo, English ambassador at Constantinople, to acquaint the Queen with the doings of the French, 265, 272, 273; ambassador's accounts sent home by him, 266.
Pinnaces, *see Ships*; "*Godspeed;*" "*Discovery;*" committee to find suitable ones in the river, 22; no pinnaces to be used, but small lancher pinnaces to be carried in the ships, 28; "The Pynnace" rated at 40 men, tonnage 100, p. 34; proportion of aquavitæ, 35; a pinnace for the "Hector," 167; pinnaces for the North West voyage, 182; committee to set down the cost of three pinnaces, &c., 183; two pinnaces of 50 and 40 tons manned with 16 and 14 men resolved on, 184, 185; two ships or pinnaces finally resolved on, 199; Edward Pullison, *purser*, of one of the pinnaces for the North West voyage, 216, *see Pullison*; various warrants for the provision of sails, iron work, beer, pullies, timber, powder, &c., 221, *see warrants*; return to Dartmouth and ordered to London without breaking bulk, 227; all stores suitable for a second voyage to be carefully preserved, 228; arrival in the Thames, 229; ordered to be sold with all stores, &c., 230; warrant to pay the mariners hired at Dartmouth, 231; warrants 24s. to Thomas Smith for keeping the pinnaces, 234, 240, 241, 242; various warrants for wages in the late voyage, 234; the two "barks," order to be sold, 239; the sale deferred, 241; to be sold for £300 each, 242.
Piott, Richard, assembly, 60; bill of adventure sealed, £240, p. 253.
Pipes, *see Casks*.
Pitch, tar, cordage, &c., ordered to be bought of Browne and Co., 121.
Planks, 169.
Plate, *see silver plate*.
Platters, 157.
Plompton, warrant £67 9s. for rape oil, 119.
Plumber, *see William Edward*.
Plumes of feathers, 141, 151.
Plymouth, 29, 80; the "Mare Scurge's" boat lying there to be sent up, 40; recommended for the purchase of biscuit, 48; wine there and the price, 50; letters to the principal merchants to give credit to the "Assention" on her return, 243-4; warrant £5 to Mr. Midleton for riding with the first report of the return of the "Assention," 247.
Poalstedd, Henrye, adventurer with George Whitmor, £200, p. 4; assembly, 60; bill of adventure sealed, £240, 252.
Pockets; suits without pockets for the porters to fill bags with pepper brought home in the "Assention," 247.

Polldavies, to be bought for making bags, 85; 50 or 60 pieces to be bought to make bags for pepper, 247.
Polsted, *see Poalstedd*.
Pomtell, Richard, assembly, 59; to bring in his bill, 159; bill of adventure sealed, £240, p. 254.
Poole, 129.
Pope, Lewis, bill of exchange, £40, p. 104; bill of adventure sealed, £240, p. 259.
Pope (Mr.), serjeant of the admiralty, warrant £2 13s. for the burial of those slain in the "Hector," 141.
Pope, Robarte, committee, 68; sent to join Captain Davies in the West Country, 29; commissions for buying provisions, &c., in the West Country, 41, 46, 48, 52, 53, 54; bills of exchange, 54, 57, 58, 68, 73, 74. 79, 81, 82, 84, 85, 88, 89, 104, 115, 129, 141; letters touching provisions and money, 64, 66, 74; nominated factor, 77; elected factor of the second sort, 82; letter from Mr. Howe to provide no more bread, &c., 88; paid £50 for his trouble in the West Country, 101; appointed second factor in the "Red Dragon," 101; Mr. Howe ordered to give him a remembrancer for the managing of business, 103; to confer with Mr. Ellicott as to shipping the Spanish money, 119; bill of adventure £100, sealed, 152.
Pork; estimate of quantity, 26; 40 tonnes of cask required, 30; estimate of quantity and price, 34; cheap in the West Country, 54; committee for ordering, 68, 75; do. for caske, 76; warrant £54 18s., p. 208; committee to provide for the North West Voyage, 209; warrant £111 5s. for pork and beef, for the North West Voyage, 214; pork brought back from the North West Voyage to be sold, 230.
Port of London, 229.
Portage; warrant £34 16s. 8d. for lighterage and portage of goods to the ships, 158.
Porter, Walter, adventurer with William Barrell, £400, 4.
Porterage, warrant £4 for landing goods from Porters, the "Godspeed" and "Discovery," 238; clothes to be made without pockets for the porters to fill bags with pepper, 247.
Portman, Sir { Hugh, } warrant £400 on bill { Hewghe, } of exchange from the West Country, 68; do. £1,000, p. 115.
Portman, John, warrant £200 to be delivered by him to the company's agent in the West Country, 87.
Post; letters to and from Exeter, 66, 74.
Pots of brass, 222.
Potter, John, adventurer with Robert Bell, £200, p. 3.
Poulsteede, *see Poalstedd*.
Powder, *see Gunpowder*.
Poyner, Walter, recommended by Mr. Chambers as a factor, 97; admitted as an extra factor, 102.
Poyntell, *see Pomtell*.
Preachers, *see Thomas Pulleyn, John Cartwright, Mr. Byddell*.
Premiums on the sale or assignment of Clement Moseley's stock, 193; William Nelson pays £30 on his admission as an adventurer of £240, p. 205.
Presents for the Kings of the East Indies, 36; looking glasses, 116; silver cups, &c., 118;

list of plate and other presents, 141; how distributed among the several ships, 151-2.
Prices and quantity of provisions for the voyage estimated, 34.
Princes and Potentates in the East Indies; letters from the Queen, 91, 131, 134, 139; presents for, 141, 151.
Prisoners in the East Indies, 194; an Englishman brought home by the Dutch, 194.
Private trade, all factors to abstain from, 86; sixty pieces of Chamlettes shipped without warrant, 123; committee to devise orders to prevent, 124; ordinances for the prevention of, 130; do. from Aleppo to Marseilles, &c., 272.
Privilege, *see also Patent*; suit to be made to the Queen for sole privilege for as many years as can be obtained, 6; committee to solicit the Privy Council, 8; petition to the Privy Council, 8; petition for leave to prepare a grant of privilege, 10; privileges promised, 11-12, 25; 200 marks awarded to Richard Wright, Secretary, for his pains in procuring the privileges, &c., 203.
Privy Council, committee to solicit privilege, &c., 8; petition praying for privileges and incorporation as a company, that the shipping when ready be not stayed for any service; for leave to send out foreign money and to coin the same in the mint; for freedom from customs, &c., 7-8; the enterprise favoured by the Council and recommended to the Queen, 9; committee to solicit an answer to the petition, 9; committee required to attend and receive their lordships' orders, also to tender a petition praying that the voyage may proceed without impeachment; leave to carry out 5 m¹. weight of bullion without charge, and for leave to prepare a grant of privilege, &c., 10; by reason of a treaty of peace in hand with Spain their lordships decline to give a warrant for the proceeding of the voyage without impeachment, October, 1599, 10; in September, 1600, their lordships favour the enterprise and obtain the royal assent to favours sought in the petition, 11-12; general court summoned to take notice of a letter signifying Her Majesty's pleasure, 57; general court, 58-63; letter promising no hindrance shall be given to the voyage, 60; all adventurers in arrears to be certified to their lordships, 61; the patent, 62; a complaint to be lodged against all adventurers in arrears, 110; order in council for defaulting adventurers to bring in their money at once on pain of imprisonment, 112-13; order in council touching the remissness of the company in paying their debts and ordering all defaulting adventurers to appear and be punished for contempt, 164-65; warrant summoning all adventurers who refuse payment to be brought before their lordships and list of such defaulters, 169-70; defaulters committed, 170-1; complaints of the hindrances offered to the North West Voyage by the Muscovia Company, 191; letter signifying Her Majesty's mislike to the delay in the second voyage and propounding unto them the example of the Dutch, 191; suit to be made for an order approving the company's act for the forfeiture of five times the value of the levy for the North West voyage to be made on the stock of all defaulters, 207; proceedings touching the return of Captain Waymouth from the North West voyage, 233; petition of the

INDEX

Privy Council, *continued*.
 Levant Company respecting their ships seized at Venice as restitution for the late prize taken by the English men-of-war, 277-78, *see also* 280, 282, 283.
Privy Seal, 107.
Prizes and prize money, resolution respecting, 118; tithes due to the Lord Admiral, 246-47.
Prockter, James, warrant £100 on bill of exchange, 73.
Profit of the voyage to be allotted in proportion to the adventure, 146; respecting the North West voyage, 200.
Prosperous, *ship*, viewed, 13.
Provisions, *see Victuals*.
Prunes, 118.
Pulleymakers, *see Arnold Mabanck, John Crane, William Denham*.
Pulleyn, Thomas, *preacher*, warrant £26 13s. 4d. for his provision to sea, 116; bill of adventure £50 sealed, 150.
Pulleys, 167, 221.
Pullison, } Edward, engaged as one of the
Pullyson, } pursers for the North West voyage, 216; salary contingent on the discovery of the passage, 216; to give a bond of £100 for his good behaviour, 216; only to be employed if the captain thinks it needful, 219; warrant £6 in full of wages and demands, 240.
Purnell, John, warrant £50 for royals, 64.
Pursers, *see the various ships*. Francis Wilson recommended, 27; the fidelity of the pursers of the " Susan," " Hector," and " Assention," guaranteed, 33; letters commending several men to be employed, 39; order to bring in accounts, 97; committee to audit and certify accounts, 98; wages fixed 40s. a month at sea, 20s. a month and board wages in harbour, 116; the " Scourge " to have two pursers, 116; Thomas Yerworth appointed one of the pursers for the North West voyage with wages contingent on the discovery of the passage and to give a bond of 100 marks for his good behaviour, 205; Edward Pullison, do. do., 216; Yerworth, purser of the " Discouery," 210; in the North West voyage pursers to keep a register and account of goods laden and disposed of, also to make notes, journals, and observations for the direction and help of posterity, 213; to deliver their bills of provisions to Mr. Burrell to receive allowance, 215; dislike taken to Thomas Yerworth, 219; differences with Edward Pullison, 219; warrant £6 13s. 4d. to Thomas Yerworth for his wages and expenses, 235; do. £6 to Edward Pullison, 240.
Pywell, John, warrant £7 10s. for head peces and morrens, 149.

Quarles, William, bill of adventure sealed, £240, p. 251.
Quays, *see Wharves*.
Queen (Elizabeth), *see also Privy Council*; suit to be made for sole privilege, also immunities from customs, &c., 6; letters to potentates in the East Indies, 91, 131, 134, 157; letters to the Emperor of China and Kathia to be carried in the North West voyage, 217, 222; letter respecting peace with Spain, 282; £4,000 per annum to be paid by the Levant Company in lieu of imposts, 280, 282, 283.

Radcliff, *see Ratcliffe*.
Raisins, 118.
Ramridge, John, adventurer with Thomas Bostocke, £200, p. 3.
Ranton, Nicholas, warrant £50 on bill of exchange, 84.
Rape oil, 2½ tonne of caske required, 30; estimate of quantity and price, 35; warrant £67 9s., p. 119.
Ratcliffe, }
Ratclyff, } 147, 154, 208.
Reddereth, committee to inspect ships lying there, 13.
Red Dragon, *ship*, the " Mare Scourge " renamed, *see also* " *Mare Scourge*;" the " Scourge " ordered to be launched and renamed the " Red Dragon," 96; Admiral ship, 100; list of officers, 100; list of factors, 101; warrant £100 to Henry Middleton, purser, 104; do. £100 to William Bradbanck, master, 104; do. £50 to William Dixson, purser, for the use of the ship, 105; do. £200 to Edward Highlord, purser, for preparations, 106; do. £50 to Edward Stephens on account for timber, 106; do. £100 to William Dyckes on account of necessaries, 108; do. £100 to William Dixon, purser, 111; do. £150 to William Dixsy, purser, for repairs, 114; ordered to have two pursers, 116; committee to provide stores, 117; warrant £250 to William Dixson, purser, 117; do. £250, p. 120; the amount of new and Spanish money appointed to be carried and how packed, 122; Mr. Wattes to inquire into the damage done to a ship by the anchor of the " Scourge," 125; warrant £200 to William Dixon, purser, 127; committee to wait on Lord Cumberland respecting the damage done to a ship by the anchor of the " Red Dragon," 128; warrant £200 to William Dickson, purser, 140; do. £100 for clearing expenses, 144; the pursers' accounts to be audited, 147; warrant £29 for ancients and streamers, 149; list of presents to be carried, 151; Mr. Brodebent's bill of adventure, 153; warrant £180 for wages and for clearing away the ship, 154; do. £15 7s. for 59 barrels of beer, 154; do. £100 for iron work, 157; do. £50 for painting the ship, 157; do. £18 for turnery, &c., 157; do. £13 2s. 10d. for porterage and lading, 158; do. £50 for shipwright's work, 163; do. £86 15s. 4d. for sails for the " Dragon " and " Hector," 168; do. £29 1s. 4d. for iron work, 172; do. £48 for painting work, 172; do. £227 for iron work for the " Dragon " and " Susan," 173; memorandum tonnage, 600, men, 180, p. 263.
Remembrancers, committee to act as, and prepare the business for the general committee, 40.
Rent, warrant £6 for 6 quarters' rent of Founder's Hall for the Company's meetings, 227.
Reprisals, resolution respecting mariners' shares of, 118; tithes due to the Lord Admiral, 246-47.
Rewler, Mr., called on to bring in his account, 159.
Rice, one tonne of drie caske required, 30; estimate of quantity and price, 35; committee to provide, 75.
Richardson, Thomas, surveyor for the " Susan," 14; bill of adventure sealed, £240, p. 257.
Rickman, Robert, warrant £133 6s. 8d. for his 6th part of the " Assention," 115; order to

Rickman, Robert, *continued*.
  make Maurice Abbott creditor by Mr. Rickman for £100, p. 127.
Roan canvas, } warrant £28 14s., p. 97.
Roan cloth,
Robinson, Henrye, adventurer with Richarde Howse, £200, p. 3; assembly, 5; bill of adventure sealed, £240, p. 260.
Robinson, Humfrie, bill of adventure sealed, £240, p. 260.
Robinson, John, senior *Merchant Tailor*, adventurer, £200, p. 2.
Robinson, Robert, bill of adventure sealed, £240, p. 261.
Robinson, Thomas, warrant £29 18s. for cables, &c., 219.
Romney, *see Rumney*.
Rose, Edward, late factor at Aleppo, 278-79.
Rouen, £5,000 worth of royals to be provided there and at Calais, 58.
Rowe Buck, *ship*, viewed, 13.
Royal assent to the formation of the Company, 5; to the preparation of the voyage and the favours sought in the petitions, 11, 25, *see also Privy Council*.
Royals, } *see also Dollars and Spanish*
Royals of Plate, } *Money*; the provision of,
Royals of 8, } in the West Country, 21, 57; two adventures brought in in Spanish money Royals of 8 at xviij the £ profit, 31; Mr. Allabaster commissioned to take up £3,000 in Royals of Plate at Calais, 41; do. £5,000, p. 58; instructions for taking up in the West Country, 51, 53; may be taken in the West Country as payment of adventure money, 54; payment for, *see Warrants*; Mr. Ellycott buys Royals and sells to the Company at London rate, 64; his conduct deprecated, 65; letter to him expressing dislike to his course, 66; letter to Mr. Sandy advising him not to exceed the price of 12d., p. 66; warrant £500 to Mr. Allabaster, 68; do. £500, p. 82; Mr. Allabaster commissioned to convey bullion and Royals from Calais, 84; warrant £500 to Mr. Allabaster, 91; Mr. Allabaster's commission continued, 91; warrant £105 12s. 4d. to Walter Clark for Royals taken up at Exeter, 102; Mr. Allabaster to buy no more, 102; instruction concerning, 103; warrant £500 to Robert Stephen on account, 105; do. £700 to Mr. Allabaster on account, 106; instructions for shipping from the West Country, 119; committee to attend to the shipping in the West Country, 120; the amount apportioned to be carried in each ship and how packed, 122; Mr. Skinner's adventure, £200, received in Royals, 124.
Rudd, Richard, warrant £60 on bill of exchange, 84.
Rules for the working of the Company, *see also East India Company*. No ship to be received as a portion of an adventure; all shipping to be bought for ready money only; no commodities to be accepted as portions of adventure, but all to be bought by committees appointed; committee of 15 appointed for the direction of the voyage, 6; any adventurer to be employed by the directors in any service, 12; no sum above £10 to be disbursed by the treasurers without a warrant, 24; no gentlemen to be employed, 28; all business in the hands of the governor and committee, 63; committee to devise rules for the prevention of private trade, 124; laws and decrees for the guidance of the traffic of the voyage, 129; committee to devise laws and ordinances for the better guidance of general business, 197; the laws and ordinances devised, 197-202, *see East India Company*.

Rumney, William, adventurer, £200, p. 2; assemblies, 4, 64, 68, 71, 77, 78, 80, 82, 96, 99, 100, 103, 109, 114, 116, 118, 121, 122, 123, 124, 125, 126, 128, 129, 138, 139, 140, 142, 143, 144, 148, 150, 151, 154, 155, 156, 158, 159, 162, 163, 164, 171, 172, 176, 180, 181, 182, 183, 184, 185, 186, 187, 190, 194, 196, 197, 203, 204, 205, 206, 208, 214, 215, 216, 217, 218, 224, 225, 226, 227, 228, 229, 231, 232, 233, 235, 236, 237, 238; committees, 77, 147, 183, 186, 191, 194, 197, 203, 209, 234, 237, 239, 240; appointed treasurer, 7; general committee, 63; elected deputy governor, 111; warrant £42 8s. 11d. for disbursements, 158; on account of Mr. Rumney's bad health and Sir Thomas Smyth being in prison, Mr. Wattes elected governor, 166; elected deputy governor to Mr. Wattes, 179; the oath of office, 179; to receive all contributions for the North West Passage, 195; signatures to treasurers' warrants, 206; warrant £13 19s. 6d. for money delivered to Mr. Burrell, 208; the dislike to Thomas Yerworth, purser, 219; warrant £2 6s. 8d. for boat hire, 224; re-elected deputy governor, 225; orders to Captain Waymouth at Dartmouth to bring his ships round to London, 231; relates the proceedings against Waymouth before the Lords of the Council, 233; thinks that only one ship should be employed in the second North West voyage, 236; being chosen an alderman, resigns the deputy governorship of the company, 239; bill of adventure sealed, £240, p. 255.
Running glasses, 218.
Russell, William, nominated factor, 77.
Russell, William, *butcher*, warrant £111 5s. for beef and pork, 214.
Rutton, William, nominated factor, 77.
Ryalles, }
Ryalls, } *see Royals*.
Ryals, }
Rylance, Humfrey, administrator of Edward Rose, late factor at Aleppo, 278-79.
Ryvelles, Henry, warrant £61 for casks, 146.

Sack wine, 169, 209, 230.
Sailmakers, *see George Barbor*. *Mr. Bolton, John Bowden, Robert Bradbury, Robert Hughes, Hildebrand Sprusen*.
Sails, 163, 167, 168, 220, 221.
St. Mallowes, Royals to be provided there, 51.
Salamon, } Joseph, *purser of the "Susan;"*
Salbanck, } guaranteed by Mr. Bannyng, 33; warrant £100 for the "Susan," 41; order to let Mr. Burrell take men for the "Mare Scourge," 56; warrant 100 marks for the "Susan," 65; do. £80, p. 74; do. £66 13s. 4d., p. 79; do. £120, p. 92; do. £250, p. 108; do. £200, p. 117; do. £100, p. 129; do. £100, p. 148; do. £100, p. 154; bill of adventure sealed, £240, p. 260.
Salbanck, Robert, *see Salbanck, Joseph*.
Salt, estimate of quantity and price, 36; committee to provide 16 tons, 75; warrant £38 for 12 way of salt, 121; warrant for salt for the North West voyage, 208.
Salt beef, 120 oxen to be bought to make, 114.
Salter, Mr., money taken up from his factor for the use of the ambassador at Constantinople, 280.
Salter, Nicholas, assembly, 59; will bring in

INDEX

Salter, Nicholas, *continued.*
his money, 73; general committee, 179; bill of adventure sealed, £240, p. 261.
Salter, Raphe, *surgeon,* warrant £32 for furnishing remedies, &c., 95.
Salter, } Thomas, nominated factor, 77;
Salterne, } elected factor of the second sort, 82; to sail in the "Assention," 101; warrant £50 for his entertainment, 120; bill of adventure sealed, £100, p. 149.
Salters, warrant to pay the Salters' porters for lading, &c., 158; George Bennett, 175.
Saltonstall, Sir Richard, adventurer with his children, £200, p. 3.
Saltpetre, 142.
Sampson, Peter, warrant £44 on bill of exchange, 58.
Sampson, Roberte, bill of adventure sealed, £360, p. 256.
Sandie, *see Sandy.*
Sandy (John), *of Exeter,* bills of exchange for money taken up in the West Country, 58, 70, 83, 84, 102, 106; letter to, respecting the price to be paid for Royals, 66; letter from, as to business in the West Country, 74; letter from, asking for Lord Treasurer's warrant to transport provisions, 78; letter to provide no more bread, 88.
Sandy, } Robert, *Grocer,* adventurer, £200, p.
Sandye, } 1; assemblies, 4, 59, 64, 65, 66, 67, 68, 69, 71, 74, 76, 78, 80, 82, 83, 85, 86, 88, 89, 94, 96, 98, 99, 100, 102, 104, 106, 107, 108, 109, 112, 113, 115, 116, 118, 119, 121, 123, 124, 127, 128, 138, 139, 142, 144, 148, 150, 151, 154, 155, 158, 160, 162, 164, 167, 168, 170, 171, 175, 176; committees, 75, 76, 79, 120, 127, 147; respecting the supply of Royals in the West Country, 57; general committee, 63; letter from Mr. Ellycott as to Royals, 64; reply to Mr. Ellycott, 66; warrant for £300 to be remitted to Exeter, 84; warrant £71 13s. 4d. for charges disbursed for the patent and warrant for coining, 96; recommends William Martin to be employed, 97; iron ordered, 104; orders lead, 105; to provide soap, 107; bill of exchange £100 from John Ellicott, 108; do. £100, p. 109; warrant £128 1s. 8d. for sundries, 115; buys vinegar, 115; to provide prunes, currants, and raisins, 118; to write to Mr. Ellicott and Mr. Pope as to shipping Spanish money now in the West Country, 119; respecting Mr. Skinner's adventure of £200 being received in Royals, 124; buys cheese, 125; to clear accounts with Mr. Peard and Mr. Howe, 127; buys pewter, 129; buys currance, 168; warrant £60 on bill of exchange, 209; bill of adventure sealed, £260, p. 258.
Saunderson, Edmond, *turner,* warrant £18 for turner's work, 157.
Saunderson, John, *merchant in Constantinople,* as to Mr. Bate's account, 268; letters from the Levant Company, 273; 279-80, *see Company of Levant merchants.*
Saundye, *see Sandy.*
Savadge, } Robert, warrant £210 for Canary
Savage, } wine, 104; do. £102 for wastes and deales, 171; do. £3 for a spare mast, 222.
Scanderona, 277.
Scott, Edmond, nominated factor, 77; adventures £200, and is employed in the voyage to choose drugs and spices, 109; made free, though not named in the patent, 177; bill of adventure sealed, £240, p. 257.
Scourge } *ship, see Mare Scourge.*
Scurge }

Seacoals, 210.
Seals, the Signet, Privy Seal, and Great Seal, 107; a Common Seal ordered, 113.
Seaton, a fit place to buy cider, 49.
Secretary of the Company, *see Wright, Richard.*
Security, *see Guarantees, Bonds;* all factors to put in security, 86, 105.
Segar, William, *Herald,* warrant £13 7s. 8d. for writing the Queen's letters to the Kings of the East Indies, 139.
Sething Lane, the great house in, nominated as a warehouse, 245.
Shaw, Leonard, warrant £52 for butter and cheese, 125.
Sheer, } John, *of Exeter,* bill of exchange £25,
Sheir, } p. 106.
Shere, Thomas, *of Exeter,* warrant £60 for money advanced, 125.
Shipping, *see Ships.*
Shipping mark for all goods shipped by the Company, 107.
Ships and shipping, *see "Assention," "Carnation," "Discovery," "Exchange," "Globe," "Godspeed," "Guift," "Hector," "Hercules," "Lioness," "Mare Scourge"* (or "*Red Dragon*"), "*Mayflower,*" "*Newcastleship,*" "*Paragon,*" "*Phoenix,*" "*Prosperous,*" "*Red Dragon*" (or "*Mare Scourge*"), "*Rowe Buck,*" "*Susan*"; *see also Pinnaces, Masters, Mariners, Factors;* no ship to be received as portion of any adventure, 6; all to be bought for ready money only, 6; committee to purchase, &c., 6, 8; ships bought in England by the Dutch, 8; petition to the Privy Council that the shipping when ready be not stayed for any s rvice, 8, 10; ships viewed at Deptford, &c., 13; surveyors appointed, 13; the provision of victuals in the West Country, 15; the surveyors to report the wants of each ship to the committee, and then by their orders supply the same, 21; Mr. Burrell ordered to supply timber, 21; more shipping required and the "Mare Scourge" surveyed, 27; bargains and sales of the ships to be made to feoffees in trust, 32; a computation of quantity and price agreed on for victualling, 34; number of men and tonnage of ships, 34; total bulk and value of provisions, 36; quantity and value of merchandise to be taken, 36-7; Alderman Watts's opinion to be taken on all proceedings, 67; biscuit and fish to be bought to carry the ships to the West Country, 67; order for ships to be "symented vppon ther sheething" before they come out of the docks, 69; number of men to go in each ship, 72; officers and mariners to be engaged by the masters, 78; factors elected, 81-3; committee to hire masters and officers, 87; list of officers engaged, 89; the state of the ships to be discussed at a general court, 92; ships ready, 93; ballast, 97; shipping mark or brand, 107; committee to provide gunners', stewards', cooks', and carpenters' stores, 117; the bargain and sale of the "Susan" sealed at £1,600, p. 120; amount of new and Spanish money apportioned to be carried in each ship and how packed, 122; the Earl of Oxford's runaway servant to be sought for and not allowed to sail in any of the ships, 126; authority for the committee to call on all officers for an account of provisions brought into the ships, 126; committee to see the discharge of the ships from the West Country, 128, 146; all the ships to be examined that

Ships and Shipping, *continued.*
no private merchandise be shipped, 130; the commission to Captain Lancaster to the chief command and others in succession, 132-7, *see Commissions;* ships 100 heavily laden, suggestion for a small ship to accompany the fleet part way and stow the spending provisions; ships to be surveyed at Gravesend before deciding, 141; committee to see the moneys shipped, 142; ships reported overladen, 143; committee to find a small ship to stow the provisions and accompany the fleet part way, 143; £20 paid to Henry Napper, master of the "Hector," for his extraordinary pains in the preparation of the ships, 143; committee to see the discharge of the ships at Gravesend, 147; the "Guift" bought to accompany the fleet with victuals, 147-8; lighterage, wharfage, and porterage, 158; all stores, &c., left behind to be gathered together into a storehouse and sold, 159; £15 allowed to Mr. Burrell for his pains in the providing of timber and surveying the work, 181; pinnaces for the North West Voyages, 182, *see Pinnaces, also North West Passage;* committee to set down the cost of 3 pinnaces, &c., 183; two pinnaces of 50 and 40 tons manned with 16 and 14 men resolved on, 184, 185; no ships for the second voyage by the Cape to be prepared without the consent of a general court, 189; two ships or pinnaces to be employed for the North West Voyage, 199; two ships, the "Godspeed" and the "Discovery" selected and provisioned and furnished for 16 months under Captain Waymouth's own instructions, 211-12; all pursers to deliver the bills of their provisions to Mr. Burrell to receive allowance, 215; the ships for the North West Voyage described as "flyboats," 220, 221; do. pinnaces, 221; several warrants for stores and necessaries for the North West Voyage, 220-24, *see Warrants;* return of the pinnaces to Dartmouth, 227; arrival in the Thames, 229; ordered to be sold, 230, *see North West Passage;* committee to prepare ships for a second North West Voyage, 234, 237; conference as to the practicability of attempting a second North West Voyage with one ship, 236; the idea of a second voyage abandoned and ships ordered to be sold, 239; the sale deferred, 241; ordered to be sold if £300 each can be obtained, 242; the return of the "Assention," 242, *see "Assention";* memoranda of tonnage and men employed, 263; orders for the prevention of private trade on French ships between Aleppo and Marseilles, 272; English ships seized at Venice, 277-78; outrages by English men-of-war in the Levant seas, 280, 282, 283.
Shipton, Thomas, bill of adventure sealed, £240, p. 252.
Shipwrights, *see William Denham, Joseph Pett, Peter Pett, Edward Stephens;* warrant by the Lord Treasurer for taking up shipwrights, 40, 263; committee to settle disputed accounts for timber, 155.
Shirts, 136.
Shirts of mail, warrant £36 10s. 10d. for 22, p. 123.
Shurley, Sir Anthony, his doings in Persia, 272.
Signet, 107.
Silver plate, warrant £69 8s. 2d. for a silver fountain and case, 116; a basin and ewer ordered, also two standing cups and two other pieces, 117; four standing cups ordered, size and price, 118; warrant £183 16s. 3d., p. 127; committee to solicit the Lord Treasurer for a warrant to remove the plate from Mr. Governor's house, 141; list of the plate and other presents, 141; how distributed among the four ships, 151.
Simes, Thomas, *ef Charde,* respecting the providing of Royals in the West Country, 51, 53.
Skelton, James, *chandler,* warrant £9 for tallow, 171; do. £92 10s. for buttter, candles, &c., 219; do. £7 11s. for powder, 221.
Skidmore, William, warrant £333 6s. 8d. for his sixth part of the "Assention," 117.
Skins, levy at Turkish ports to maintain the charges of the ambassador and consuls, 267, 270, 271, 274, 279.
Skinner, } *see Skynner.*
Skynner, } Augustine, adventurer with Roberte Brooke and Thomas Westray, £300, p. 3; assembly, 59; will bring in his money in dollars, 63; ordered to do so, 124; appointed auditor, 218; bill of adventure sealed, £240, p. 257.
Skynners, *see Nicholas Farrer, John Harbie, William Starky;* warrant to pay the porters employed in lading, 158.
Smalwood ( ), *locksmith,* warrant 37s. for lock staples, &c., 223.
Smith, (Sir) Thomas, alderman and governor of the company, *see Smythe.*
Smith, Thomas, warrant 24s. for keeping pinnaces returned from the North West Voyage, 234; do. 24s., p. 240; do. 24s., p. 241; do. 24s., p. 242.
Smithe, Humfrey, }
Smithe, Thomas, } *see Smythe.*
Smithe, William, }
Smithers, *see Smythes.*
Smithery, warrant £100, p. 104; do. £100, p. 104.
Smithes, George, *see Smythes.*
Smiths, *see Roger Frythe, Richard Hart, Justice Mullett, Lewis Tate, Christopher Thompson, William Woodfield;* payment of a smith's bill stopped because he had not paid for his iron, 126, 147.
Smithyes, George, *see Smythes.*
Smyth, Thomas, } *see Smythe.*
Smyth, William, }
Smythe, Humfrey, assembly, 59; bill of adventure sealed, £240, p. 260.
Smythe, John, admitted as an extra factor, 102.
Smythe, (Sir) Thomas, *Haberdasher,* adventurer, £200, p. 3; alderman, first governor of the East India Company, also governor of the Levant Company, *see* 275 and 281; assemblies, 26, 27, 33, 58, [65], 68, 69, 76, 80, 82, 83, 85, 87, 92, 93, 94, 99, 100, 104, 106, 107, 109, 111, 119, 122, 124, 126, 129; committees, 12, 37, 38, 73, 77, 111; elected governor of the company, 62; being still in prison Mr. Watts elected governor in his place, 166; bill of adventure sealed, £360, p. 256; letter to Mr. Dyddell, preacher at Aleppo, 275; signed letter to Mr. Saunderson, merchant at Constantinople, 279-81.
Smythe, William, freedom refused for £105, and ordered to bring in the balance of his adventure, 174-75; bill of adventure sealed, £240, p. 259.
Smythes, George, *Goldsmith,* adventurer, £200, and will pay in Spanish money, 31; warrant £88 16s. 3d. for plate, 127; general committee and sworn, 225; assemblies, 229, 230, 240, 242, 244.

INDEX

Soame, Sir Stephin, Lord Mayor of London, adventurer, £200, p. 1; do. with Richard Carter and Co., £400, p. 1.
Soap ordered, 107.
Sole Privilege, *see Privilege.*
Southacke, } Thomas, committee, 245; bill of
Southewyke, } adventure sealed, £240, p. 251.
Southseas, Captain Waymouth's hope of the discovery of a passage "by divers inlets that treat through the coast of America," 233.
Spain: by reason of the treaty of peace in hand, the East India Company fearing delays, postponed the preparation of their first voyage from October, 1599, to September, 1600, p. 11; the alledged false translation by the French King of the Queen's letter to him respecting the motion of peace with Spain, 282.
Spanish money, *see also Royals, Dollars, West Country, &c.;* two adventures paid in, 31; the amount apportioned to be carried in each ship and how packed, 122.
Spanish Royals, or Ryalles, *see Royals.*
Speake, George, warrant £200 for money provided in the West Country, 66.
Spectacles, 155.
Speeke, *see Speake.*
Spencer, Edmund, bill of adventure sealed, £240, p. 254.
Spencer, Sir John, adventurer, £800, p. 1; assemblies, 109, 176, 181, 177, 244; general committee, 179; takes over the £200 adventure of Robert Bayly for £180, and to have the nomination of a freeman, 181; nominates Joseph Jackson for a freeman, 187; his warehouse suggested for storing the goods brought home in the "Assention," 245; bill of adventure sealed, £360, p. 256.
Spencer, John, *cooper,* warrant £19 6s. for casks, 148.
Spencer, Samuel, to sail as master in the "Susan," 100; warrant £30 on account as agreed, 116; order to receive a barrel of oil, 123.
Spenser, *see Spencer.*
Spices, estimate of quantity for the voyage and price, 35; quantity ordered and committee to purchase, 75; Edmund Scott to go in the voyage in the hope of his service in the choice of drugs and spices, 109; mentioned as one of the articles to be traded in, 198; quantity brought home by the "Assention" and entered at the Custom House, 247.
Spits, 222.
Spruson, Hildebrand, *sailmaker,* warrant £13, p. 168.
Stace ( ), *pilot,* hired for £6 to go with Captain Waymouth to Newcastle, 223.
Stamps, warrant £29 10s. for stamps made for the East India monies, 174.
Stanfeld, John, warrant £110 on bill of exchange, 70.
Staper, } Richard, adventurer, £500, p. 1;
Stapers, } assemblies, 4, 7, 9, 10, 20, 22, 24, 26, 28, 30, 31, 43, 44, 45, 46, 56, 58, 65, 67, 68, 69, 71, 78, 80, 82, 83, 89, 90, 94, 96, 98, 100, 103, 106, 107, 108, 114, 116, 118, 119, 123, 124, 125, 126, 129, 138, 139, 142, 144, 148, 150, 155, 158, 159, 162, 164, 167, 171, 173, 174, 175, 176, 177, 180, 181, 182, 183, 184, 185, 187, 190, 192, 193, 194, 196, 197, 203, 204, 205, 206, 208, 214, 215, 216, 217, 218, 219, 225, 227, 231, 235, 236, 237, 238, 242; committees, 6, 8, 9, 10, 12, 31, 37, 38, 40, 67, 75, 77, 80, 87, 90, 97, 118, 155, 156, 183, 197, 203, 209, 210, 234, 237, 239; views ships, 13; proposes the "Mare Scurge," 20; guarantees George Parsons as purser of the "Hector," 33; commends Richard Babington as a purser, 39; compounds for iron, 41; signature to West Country commission, 52; general committee, 61; letter from Mr. Sandy respecting Spanish money, 66; compounds with William Tavernor, *Mariner,* 68; ordered to bring in his account, 159; receives bond for the payment of Mr. Tailby's adventure, 176; general committee and sworn, 179; do. 223; signature to treasurer's warrant, 206; warrant £28 18s. for hides, 208; warrant £150 to be disbursed for wages, 215; do. £200 for necessaries, &c., 217; do. £40 15s. 8d. for balance of account, 222; do. £7 8s. 8d. for disbursements, 223; bill of adventure sealed, £800 p. 261; a private letter written to Mr. Lyllo, ambassador at Constantinople, as to the complaints made by the French ambassador, 265; *see Company of Levant Merchants.*

Starkey, } William, nominated factor, 77; elect-
Starkie, } ed factor of the second sort, 82; to
Starky, } sail in the "Hector," 101; warrant
Starkye, } £50 for his preparation, 106; bill of adventure £100 sealed, 149; bill of adventure sealed £100, 261.
Starky, William, *Skynner,* bill of adventure with Raphe Allen £400 sealed, 149.
Steel, warrant £40, p. 138.
Steephens, *see Stephens.*
Stephens, Edward, *Carpenter,* warrant £100 for timber for the "Malice Scourge," 74; do. £50 for repairs, 87; do. £50, p. 95; do. £50 for timber, 106; £50 for work on the "Red Dragon," 163.
Stephens, Richard, adventurer, £200, p. 2; assemblies, 4, 30.
Stephens, Robert, warrant £1,100 on bill of exchange from Mr. Ellicott, 56; do. £100, p. 58; do. £1,000, p. 65; do. £900, p. 69; do. £800, p. 102; do. £600, p. 102; do. £500, p. 105; do. £100, p. 108; do. £100, p. 109; do. £100, p. 115.
Stephens, Thomas, appointed book-keeper at a salary of £30, p. 210; re-appointed book-keeper, 226; desires the freedom of the company, but his suit deferred, 227; ordered to charge up all debtors' accounts that the amounts due may be defaulted on their several stocks, 223; warrant £23 6s. 8d. for salary, 235; admitted to the freedom, 239; to make out carmen's tickets for the goods from the "Assention" sent to the Exchange, 248; warrant to pay 56s. to the wife of John May, master's mate of the "Susan," 248; do. £6 for pilotage of the "Assention" into the River, 248.
Stephins, } *see Stephens.*
Stevens, }
Stewards, *see Thomas Bourne or Bowrne?* the number to be employed in each ship, 90; committee to provide stores, 117.
Stile, *see Style.*
Stoackly, John, bill of adventure sealed, £240, p. 250.
Stoane, William, adventurer with William Chambre, £500, p. 2; assembly, 59; bill of adventure sealed £600, p. 254.
Stock, *see adventure.*
Stockfish, 209.
Stone, *see Stoane.*
Storehouses, *see Warehouses,* for the gathering together of things left behind by the ships, 159.
Stoves, for the North West Voyage, 209.

T T

Stradling, } Christopher or Percival, elected fac-
Stragling, } tor of the fourth sort, 83; to sail in the "Red Dragon," 101; warrant £20 for his preparation, 119; bill of adventure sealed, £40, p. 152.
Straits of Magelano, 183.
Stratford, Anthonie, bill of adventure sealed, £240, p 257.
Stratford, Richard, warrant £50 on bill of exchange, 83.
Stratford, Robert, bill of adventure sealed, £240, p. 258.
Streamers, ancients and flags, 108, 149, 163.
Style, Humfrey, assembly, 59; bill of adventure sealed, £240, p. 252.
Style, Nicholas, *Grocer*, adventurer, £200, p. 2; assemblies, 4, 7; appointed director, 6; committee, 8.
Style, Oliver, *Grocer*, adventurer, £300, p. 2; assemblies, 59, 64, 65, 67, 68, 71, 74, 76, 79, 80, 82, 83, 85, 88, 89, 90, 91, 92, 93, 94, 95, 96, 98, 99, 100, 102, 103, 104, 107, 108, 109, 112, 113, 115, 116, 118, 119, 124, 143, 144, 151, 154, 156, 159, 173, 175, 176, 204, 242; committees, 77, 107, 117, 124, 147, 191. 203; general committee, 63; respecting Roger Style, 86; adventures £200 on behalf of Roger Style, 105; appointed auditor, 166, 218; bill of adventure sealed, £560, p. 253.
Style, Persevall, seeks to be employed, 65.
Style, Roger, seeks to be employed; nominated a factor, 77; offers to serve as factor without salary, also to reside in the East Indies and learn the language, 86; appointed third factor in the "Assention," 101; to take the place of Richard Collymore, 105; Oliver Style adventures £200 on his behalf, 105; warrant £30 for his preparations, 108; do. £30 for his entertainment, 120; bill of adventure sealed, £50, p. 149; bill of adventure £40 sealed, 153; letter received from him from the East Indies, by which good hope is conceived of the success of the voyage and encouragement given for another voyage for further discoveries, &c., 243; order to attend on board the "Assention" till ship is discharged, 246; bill of adventure sealed, £40, p. 262.
Suckley, Mr., Lord Treasurer's secretary. 85.
Sugar, estimate of quantity of price, 35; quantity ordered and committee to purchase, 75; warrant £27 6s. 6d., p. 149.
Suger, Jerome, adventurer with Clement Moseley, £250, p. 2.
Sumatra, 194, 198.
Supplies, *see Adventures, also Levies*.
Sureties, *see Security, Guarantees*, all factors to put in, 86.
Surgeons, *see also Medicine*, the number to be carried in each ship, 90; warrant £32 to Raphe Salter for furnishing his medicine chest, 95; do. £25 to James Lovering of the "Hector," 98; do. £20 to Christopher Newchurch of the "Assention," 98; do. £20 to John Gamond of the "Susan," 98.
Surveyors for the ships "Hector," "Assention," and "Susan," 14; power with the advice of the carpenters to supply all defects and repairs, 14; Mr. Burrell appointed general surveyor, 21; all surveyors to report the wants of their ships to the committee, and then by their orders to supply the same, 22; for the "Mare Scourge," 27, 29, 32.
Susan, *ship*, 240 tons, 80 men; Samuel Spencer, *Master*; John May, *Master's Mate*; John Havard, *Principal Factor*; Henry Middleton, *Second Factor*; William Wilford. *Third Factor*; Thomas Morgan, *Fourth Factor*; John Gamond, *Surgeon*; Peter Fenton, *Carpenter*; viewed, 13; chosen and bought with her furniture of Alderman Banning, for £1,600, p. 13; surveyors appointed, 14; inventory, 17; Joseph Salaman, the purser, guaranteed by Mr. Kannyng, 33; rated 80 men, tonnage 240, p. 34; proportion of aquavitæ, 35; order to the purser to give up any men required to complete the "Mare Scourge," 56; warrant £50 on account of repairs, 57; do. 100 markes, 65; to be manned with 80 men, 72; warrant £50 for timber, 79; do. £66 13s. 4d. for necessaries and wages, 79; the number of carpenters, caulkers, gunners, stewards, cooks, surgeons, and barbers, to be employed, 89-90; John Havard to sail as principal factor, 94; warrant £20 to John Gamond, *Surgeon*, for furnishing his medicine chest, 98; officers appointed, 100; factors appointed, 101; warrant £250 for necessaries, 108; warrant £30 to Samuel Spencer, *Master*, on account, 116; Peter Francis, a Portugal, to sail in the "Susan," wages £5 a month, 117; committee to provide stores, 117; warrant £250 for men's wages, 117; the bargain and sale of the ship made absolute, and sealed at £1,600, p. 120; abuses and overcharges by the carpenter for masts, 121, 157; amount of new and Spanish money to be carried and how packed, 122; a barrel of oil allowed to the master, 123; warrant £100 to the purser for charges, 129; being found overladen, a committee appointed to find a small ship to accompany the fleet part way, 143, *see* 141; warrant £100 to the purser for clearing the ship, 148; list of presents to be carried, 152; warrant £100 for wages and for clearing away the ship, 154; do. £30 12s. 4d. for gunners' stores, 157; do. £100 for timber, &c., 157; do. £6 16s. 8d. for porterage and lading, 158; do. £27 5s. for sails, 167; do. £71 15s. for timber, 172; do. £227 for iron work, 173; do. 30s. to Faith May in part of wages of John May, *Master Mate*, 224; do. 56s. to the wife of John May for a month of his wages, 248; memorandum, 240 tons, 80 men. 263.
Suzan, John, adventurer with Samewell Garrard, £200, p. 4.
Swinerton, } John, junior, alderman, adventu-
Swynerton, } rer, £300, p. 4; assembly, 244; bill of adventure sealed, £360, p 252.
Symondes, } Thomas, adventurer, £200, p. 1;
Symonds, } assemblies, 4, 7, 9, 10, 180; appointed director, 6; committees, 8, 10; warrant £6 13s. 4d., p. 117; respecting the account with John Hedland, 163; appointed auditor, 166; general committee, 179; bill of adventure sealed, £240, p. 258.
Symonds, } Nicholas, *Carpenter*, assembly,
Symondson, } 30; warrant £50 for timber for
Symons, } the "Susan," 79; do. £80, p.
Symonson, } 92; do. £100, p. 157; do. £71 15s, p. 172: do. for work on the "Discovery," &c., £71 13s.
Syms, *see Simes*.
Synamon, *see Cinnamon*.

Tailby, } Richard, assembly, 59; promises to
Tailbye, } pay £73 6s. 8d. to Mr. Atye, and
Taileby, } £100 to the Muscovia Company as part payment of his adventure, 176; committees, 245, 246; bill of adventure sealed, £240, p. 256.

Tailor, Francis, *Vintner*, warrant £18 for claret, 169;
Talbutt, Thomas, bill of adventure sealed, £240, p. 250.
Tallow, 171.
Tar, committee to provide casks, 76; ordered to be bought of Browne & Co., 121.
Tate, Lewis, *Smith*, warrant £100 for smith's work, 104; do. £100, p. 163; do. £227, p. 173.
Tavernor, William, *Mariner*, compounds for his employment at £6 per month, 68.
Taylby, *see Tailby*.
Tayler, } Francis, appointed auditor, 218; bill of
Taylor, } adventure sealed, £240, p. 260.
Taylor, John, adventurer, £200, p. 77 : nominated factor, 77.
Tayte, *see Tait*.
Terrell, Fraunces, adventurer, £200, p. 2
Thames, River, the return of the ships from the North West, 229; the return of the "Assention," 244, *see also Gravesend, Woolwich, Deptford, &c.*
Thomas, William, warrant 26s. for lanthornes, 223.
Thompson, } Christopher, *Smith*, warrant £50
Thomson, } for ironwork for the "Hector," 195; do. £60, p. 111; do. £100, p. 149; do. £34 4s. 2d., p. 163; do. £22 6s., p. 221; do. 13s. 10d. for plates, 224.
Thurston, John, master of the ship "Carnation," 263.
Timber, Mr. Burrell ordered to supply, 21, 46, 89; warrant £100, p. 47; do. £100, p. 74; do. £100, p. 86; quantity borrowed from Her Majesty's storehouse at Woolwich for the repairs of the "Scourge," 71; warrant £50 for the "Susan," 79; do. £80, p. 92; do. £80, p. 92; do. £50 for the "Red Dragon," 106; do. £100 for the "Hector" and "Assention," 114; committee to agree with the carpenters on the disputed prices of timber, 124; committee to agree with Mr. Ady and other shipwrights, 155; warrant £100 for the "Susan," 157; do. £50, p. 164; do. £102 for the wastes and deales, 171; do. £71 15s. for the "Susan," 172; arbitrators appointed to agree on Mr. Adye's account, 173; warrant £16 16s. 11d. for timber, &c., for the "Assention," 180; £15 allowed to Mr. Burrell for his paines in the providing of timber and surveying the work, 181; warrant for timber for the "Discovery," 221.
Tin, quantity to be sent out in the ships and price, 36; committee to provide, 79; duty at Constantinople and Aleppo to support the ambassador's and consuls' charges, 267, 270, 271, 274, 279.
Tithes due to the Lord Admiral on a prize taken in the East Indies, 246-7.
Tonnage of ships and number of men for the East India voyage, 34, 263; do. for the North West Voyage, 184, 185.
Toomes, Mr., assembly, 227 (? Coombes).
Toppesfelde, Mr., offers the ship "Phenixe."
Tower of London, as to coining, 78; bullion stored there, 87; coining, 114, 120.
Towerson, Robert, disfranchised, 178.
Trade, the chief articles of trade in the East Indies, 198; the object of the attempt to discover a North West Passage was to open up trade in English merchandise with China and other temperate climates, 199.
Treasurer, Lord, *see Lord Treasurer*.
Treasurers, *see also Warrants, Bannyng,*

Holliday, Cambell, and Chamberlaine, *&c.* John Highlord and William Romney elected, 7; immediate levy of 12d. per £100 for petty charges, 7; to pay all sums by warrants signed by four of the committee, but not to disburse above £10 without a warrant, 24; Mr. Bannyng elected, 25; committee appointed to audit the accounts, 107, 156, 166; Mr. Bannyng and Mr. Holliday desired to borrow £1,500 at interest on their own credits, 146; the state of the accounts on March 6, 1600-1, showing amount of debts and amount of adventure not yet brought in, 156; indemnity for the money borrowed at interest, 161; conference as to money in hand to pay debts, 167; to deliver bills of adventure to all who have cleared their adventures and supplies and to charge 6d. each for the same, 175; Mr. Alderman Cambell appointed treasurer for the North West Voyage, 200; the treasurer for the North West voyage not to receive any contributions after the end of March, 1602, without the consent of a general court, 208; Mr. Robert Chamberlaine elected, 226; the cashiers ordered to be reimbursed for money lost in the receiving and paying of money, 227; Mr. Holliday ordered to bring in £38 6s. 9d. balance of his accounts and the sum of eight or nine pounds disbursed by his wife not allowed, 231.
Trowbridge, Thomas, money in the West Country, 73.
Tucker, Daniel, nominated factor, 77.
Tudd, Thomas, nominated factor, 77; elected factor of the fourth sort, 83; to sail in the "Hector," 101; warrant £20 for his preparations, 122; bill of adventure sealed, £40, p. 153.
Turkey, trade in, 268; the trade by the Dutch, 270, 273; duties on certain goods entering Turkish ports to maintain the charges of the ambassador and consuls, 271; Mr. Coltherst's favour with the Bashaw, 272.
Turner, Edward, adventurer with William Turner, £200, p. 3.
Turner, James, adventurer with John Buzbridge, £200, p. 3; assembly, 59; committee, 246; bill of adventure sealed, £240. p. 254.
Turner, William, adventurer with Edward Turner, £200, p. 3; assembly; warrant £24 for money supplied in Plymouth, 64; bill of adventure sealed, £240, p. 258.
Turnery, 157.
Turnor, *see Turner*.
Tyght, Lewys, *Blacksmith*, warrant £100 for ironwork, 157.
Tyler, Thomas, *Painter*, warrant £13 6s. 8d. for work done, 221.

Uffington, William, warrant £86 for wax candles, 142.
Utley, George, disfranchised, 178.

Vale, Richard, warrant £24 19s. for spectacles, &c., 155.
Value, of the original adventures subscribed, 4; of the provisions for the voyage, 36; of the merchandise to be sent out, 37; of the goods brought home by the "Assention," 247.
Vaults under the Exchange used as a warehouse, 245, 248.
Venice, bills of exchange from the ambassador at Constantinople, 266, 271; petition to the Privy Council respecting the Levant Company's ships seized at Venice as restitution

Venice, *continued*.
for the late prize taken by English men-of-war, 277-8, *see also* 280, 282, 284.
Victuals, *see also Bread, Butter, Beer, Beef, Pork, Cheese, Peas, Wine, Oil, &c., &c.* The providing of, in the West Country, 15, 21; Captain Davies ordered to draw out a proportion for 500 men, 22; Captain Davies presents his estimate, which is referred to a committee, 26; peas, 26, 29; a commission to be prepared for Captain Davies, 28; committee appointed to go to the West Country and purchase, 29; the quantity of caske required for victuals, &c., 30; a computation agreed on for the victualling of the ships, quantity and price, 34-6; total bulk and value, 36; commission for Captain Baker to purchase, 38, 54; the quantities to be provided in the West Country, 41, 52, 54-5; prices to be certified, 49; commission for Captain Davies to purchase, 52-4; bills of exchange for the purchases in the West Country, *see Warrants*; letters of advice as to business in the West Country, 64; Admiral Wattes joined to the committee on victuals, 70; committee to review the estimate and the progress of the victualling, 72; quantities required and committees to purchase, 75-6; commissions given to the committees to purchase, 77; committee to solicit Lord Treasurer's warrant for transporting provisions in the West Country, 78; all ready for the voyage, 93; £50 paid to Robert Pope for his pains in the West Country, 101; committee to attend to the shipping of in the West Country, 120; the committee authorized to call on all officers for an account of all provisions supplied, 126; the ships appearing overladen it is suggested that a small ship be bought to stow part of the provisions and accompany the fleet part way, 141; the "Guift" bought, 147-8; all stores, &c., left behind to be gathered together and sold, 159; warrant £22 4s. for chaundler's provisions, 164; three committees appointed for the provision of victuals and other necessaries for the North West voyage, 209; the North West ships victualled, &c., after Captain Waymouth's own desires, 211-12; various warrants for stores for the North West voyage, 217-21; the stores returned from the North West voyage to be preserved for a second voyage, 228; certain provisions to be sold, 230; all ordered to be sold, 239.
Vinegar, 30 tonne of caske required, 30; estimate of quantity and price, 35; price and quantity in the West Country to be ascertained, 49; committee to provide, 76; do. casks for, 76; warrant £70 for 7 tons, 114; do. £25 10s., and £20, p. 115; do. £14 12s., p. 116; committee to provide for the North West voyage, 209.
Vintners, *see Mr. Crosse, Francis Cheric, Thomas Farrington, Francis Tailor*.
Voyage, first by the Cape to the East Indies, *see also Adventurers, East India Company, Ships, Pursers, &c.* Committee for the general direction of the voyage, 6, 63; Oct. 1599, the voyage postponed for a year, 11; September, 1600, on receiving the royal assent the preparation of the voyage determined on and committee appointed for its direction, 11, 12; Captain Davies principal director, 25; victuals, 22, 26, 28, *see Victuals*; merchandise, 26, &c., *see Merchandise;* more shipping required, 27; no gentlemen to be employed, 28; number of men and tonnage of ships, 34; quantity and value of provisions, 34-6; do. of merchandise, 36-7; number of men to go in each ship, 72; the hindrance and damage to the voyage by reason of certain persons not bringing in their adventure, 110; action of the Privy Council to compel adventurers to bring in their sums subscribed, 112-13; the amount of money apportioned to be carried in each ship and how packed, 122; all things to be managed as a joint stock and no private trade to be practised, 130; the commissions for the general or principal merchants, 132-7, *see Commissions;* ships appearing too heavily laden, suggestion for a small ship to accompany the fleet part way and stow the provisions, 141; Mr. Hacklett paid £10 for his advice and instructions, 30s. for 3 maps, 143; forms of the bills of adventure, 145; the return of the "Assention," *see "Assention."*
Voyage, second by the Cape to the East Indies. A second voyage proposed, 182; Mr. Governor to peruse the charters to see if power is given to compel any one to contribute to a second voyage, 183; a second voyage resolved on and a book to be sent round that adventurers may set down their contributions under their own hands, and not less than £100 to be received, 186; the title or preface to the book agreed on and ordered to be sent round to all the freemen, 187; the total subscribed amounts to only £11,000, which is insufficient, 189; enquiries by the Lord Admiral and Mr. Secretary as to the cause of the great delay in the second voyage as compared with the Dutch, 189-90; letter from the Privy Council notifying Her Majesty's mislike to the delays, and propounding the example of the Dutch, 191; a general court convened to deal with the matter and a penalty of 20s. imposed for non-attendance, 191.
Voyage to discover the North West Passage, *see North West Passage, Waymouth, East India Company, &c.*

Wages, *see also Warrants, Agreements*. Pursers 40s. the month at sea, and 20s. and board wages in harbor, 116; in the North West voyage contingent on the discovery of the passage, 205; agreement with Waymouth, 214; do. with Thomas Cartwright, preacher, for the North West voyage, 216; do. with Edward Pullison, *purser*, 216; covenant for the payment of the wages of John Drew, master of the "Godspeed," 220-1.
Walcott, Humfrey, assembly, 59, 229, 232, 233, 238, 240, 241, 244; general committee and sworn, 226; bill of adventure sealed, £240, p. 252.
Waldo, Laurence, assembly, 59; recommends Francis Wilson as a purser, 27; warrant £50 to be repaid at Exeter, 55; do. £25, p. 106; bill of adventure sealed, £240, p. 251.
Waldo, Robert, assembly, 59; bill of adventure sealed, £240, p. 252.
Walker, Edward, bill of adventure sealed, £240, p. 258.
Wallcott, *see Walcott*.
Walter, William, ordered to be gratified with £20 (? 20s.) for dedicating to the company the book of the Flemynges Voyage, 125.
Walthall, William, warrant £224 2s. for lead, 95.

INDEX

Walton, Richard, warrant £40 on bill of exchange, 84.
Wapping, 223.
Warde, Thomas, admitted as an extra factor, 102.
Warehouses, for the beef and pork returned from the North West voyage, 230; for the goods brought home in the "Assention," 245; committee to prepare the vaults under the Exchange, 248; committee to see the goods sent to the warehouses, 248; committee to receive and weigh the goods, 248.
Warner, Robert, warrant £100 for iron, 104; do. £43 16s. 6d. for glasses, 129.
Warrants. No sum above £10 to be disbursed by the Treasurers without a warrant, 24; warrant to take up shipwrights, 40; Lord Treasurer's warrant for the transport of peas and beans from Norfolk and Cambridge, 66; do. from the West Country, 78, 79; warrant for coining, 78; charges on the warrant for coining, &c., 96; warrant summoning the adventurers who have not brought in their payments, 169-70; two warrants warning defaulting adventurers to appear before the the Privy Council to answer for their contempt, 173; warrant to take up carpenters, 263.
Warrants entered in Mr. Allabaster's book: £300 to John Busbridge for iron, 111; £100 to William Dixon, Purser of the "Dragon," 111; £60 to Xpofer Thompson, *smith*, for the "Hector," 111; £100 to Mr. Wyseman for the "Hector," 111; £20 to Nicholas Lynge for charges, 111; £213 6s. 8d. to Andrew Bannyng for oil, 111; £100 to William Dixon for the "Hector," 111.
Warrants to the Treasurer (no name): £100 to Mr. Wiseman for necessaries for the "Hector," 25; £100 to Mr. Chambers for casks and iron hoopes, 33; £100 to do. for casks and iron hoopes, 56; £30 to William Kempe on a bill of exchange from Captain Baker, 80; £20 to Mr. Governor to gratify William Walter, who dedicated to the Company the book of the "Flemyngs" voyage, 125; £2 to Mr. Worsenham, *Searcher*, for clearing the ships, 156.
Warrants per Mr. Banning, Treasurer : £4 to Mr. Altham for making the draft of the patent, 25; £500 to Mr. Howe, to be sent into the West Country for purchases, &c., 29; £200 to Captain Lancaster and Mr. Chambers for iron work and caske, 41; £100 to Joseph Salamon, necessaries for the "Susan," 41; £600 to Francis Elington for cloth, 45; £1,000 to the Earl of Cumberland on account of the purchase of the "Mare Scurge," 45; £100 to Mr. Burrell for timber, 47; £20 to Captain Davis for travelling expenses, 47; £50 to Laurence Waldo for a bill of exchange on Exeter, 55; £100 to Henry Middleton, Purser, for charges about the "Scourge," 56; £1,100 to Robert Stephens on bill of exchange from Exeter, 56; £200 to Mr. Coles on bill of exchange from the West Country, 57; 100 markes to Mr. Garway on account of the repairs of the "Assention," 57; £50 on account of the repairs of the "Susan," 57; £50 to John Purnell for Royals delivered at Plymouth, 64; £24 to William Turner on bill of exchange from Plymouth, 64; £1,000 to the Purser of the "Scourge" on account of repairs, 65; £1,000 to Robert Stevens on a bill of exchange from Exeter, 65; £100 to Richard Wiseman for repairs and provisions for the "Hector," 65; £200 to William Burrell for timber, 65; 100 markes to Joseph Salbancke, *Purser*, for repairs, &c., on the "Susan," 65; £900 to Robert Stephens on two bills of exchange from Exeter, 69; £30 to Thomas Bowles on a bill of exchange from Captain Baker, 69; £110 to John Stanfeld on a bill of exchange from Dartmouth, 70; £100 to Purser of the "Malice Scurge" for preparations, 70; £40 to William Harvy on bill of exchange from Robert Pope, 74; £110 to William Lacy on bill of exchange from Robert Pope, 74; £80 to Joseph Sulman, Purser of the "Scurge," for preparations, 74; £100 to Henry Middleton, Purser of the "Scurge," for preparations, 78; £40 to John Wyndham on a bill of exchange from Robert Pope, 79; £50 to Nicholas Symons for timber for the "Susan," 79; £66 13s. 4d. to Joseph Salbanck for necessaries and wages for the "Susan," 79; £39 to Roger Gibbons on a bill of exchange from Robert Pope, 79; £100 to Richard Wyseman for the Hector's provision, 79; £40 to Thomas Northeover on bill of exchange from Robert Pope, 81; £150 to John Lant on bill of exchange from Robert Pope, 81; £40 to John God on bill of exchange from Robert Pope, 82; £100 to Francis Covell for peas and beans, 82; £500 to Mr. Allabaster for royals of plate, 82; £300 to Mr. Robert Sandy, to be repaid to Mr. John Sandy at Exeter, 84; £100 to Edward Highlord, Purser, on account of repairs of the "Scourge," 87; £112 to William Dale on a bill of exchange from Robert Pope, 88; £120 to Joseph Salbanck, 92; £80 to Nicholas Symondson for timber, 92; £50 to William Angell for fish, 92; £300 to Henry Middleton, Purser, for the provision of the "Scourge," 93; £224 2s. to William Walthall for lead, 95; £100 to Edwin Babington for canary wine, 95; £100 to Francis Covell for beans and peas, 96; £100 to Richard Wyseman on account of the preparation of the "Hector," 96; £73 13s. 4d. to Mr. Attorney and Clerks for drawing and engrossing the patent and warrant for coining, 96; £125 10s. to John Busbridge for linen cloths, 97; £100 to the Pursers of the "Hector" for repairs and preparations, 99; £800 to Robert Stevens on a bill of exchange from John Ellacott, 102; £105 12s. 4d. to Walter Clarck for royals of plate delivered in Exeter, 102; £30 to William Wilford, factor, for his salary, 103; £231 10s. to George Hanger for canary wine, 103; £378 10s. to William Harrison for canary wine, 103; £160 to Edwin Babington for canary wine, 103; £100 to Lewis Tate for smithery, 104; £100 to Henry Middleton, Purser of the "Red Dragon," 104; £50 to Roger Hanckey, Master of the "Assention," on account of his wages, 104; £100 to William Burrell, for the provision of the ships, 104; £40 to John Coles on bill of exchange from Lewis Pope, 104; £200 to Mr. Wyseman for wax candles and provision of the "Hector," 104; £30 to Thomas Dassell for his wages, 104; £100 to William Bradbanck, Master of the "Red Dragon," on account, 104; £150 to John Buzbridge on account of iron, 104; £100 to Robert Warner on account of iron, 104; £100 to Robert Savage for canary wine, 104; £100 to William Chambers towards the provision of caske, 104; £10 5s. 8d. to Henry Lambard for black jacks, 105; £50 to Xpofer Thomson, *Smith*, on account of iron work

Warrants per Mr. Bannyng, *continued.*
for the "Hector," 105; £17 4s. 11d. to Francis Covell in full of provisions made by him, 105; £50 to William Dixson, Purser of the "Red Dragon," for the use of the ship, 105; £500 to Robert Stephens on account of £700 taken up in royalles of plate, 105; £200 to Edward Highlord, Purser of the "Red Dragon," for preparations, 106; £50 to Edward Stephens on account of timber for the "Red Dragon," 106; £700 to Mr. Allabaster on account of £880 bills of exchange for royalles, 106; £96 8s. to John Gover for aquavitæ, 107; £250 to Joseph Salbanck, Purser of the "Susan," for necessaries, 108; £30 to Roger Style, factor, being the allowance for his provisions, 108; £100 to John Ady, Carpenter, on account of timber for the "Hector" and "Assention," 114; £80 to William Fisher for candy oil, 114; £70 to William Harrison for vinegar, 114; £200 to Thomas Babar on account of canvas for the ships, 114; £133 6s. 8d. to Robert Rickman for his sixth part of the "Assention," 115; £128 1s. 8d. to Robert Sandy for sundry disbursements, 115; £200 to Robert Stevens on bills of exchange, &c., 115; £500 to Sir Hugh Portman on a bill of exchange from Robert Pope, 115; £333 6s. 8d. to William Skidmore for his sixth part of the "Assention," 117; £200 to Joseph Salbanck to be employed on the "Susan," 117; £67 0s. to Henry Plompton for rope oil, 119; £30 to Roger Style, factor, for his entertainment, 120; £250 to William Dixon, Purser, for the preparation of the "Red Dragon," 120; £6 13s. 4d. to —— Bradley for ballast, 121; £36 10s. 10d. to Mr. Wattes for 22 shirts of mail, 123; £20 1s. to Thomas Parkins for 32 jars of honey, 125; £52 to Leonard Shaw for butter and cheese, 125; £20 to Thomas Morgan, factor, for his provision to sea, 126; £180 to John Lacy for cordage bought of the Muscovia Company, 126; £300 to John Davies, Pilot Major, for his salary, 127; £200 to William Dixon, Purser of the "Red Dragon," on account of her provisions, 127; £100 to Joseph Salbanck, Purser of the "Susan," for the provision of the voyage, 129; £36 to Alderman Watts for iron hoops, 129; £207 to Frances Parrett for Norromborough ware, 138; £11 1s. to George Davyes for chests, 138; £200 to Captain Lancaster as per agreement, 139; £11 to Captain Lancaster for so much laid out by him, 139; £200 to William Dickson, Purser of the "Red Dragon," on account of her provision, 139; £78 16s. 4d. to Thomas Perkins, Couper, for caske, 143; £20 to Henry Napper, Master of the "Hector," for his extraordinary pains in the preparation of that ship, 143; £100 to Joseph Salbanck, Purser of the "Susan," for the clearing away of the ship, 148; £19 16s. 4d. to John Spencer, *Cooper*, for caske, 148; £27 6s. 6d. to Robert Myddleton for sugar, 149; £100 to Nicholas Symondson for timber and planks for the "Susan," 157; £14 7s. 2d. to Mr. Highlord for disbursements, 162; £12 to Thomas Duck for streamers, 163; £50 to Edward Stephens, Shipwright, for work on the "Red Dragon," 163; £50 to Adam Wood for deals, masts, and timber, 163-4; £27 5s. to George Barber for sails for the "Susan," 167; £4 0s. 8d. to John Crane for pulleys, 167; £46 17s. to George Bowles, *Grocer*, for currance, 168; £6 to William Denham, Shipwright, in part of his bill, 169; £9 15s. to James Marshe for deales and planckes, 169; £22 4s. to Francis Covell, *Chaundeler*, for provisions for the "Assention," 169; £18 to Francis Tailor, *Girdeler*, for a tun of claret wine, 169; £9 to Jeames Skelton for tallow, 171; £500 to Abraham Campion on account of beer, 171; £71 15s. to Nicholas Symonson, Carpenter, in full for timber, 172; £39 16s. 6d. to Richard Wryte in full payment of his account for disbursements, 173; £16 16s. 11d. to William Brett for timber, &c., for the "Assention," 180; £16 10s. to Symon Turner for powder, 184; £57 16s. 8d. to Benjamin Decro, agent of the Muskovia Company, for cordage, 187; £39 2s. 4d. to Abraham Campion for the rest of his account for beer, 193.

Warrants per Mr. Cambell, Treasurer of the North West Voyage: £30 to Captain Waymouth to provide his instruments, 204; £30 to do. for provisions for the voyage, 204; £20 to do. to provide needful instruments, 204; £5 to John Drewe, a master to go in the North West Voyage, as an advance on his wages agreed on, 206; £80 to Thomas Yerworth, purser, for clearing carpenters' wages, 206; £54 18s. to Austyn Bandicott, *Butcher*, for pork, 208; £30 to Thomas Yerworth, purser, to be paid to workmen at Ratcliffe and Lymehouse, and for salt and mariners' board wages, 208; £28 18s. to Richard Staper for hides to make the mariners' cassocks, breeches, and gowns, 208; £13 19s. 6d. to Mr. Rumney for so much delivered by his servant to Mr. Burrell in gildernes, 208; £60 to Mr. Sandy on bill of exchange, for so much taken up at Exeter by Captain Waymouth for the hiring of mariners, 209; £100 to Thomas Yarworth, purser of the "Discovery," for anchors and other necessaries, 210; £10 to John Drewe, Master of the "Godspede," in part of his wages, 210; £100 to Thomas Yerworth, purser, for sea coals, wood, lead, and divers other necessaries, 210; £100 to Captain Waymouth by parcels, as he shall call for it, for men's wages, &c., 211; £111 3s. to William Russell, *Butcher*, for beef and pork, 214; £150 to William Chambers for cloth and other necessaries, 215; £150 to Nicholas Leat for further necessaries, 215; £150 to Mr. Staper to disburse for wages as called for, 215; £60 to Joseph Page, Baker, for biskett, 215; 100 to Thomas Yerworth for necessary provisions, 215; £100 to William Chambers for necessary provisions, 217; £200 to Richard Stapers for necessaries and disbursements, 217; £50 to Captain Waymouth for his expenses attending the preparation of the voyage, 218; £30 to Robert Grynken for watches, compasses, running glasses, and instruments, 218; £20 to Mr. Leat for mariners' clothes, 218; £50 11s. 8d. to John Davies, *Cooper*, for casks, 218; £7 8s. to Adam Wood for deals, oars, &c., 218; £6 10s. to William Woodfield, *Smith*, for iron hoops, 219; £29 18s. to Thomas Robinson for cables and skeytes, 219; £92 10s. to Mr. Skelton, *Chaundler*, for butter, candles, powder, &c., 219; £11 6s. 8d. to Mr. Johnson for bay salt, 219; £143 to Thomas Barber for canvas for sails for the two flyboats for the North

INDEX

Warrants per Mr. Cambell—*continued*.
West voyage, 220; £32 10s. to Robert Hewhes, *Sailmaker*, for making sails, 221; £9 10s. to Arnold Mabancke for pullies, 221; £13 6s. 8d. to Thomas Tyler, *Painter*, for work done on the pinnaces, 221; £19 to Roger Frythe, *Smith*, for iron work for ships' stores, 221; £26 to Richard Hall, *Blacksmith*, for iron work, 221; £3 8s. to George Gryce, *Carriage Maker*, 221; £22 6s. to Xpofer Thompson, *Smith*, for iron work, 221; £12 to William Denham for pullies, 221; £120 3s. to Abraham Campion for beer, 221; £58 13s. to Nic. Symonson, *Carpenter*, for work on the "Discovery," 221; £13 to do. do. for timber and a boat, 221; £7 11s. to Mr. Skelton for powder for the pinnaces, 221; £4 15s. to Richard Wright for charges on procuring the Queen's letters, 222; £34 7s. 10d. to Xpofer and Thomas Nicholls for cordage, 222; £3 to Mr. Savage for a spare mast, 222; £40 15s. 8d. to Richard Stapers, due to him, as appears by his audited account, 222; 30s. 8d. to William Deyns, *Ironmonger*, for spits, &c., 222; £17 17s. to John Makesfield, *Brasier*, for pots of brass, copper kettles, &c., 222; £41 8s. to Joseph Page for biskett and biskett bags, 222; £42 to Alderman Watts for iron hoops, 222; £4 7s. to Tristram Eldrich for mariners' lodgings, &c., 222; £2 3s. to Peter Wright for lanthorns, &c., 223; 26s. to William Thomas for lanthorns, &c., 223; 37s. to William Smalwood for locks, staples, &c., 223; £52 to Joseph Pett, *Shipwright*, for work on the "Godspeed," 223; 28s. 8d. to Richard Stapers, amount disbursed by him to John Franklyn for carrying a letter to Captain Waymouth in the Downs, 223; £6 to Richard Staper, the amount disbursed to one Stace, a pilot hired to go with the captain to Newcastle, 223; £5 10s. to William Hedger of Wapping for a boat for the "Discovery," 223; £51 3s. 3d. to Nicholas Leat for money laid out in merchandise, 223; £129 9s. to John Fletcher for cordage, 224; £3 to William Kymber for wharfage, 224; 30s. to Faith May, wife of John May, master's mate on the "Susan," 224; 13s. 10d. to Xpofer Thomson for plates for the pinnaces, 224; £8 8s. to William Edward, *Plumber*, for lead, &c., 224; £2 to John Watts for iron hoops, 224; 46s. 8d. to Mr. Rumney for boat hire, &c., 224.

Warrants per Mr. Chamberlaine: £6 13s. 4d. to Tristram Eldred, purser, for his pains taken on the Company's affairs, 226; £6 to John Bowen for six quarters' rent of Founders Hall for the Company's meetings, 227; to pay mariners hired at Dartmouth to bring the pinnaces to London, 231; 24s. to Thomas Smith for keeping the pinnaces, 234; £5 to John Drew, Master of the "Godspeed," for wages in the late North West voyage, 234; 30s. to John Lane for wages in the late North West voyage, 234; £3 to Thomas Bearne for wages in the late North West Voyage, 234; £2 6s. 8d. to Thomas Branskom for wages in the late North West voyage, 234; £6 13s. 4d. to Thomas Yerworth, *Purser*, for wages and expenses, 235; £23 6s. 8d. to Thomas Stevens, *Accountant*, for three quarters' salary, 235; £4 to the porters for landing and housing of stores from the North West ships, 238; 25s. 7d. to Thomas Evesed for disbursements, 238; 24s. to Thomas Smith for keeping the pinnaces two months, 240; £6 to Edward Pullyson, *Purser*, in full of his account and for wages, 240; 20s. to the wife of Thomas Bowrne, steward of the "Godspeed," in full of all demands, 240; 24s. to Thomas Smith for keeping the pinnaces two months, 241; 24s. to Thomas Smith for keeping the pinnaces two months, 242.

Warrants per Mr. Chambers: 34s. 3d. to Captain Mydleton as by a bill of particulars, 142.

Warrants per Mr. Holliday, Treasurer: £100 to the purser of the "Scourge," 45; £700 to the Earl of Cumberland on account of the "Mare Scurge," 45; £200 to Sergeant Hill for a bill of exchange on Plymouth, 55; £30 to Philip Grove on account of his wages, 56; £120 to Francis Evington on a bill of exchange from the West Country, 56; £50 to Nicholas Holway on a bill of exchange from Robert Pope, 58; £1,000 to Robert Stephens on a bill of exchange from John Ellacott of Exeter, 58; £44 to Peter Sampson on a bill of exchange from John Sandy of Exeter, 58; £200 to George Speake on a bill of exchange from Robert Pope, 66; £500 to Mr. Allabaster for the provision of royals of plate, 68; £400 to Sir Hugh Portman on bill of exchange from Robert Pope, 68; £200 to Ellys Cryspe on bill of exchange from Plymouth, 68; £70 to Peter Grove in full of his agreement, 71; £50 to William Harvy on bill of exchange from Robert Pope, 73; £100 to James Prockter on bill of exchange from Robert Pope, 73; £100 to Edward Stephens for timber for the "Malice Scurge," 74; £200 to Mr. Burrell for the preparation of the shipping, 74; £50 to Richard Stratford on a bill of exchange from Exeter, 83; £500 to John Ellecott on a bill of exchange from Exeter, 83; £100 to Edward Highlord, purser, for the preparation of the "Scourge," 84; £40 to Richard Walton on a bill of exchange from Exeter, 84; £60 to Richard Rudd on a bill of exchange from Exeter, 84; £50 to Nicholas Ranton on a bill of exchange from Exeter, 84; £40 to Richard Gregory on a bill of exchange from Robert Pope, 84; £70 to William Mallett on a bill of exchange from Robert Pope, 85; £200 to William Garway for the preparation of the "Assention," 85; £100 to William Burrell for timber and necessaries for the ships, 86; £50 to Edward Stephens, Carpenter, for repairs to the "Scourge," 87; £200 to John Portman, to be paid to Robert Pope in the West Country, 87; £100 to the purser of the "Hector" on account of repairs, 88; £4 in recompence to a poor man for bulging his crane with the "Scourge's" anchor, 88; £100 to John Colles, to be repaid to Robert Pope in the West Country, 88; £100 to Captain Lancaster, on account for his entertainment in the voyage, 89; £172 7s. 9d. for meal bought of Mr. Gawldsmith, 90; £50 to Mr. Allabaster for Royals; £100 to Mr. Garway for the provision of the "Assention," 91; £100 to Mr. Chambers for the provision of caske, 92; £80 to Mr. Burrell for timber and other necessaries, 93; £500 to Mr. Allabaster for royals, 95; £50 to Edward Stephens, Carpenter, on account of repairs of the "Scourge," 95; £32 to Raphe Salter, Surgeon, for his medicine chest, 95; £28 14s. to William and George Cater for

Warrants per Mr. Holliday, *continued*.
roan cloths, 97; £36 0s. 4d. to Roger Hankin, Master of the "Assention," for ballast and charges on two hoyes to go to the ships, 97; £100 to the purser of the "Assention" for repairs and preparations, 99; £600 to Robert Stevens and Roger Howe on a bill of exchange from John Ellacott, 102; £241 to Francis West on a bill of exchange from John Sandy, 102; £100 to Richard Hart for smithery for the "Assention," 104; £100 to William Garway for the "Assention," 105; £150 to William Candish on account of lead, 105; £25 to Laurence Waldo on a bill of exchange from Exeter, 106; £50 to William Starky, a factor, for his entertainment and preparation, 106; £100 and £50 to Richard Wright for gratuities and charges for the patent, &c., 107; £100 to William Dyckes, purser of the "Red Dragon," on account of necessaries, 108; £100 to Robert Stephens on a bill of exchange from John Ellicott, 108; £100 to Robert Stephens on a bill of exchange from John Ellicott, 109; £194 5s. 6d. to William Garway for candy oil, 114; £150 to William Garway for the repairs to the "Assention," 114; £150 to William Dixsy, purser of the "Red Dragon," for repairs, 114; £500 to Sir Hugh Portman on bill of exchange from Robert Pope, 115; £100 to William Burrell for boats and other necessaries, 115; £25 10s. to Anthony Moseley for vinegar, 115; £20 to Humfrey Phipps for wine-vinegar, 115; £14 12s. to John Combe for wine-vinegar, 116; £69 8s. 2d. to Christopher Wasse for a silver fountain and case, 116; £26 13s. 4d. to Thomas Pulleyn, preacher, for his provision to sea, 116; £250 to William Dixson, purser of the "Red Dragon," 117; £6 13s. 4d. to Thomas S monds, 117; £250 to Richard Wyseman for the purser of the "Hector," 117; £150 to William Leake, purser of the "Assention," for men's wages, 117; £250 to John Havard for men's wages on the "Susan," 118; £19 6s. 3d. to George Davies for chests for cloth, 118; £100 to Widowe Bennett for iron, 119; £20 to Percival Stradling, *factor*, for his preparation, 119; £500 to Sergeant Helle for exchange at Exeter, 119; £50 to Thomas Salterne, *factor*, for his entertainment, 120; £20 to Phillip Winchecomb, *factor*, for his preparation for sea, 121; £100 to George Persons, purser of the "Hector," for provisions, 121; £38 to Patrick Johnson for salt, 121; £326 13s. 4d. to Symon Furner for powder, 121; £20 to Thomas Tudd, factor, to make h's provision, 122; £100 to John Havard, *factor*, for his entertainment, 123; £60 to Thomas Shere of Exeter for so much paid to John Sandy, 125; £100 to William Brunde, *factor*, for his entertainment, 125; £100 to Mr. Garway, purser of the "Assention," for necessaries, 126; £90 10s. to Mr. Robert Bell for paper, 126; £88 16s. 3d. to George Smithyes for plate, 127; £100 to William Drodebent, Master of the "Dragon," an advance on mortgage, 128; £200 to the assignee of Thomas Billett on a bill of exchange from Robert Pope, 129; £68 18s to Thomas Lieth for pewter, 129; £43 16s. 6d. to Robert Warner for glasses, 129; £40 to Derick Lypson for steel, 138; £11 to Phillip Grove for travelling expenses, 138; £30 to Nathaniel Jamryn, *factor*, as per agreement, 139; £100 to Mr. Wyseman for the purser of the "Hector," for men's wages, 139; £38 7s. 7d. to William Dove, *Cooper*, for work done, 139; £13 7s. 8d. to William Segar, *Herald*, for writing the Queen's letters to the Kings of the East Indies, 139; £100 to Captain Mydleton for his entertainment in the voyage, 140; £100 to William Garway on account for the provision of the "Assention," 140; £8 3s. 7d. to Captain Mydleton for disbursements, 140; £400 to William Harvey on a bill of exchange from Robert Pope, 141; £2 13s. to Mr. Pope, Sergeant of the Admiralty, on a bill of charges for the burial of those slain in the "Hector," 141; £50 to Henry Mydleton, *factor*, for his entertainment in the voyage, 141; £371 15s. to Simon Furnor for powder, brimstone, and saltpetre, 142; £61 5s. 9d. to Simon Yomans for butter and cheese, 142; £86 to William Uffington for wax candles, 142; £100 to Mr. Wiseman for the purser of the "Hector" for charges, 142; £49 to William Candishe for lead, 143; £30 to James Emerson for aquavitæ, 143; £11 10s. to Mr. Hacklett for advice and maps, 143; £100 to William Dixon, purser of the "Red Dragon," for the clearing of the ship, 144; £50 to the purser of the "Hector" for the clearing of the ship, 144; to take 4, 5, or £600 to Gravesend for the payment of harbor-wages and other expenses in clearing the ships, 146; £61 to Henry Ryvelles, *Cooper*, for caske, 147; £57 15s. to John Hardway, *Cooper*, for caske, 147; £40 12s. to Leonard Onnyslowe, *Cooper*, for caske, 148; £36 19s. to George Chapman, *Cooper*, for caske, 148; £29 to Thomas Duck for ancients and streamers for the "Dragon," 149; £80 to Josephe Page, Baker, for bread, 149; £7 10s. to John Pywell for head pieces and morrens, 149; £100 to Christopher Thomson, *Smith*, for iron, 149; £30 10s. to Richard Hall, *Smith*, for two anchors for the "Hector," 150; £100 to William Leake, purser of the "Assention," for wages and clearing expenses, 154; £100 to George Parsons, purser of the "Hector," for wages and clearing expenses, 154; £100 to Joseph Salbanck, purser of the "Susan," for wages and clearing expenses, 154; £180 to William Dixon, purser of the "Red Dragon," for wages and clearing expenses, 154; £15 7s. to Anthonie Duffeilde for beer, 154; £300 to Robert Golding for the ship "Guift," 154; £24 19s. to James Bover and Richard Vale for spectacles and boxes, 155; £200 to Abraham Campion, part of his account for beer, 155; £100 to Lewys Tyght, *Blacksmith*, for iron work for the "Red Dragon," 157; £50 to Joseph Page, *Baker*, for biskett, 157; £30 to Francis Caudell, *Painter*, for painting the "Red Dragon," 157; £161 13s. 1d. to Richard Hart, *Smith*, for nails and iron work for the "Assention," 157; £18 to Edmond Saunderson for Turner's work for the "Red Dragon," 157; £100 to William Burrell for money owing, 157; £16 0s. 10d. to William Bacon for masts and stores, 157; £30 12s. 4d. to James Waters, Ironmonger, for gunners' stores for the "Susan." 157; £34 16s. 8d. to William Kymber, *Wharfinger*, for lighterage and porterage, 158; £34 13s. 4d. to various porters for portage and lading of the ships, 158; £11 6s. 8d. to Robert Wood, *Wharfinger*, for wharfage and lighterage, 158; £42

INDEX

Warrants per Mr. Holliday, *continued*.
8s. 11d. to Mr. Rumney for disbursements, 158; £12 8s. 6d. to Thomas Hewys, *Clothworker*, for work done, 159; £30 to Arnold Mabanck, *Pullymaker*, for work done, 163; £34 4s. 2d. to Christopher Thomson, *Smith*, for work done, 163; £16 1s. 8d. to John Hedland for carriages for the ships, 163; £100 to Lewis Tate, *Smith*, for iron-work, 163; £100 to Thomas Barbor for canvas, 163; £11 to John Maxfield, *Brasier*, for copper vessels, 164; £42 15s. to Robert Heighoo for canvas, 164; £22 4s. to Francis Covell, *Chaundler*, for provisions, 164; £45 10s. 11d. to Joseph Page, *Baker*, for biskett, 167; £200 to Thomas Barber for canvas, 167; £6 to William Hedger for building a pinnace for the "Hector," 167; £49 to Robert Huse, *Sailmaker*, for sails, 167; £40 to John Bowden, *Sailmaker*, for sails, 168; £42 5s. 4d. to Adam Wood, *Carpenter*, in full of his account, 168; £86 15s. 4d. to Robert Bradbury, *Sailmaker*, for sails for the "Dragon" and "Hector," 168; £42 15s. to Robert Highhoe for *canvas* for the "Assention," 168; £27 to James Waters, *Ironmonger*, for iron-work, 168; £13 to Hildebrand Sprusen, *Sailmaker*, in full of his bill, 168; £17 12s. 6d. to Peter Pett, *Shipwright*, for work and charges, 169; £14 to Mr. Crosse for a pipe of Malaga wine, 169; 20 merkes to the King of Heralds for assigning the Company's arms, 171; £102 to Robert Savadge for wastes and deales, 171; £29 1s. 4d. to Justice Mullett, *Smith*, for iron work for the "Dragon," 172; £300 to Thomas Barbar on account of canvas, 172; £90 to Elizabeth Bennett for nails, &c., 172; £3 15s. to Peter Hiller for caske for the "Hector," 172; £48 to Francis Caudell, *Painter*, for work done on the "Dragon," 172; £10 to William Allom, *Lighterman*, for lighterage of goods, 173; £227 to Lewis Tate, *Blacksmith*, for iron work for the "Red Dragon," 173; £2 to Agnes Haselton to relieve her husband, hurt in the "Hector," 173; £29 10s. to Charles Anthony for stamps made for the East India monies, 174; £13 3s. 2d. to Robert Bell for disbursements for wharfage and cutting of lead, 203; £4 7s. 5d. to Alderman Bannyng, *Treasurer*, for so much disbursed by him beyond his receipts, 203; £109 16s. 8d. to Benjamin Deycro, agent of the Muskovia Company for cordage, 204.

Warrants per Thomas Stephens: £2 16s. to the wife of John May, master's mate in the "Susan," for a month's wages, 248; £6 for pilotage of the "Assention" into the river, 248.

Warwicke, *see* Heale.

Washer, Richard, assembly, 60; bill of adventure sealed, £240, p. 252.

Wasse, Christopher, warrant £69 8s. 2d. for silver plate, 116.

Wasse, Thomas, desires to be employed as a factor, 56.

Wastall, } William, adventurer, assembly 59;
Wastell, } will bring in his money in dollars, 63; committee, 246; bill of adventure sealed, £240, p. 260.

Watches, 218.

Water caske, 150 tonnes of caske required, whereof 40 tonnes of hogsheads, 30, 36; committee to provide 150 tonnes, 76; committee to provide for the North West Voyage, 209.

Waters, James, *Ironmonger*, warrant £30 12s. 4d. for gunner's stores, 157; do. £27 for iron work, 168.

Wattes, John, Alderman, assemblies, 68, 69, 71, 78, 79, 80, 82, 83, 85, 87, 89, 91, 96, 99, 100, 102, 104, 106, 109, 112, 115, 122, 124, 128, 138, 140, 143, 144, 148, 151, 155, 159, 164, 167, 168, 170, 171, 173, 174, 175, 176, 180, 181, 182, 183, 184, 185, 186, 187, 190, 192, 193, 194, 203, 204, 205, 206, 208, 214, 215, 216, 217, 219, 224, 225, 244, 248; committees, 57, 67, 69, 70, 71, 72, 73, 77, 90, 99, 115, 147, 155, 183, 186, 191, 194, 209; warrant £36 10s. 10d. for shirts of mail, 123; to confer as to the damage done to a ship by the anchor of the "Scourge," 125; elected governor, 166, 179; the oath of office, 179; to examine the charters as to authority for compelling contributions for a second voyage, 183; conference with Lord Admiral and Mr. Secretary (Herbert) as to the delay in the second voyage, 189; advice from Midleboroughe of the return of two Dutch ships from the East Indies, 194; an Englishman returned from the East Indies to be conferred with as to the state of trade, &c., 194; signatures to treasurer's warrant, 206, 210; warrant £42 for iron hoops, 222; do. £42, p. 224; general committee and sworn, 225; requested to give his bond with Mr. Bannyng for £1,000 as security for money to be taken up at interest for the payment of wages of mariners returned in the "Assention," 249; bill of adventure sealed, £600, p. 256; do. £240, p. 261.

Waymoth, } Captain George, *see also* North
Waymouth, } *West Passage*; assemblies,
Waymouthe, } 183, 204, 208; letter from him proposing the Company should undertake a voyage for the discovery of a North West passage to the East Indies, 182; conference and resolutions that the voyage be made, 183-4; the terms agreed on with Waymouth, 184; report of the committee, 185; warrant £30 for instruments, 204; do. £30, p. 204; do. £20, p. 204; £60 taken up at Exeter for the hiring of mariners, 209; warrant £100 for men's wages, 211; formal agreement with Waymouth containing his commission and instructions, 211-14; *see* North West Passage; John Cartwright, *Preacher*, engaged to go in the voyage, 216; the articles of agreement read, 217; warrant £50 for expenses prior to sailing, 218; return to Dartmouth; his journal read; ordered to bring ships round to London, 227; delay in coming to London, 229; arrival in London, 229; Mr. Cartwright accused of being the main persuader for the return of the expedition, 232; proceedings before the Privy Council as to his return; his hope of discoveries in a second voyage, and a second and final voyage resolved on; re-appointed chief in command, confident of success in finding a passage, 233; proposed conference as to a second voyage, 236-7; his demands for charges and expenses in the voyage referred to arbitration, 240; *see his Agreement*, 211-14.

Webbe, Thomas, admitted as an extra factor, 102.

Welbye, Richard, adventurer with Giles Dohcomb, £200, p. 4.

Wellington, Peter, being the assign of Peter Helms, deceased, he desires the transfer of his stock and the freedom of the Company, 226; stock transferred but the freedom denied, 227.

West, Francis, warrant £241 on bill of exchange, 102.
West Country; Mr. Howe requested to travel there to make provision for dollars and victuals for the ships, 15; he agrees to go with Captain Davies, 21; a commission to be prepared, 28; committee appointed to purchase, 29; letter from the Lord Treasurer to Her Majesty's receivers of Devon and Cornwall, authorizing credit to be given to the agents of the Company, 38; Captain Baker's commission for the purchase of victuals, 38, 40, 48-50; the quantities of provisions to be purchased, 41; money and bills of exchange, 45, 47, *see Warrants*, commissions for the purchase of provisions, 48-54; letters of advice respecting the providing of victuals, money, &c., 64; provisions to be bought to carry the ships to the West Country, 67; committee to solicit the Lord Treasurer's warrant to transport provisions, 78; the warrant sent, 79; poll davies to be bought and made up into bags, 86; order for no more biscuit or meal to be bought, 88; instructions for shipping the Spanish money, 119; committee to see the discharge of the ships, 128, 140; Mr. Howe's and Mr. Combe's commission, 147; Mr. Howe and Mr. Combe to bring in their accounts, 172-3; letters sent down for the purser and officers of the "Assention," 243.
Westray, } Thomas, adventurer with others, Westrow, } £300, p. 3; bill of adventure sealed, £240, p. 254.
Westwray, John, made free though not named in the patent, 177; bill of adventure sealed, £360, p. 256.
Wethrall, Larance, adventurer with Thomas Wheeler, £200, p. 2.
Wharfage, 203, 224.
Wharfingers, *see William Kymber, Robert Wood.*
Wharfs, Gully Key, 158; Wiggens Key, 203; Wooll Key, 158.
Wheat, estimate of quantity and price, 35; revised estimate, 46, 54-5; quantity to be bought in the West Country, 41, 52.
Wheeler, Ambrose, committees, 246; bill of adventure sealed, £240, p. 257.
Wheeler, Thomas, adventurer with Larance Wethrall, £200, p. 2; assembly, 4.
White, Leonarde, adventurer, £200, p. 2; assemblies, 5, 59; bill of adventure sealed, £240, p. 259.
White, Thomas: assembly, 59; committee, 245; to keep a note of the weight of the goods from the "Assention" received at the Exchange vaults, 248; bill of adventure sealed, £240, p. 255.
Whitehall, 112, 164.
Whitmore, George, adventurer with Henrye Poalstedd, £200, p. 4; bill of adventure sealed, £240, p. 252.
Whyte, *see White*.
Wiggens Key, *Wharf*, 203.
Wilford, nominated factor, 77; elected factor of the third sort, 83; to sail in the "Susan," 101; warrant £30 for salary, 103; bill of adventure sealed, £50, p. 150.
Willoughby, Lord, warrant to buy the Spanish meal taken prize by his ship, 86.
Wilson, Francis, offers as a purser, 27.
Winchcomb, } Phillip, nominated factor, 77; Winchcombe, } elected factor of the fourth sort, 83; to sail in the "Assention," 101;
warrant £20 for his preparation, 121; bill of adventure sealed, £40, p. 149.
Wine, an estimate to be made, 26; to be in good casks iron bound, 30; estimate of quantity and price, 34; quantity and price in the West Country to be ascertained, 49; wine out of a prize ship to be purchased at Plymouth and price, 50; committee to provide 66 tuns, 75; warrant £100 for Canary, 95; do. £231 10*s*., £378, and £160, p. 103; do. £210, p. 104; do. £14 10*s*. for a pipe of Malaga wine given to the Lord Admiral in lieu of the deodand claimed for the "Hector," 169; do. £18 for a tun of claret for the like purpose, 169.
Wiseman, Richard, *Goldsmith*, adventurer, £100, p. 2; assemblies, 4, 9, 14, 20, 22, 24, 26, 28, 30, 31, 39, 44, 46, 47, 56, 57, 58, 67, 68, 69, 73, 74, 76, 78, 79, 80, 82, 83, 86, 88, 89, 90, 91, 93, 94, 95, 96, 98, 99, 100, 102, 103, 104, 106, 109, 112, 123, 124, 125, 126, 138, 140, 142, 144, 155, 156, 158, 160, 162, 163, 164, 167, 168, 170, 171, 172, 174, 175, 176, 177, 180, 182, 183, 184, 185, 192, 203, 214, 216, 217, 218, 224, 225, 227, 231, 232, 241, 242, 244; committees, 6, 8, 9, 12, 27, 68, 75, 76, 80, 91, 99, 107, 114, 115, 117, 124, 155, 156, 183, 186, 203, 209, 214; views ships, 13; surveyor for the "Hector," 14; warrant £100 for provisioning the "Hector," 25; signatures to the West Country commissions, 52, 54, 55; general committee, 63; warrant £100 for the use of the "Hector," 65; compounds with William Tavernor, mariner, 68; order to use a mast for the "Hector," 71; warrant £100 for the preparation of the "Hector," 79; do. £100, p. 96; do. £200, p. 104; do. £100, p. 111; do. £250, p. 117; do. £100, p. 139; do. £100, p. 142; to pay dock charges, 80; to clear accounts with Mr. Burrell, 127; appointed auditor, 166; general committee and sworn, 179; do. 225; allows the chests of merchandise returned from the North West voyage to be stored and viewed at his house, 231; bill of adventure sealed, £600, p. 255.
Wollastone, William, bill of adventure sealed, £240, p. 252.
Wollstenham, John, bill of adventure sealed, £240, p. 255.
Wood, committee to provide for the North West voyage, 209; warrant for wood, 211.
Wood, Adam, warrant £50 for masts and timber, 164; do. £42 5*s*. 4*d*., p. 168; do. £7 8*s*. for deals, &c., 218.
Wood, Robert, Wharfinger, warrant £11 6*s*. 8*d*. for wharfage, 158.
Woodfield, William, *Smith*, warrant £6 10*s*. for iron hoops, 219.
Woodwarde, John, *Ironmonger*, adventurer, £300, p. 2.
Wooll Key, *Wharf*, 158.
Woolwich, committee to inspect ships lying there, 13; the use of the docks requested, 13; the "Mare Scourge" in dock there, 27; a committee to lie at Woolwich to superintend the preparation of the "Mare Scourge," 39; Justice Mullett, a smith, to be employed, 40; timber borrowed from Her Majesty's storehouse, 71.
Worsenham, Mr., *The Searcher*, warrant £2 for the clearing of the ships, 156.
Wragge, John, bill of adventure sealed, £240, p. 261.

INDEX

Wragge, Richard, adventurer £200, p. 2; bill of adventure sealed, £240, p. 261.
Wray, John, nominated factor, 77.
Wright, Peter, warrant 43s. for lanthorns, &c., 223.
Wright, } Richard, *Secretary of the Company:*
Wryght, } assemblies, 228, 249; committees, 31, 33, 65, 75, 87, 91, 106, 115, 124, 141, 152; elected secretary, 38; ordered to request the Queen's Attorney to finish the patent, 88; warrant £100 and £50 for the expenses of the patent, &c., 107; do. £39 16s. 6d. for disbursements, 173; order to make out bills of adventure for every adventurer, 175; sixpence to be paid for every bill of adventure, 175; warrant 20 marks for his services, 203; to make out new bills of adventure, embodying all supplies, &c., in one lump sum, 220; warrant £4 15s. for charges in procuring the Queen's letters, 222; re-elected secretary, 226.
Wryte, Hugh, nominated factor, 77.
Wich, }
Wiche, } *see Wyche.*
Witche, }
Wyche, James, adventurer with Richard Wyche, £200, p. 2.
Wyche, } Richard, adventurer with James
Wycke, } Wyche, £200, p. 2; assemblies, 4, 7, 9, 10, 14, 20, 24, 26, 27, 29, 31, 33, 37, 39, 46, 56, 57, 64, 67, 69, 71, 74, 76, 78, 80, 82, 83, 85, 86, 88, 89, 95, 98, 99, 100, 104, 108, 109, 112, 113, 116, 119, 121, 122, 123, 124, 128, 129, 139, 140, 143, 144, 148, 150, 151, 152, 154, 155, 160, 168, 170, 175, 181, 192, 193, 197, 204, 205, 225, 228, 232, 235, 236, 238, 240, 241, 244, 247; committees, 6, 8, 12, 31, 33, 40, 65, 75, 120, 124, 128, 147, 156, 229, 230, 240, 248; views ships, 13; feoffee in trust for ships bought, 32; surveyor of the "Malice Scurge," 33; money in the West Country, 45; signature to West Country commissions, 52; general committee, 63; to buy oatmeal, 75; do. mustard seed, 76; order to provide ship's stores for the "Red Dragon," 117; expenses at Gravesend, 158; general committee, 179; do. and sworn, 225; bill of adventure sealed, £240, p. 259.
Wymers, Humfrey, adventurer with Richard Edmonds, £200, p. 3.
Wynchcomb, *see Winchcomb.*
Wyndham, John, warrant £40 on bill of exchange, 79.

Yerworth, Thomas, *purser of the "Discovery,"* appointed purser of one of the ships for the North West Voyage, 205; salary contingent on the discovery of the passage, 205; to give a bond of £100 for his good behaviour, 205; warrant £80 for carpenters' wages, 206; do. £30 for mariners' wages, &c., 208; do £100 for anchors and stores for the "Discovery," 210; do. £100 for coals, &c., 210; his account, £210, to be audited, 214; warrant £100 for provisions, 215; dislike taken to him, but his employment continued, 219; warrant £6 13s. 4d. for wages, 235.
Yomans, Simon, *Chandler,* warrant £61 5s. 9d. for butter and cheese, 142.
Yonson, Richard, *Goldsmith,* adventurer £200, and will pay in Spanish money, 31.

CHISWICK PRESS:—C. WHITTINGHAM AND CO. TOOKS COURT,
CHANCERY LANE, LONDON, 1886.